THE EMOTIONAL CON... S

Jesse J. Prinz argues that recent ... ...ence, and anthropology supports two radical h... ...out the nature of morality: moral values are based on emotional responses, and these emotional responses are inculcated by culture, not hard-wired through natural selection.

In the first half of the book, Prinz defends the hypothesis that morality has an emotional foundation. Evidence from brain imaging, social psychology, and psychopathology suggest that, when we judge something to be right or wrong, we are merely expressing our emotions. Prinz argues that these emotions do not track objective features of reality; rather, the rightness and wrongness of an act consists in the fact that people are disposed to have certain emotions towards it. In the second half of the book, he turns to a defence of moral relativism. Moral facts depend on emotional responses, and emotional responses vary from culture to culture. Prinz surveys the anthropological record to establish moral variation, and he draws on cultural history to show how attitudes toward practices such as cannibalism and marriage change over time. He also criticizes evidence from animal behaviour and child development that has been taken to support the claim that moral attitudes are hard-wired by natural selection. Prinz concludes that there is no single true morality, but he also argues that some moral values are better than others; moral progress is possible.

Throughout the book, Prinz relates his views to contemporary and historical work in philosophical ethics. His views echo themes in the writings of David Hume and Friedrich Nietzsche, but Prinz supports, extends, and revises these classic theories using the resources of cutting-edge cognitive science. *The Emotional Construction of Morals* will stimulate and challenge anyone who is curious about the nature and origin of moral values.

Jesse J. Prinz is Distinguished Professor of Philosophy at The City University of New York, Graduate Center.

The Emotional Construction of Morals

JESSE J. PRINZ

OXFORD
UNIVERSITY PRESS

OXFORD
UNIVERSITY PRESS

Great Clarendon Street, Oxford OX2 6DP

Oxford University Press is a department of the University of Oxford.
It furthers the University's objective of excellence in research, scholarship,
and education by publishing worldwide in

Oxford New York

Auckland Cape Town Dar es Salaam Hong Kong Karachi
Kuala Lumpur Madrid Melbourne Mexico City Nairobi
New Delhi Shanghai Taipei Toronto

With offices in

Argentina Austria Brazil Chile Czech Republic France Greece
Guatemala Hungary Italy Japan Poland Portugal Singapore
South Korea Switzerland Thailand Turkey Ukraine Vietnam

Oxford is a registered trade mark of Oxford University Press
in the UK and in certain other countries

Published in the United States
by Oxford University Press Inc., New York

British Library Cataloguing in Publication Data

Data available

Library of Congress Cataloging in Publication Data

Data available

Typeset by Laserwords Private Limited, Chennai, India
Printed in Great Britain
on acid-free paper by
Clays Ltd., Bungay, Suffolk

ISBN 978-0-19-928301-9 (Hbk.)
ISBN 978-0-19-957154-3 (Pbk.)

1 3 5 7 9 10 8 6 4 2

To my parents, Phyllis and Jonathan Prinz, who taught me the difference between right and wrong.

Preface

David Hume's *Treatise of Human Nature* is divided into three books: "Of the Understanding", "Of the Passions", and "Of Morals". One might wonder how these disparate topics are related, other than by virtue of the fact that they have something to do with the mind. But the links become clear on reading the text. Hume develops a theory of concepts (or "ideas") in the first book and a theory of emotions in the second book, and then he integrates these in the third by arguing that our moral concepts have an emotional foundation. The project is also unified by Hume's allegiance to empiricism. His theory of concepts is based on the premise that ideas are stored copies of sensory impressions, and his theory of emotions is designed to be compatible with this empiricist view (he defines emotions as impressions of impressions). Hume's moral theory is empiricist too. Moral concepts seem especially problematic for an empiricist because there can be no image of virtue, no taste of goodness, and no smell of evil. By appealing to sentiments, Hume is able to argue that all concepts bottom out in impressions, after all. The concept of goodness consists in a feeling of approbation and the concept of badness consists in a feeling of disapprobation. The class of virtues has no common appearance, but good things just feel right; the class of vices would be impossible to paint, but each instance elicits a palpable pang of blame. In sum, Hume's *Treatise* has a coherent structure, and the culminating moral theory can be read as the resolution of an apparent counter-example to his theory of concepts, or as the payoff for those who take the time to understand how the mind works. No matter where you place the emphasis, Hume's theory of concepts and his theory of morals hang together, and passions are the glue.

Philosophers like to reinvent wheels, and I am no exception. The views that I defend here owe a tremendous debt to Hume. This book defends a sentimentalist theory of morality that builds on the ideas developed by Hume and some his contemporaries. I depart from Hume in various ways, but the basic thrust of the theory is Humean, and, in this respect, my proposals are footnotes to Book III of the *Treatise*. And this is not the first Humean footnote I've written. My first book, *Furnishing the Mind*, defends an empiricist theory of concepts, and my second book, *Gut Reactions*, defends an empiricist theory of emotions (which is more Jamesian than Humean, but, with Hume, my goal there is to show that emotions are a kind of impression). So here, in my third book, I am simply completing a trilogy that parallels the structure of Hume's *Treatise*. These works are independent in one sense—you can reject one while accepting the others—but they hang together in just the way that Hume's *Treatise* hangs together. I view them as parts of a whole, and I view that whole as a tribute and modest extension of Hume's masterwork.

I have three main goals in extending Hume's project. The first is to provide empirical support for a theory that was first developed from an armchair. The second is to add some details to Hume's theory, including an account of the sentiments that undergird our moral judgments, and an account of the ontology that results from taking a sentimentalist view seriously. My third goal is to show that this approach leads to moral relativism. Hume resisted relativism, and I argue that he shouldn't have. I also investigate the origin of our moral sentiments, and I suggest that Nietzsche"s genealogical approach to morality has much to contribute here. The resulting story is half Humean and half Nietzschean, but I take the Nietzschean part to fit naturally with the Humean part.

I mention Hume and Nietzsche by way of acknowledgement. Within the pantheon of dead philosophers, they are ones to whom I owe the greatest philosophical debts. I must also mention Edward Westermarck, because he recognized the link between sentimentalism and relativism a hundred years ago, and recognized the value of anthropology and history in investigating morals. This book continues in the tradition of Westermarck. Among living philosophers, I have been especially inspired by Gil Harman, Shaun Nichols, David Wiggins, and John McDowell. Steve Stich also deserves special mention for his efforts to promote an approach to philosophy that makes liberal use of empirical results. On that note, I also owe tremendous debts to the scientists who have been providing data to help assess philosophical theories. Among psychologists, Jon Haidt and James Blair have been an especially influential, and I would also single out the late Marvis Harris, whose cultural materialism leaves its mark on the second half of this book. These authors have educated me through their published work, but many others have offered guidance through discussion and written commentaries on material from this book. I have benefited from giving talks at numerous philosophy departments and conferences, spanning four continents and twice that many countries. I wish I could list the name of everyone who offered suggestions or objections along the way. I also want to thank all the members of the Moral Psychology Research Group, who have created one of the most conducive environments for exchanging philosophical ideas that I have ever seen. I have also benefited from written feedback, which led to improvements large and small throughout. In this context, let me first mention participants in seminars taught by Steve Stich, Eric Schwitzgebel, and John Mikhail who endured earlier versions of this manuscript or related papers. I also received philosophical and typographical corrections on the entire manuscript from Nigel Hope, Mark Jenkins, Joel Marks, and Jonathan Prinz, as well as helpful comments on selected parts or related materials from Ruth Chang, Matthew Chrisman, Justin D'Arms, Karen Jones, Matt Smith, Valerie Tiberius, Teemu Toppinen, Brian Weatherson, and others whom I am undoubtedly forgetting. Among readers, my biggest debt goes to Shaun Nichols, Richard Joyce, and two anonymous referees for Oxford University Press, who provided me with detailed comments on drafts of the manuscript. They each caught embarrassing mistakes and pressed me on dozens of philosophical issues. The book is much better because of them, and it would have been better still had I been more successful in accommodating all of their suggestions. I will remain forever grateful. Of course, I would not have received such helpful feedback were it not for my patient and outstanding editor, Peter Momtchiloff. Peter has been a great source of support at every stage.

In writing this book, I also benefited from several institutions. I was a fellow at the Collegium Budapest and did some writing there. Tamar Gendler was instrumental in orchestrating that visit, and in assembling a wonderful group of summer colleagues. I also owe special thanks to the Center for Advanced Study in the Behavioral Sciences, in Palo Alto. CASBS is a magical place, and I finished this manuscript there. In so doing, I benefited from the abundant intellectual resources and the outstanding staff, who contribute to making it an ideal environment for research. I was able to go to CASBS because of a research leave from my home institution, the University of North Carolina at Chapel Hill. I am grateful to UNC for that, but also and especially to my students and colleagues. There is no better place to work.

Finally, I wanted to mention my family. I feel fortunate to have been raised by two parents with strong moral convictions, and I grew up alongside an older brother with a keen moral sense. My views about right and wrong would be very different without them, and they continue to provide support in many ways. As always, my deepest gratitude goes to Rachel, who was nearby as I wrote almost every page of this book, and she has patiently endured every mood swing that comes along with the writing process. Her support has been essential.

Contents

Preamble
Naturalism and Hume's Law

Morality is a normative domain. It concerns how the world ought to be, not how it is. The investigation of morality seems to require a methodology that differs from the methods used in the sciences. At least, that seems to be the case if the investigator has normative ambitions. If the investigator wants to proscribe, it is not enough to describe. As Hume taught us, there is no way to derive an ought from an is. More precisely, there is no way to deduce a statement that has prescriptive force (a statement that expresses on unconditional obligation) from statements that are purely descriptive. No facts about how the world is configured entails that you ought to refrain from stealing or killing or blowing up buildings. Hume's Law is appealing because it makes morality seem special; moral truths are unlike the cool truths of science. But, on one reading, Hume's Law is a recipe for moral nihilism. By insulating moral truths from scientific methods, it may imply that morality is supernatural. If so, morality should go the way of spirits and fairies. That is a path I want to resist.

Defenders of Hume's Law acknowledge the viability of certain kinds of descriptive projects in morality. One can describe the moral convictions that obtain in a culture. One can describe the nature of the concepts that people deploy when they make moral judgments. One can say something descriptive about the nature of moral facts and how they relate to other kinds of facts. These questions will be my concern. But, I want to begin by discussing how the descriptive truths about morality bear on the prescriptive. The metaethical theory and moral psychology that I will be defending in the chapters that follow offers a way to cross the is/ought boundary.

I will argue that morality derives from us. The good is that which we regard as good. The obligatory is that which we regard as obligatory. The 'we' here refers to the person making a moral claim and the cultural group with which that individual affiliates. If the good is that which we regard as good, then we can figure out what our obligations are by figuring what our moral beliefs commit us to. Figuring out what we believe about morality is a descriptive task *par excellence*, and one that can be fruitfully pursued empirically. Thus, normative ethics can be approached as a social science.

This suggestion is difficult to square with the intuition underlying Hume's Law. There is a nagging intuition that no empirically discoverable facts about our beliefs can entail that we ought to behave in a certain way. I do not want to trample on this intuition. Hume's Law is true in one sense, and false in another. That is what I hope to show here. More precisely, I want to show how a thoroughgoing naturalist—one who is repelled by spirits and fairies—can find a place for the normative. I regard Hume as such a naturalist, and I will be defending a view of morality that is deeply indebted to Hume. The view that I favor preserves many of our intuitions about the moral domain, but not all. I reject nihilism, but embrace subjectivism, relativism, and arationalism. Morality is a human construction that issues from our passions. But that does not mean we ought to give it up.

0.1 FOUR KINDS OF NATURALISM

The term 'naturalism' is used in a variety of ways, sometimes with a derogatory intonation, and sometimes as a battle cry. I want to discuss four different species of naturalism, all of which I support. I will not argue for naturalism here. I will just pledge my allegiance.

One kind of naturalism, already suggested by my remarks about fairies and spirits, is best understood in contrast to supernaturalism. It is the view that our world is limited by the postulates and laws of the natural sciences. Nothing can exist that violates these laws, and all entities that exist must, in some sense, be composed of the entities that our best scientific theories require. This is a metaphysical thesis; it concerns the fundamental nature of reality. I will call it metaphysical naturalism.

Metaphysical naturalism entails a kind of explanatory naturalism. If everything that exists is composed of natural stuff and constrained by natural law, then everything that is not described in the language of a natural science must ultimately be describable in such terms. This is not equivalent to reductionism in the strong sense of that word. Strong reductionists say that the relation between natural sciences and 'higher-level' domains is deductive. We should be able to deduce higher-level facts from their lower-level substrates. Antireductionists deny this. They think, for example, that there are higher-level laws or generalizations that could be implemented in an open-ended range of ways. Regularities captured at a low level would miss out on generalizations of that kind. The explanatory naturalist can be an antireductionist. The explanatory naturalist does not need to claim that low-level explanations are the only explanations. The key idea is that there must be some kind of systematic correspondence between levels. One must be able to map any entity at a high level onto entities at a lower level, and one must be able to explain the instantiation of any high-level generalization by appeal to lower-level features that realize those generalizations.

A third kind of naturalism can be termed methodological. If all facts are, in some sense, natural facts (according to metaphysical naturalism), then the methods by which we investigate facts must be suitable to the investigation of natural facts. Philosophers sometimes claim to have a distinctive method for making discoveries: the method of conceptual analysis. If metaphysical naturalism is true, this cannot be a supernatural method of discovering supernatural truths. Concepts themselves are natural entities, and they can be investigated using natural processes. Conceptual analysis is, like all legitimate investigatory tools, an empirical method. As empirical methods go, it is not especially powerful. Conceptual analysis proceeds through first-person access to psychological structures, or introspection. Introspection is error-prone, and there are methodological perils associated with drawing conclusions from investigation using a single subject (oneself). We can investigate concepts using the tools of social science. If concepts are natural entities, then they come about in natural ways. For example, concepts can be acquired through experience, and they can be revised through experience. They have no special status when it comes to revealing facts about the world.

Methodological naturalism, as I have defined it, is associated with Quine. In his (1969) critique of epistemology, Quine tells us that the investigation of knowledge should be pursued using the resources of the social sciences. In his (1953) defense of confirmation holism, Quine argues that all claims are subject to empirical revision. There is a further kind of naturalism associated with Quine's holism. We are always operating from within our current theories of the world. In making theoretical revisions, we cannot step outside our theories and adopt a transcendental stance. To do so would be to suppose that we have a way of thinking about the world that is independent of our theories of the world. If theories of the world encompass all of our beliefs, then no such stance is possible. Call this transformation naturalism, because it is a view about how we change our views.

Each form of naturalism has implications for normativity. Metaphysical naturalism entails that moral norms, if they exist, do not require postulating anything that goes beyond what the natural sciences allow. Explanatory naturalism entails that we can ultimately describe how any moral norm is realized by natural entities. Methodological naturalism entails that we should investigate norms using all available empirical resources tools. Transformation naturalism entails that we must investigate norms from within our current belief systems, and, as a result, the norms we currently accept will influence our intuitions about what norms we ought to uphold. If we chose to change our norms, we cannot do so by adopting a transcendental stance that brackets off the norms we currently accept.

0.2 BREAKING HUME'S LAW

If naturalism is right, then moral facts are natural facts, or they are not facts at all. Natural facts are facts that are consistent with the four strictures of naturalism just adduced. The world is as it is, and not any other way. If the world includes facts about what ought to be, those facts must be explicable in terms of how things are. Every ought must supervene on an is. Since naturalism does not entail reductionism, naturalism does not entail that prescriptive facts reduce to descriptive facts. Naturalism does, however, entail that prescriptive facts are descriptive facts in another sense. Every prescriptive fact must be realized by, or made true by, facts that can be described without use of prescriptive vocabulary. For every prescriptive fact there is some underlying descriptive fact that makes it true. As it happens, I think that naturalism does allow us to infer prescriptive facts from normative facts, and, thus, there is a way to break Hume's Law. But naturalism does not entail that Hume's Law is violable, for reasons that I will discuss in the next section.

First, I want to offer a quick and dirty argument for how to derive an ought from an is. A full defense of the argument would require a more labored excursion into the philosophy of language. My goal here is more modest. I want to indicate one way in which a naturalist might simultaneously regard moral facts as natural (hence entailed by descriptive facts), but also irreducible (and thus not so entailed). The arguments in this section and the next illustrate how that seemingly paradoxical pair of demands might be met.

To see how an ought might be derived from an is, we must first figure out what oughts are. The way to do that is to figure out what the word 'ought' means (here I restrict myself to the moral use of 'ought'). What concept does that word express? To answer this question, we need to do some psychology (introspective or otherwise). We need to determine what people have in mind when they say that something is obligatory. Much of this book is about that question. For now, I want to sketch a very simplified version of the kind of answer that I will defend. On the theory I favor, when a person says that a course of action is obligatory, that judgment expresses what might be called a prescriptive sentiment. A prescriptive sentiment is a complex emotional disposition. If one has this sentiment about a particular form of conduct, then one is disposed to engage in that conduct, and one is disposed to feel badly if one doesn't. One is also disposed to condemn those who don't engage in that form of conduct. Suppose that Smith honestly judges that one ought to give to charity. Smith is expressing a sentiment that disposes him to feel badly if he doesn't give to charity and angry if you don't give to charity. This resembles the philosophical view called emotivism, but, as will become clear in chapter 3, my approach differs in important details.

Many refinements will follow in the coming chapters. I want to dwell here on implications. If the word 'ought' expresses a prescriptive sentiment, then that is what the word means. The concept underlying the word can be nothing more than what we use the word to express. So, if this simplified psychological theory is right, then we have learned what it means to say that someone ought to do something. We have learned what conditions satisfy the judgment that something is obligatory.

Now we are in a position to try to get an ought from an is. I offer the following argument:

1. Smith has an obligation to give to charity if 'Smith ought to give to charity' is true.
2. 'Smith ought to give to charity' is true, if the word 'ought' expresses a concept that applies to Smith's relationship to giving to charity.
3. The word 'ought' expresses a prescriptive sentiment.
4. Smith has a prescriptive sentiment towards giving to charity.
5. Thus, the sentence 'Smith ought to give to charity' is true.
6. Thus, Smith has an obligation to give to charity.

The conclusion of this argument is a prescriptive fact. The premises are descriptive. The word 'ought' is mentioned, but never used. Hume's Law has been violated.

My argument contrasts with an argument defended by Searle (1964). Searle also pursues a metalinguistic strategy. Simplifying a bit, he says that, when a person utters a sentence of the form, 'I promise to do X', that person places herself under an obligation. This is part of the meaning of promising. Then Searle infers that a person who has placed herself under an obligation is under that obligation. I am not convinced by Searle's argument. There may be trouble with both steps (for a more thorough critique, see, e.g., Downing, 1972). To promise is only to place oneself under an obligation if people ought to keep their promises. Thus, there is a suppressed normative premise. The move from placing oneself under an obligation to being under an obligation is also suspect. Placing oneself under an obligation can be interpreted conventionally. It can be a matter of being regarded as falling under an obligation in the eyes of a community. The community can regard a person as having an obligation—can place her under an obligation—even if the person is not actually obligated.

I think we need a stronger metalinguisitic premise than Searle offers. We need a substantive theory of the meaning of normative terms. Premise 3 in my argument articulates such a theory. That's where all the action is. The other premises are hard to deny. Premise 3 is controversial, and one goal of the chapters ahead is to provide arguments that make it more convincing. But I hasten to note that the argument can be modified to accommodate other theories. If naturalism is true then moral concepts are either vacuous, or they express properties that can ultimately be described without moral vocabulary. If my analysis of ought is incorrect, substitute another analysis, and replace premise 3 with the corresponding description of the natural facts underlying obligation. Now revise premise 4 accordingly, and the argument will go through. If there are obligations, then they can be derived in this purely descriptive way on any naturalist account.

0.3 SAVING HUME'S LAW

This is all a bit unsettling. First of all, there is an intuition favoring Hume's Law. There seems to be a logical leap from premises about how things are to conclusions about how things ought to be. Second of all, the theory of norms given in premise 3 makes it too easy to derive obligations. A sadistic person might have a prescriptive sentiment towards making people suffer. The argument just presented would entail that the sadist is obligated to be cruel. Something must have gone wrong.

I think these concerns can be addressed. With regard to the first concern, I begin by noting that the argument that I have offered does not violate Hume's Law. The argument does show how we can use descriptive premises to derive prescriptive facts, but the phrase 'prescriptive fact' turns out to be ambiguous. On one reading, a prescriptive fact is just a fact about what someone is obligated to do. But, a prescriptive fact can also be interpreted as a prescriptive judgment or, more succinctly, a prescription. Notice how the conclusion is expressed in the argument above. I said, 'Smith has an obligation to give to charity.' I did not say, 'Smith ought to give to charity.' Indeed, the argument itself shows why this conclusion could not follow. 'Ought' expresses a prescriptive sentiment. It can only be used truly by a speaker who has that sentiment. No premise in the argument entails that I, the author of the argument, have any disposition to react emotionally to charity. So no premise in the argument could entail, in my voice, that Smith ought to give to charity. If 'oughts' are prescriptions, then I have not shown how to derive an ought from an is. Premise 3, which gives the meaning of ought, shows why such a derivation won't work. That premise does not abrogate Hume's Law; it is the key to defending it.

In the end of the last section, I said that Premise 3 could be replaced with premises describing other naturalistic theories of normative terms. Other theories do not necessarily entail the result that I have just presented. They do not necessarily explain why there is no direct inference from obligation to ought. It is an advantage of the approach that I favor that it explains why Hume's Law is so compelling. Normative claims seem as if they can't be derived from descriptive claims, because there is no way to derive a prescriptive sentiment. Identifying normative concepts with prescriptive sentiments captures the truth in Hume's Law.

One might object that my attempt to save Hume cannot work because it violates a basic semantic principle. In the argument above, the final step moves from the semantic premise that 'Smith ought to give to charity' is true, to the claim that Smith has an obligation to give to charity. One might think that the semantic premise entails something stronger. If 'Smith ought to give to charity is true', then Smith ought to give to charity. This is just an instance of disquotation.

We can always infer P from 'P' is true. Or can we? I think that the argument that I have presented is a counterexample to the principle of disquotation. This is not a bad bullet to bite, because there are other counterexamples. Suppose Smith utters the sentence, 'I am Smith.' That sentence is true. It does not follow that I am Smith. Disquotation is not always allowed when we use indexicals such as 'I.' I believe that 'ought' is like an indexical in that its meaning is not exhausted by its contribution to a proposition expressed. I will argue for this conclusion in chapter 5. For now, the case of 'I' simply shows that disquotation has well-known exceptions. If 'ought' is an exception, and if it works like 'I', then my argument is sound.

The fact that we cannot derive oughts may come as cold comfort to some. Isn't it bad enough that we can infer obligations? Inferring obligations from descriptive premises is a little bit disturbing, but I think we can now diagnose why. We are uncomfortable asserting that people have obligations that we do not endorse. We would not want to assert that sadists are obliged to be cruel. I think that this discomfort has a pragmatic origin. Ascriptions of obligations conversationally implicate prescriptive judgments. If I tell you that someone is obligated to give to charity, I probably have an interest in conveying how I feel. Asserting the existence of an obligation is a way of conveying that I think the person ought to do something. But 'ought' is a conversational implicature of 'obligation,' not a semantic entailment. To see that, notice that the inference from 'obligation' to 'ought' can be cancelled. It sounds utterly contradictory to say, 'Smith ought to give to charity, though he ought not to give to charity.' But it does not sound contradictory to say, 'Smith has an obligation to give to charity, but he ought not.' We say things like this quite frequently when talking about the moral values of other people. We might say that the Japanese soldiers of World War II had an obligation to sacrifice their lives as Kamikaze pilots, but they ought not to have done that. Likewise, I can consistently admit that sadists have an obligation to be cruel while insisting that they ought to refrain from cruelty. This addresses the second concern raised at the beginning of this section. Obligations can be deduced from descriptive premises, but they need not be endorsed by their deducers. Endorsements are merely implicated. They cannot be deduced. Believing that Smith ought to give to charity requires making a prescriptive judgment. To make a prescription, we need to be in a particular psychological state—we need to prescribe. That is the sense in which we cannot derive an ought from an is.

0.4 DEFENDING SUBJECTIVISM

I have been arguing that Hume's Law is basically true. My defense depends on a theory of normative concepts that I presented in the form of a simple sketch. 'Ought,' I said, expresses a prescriptive sentiment. My primary goal in the chapters that follow will be to defend this claim, and to bring out some implications. I will focus on concepts such as GOOD and BAD or RIGHT and WRONG (capital letters denote concepts). These, like the concept OUGHT, essentially involve sentiments. Such concepts are fundamentally *subjective*.

My goal will not be to derive prescriptions from descriptions. That is a normative project and, if the preceding arguments are right, it is not one that can be taken very far. But I will try to derive metaphysical facts from psychological ones. Right and wrong are the referents of our concepts of RIGHT and WRONG if they are anything at all. If the analysis of our concepts uncovers a strong connection to subjective responses, then these terms may refer to something subjective. Moral psychology entails facts about moral ontology, and a sentimental psychology can entail a subjectivist ontology.

If morality is subjective, then why should moral judgments matter to us? One answer, inspired by Hume, is that we can't help caring about morality. There is something right about this, but it only pushes the question back a level. Why can't we help caring about morality? This question may actually be harder to answer than the question of why we *do* care. There is no single answer to the latter question. Moral systems serve various ends. They regulate behavior, they imbue life with a sense of meaning, and they define group membership. The question 'Why does morality matter?' is like the question 'Why does law matter?' or why does 'Culture matter?' People who feel uncomfortable with the idea that morality derives from us, should consider some other things that derive from us, such as medicine, governments, and art. The fact that art is a social construction does not deprive it of value. We don't expect institutions of art to collapse upon discovering that art is a product of human invention.

The discussion ahead divides into two parts, corresponding to themes that emerged in this discussion. In part I, I argue that morality depends on emotions, and, in part II, I discuss what I take to be an implication of this view: the hypothesis that morality varies across cultures. If morality depends on sentiments, I argue, then it is a construction, and, if it is a construction, it can vary across time and space.

The first chapter in part I presents a survey of different ways in which emotions can be involved in morality. I introduce the term 'emotionism' to label any view that makes emotions essential, and I offer some reasons for thinking that a strong form of emotionism is true. In chapter 2, I lay the foundations for an emotionist theory by presenting a general theory of the emotions. If morality has an emotional basis, then it is best to begin with an independently motivated theory of what emotions are. In that chapter, I also present an overview of the moral emotions, and I suggest that moral emotions derive from non-moral emotions. In chapter 3, I begin to present my positive account. It is what contemporary ethicists call a 'sensibility theory,' though my particular version departs in subtle ways from prevailing accounts (namely, it draws on an account of moral sentiments forecast in chapter 2, and it is not metacognitive). I argue that this theory can cope with ten major objections that have been levied against sensibility theories. Chapter 4 addresses a further objection not addressed in chapter 3: sensibility theories are subjectivist, and many people assume that morality is objective. I argue against this assumption by distinguishing several kinds of objectivity and critically assessing leading ethical theories that purport to show that morality is objective in each sense of the term. I conclude that morality is thoroughly subjective.

I call the account developed in part I 'constructive sentimentalism.' The term sentimentalism refers to the role of sentiments, and the term 'constructive' refers to the fact that sentiments literally create morals, and moral systems can be created in different ways. Part II focuses on this implication of sentimentalism. More specifically, it explores the role of culture in shaping moral values. In chapter 5, I draw out the relativist consequences of my case against objectivism, and I respond to standard arguments against relativism. The sixth chapter concerns the genealogy of morals, in Nietzsche's sense. I argue that historical anthropology can be used to explain why certain values persist, and why others have disappeared. I also assess the degree to which such analyses can be used to criticize morality. Chapter 7 turns from genealogy to genes. Even if some values are historical in origin, others may be biological. Evolutionary ethicists have been pushing this line in recent years. I argue that evolutionary ethics falls short of explaining any of our specific values. The only biologically based moral rules are too abstract to guide action, and their status as moral is epigenetic. Morality essentially involves learning. This conclusion bears on the prospect for moral progress, which is the theme in the final chapter. I discuss the nature of moral debates and argue that we can improve on morality. Moral improvement sometimes requires us to look beyond the categories of good and evil, but we should not attempt to abandon morality or replace it with another kind of normative enterprise.

My approach in defending these claims will be naturalistic in all the senses that I characterized above. My most obvious commitment is to methodological naturalism, because I will draw on empirical findings throughout, including findings from neuroscience, psychology, psychiatry, anthropology, cultural history, and ethology. I think enduring philosophical questions can be illuminated by empirical results, and, indeed, they might not endure so long if we use the resources of science. That said, I do not reject traditional philosophical methods, such as conceptual analysis. Indeed, I think that conceptual analysis is an empirical method in some sense: a kind of lexical semantics achieved by means of careful introspection. I think that method often bears fruit, but sometimes introspections clash or fail to reveal the real structure of our concepts. So it is helpful to find other methods to help adjudicate between competing philosophical theories. These other methods cannot replace philosophy. Philosophy poses the problems we investigate, devises useful tools for probing concepts (such as thought experiments), and allows us to move from data to theory by systematizing results into coherent packages that can guide future research. I see philosophy as continuous with science, and believe that we should be open to using any methods available when asking questions about the nature of morality.

I am also a pluralist about subject matter. This is a book about moral psychology, metaethics, and the origin and anthropology of morals; I even come into contact with some normative questions in the final chapter. Readers with a specific interest in, say, metaethics, may find little of interest in the discussions of cultural history, and readers with an anthropological orientation may be put off by the discussions of moral ontology. I hope this isn't the case. I think a complete account of morality should touch on each of these dimensions, and I think the dimensions are mutually illuminating. For example, one can argue for relativism by presenting semantic evidence and one can argue by studying cultural variation. Both may provide converging evidence, and the cultural observations motivate semantic inquiry and help to reveal why the semantic thesis may be so deeply important.

PART I

MORALITY AND EMOTION

1

Emotionism

1.1 AFFECTIVE MORALITY

1.1.1 Two Species of Emotionism

Judging that something is right or wrong is not like judging that 3 is a prime number or that trees photosynthesize. We can form those latter judgments without the slightest stirring of passion. We can be utterly indifferent to them. But moral judgments are anything but indifferent. They ooze with sentiment. We are passionate about our values. Consider the questions, "How do you feel about capital punishment?" An appropriate answer might be, "I feel it is completely unjustifiable." This figure of speech is awkward outside the evaluative domain. We would not ask, "How do you feel about trees," and answer, "I feel they photosynthesize." Rightness and wrongness, unlike primeness and photosynthesis, are things we feel.

Of course, many ethical theorists are prepared to reject this contrast. No one can deny that we feel strongly about our moral values, but one can reasonably doubt whether such strong feelings are constitutive of what it is to value or to be valuable. One can agree that moral judgments stir up our feelings while denying that something's status as a moral judgment depends on our having such feelings. One can admit that we feel strongly about moral facts while denying that those facts depend on our feelings. One can contend that there are things we ought to do and ought not to do, regardless of how we feel. The division between those theorists who think feelings are essential to morality and those who think emotions are incidental is perhaps the most fundamental rift in moral philosophy. I side with the members of the first camp. The claim that emotions figure into morality can be cashed out in various ways. I will use the term "emotionism" as an overarching label for any theory that says emotions are somehow essential. The term should not be confused with "emotivism," which is a specific version of emotionism.

I want to distinguish two dissociable emotionist theses. According to the first, moral properties could not exist without emotions. In other words there is no way to specify the identity conditions of a moral property as such without reference to an emotion or class of emotions. More succinctly, we can say:

Metaphysical Emotionism
Moral properties are essentially related to emotions

Defenders of this view are committed to moral realism, if we define moral realism as the view that there are moral facts. When a moral property is instantiated, there is a fact that consists in its instantiation. If one believes in moral properties, it follows that there are moral facts. The metaphysical emotionist embraces moral facts and claims that these facts depend on emotions. Some forms of utilitarianism qualify. Consider, especially, the classical utilitarianism of Bentham and Mill. They define the good as that which maximizes utility, and they define utility as happiness. There are moral facts, on this view, because there are actions that maximize happiness. And these facts are essentially emotional, because happiness is an emotion.

The term "realism" is sometimes reserved for a kind of mind-independence: the fact that *a* is *F* is real, on this interpretation, if *a*'s being *F* does not depend on our regarding *a* as *F*. Utilitarians are realists in this strong sense, about good. Call this external realism. Internal realism, in contrast, is the view that *a*'s being *F* is a fact, but that fact depends on our regarding *a* as *F* (see Putnam, 1980). Internal realism is factualism without mind-independence. Some metaphysical emotionists are internal realists. Consider the view that moral properties are secondary qualities. Secondary qualities are response-dependent properties. According to Locke, colors, tastes, and smells fit into this category. Lemons are tart—that's a fact—but they have this property only insofar as they cause a certain tart experience in us when we taste them. Accounts that develop the analogy between secondary qualities and morals have been dubbed "sensibility theories" (Darwall et al., 1992). The most influential recent versions we owe to McDowell (1985) and Wiggins (1987).

Sensibility theories descend from the "sentimentalist" theory of British moralists, such as Shaftesbury, Hutcheson, Hume, and Smith. Hutcheson tells us:

The word *moral goodness* . . . denotes our idea of some quality apprehended in actions, which procures approbation . . . *Moral evil* denotes our idea of a contrary quality, which excites condemnation or dislike.   (1738: 67)

Hume goes further, explicitly drawing an analogy between morals and secondary qualities:

Examine it in all lights, and see if you can find that matter of fact, or real existence, which you call vice. In which-ever way you take it, you find only certain passions, motives, volitions and thoughts. There is no other matter of fact in the case. The vice entirely escapes you, as long as you consider the object. You never can find it, till you turn your reflection into your own breast, and find a sentiment of disapprobation, which arises in you, toward this action. Here is a matter of fact; but 'tis the object of feeling, not of reason. It lies in yourself, not in the object. So that when you pronounce any action or character to be vicious, you mean nothing, but that from the constitution of your nature you have a feeling or sentiment of blame from the contemplation of it. Vice and virtue, therefore, may be compar'd to sounds, colours, heat and cold, which, according to modern philosophy, are not qualities in objects, but perceptions in the mind.   (1739: III.i.i)

Hume's moral theory has features that distinguish it from modern sensibility theories. One difference is that, in this passage, Hume can be read as implying that moral properties do not exist (the question of whether that was Hume's considered view I leave to the scholars). It's easy to arrive at a skeptical view about moral properties if you begin with an antirealist conception of secondary qualities. The Lockean conception of secondary qualities is different. According to Locke, sounds and colors are real, but relational (powers to cause sensations in us). If one is a realist about secondary qualities, one can adopt a realist analogue of Hume's thesis. Contemporary sensibility theories tend to have that flavor. In modern parlance, sensibility theories are committed to perceptivism rather than projectivism (D'Arms and Jacobson, 2006). Perceptivists say that we perceive moral properties in virtue of having certain emotions, and projectivists say we do not perceive them, but instead project them onto the world. As perceptivists, sensibility theorists are committed to metaphysical emotionism.

I will have more to say about sensibility theories below, but I want to turn now to another feature of Hume's moral philosophy. Hume emphasizes the priority of character over action. Being right or wrong is a function of causing certain emotions, but we must distinguish the emotions that matter to moral evaluation from those that don't. The question of which emotions matter is analyzed by Hume as a question about whose emotions matter. Hume thinks that right and wrong are determined by the emotional responses of a person of character:

'Tis only when a character is considered in general, without reference to our particular interest, that it causes such a feeling or sentiment, as denominates it morally good or evil. 'Tis true, those sentiments, from interest and morals, are apt to be confounded, and naturally run into one another. It seldom happens, that we do not think an enemy vicious, and can distinguish betwixt his opposition to our interest and real villainy or baseness. But this hinders not, but that the sentiments are, in themselves, distinct; and a man of temper and judgment may preserve himself from these illusions.   (1739: III.i.ii)

In this respect, Hume's sensibility theory is also an example of another kind of theory: it is a virtue ethics. Some versions of virtue ethics qualify as forms of metaphysical emotionism. Consider the following view. An action is good if and only if it is that which a virtuous person would do. A virtuous person is a person who has certain character traits. Virtuous character traits are or include emotional dispositions. It follows that an action is good just in case it would be performed by an emotional agent.

Utilitarianism, sensibility theories, and virtue ethics all make metaphysical claims about the nature of moral properties. Many of their defenders are also committed to epistemic claims. To recognize a moral fact, one must grasp the corresponding moral concepts. If moral concepts refer to moral properties and moral properties are constitutively related to emotions, then it is reasonable to think that grasping moral concepts involves emotions in some way. For example, utilitarians might say you cannot understand what the good is unless you possess the concept of happiness. Thus, for classical utilitarians, moral concepts may be essentially related to emotion concepts. Sensibility theories generally make an even stronger claim. They generally say that moral concepts must be defined, not in terms of emotion *concepts*, but in terms of emotions *themselves*. I will refer to this thesis as:

Epistemic Emotionism
Moral concepts are essentially related to emotions

To make this thesis plausible, it is important to draw a distinction between standard ways of possessing moral concepts, and deviant ways. Consider the analogy with color. There is a sense in which a congenitally blind person can grasp color concepts (see Crimmins, 1989). She might master the kinds of sentences that contain color words or she might even detect colors using a special apparatus that converts spectral information into another format. But this is not the way sighted people grasp color concepts. If colors are secondary qualities, we could say that a blind person is unable to grasp colors by their essential properties. A blind person cannot think about colors as such. Epistemic emotionism is supposed to be a thesis about our capacity to grasp moral properties in a standard way. The epistemic emotionist does not deny that there may be other ways of thinking about morality. A Martian without emotions could have deferential moral concepts, for example ("Wrong is what Earthlings call 'wrong'"). I will have more to say about standard concepts below.

Another point of clarification is in order. In defining epistemic emotionism, I used the phrase "essentially related." The most obvious form of essential relation is a constitution relation. Moral concepts are essentially related to emotions if they are constituted by emotions. On this approach, token instance of concepts such as WRONG and RIGHT are emotional states or have emotional states as component parts. This is what epistemic emotionists often have in mind. But some epistemic emotionists will want to allow for a dispositional relationship between moral concepts and emotions. They will want to allow that on some occasions people may make moral judgments without feeling anything, but they will insist that on such occasions, the people making those judgments are disposed to have emotional responses. By analogy, suppose you think the concept FUNNY is essentially related to amusement. On some occasions, you may judge, from memory for example, that someone is funny without actually feeling amused. On those occasions, however, you are being sincere only if you are disposed to feel amused when you are interacting with that person.

One can be a metaphysical emotionist without being an epistemic emotionist. Classical utilitarians are a case in point. One can also be an epistemic emotionist without being a metaphysical emotionist. Consider those who deny that moral properties exist. If moral realism is false, then metaphysical emotionism cannot be true. But a moral antirealist can defend epistemic emotionism.

Emotivism is a theory of this kind. Emotivists maintain that moral judgments do not describe the world; rather, they express our attitudes. Ayer (1952) says that the sentence "stealing is wrong" is equivalent to saying "stealing!" with a tone of horror. It does not ascribe any property to stealing money; it merely communicates a feeling. Stevenson (1937) defends a slightly different version of emotivism. He says that "stealing is wrong" does assert something, namely that I don't like stealing, but does not merely assert that fact; it asserts it in a "dynamic" way that expresses my dislike emotionally and thereby enjoins you to share in that attitude. Thus, even though Stevenson admits that moral terms express facts (likes and dislikes), their primary function is to express and commend emotions. Emotivism has sometimes been dubbed the boo/hurrah theory, because its defenders sometimes compare moral terms to expletives. Saying that stealing is wrong is somewhat like saying "boo to stealing!" because both "wrong" and "boo" are principally used to convey and prescribe feelings rather than to report facts.

Recent authors have defended more sophisticated expressivist theories. Blackburn (1984) is close to traditional emotivism, but he emphasizes the projective nature of moral judgments. We talk about moral properties *as if* they were in the world, but do not take on any serious ontological commitment in so doing. Blackburn and the classical emotivists are epistemic emotionists, but they reject metaphysical emotionism. Blackburn's account is often compared to another theory, called norm expressivism, which has been advanced by Gibbard (1990), but the two are importantly different. Gibbard claims that moral judgments express our acceptance of emotional norms. To say that stealing is wrong is to express acceptance of a norm that mandates feeling guilty when I steal and angry if someone else steals. Gibbard's view is different from emotivism because moral judgments do not express emotions directly; rather they express norms that commit us to the appropriateness of emotions. Thus, Gibbard is not strictly an epistemic emotionist; on his view, one might say that moral judgments mention emotions (they express the attitude that I have the right to be angry), but they don't use emotions (they don't express anger).

Epistemic emotionism is a psychological thesis. It is a thesis about moral concepts. The label "epistemic" adverts to the fact that concepts are the psychological tools by which we come to understand morality. But psychology has another dimension. It is the locus of action. And it is in this domain that emotionism shows another face. In order to act, we must be motivated. Emotions and motivation are linked. Emotions exert motivating force. There is clinical evidence that, without emotions, people feel no inclination to act. Damasio and Van Hoesen (1983) describe a condition called akinetic mutism, in which patients who have sustained injuries to emotional areas of the brain lie motionless in bed; upon recovery, they report that they were fully conscious, but they felt no emotions, and hence, no inclination to act. Moral emotions may be especially important in motivating decent behavior. For example, there is evidence that guilt promotes helping. In one study, McMillen and Austin (1971) induced some subjects to cheat in an exam, and then they asked those subjects to help score some questionnaires; subjects who hadn't been induced to cheat helped for only 2 minutes, but the cheaters helped for 63 minutes. If you feel guilty about doing something, you will try to make up for it, and if you anticipate feeling guilty about doing something, there's a good chance you'll resist the temptation to doing it. Therefore, if moral concepts *contain* emotions, then moral judgments will promote behavior that aligns with those judgments.

In philosophical jargon, this means that epistemic emotionism may entail motivational internalism. Motivational internalists believe that there is a necessary connection between moral judgments and the motivation to act in accordance with those judgments (Brink, 1989): if one believes that stealing is wrong, one is thereby motivated to act in a certain way (e.g., to refrain from stealing or work to prevent others from stealing) even if, under some circumstances, those motivations get swamped out by other motivational demands on action. As the name "internalism" implies, motivational internalists think that moral judgments carry motivational force on their own, with no need for help from the outside. For example, if you believe that stealing is wrong, you don't need an overarching desire to avoid the wrong in order to be motivated not to steal. But how might a moral judgment be intrinsically motivating? The answer is clear on an epistemic emotionist picture. Moral judgments contain moral concepts, and, epistemic emotionists claim that there is a necessary connection between moral concepts and emotions. Suppose that the necessary connection is such that tokening moral concepts always results in an emotional state. Empirical evidence demonstrates that emotions have motivational force. Thus, if this version of epistemic emotionism is correct, then moral judgments cannot occur without motivation.

Motivational internalism is a controversial doctrine. My point here is that epistemic emotionists have an explanation of how it could be true. It must also be noted that different forms of epistemic emotionalism would entail different forms of motivational internalism. On the form that I hinted at in my example, motivational internalists claim that moral judgments are *always* intrinsically motivating. There are also weaker forms of motivational internalism. For example, one might claim that moral judgments are ordinarily motivating, or capable of being intrinsically motivating, or dispositionally linked to motivation. Likewise, epistemic emotionism might come in different varieties. One might have the view that one cannot token a moral concept without tokening an emotion. Or one might have the view that tokening moral concepts disposes us to emotions. And so on. Each version of epistemic emotionism seems to entail a corresponding form or motivational internalism. In each case, there is a link between moral concepts and states that are motivating.

1.1.2 Essential Relations

In the definitions just presented, I said that emotionists postulate an "essential relation" between emotions and things in the moral domain. What is it to be essentially related? I chose this phrase, rather than "necessarily related" because there can be some leeway between necessity and essence. Something A belongs to the essence of another thing B if one cannot specify what it is to be B without mentioning A. This formulation does not invoke necessity in a strong modal sense. It does not say that all Bs are necessarily As. One *might* construe essential relations in this strong way. It is not uncommon for philosophers to think of essences as necessary and sufficient for membership in a category. The kind of essentialism associated with modern philosophy of language has this tone. When Kripke (1980) says that "water" refers to H_2O, he means water is H_2O in every possible world. This might give the impression that emotionists are committed to the view that emotions are present every time moral judgments or properties are present, just as oxygen in present in every sample of water. That impression is misleading.

Fist of all, there are other ways of construing essences. For example, Boyd (1988) defines an essence as a homeostatic property cluster: a collection of properties that tend to co-occur and promote each other's occurrence. On this view, some particular property could be part of the essence of some kind of thing even though it didn't always occur in every instance of that kind.

Second of all, even on a Kripkean view of essences, the phrase "essentially related to emotions" does not entail that emotions are active whenever there is a moral property or judgment instantiated. Suppose, for example, that moral concepts are constituted in part by *dispositions* to have emotions. Suppose, further, that such dispositions are essential to moral concepts in a Kripkean sense (in every token of a moral concept in every world, that token is constituted in part by an emotional disposition). It would follow that moral concepts are essentially related to emotions, because they are essentially related to emotional dispositions, and an emotional disposition is a relation to emotion. Essential relations are transitive. As long as the relations in question are not constitution relations, the emotionist can say that there is a strong modal connection between morality and emotion while conceding that emotions and morals are not always co-instantiated.

1.1.3 Strong Emotionism

The two species of emotionism that I have described can be accepted together or separately. I have already mentioned some of the theories that take on one or another species without embracing all of them. A partial breakdown is presented in the Table 1.1.

Table 1.1. Species of emotionism

	Sensibility Theories	Emotivism	Classical Utilitarianism	Kantian Ethics
Metaphysical Emotionism	Yes	No	Yes	No
Epistemic Emotionism	Yes	Yes	No	No

Kantians reject both forms of emotionism. Morally bad actions are those that I could not will as a universal law. This is not intended as an axiom about my passions or tastes. The bad is not that which I detest. Universalizability is a rational requirement on morality. Certain forms of conduct cannot coherently be universalizable. Kant (1785) gives lying promises as an example. If everyone lied when promising, the whole construct of promising would collapse. Promising makes sense only against a background where promises are generally reliable and honest. Kant sees a similar rational foundation to positive prescriptions. Helping the needy is morally required because one cannot universalize a lack of help for the needy. Everyone is needy or potentially needy some time, so it would be irrational for any one to will a world where no one helps the needy.

Kantians also reject epistemic emotionism, because conceptualizing something as right or wrong is a matter of forming a judgment about what is rational. Generally speaking, one can do that without being in any emotional state. Kant thinks, in making successful moral judgments, we would generally do well to ignore our passions.

Classical utilitarians agree with Kantians in denying epistemic emotionalism. They deny that moral concepts are essentially related to emotions. One could token a moral concept without having any disposition to experience an emotion. On the other hand, utilitarians think that metaphysical emotionism is true. The good is defined in terms of happiness. Emotivism is, in this respect, the inverse of utilitarianism. Emotivists claim that emotions are essential to moral concepts, but they reject the metaphysical thesis. They claim that there are no moral facts.

Utilitarianism and emotivism can be called weak emotionist theories, because they entail one emotionist thesis and not the other. A strong emotionist theory would entail both. Sensibility theory is the most salient instance. Here is a schematic statement of the view:

(S1) *Metaphysical Thesis:* An action has the property of being morally right (wrong) just in case it causes feelings of approbation (disapprobation) in normal observers under certain conditions.

(S2) *Epistemic Thesis:* The disposition to feel the emotions mentioned in S1 is a possession condition on the normal concept RIGHT (WRONG).

I think a theory of this kind can be defended. I endorse strong emotionism. Much of this book will be dedicated to justifying and elucidating that endorsement.

1.2 MIGHT EMOTIONISM BE TRUE?

Evidence from a variety of sources suggests that emotions are central to morality. In the remainder of this chapter, I will focus on evidence for epistemic emotionism, though I will offer some support for the metaphysical thesis at the end. I will add further arguments and responses to objections in the chapters that follow.

1.2.1 Moral Judgments Are Accompanied By Emotions

The most obvious reason for taking emotionism seriously stems from the mundane observation that moral judgments are often accompanied by emotions. It is hard to remain dispassionate when you read newspaper stories about child molesters, atrocities of war, or institutionalized racism. The intensity of our emotions is often a very reliable guide to the strength of our moral judgments. For example, crimes against children are often deemed worse than crimes against adults and they also seem to stir up stronger emotional responses.

The emotional impact of moral judgment is apparent from the fact that we tend to avoid bad behavior. Violating moral rules is often advantageous. If we steal things, we get to have them for free. If we cheat on our lovers, we can multiply our pleasures. Even killing can be advantageous; if you enter an essay contest, there is no better way to increase your chances of winning than to kill off the best writers in the competition. As it happens, we don't make a habit of doing these things, even when we can get away with them. Why not? The obvious answer is that doing bad things makes us feel bad.

This is poignantly illustrated by an experiment that Stanley Milgram conducted in the early 1970s. He asked his graduate students to board a New York City subway train and ask strangers to give up their seats. This violates a norm. We ordinarily obey a rule according to which anyone who finds an empty seat first is entitled to that seat. If you found the last free seat at 14th Street, and I board at 23rd Street, I have no right to your seat; it would be wrong of me to ask for it unless I was old, injured, or otherwise incapable of standing without risk. Milgrim asked his students to violate this norm, because he wanted to know how people would react. He had a general interest in obedience. But almost all of his students refused. He could only coax one student into performing the study. That student dutifully boarded the subway and asked people to give up their seats. When he came back, he said that the experience was incredibly difficult, and that he could not collect as much data as Milgrim had requested. Rather than asking twenty people for their seats, he stopped at fourteen. The difficulty had nothing to do with the fact that people were uncooperative. On the contrary, the majority of people willingly gave up their seats. The assignment was difficult because it was emotionally painful to break a norm.

Milgrim discovered this for himself after losing patience with his reluctant graduate students and performing the study himself. This is how he describes the experience in a 1974 interview:

The words seemed lodged in my trachea and would simply not emerge. Retreating, I berated myself: "What kind of craven coward are you?" Finally after several unsuccessful tries, I went up to a passenger and choked out the request, "Excuse me sir, may I have your seat?" A moment of stark anomic panic overcame me. But the man got right up and gave me the seat. A second blow was yet to come. Taking the man's seat, I was overwhelmed by the need to behave in a way that would justify my request. My head sank between my knees, and I could feel my face blanching. I was not role-playing. I actually felt as if I were going to perish.   (Quoted in Blass, 2004: 174)

This anecdote illustrates an important fact about moral norms. When we do things that violate moral values, we incur emotional costs.

There is now abundant empirical evidence that emotions occur when we make moral judgments. It is of particular interest that every neuroimaging study of moral cognition seems to implicate brain areas associated with emotion (Greene and Haidt, 2002). Consider some examples. Heekeren et al. (2003) asked subjects to evaluate whether sentences are morally incorrect (such as, "A steals B's car") or semantically incorrect (such as, "A drinks the newspaper"). In the moral judgment condition, subjects showed significantly more activation in emotion areas. In a similar study, Moll et al. (2003) had subjects make "right" or "wrong" judgments about both moral sentences such as, "They hung an innocent person," and factual sentences such as, "Stones are made of water." Once again, emotion areas were more active for the moral judgments. Moll et al. (2002) also found emotional activation when subjects listened to morally offensive sentences as opposed to neutral sentences (e.g., "The elderly are useless" versus "The elderly sleep more at night"). Sanfey et al. (2003) asked subjects to play an "ultimatum game" in which one player was asked to divide a monetary sum with another player. When the second player judged a division to be unfair, emotional regions of the brain were active. Singer et al. (2006) had subjects watch as electric shocks were administered to people (actually experimental confederates) who had played either fairly or unfairly in a prior prisoner's dilemma game. Areas associated with negative emotions and vicarious distress were more active when subjects watched fair people being shocked. Berthoz et al. (2002) gave subjects stories in which social rules were broken and contrasted these with cases of situations that are merely socially awkward. For example, subjects either heard about a person who rudely spits food into a napkin at a dinner party or about a person who innocently spits out food while choking at a dinner party. The social rule violations were associated with greater emotional activation.

The structures that are implicated in these studies include the insula, anterior cigulate cortex, the temporal pole, the medial frontal gyrus, and oribitofrontal cortex, which are all regular players in emotion studies (Phan et al., 2002). Moral judgments and emotions seem to coincide in the brain, just as epistemic emotionism predicts. A natural explanation of these findings is that moral judgments are constituted by emotional responses.

It must be conceded, however, that this is not the only explanation. The Milgrim anecdote and neuroimaging studies show that moral judgments have emotional costs, but that is consistent with two different models of how emotions relate to moral judgments: a causal model and a constitution model. The causal model says that moral judgments can have emotional effects. This is uncontroversial. Anyone who thinks we care about morality might be willing to say that moral judgments cause emotions. Music, sporting events, and sunny weather all cause emotions too, but they are not constituted by emotions. On a causal model, moral judgments occur prior to emotions, and are hence independent of emotions. On the constitution model, concepts such as RIGHT and WRONG literally contain emotions as component parts. This is what epistemic emotionists have in mind. The evidence so far cannot decide between these two possibilities. To support the constitution model, further evidence is needed.

1.2.2 Emotions Influence Moral Judgments

The emotionist can make progress showing that emotions actually influence our moral judgments. If moral judgments comprise emotions, then this influence can be explained. If the judgment that something is wrong contains indignation, then becoming indignant would promote that judgment. By analogy, suppose that the judgment that something is amusing contains amusement. More specifically, imagine that when we judge something to be amusing we are making a judgment of the form "that thing causes this state," where "this state" is an inner demonstrative pointing to amusement. Becoming amused promotes the judgment that something is amusing by furnishing us with one of its constituent parts.

There are various ways to show that emotions promote and influence moral judgments. Consider, for example, moral intuitions about killing and letting die. We tend to think killing is worse. Why is that? One answer is that killing arouses stronger negative emotions. Think about this from the first-person perspective. If your actions allow someone to die, and this is not your primary intention, you can focus away from the victim and concentrate on whatever your primary intention happens to be. When you imagine deliberately taking a life, you cannot focus away from the victim, so negative feelings brought out by sympathy with the victim are likely be strong and ineluctable. It may be that killing seems worse as a result of these stronger emotions.

This idea can explain intuitions about trolley cases (Thomson, 1976). In these thought experiments, we are typically asked to compare two scenarios. In both, a trolley is heading toward five people who have been tied down to the tracks. You are not close enough to free them, but you can save them. In one scenario, you can do this by pushing a person off a footbridge into the trolley's path, killing him, and causing the trolley to stop. In the other scenario, you can save the five by pulling a lever that switches the trolley to another track where you know that one person is tied down, instead of five. In both cases, your intervention would result in there being one death instead of five. Many people have the intuition that it is morally impermissible to intervene in the first case, and morally permissible to intervene in the second (Mikhail, 2000). Pushing someone in front of a trolley seems wrong, but it seems okay to divert a trolley away from five people and toward one. Why is this? A popular answer among philosophers is that killing a person is morally worse than letting someone die. In the pushing case, we are killing someone, but in the lever case we are merely allowing someone to die. Another explanation is that killing just stirs up more intense emotions. We don't want to push anyone into the trolley tracks because doing so fills us with horror, and the negative feeling causes us to think that the action is wrong.

The philosophical answer is compatible with the emotional answer. On the philosophical story, we have two rules: one that says we should not kill and another that says we should save lives, and the former is stronger than the latter. We don't have a rule against letting people die, or at least not a very strong rule. Thus, saving trumps letting die, and killing trumps saving. But what exactly are these rules, psychologically speaking? One answer is that they are grounded in emotions. We have negative feelings about killing, and positive feelings about saving lives, and few feelings about letting die. When considering dilemmas, the stronger feeling wins. This story makes two key predictions. One is that emotions should come on line when considering moral dilemmas, and the other is that our intuitions about what's right should be influenced by changes in the emotional content of the scenarios we consider. If moral rules are grounded in emotion, then factors that alter our emotions should affect our application of those rules.

Greene et al. (2001) have used functional magnetic resonance imaging to measure brain activity as subjects consider trolley cases. They showed significant activation in emotional areas of the brain when subjects were asked whether it is appropriate to push someone off a footbridge into the path of a trolley. Emotion activations were lower when subjects were asked whether it is appropriate to pull a lever that would divert a trolley away from five people toward one person. Greene et al. also note that, in the lever-pulling scenarios, subjects also show brain activations in areas associated with working memory. On this basis, the authors suggest that moral reasoning is driven by two dissociable processes: a cool rational process and an emotional process. I interpret their data differently. I suspect that emotions are involved in both cases. On the emotionist account that I just sketched, we have an emotion-backed rule that it's bad to kill, and a somewhat weaker emotion-backed rule that it's good to save lives. In the pushing case, we imagine killing in a very vivid way, and the emotional wallop packed by the "don't kill!" rule overwhelms the weaker emotions associated with the "save lives!" rule. In the lever-pulling case, we don't imagine the harm we are causing very vividly, so the "save lives!" rule can guide our actions. Here the numbers matter. We calculate that pulling the lever will result in more lives saved, and that results in an emotional preference for pulling the lever. The activations in working memory areas result from the fact that our decision depends on thinking about the numbers. We can coolly calculate which course of action will save more lives, but once we figure out that it's morally best to pull the lever, *that* judgment may be backed by an emotional response. This is consistent with the data. Greene et al. found that emotions are active during both the pushing scenario and the lever scenario. Emotions are more intense in the pushing case, but that's no surprise: pushing someone to his death is a very evocative activity.

If I am right, we deliberate about moral dilemmas by pitting emotions against emotions. Conflicting rules have different emotional strength, and the stronger emotions win out. If that's right, then it should be possible to alter intuitions about trolley cases by changing the scenarios in emotionally significant ways. Here's a prediction. When subjects say it is morally acceptable to pull the lever to save five people and kill one, they are imagining that the lever is far away from the tracks. Now suppose we tell subjects that the lever is just a few inches away from the person who would be killed if the lever were pulled. Imagine yourself in that situation. A man is tied down to the tracks right next to you. You cannot free him. He is writhing around and howling in terror. You know that there are five people on another track, which is some distance away, and you know that the trolley is heading that way. Would you sacrifice the person at your feet? Would that be morally acceptable? Here, I think intuitions would change. This is more like the pushing case. People who had not been exposed to many of these examples would, by default, have serious moral misgiving about sacrificing the life of someone inches away. The strong emotions elicited by proximity to the victim would, I predict, influence the judgment.

Conversely, we can imagine an emotionally attenuated variant on the footbridge case. Now you are located in a control room, and learn that a trolley is heading toward five people. By pulling a lever, you can open a trap door, causing a person standing on a footbridge to fall in the trolley's path and derail it. In this scenario, no physical contact with the victim is required. This has recently been tested by Greene et al. (forthcoming), and they found that most people think it is permissible to kill the man on the footbridge in this variant. If subjects are told that they have to push the man off the bridge, only 31 percent say it is permissible, and if they are told they just need to pull a lever that opens a trap door, 63 percent think it's permissible. Diminishing the emotional intensity of the method of killing doubles the approval rating.

These examples suggest that we are not slaves to a principle that killing is worse than letting die. We normally adhere to such a principle, but a change in emotional intensity can lead us to endorse clear violations of it. Moreover, the principle itself may be partially underwritten by the fact that killing is usually more emotionally charged than letting die. Killing usually involves physically contacting another person and perceptually experiencing that person's suffering. We can let someone die without any contact (as we so often do with distant crises around the world). I am not claiming that there is no moral difference between these cases (for that view, see Kagan, 1989). My point is that our moral intuitions about such cases are influenced by emotions.

Consider one more trolley case (for a more complete survey, see chapter 7 below and Prinz, forthcoming *a*). When you refuse to push a person in front of a speeding trolley to save five lives, you are making a deontological moral judgment. You are siding with those moral philosophers who claim that intentionally killing a person is wrong regardless of the consequences. You must obey the principle of humanity: you cannot use a human being as a means, rather than as an end. But such deontological intuitions can, famously, be overridden by changing the numbers. Suppose that, instead of five people tied to the track, the trolley is filled with powerful explosives and heading toward a village where it will detonate, killing five hundred people. Now it seems that pushing the person into the tracks and causing the trolley to derail would be morally commendable. We shift from being deontologists to being consequentialists. This switch in intuitions is an embarrassment for philosophers who think that deontological theories and consequentialism are in competition. But suppose that neither theory is right. Suppose that the concept of the good is not the concept of bringing about the best consequences or the concept of strictly following rules that obey the principle of humanity. Suppose instead that the concept of the good is the concept of that which causes strong emotions of approbation. In some cases, the action proscribed by deontological principles causes approbation, and in other cases, we approve of the consequentialist demand. In the present example, that shift is explained by the fact that imagining five hundred deaths fills us with an acute sense of horror. The scale of the loss pulls on our heartstrings. The emotional difference between five lives lost and one is big, but not enormous. It is not big enough to outweigh the revulsion we would feel pushing a person into the path of a speeding trolley. But the enormity of loss in the explosives case trumps the revulsion of killing a single individual. I think our emotions are influencing our judgments.

These examples suggest that moral judgments are linked in an essential way to emotions. If emotions were merely concomitants of moral judgments, then they should not influence those judgments. The fact that we are influenced by our emotions is predicted by the hypothesis that emotions are the basis of our judgments and, perhaps, constituent parts.

One might respond to this line of argument by pointing out that, while emotions *can* guide moral judgments, they need not. A dedicated deontologist might say, "It would fill me with unspeakable anguish to allow the decimation of a village, but it is still wrong for me to prevent that outcome by taking a human life." Moral judgments and emotions seem to be dissociable in this way. Doesn't this undermine the emotionist claim?

I will postpone serious discussion of this kind of objection until chapter 3. For now, I will mention four ways in which an emotionist theory could accommodate the deontologist who insists that it's okay to decimate the village. First of all, the deontologist might be quite passionate about the principle of humanity. Her emotional investment in the principle that it is wrong to use one person as a means to save others might be strong enough to trump countervailing considerations. Second, moral judgments may depend on particular kinds of emotions, and not others. When the deontologist says it is right not to push the person into the tracks, she may be recognizing that she would feel guilty if she did. If she lets the villagers die, she might feel intense sadness but not guilt. The sadness may be more intense than the guilt she would feel if she pushed the person into the tracks, but it would be the wrong emotion. Non-moral emotions can fuel moral emotions, but careful deliberators can keep these apart. Third, the deontologist may be judging that our emotions are misplaced in this case. By analogy, imagine the anguished victim of a crime who condemns a falsely accused suspect. The anguish causes the condemnation, but it is directed toward the wrong person. Likewise, when we imagine five hundred villagers dying, the anguish causes us to look for a perpetrator, and we may condemn a person whose actions or inactions would seem blameless if we considered the scenario in a cooler moment, with all the facts in. Finally, the deontologist might be self-deceived. Suppose she allows five hundred people to die, and then feels intense guilt. She might continue to insist that she doesn't believe the action was wrong, but we can challenge her self-assessment. We can say, "Clearly, you have moral misgivings about this action; clearly, it seems wrong to you." We can claim that she is merely mouthing the words when she says her inaction was right. Or one might suppose that she correctly recognizes that the action was right in a non-moral sense (she did as reason demanded), while painfully recognizing that her inaction conflicted with her basic moral values.

Intuitions about trolley cases do not prove that moral judgments involve emotions *necessarily*, but they suggest that emotions can exert a serious influence on moral judgments. This conclusion gains further support from research on the effects of emotion induction. In one study, Wheatley and Haidt (2005) hypnotized subjects to feel a pang of disgust when they hear either the word "take" or the word "often." They are then asked to evaluate morally the protagonist of various stories containing one of these two words. For example, they hear about a congressman who "is often bribed" or "takes bribes." The wrongness evaluations go up when the word choice corresponds to the word that triggers disgust in the subject. In fact, when the trigger word is used in neutral stories, subjects tend to condemn the protagonist as well. For example, they hear about a student in charge of scheduling discussions in school, who *often* picks interesting topics. Subjects who are disgusted when they here the word "often" find this student morally suspect, though they can't say why ("He seems like he's up to something"). In another study, Schnall et al. (2005) asked subjects to make moral evaluations of stories while sitting at a desk that was either tidy or filthy. The filthy desk has an old greasy pizza carton next to it, a chewed up pencil, used tissues, and a dirty beverage cup. Subjects who are good at introspecting their emotions (as measured by a body self-awareness scale that is correlated with emotion awareness) responded differently. Those seated at the filthy desk judged the scenarios to be worse than subjects seated at the clean desk. For example, they gave higher wrongness ratings to a scenario describing a person who accidentally kills his pet dog and then eats it. These effects do not depend on disgust. Lerner et al. (1998) showed subjects film clips that were either neutral or evocative of anger. They were then asked to consider some unrelated vignettes that describe people who perpetrate relatively minor transgressions, such as selling a used car without disclosing a defect. Subjects who viewed the anger-inducing clips recommended harsher penalties for the perpetrators in these vignettes. In addition, some studies have shown that induction of sad moods can lead to more negative appraisals of people (Fogas and Bower, 1987). Conversely, physical attractiveness, which is known to induce positive affect, can promote positive appraisals of people, including appraisals of honesty and integrity (Dion et al., 1972). It has also been shown in jury studies that attractive or smiling defendants are treated more leniently (Darby and Jeffers, 1988).

Together such findings support the case for epistemic emotionism. They suggest that emotions can influence moral evaluations even when the emotions are induced by morally irrelevant factors. This is just what epistemic emotionism predicts. Epistemic emotionism provides a natural explanation of the phenomenon: if moral concepts have an emotional component, then induction of emotions should influence application of those concepts. Compare: if the concept FUNNY contains the emotion amusement, then covertly tickling people should increase their tendency to think that a joke is funny. If the tickling is too obvious, they will attribute amusement to the tickling and not the joke, but, if the tickling is subtle, they may rate the joke as more amusing than they otherwise would.

I am not suggesting that this is a knock-down argument for emotionism. The fact that emotions influence moral judgments does not entail that moral judgments contain emotions. Emotions might influence moral judgments in another way. For example, empathy for the victim of a crime could instill the desire for punishment, and that could lead us to weigh evidence selectively in assigning blame to a suspect. On this view, the assignment of blame would not need to be an emotional judgment in its own right, even though emotions played a role in bringing it about. Emotions play a causal role, here, but they are not constitutive.

I think epistemic emotionism offers a better explanation of how emotions influence moral judgments. In the controlled experiments, there is no question about whether the characters described in various vignettes are guilty. The guy who eats his pet dog is clearly responsible for his actions. So emotions cannot be affecting wrongness judgments by influencing the way people weigh evidence. Moreover, there are dissociations between the desire for punishment and judgments of wrongness. Compare a crazed axe murderer to a calculating murderer who uses a gun. Because of his insanity, we may think the axe murderer should be less harshly punished than the gun murderer, but, because axe murders are more gruesome, we may judge that his crimes are more wrong. This is just my intuition, but it would be easy to test.

Of course, the opponent of emotionism could devise other explanations for why emotions influence moral judgments if the desire for punishment doesn't accommodate all the data. I think the main reason for preferring the emotionist explanation is that it fits better with findings that I am about to describe. If emotions were not constituents of moral judgments, but merely exerted a causal influence, then emotions would be neither necessary nor sufficient for regarding something as wrong. The wrongness concept would be something above and beyond the emotions, and hence independent of them. On the causal influence account, there should be cases in which people moralize without having emotions, and there should not be cases in which emotions alone are, on reflection, the sole basis of moral judgment. As we will see, these predictions of the causal influence account are incorrect. The view that emotions constitute our moral judgments fits better with the data.

1.2.3 Dumbfounding

The evidence adduced so far shows that emotions can sway our moral judgment. But epistemic emotionists make a stronger claim. They say that having a moral attitude is a matter of having an emotional disposition. If this is right, then someone should be able to have a moral attitude in the absence of any rational justification. Emotional attitudes should be sufficient for moral attitudes. There is empirical evidence supporting this prediction. People's reflective moral judgments seem to have an emotional foundation. If we ask people why they hold a particular moral view, they may offer some reasons, but those reasons are often superficial and post hoc. If the reasons are successfully challenged, the moral judgment often remains. When pressed, people's deepest moral values are based not on decisive arguments that they discovered while pondering moral questions, but on deeply inculcated sentiments.

This conclusion has been compellingly defended by Jonathan Haidt and his collaborators. Haidt defends a "social intuitionist" account of moral decision-making, according to which we usually arrive at a moral judgment by introspecting our sentiments. Arguments for that judgment are usually contrived after the judgment is made, and play no essential role in arriving at the judgment or in sustaining the judgment.

To support this model, Murphy et al. (2000) studied moral attitudes toward consensual incest. They asked American college students to consider a case in which a brother and sister have sex. In the scenario, the siblings consent to intercourse, use contraception, enjoy the experience, and keep it a secret. Eighty percent of the subjects judged that the behavior was morally wrong, but they had great difficulty explaining why. Each time they came up with an argument to show that the siblings had done something immoral, the experimenters explained why the argument fails. Many subjects worried that the couple would have deformed children, but the experimenters reminded them that contraception was used. Some were worried about the effects on the community, but that worry is inapplicable, because the couple in the scenario did not tell anyone what they had done. Some subjects might have complained that the couple would be traumatized, but the scenario specifies that they actually enjoyed the experience and it strengthened their relationship. A few subjects suggested that incest is condemned in the Bible, but none could recall where (certainly not in the story of Lot and his daughters!). Subjects were presented with decisive counterarguments to every argument that they gave against consensual incest. They tended to concede that the counterarguments were successful, but only 17 percent changed their initial moral judgments. The others typically bottomed out in unsupported declarations and emotional exclamations. Incest is nasty! Incest is just wrong: it's gross! Reasons fell by the wayside, but moral convictions and moral emotions were recalcitrant.

Murphy et al. (2000) found the same pattern of responses when they presented subjects with a scenario involving cannibalism. A woman working alone late one night in a medical pathology lab decides to cook and eat a discarded piece of a human cadaver that was donated to the lab for medical research. Once again, subjects say this is wrong, but they cannot articulate reasons sufficient to support that conclusion. They say that their moral appraisal of the case is based on a "gut feeing."

These dumbfounding results can be interpreted in several ways. One possibility is that subjects have good reasons for their views about incest and cannibalism, but these reasons operate unconsciously. After all, a lot of problem-solving is done unconsciously, and people have limited insight into how they arrive at judgments in other domains (Nisbett and Wilson, 1977; Moscovitch, 1995). Call this the *hidden reasons* interpretation.

This interpretation strikes me as highly unlikely. We may arrive at our moral assessment of incest unconsciously, but there is no evidence that much reasoning is taking place. It is very hard to know what those reasons would be. It's one thing to say that the reasons are not accessible to consciousness when we initially arrive at our judgments, and another to say that extensive careful reflection cannot gain access to them. Coming up with arguments against consensual incest is hard, and, since there is little public discussion of incest, it is difficult to believe that subjects have internalized arguments from earlier reflection or education. Moreover, there is a straightforward explanation of how people arrive at their moral judgments that does not require postulation of hidden reasons. Incest and cannibalism have been emotionally tagged as repulsive and taboo. That fully explains the knee-jerk moral condemnations of perpetrators. And our tenacity in denouncing incest and cannibalism derives from the fact that reasons do not easily override the deeply entrenched emotional responses.

According to a second interpretation of the dumbfounding results, people always base their moral judgments on reasons, but those reasons are sometimes bad. After all, people do offer arguments against incest and cannibalism. It just turns out that their arguments are flawed. Murphy et al.'s results are consistent with the hypothesis that moral judgments derive from reason, rather than passion.

The problem with this interpretation is that people usually don't revise their moral assessment when their reasons are debunked. They recognize that the reasons are flawed but they dig in their heels about the wrongness of consensual incest and cannibalism. This suggests that the reasons they offer did not play a very central role in the formation or maintenance of their moral judgments.

Another possibility is that subjects do not really regard incest and cannibalism as immoral. Perhaps they are just saying these things are wrong because they recognize that to be the prevailing view. Endorsing a taboo behavior in public has serious social consequences, so subjects have good reason to make it appear as if they find incest and cannibalism bad.

This interpretation is also unconvincing. If taboos are powerful enough to make people say that they categorically oppose incest and cannibalism, then they should be strong enough to instill the corresponding beliefs. The issue could be tested by having people answer questions about consensual incest and cannibalism on an anonymous questionnaire. I would predict that subjects would continue to condemn.

A fourth possibility is that subjects have *no reasons* for their moral judgments. They simply have a gut reaction that consensual incest and laboratory cannibalism are wrong, and a few post hoc rationalizations, which play no important role in driving those reactions.

I think this proposal is almost right, but it's a bit misleading. Usually, if you have no reason for a belief, you are rationally required to give it up, but I don't think that people regard their moral attitudes as subject to this requirement. Values can be basic in a way that places them outside the reason-giving game. People tend to express their views about incest and cannibalism by saying, "It's just wrong!" My guess is that they would say the same thing about killing or inflicting harm on an innocent person. Consider the question, "Why is it wrong to rape a toddler who will never remember the incident?" This is an odd question. It is difficult to answer. It's just wrong to do that. Very wrong. Fundamentally wrong. And morally monstrous. When we say, "It's just wrong" we are not obviating reason; we are implicitly giving one. The "just" in "just wrong" signals that this is a basic value. We have hit rock bottom. Someone who sincerely asserts that he does not regard it as wrong to rape a toddler doesn't understand what we mean by "wrong." He is using the word differently. Compare someone who insists that strawberries are not red.

This reveals something about the practice of reason-giving in morality. When we provide a reason for thinking that some behavior is wrong, we imply that its wrongness consists in the fact that it has a particular property that makes it wrong. But suppose we iterate the why-question. Why is drunk driving wrong? The answer is that it endangers innocent lives. Why is it wrong to endanger? Because danger is risk of harm, and harming an innocent person is wrong. Why is it wrong to harm an innocent person? Here the question becomes odd. Trained philosophers might have views about this, and others may be able to come up with reasons, but it is unlikely that those reasons are the source of the moral intuition. If one could come up with some feature that makes killing wrong, we could ask what makes that feature wrong. At some point, we grasp for straws. At some point the why-question looks misplaced, bizarre, or even depraved. We might say that people have no reasons for their basic values, but it would be better to say that basic values are implemented in our psychology in a way that puts them outside certain practices of justification. Basic values provide reasons, but they are not based on reasons.

I return to basic values in chapter 3 under the label "grounding norms." I present them here as a way of explaining the Murphy et al. dumbfounding results. People get flustered when asked to explain their condemnation of incest, because this is a basic value. Moreover, basic values seem to be implemented in an emotional way. When we get down to basic values, passions rule. People say incest and cannibalism are disgusting. Murder is abhorrent. Stealing is unconscionable. A typical member of this culture would endure a considerable emotional penalty for committing any of these acts.

1.2.4 Moral Development

If this interpretation of Haidt's findings is right, normal adults have values that are not maintained by a network of carefully thought-out reasons. They are implemented by gut feelings. This picture gains further support from research on moral development.

The most widely discussed theory of moral development has been propounded by Laurence Kohlberg (1984). Kohlberg asks subjects to resolve moral dilemmas. For example, he tells them about a man named Heinz who cannot afford to pay for a drug needed to save his wife from cancer. After unsuccessfully pursuing legal means to get the drug, should Heinz break into a lab and steal it? Kohlberg assesses moral understanding by looking at how subjects justify their responses to such cases. On the basis of this research, he concluded that children go through a progression of stages in moral development. Kohlberg identifies six stages, grouped into three levels. In the first stage, children focus on obedience and punishment. They justify moral judgments by appealing to the punitive responses of authorities. After that, children begin to think instrumentally about morality; they think about the benefits to the moral agent. Kohlberg calls these two stages preconventional morality; they are characterized by an egoistic orientation. This is followed by a two-stage conventional level of moral thinking, in which children begin to think about conformity to a group. In the first stage of conventional morality—stage three of the overall sequence—children adopt a "good boy/nice girl" orientation. They begin to focus on how they will be regarded by others. In stage four, there is a focus on law and order. At this stage, there is a focus on duty to fixed rules and the maintenance of social order. Kohlberg thinks that conventional morality can be followed by postconventional morality, but he recognized, empirically, that this final level of development is rarely attained, even among adults. Postconventional morality begins with a fifth stage of moral development in which people focus on social contracts. At this stage, people continue to think in terms of law and order, but now they justify laws by appeal to broadly utilitarian principles. There is a potential sixth stage after that, which Kohlberg characterizes in terms of universal moral principles. These rules are abstract and categorical (like the Golden Rule), rather than concrete and particular (like the Ten Commandments). In other words, Kohlberg thinks that moral development should, but rarely does, bring us ultimately to a Kantian conception of morality. In a longitudinal study in the United States, Colby et al. (1983) found little evidence for reasoning at stages five and six. Most adults reason at stage four most of the time. In a review of cross-cultural research, Snarey (1985) found that stage four was the highest stage exhibited in rural and village societies.

Kohlberg's findings are consistent with the view that emotions are essential to moral judgment. First of all, the relative absence of reasoning at the fifth and sixth levels suggests that ordinary people are neither utilitarians nor Kantians. Standard moral concepts do not seem to be grounded in the kinds of principles that dominate philosophical ethics. This raises some doubts about philosophical accounts in the utilitarian and Kantian traditions. These programs may be better construed as revisionist, rather than as accurate analyses of how ordinary people understand moral concepts (see chapters 3 and 4). Second of all, Kohlberg's first three stages of moral development implicate emotions quite explicitly. In stage one, people express fear of punishment. In stage two, people appeal to hedonic gains. In stage three, people express the desire to be liked by others. Simplifying, one can say that the concept WRONG is sequentially linked to fear, frustration, and ultimately, the anticipated sadness of social rejection.

What are we to say about Kohlberg's fourth level, which is dominant in Western industrialized societies? Reasoning at this level is not explicitly emotional, but that does not mean it lacks an emotional foundation. At the fourth level people appeal to law and order. Appeals to order may have an emotional undertone. People say that moral rules are justified by the fact that society would fall apart without them. This justification lacks force if one is neutral about societal collapse. It is natural to suppose that thoughts of societal collapse evoke fear and concern for loved ones. Those who jeopardize social stability pose a threat to well-being, and are thus viewed with contempt or anger. If so, appeals to order may reflect an emotional attitude. Turn now from order to law. Sometimes, instead of raising worries about societal collapse, people try to justify their moral judgments simply by citing the existence of a law or policy. In effect, they say that something is wrong because there is a rule against it. Such people treat rules as if they had intrinsic value. This pattern of justification is actually predicted by epistemic emotionism. If we ground norms in emotional reactions, then our moral convictions lack a rational foundation. Now suppose you give subjects a reasoning task, in which they are asked to justify their belief that ϕ-ing is wrong, and they find themselves unable to articulate any reasons because the rule is grounded in emotions. At this point, justifications will begin to sound circular. Why is ϕ-ing wrong? Well, it just is. Put differently, ϕ-ing is wrong because that's the rule.

The emotionist can explain this kind of rule fetishism. In the course of moral development, we are conditioned to have a strong emotional reaction to the violation of certain rules. Merely thinking about someone violating those rules elicits negative feelings. Thus, the rules take on a kind of obviousness. They are immediately compelling to us, and we assume that they are obvious to others. Evocation of a rule that has been conditioned in this way feels sufficient for purposes of justification. Thus, stage four is like the earlier three stages of moral development, in that all of them make implicit appeal to emotions. The main change in development is that, by the time we reach the fourth stage, we assign emotional significance directly to rules, rather than derivatively. In earlier levels, ϕ-ing is wrong because it causes negative emotional consequences for me. By level four, ϕ-ing is wrong because I regard it negatively in itself. There is a transfer of emotions from egocentric consequences of transgression to transgression itself. The developmental change fits beautifully within an emotionist framework.

On the view that I have just described, people at Kohlberg's level four justify moral judgments by appeal to rules because rules are regarded as intrinsically valuable, and rules achieve this status because they are grounded in emotion, rather than reason. To test this interpretation, subjects in Kohlberg-style experiments must be pressed a bit more. When they say that ϕ-ing is wrong because of a rule against ϕ-ing, they should be asked, "Why should we do what the rules command?" I predict that most people would have difficulty articulating an answer. As in Murphy et al.'s (2000) dumbfounding research, I would expect people to become befuddled or to express emotions. They should say, "ϕ-ing is horrible," or something along those lines. In referring to stage four as "conventionalist," Kohlberg seems to have a very different interpretation in mind. The label implies that people at stage four think of morality in conventional terms. If asked, "Why should we do what the rules command?" a person with a conventional conception of morality should respond by saying "Well, that's what members of my community do."

In sum, the fact that most people progress to level four can be interpreted as evidence for emotionism. Kohlberg calls this the conventional stage, but I think that label is misleading. I do think moral rules are essentially conventional, but I don't think people view them that way. The fact that people justify their moral attitudes by appeal to law and order does not entail that they regard them as conventions. On the alternative interpretation that I just offered, people at this stage actually regard rules as having intrinsic value. Violating a moral rule just feels wrong. The appeal to law and order in moral reasoning is not an appeal to convention, but rather an appeal to emotionally grounded norms. My emotionist interpretation of Kohlberg's results makes two empirical predictions. It predicts that moral maturation is achieved through a process of emotion training, and it predicts that people at the so-called conventional stage do not really think moral rules hold simply in virtue of societal conventions. Putting these two predictions together, the emotionist account predicts that people come to regard moral rules as different from conventional rules by assigning emotional significance to moral rules. Evidence from developmental psychology supports all of these predictions.

First of all, there is evidence to suggest that moral education is a matter of emotional training. Children are given moral instruction via careful manipulation of emotions. Psychologists emphasize three primary methods used by caregivers to promote good conduct (Hoffman, 1983: Eisenberg, 2000). One method is power assertion. Caregivers punish or threaten to punish their children. Punishment promotes fear, and, by imitation, children who have been punished for doing something bad are likely to become angry at others who behave badly in the future. Another method is love withdrawal. When children do something bad caregivers sometimes express disappointment and refuse to signal affection. This makes children feel sad, and that may be the wellspring of regret. Caregivers also use a technique called induction. They call children's attention to the harms that their misdeeds cause. When children recognize that their actions have made someone suffer, they naturally feel sympathy and vicarious distress for the victim. Each of these methods has been associated with the development of guilt and shame, and with the development of pro-social behavior.

Second of all, there is evidence that ordinary children do not regard moral rules as merely conventional. Smetana (1981), Turiel (1983), and Nucci (2001) have pioneered research on this issue. They have demonstrated that children distinguish between moral and conventional rules. For example, children draw a distinction between rules prohibiting hitting and stealing, on the one hand, and rules prohibiting speaking without raising your hand in class and rules proscribing dress codes, on the other. To establish that this distinction is understood, Smetana, Turiel, and Nucci present children with examples of rule violations, not indicating which ones are moral and which ones are conventional.

They then ask children questions about seriousness (e.g., How wrong was behavior in the example?), authority dependence (e.g., Would the behavior be wrong if teachers permitted it?), and justification (e.g., Why is it wrong?). Children answer these questions differently for moral and conventional rules. They treat moral rule violations as more serious and less dependent on authorities. Hitting would be wrong no matter what the teacher says, but talking out in class would be fine if the teacher allowed it. Children tend to justify moral rules by appeal to harms inflicted on others, whereas they justify conventional rules by appealing to conventions.

Smetana, Turiel, and Nucci's results can be given an emotionist explanation. Why do children find moral transgressions more serious? Perhaps they have greater emotional consequences. Seriousness may be an emotional assessment. Why do children appeal to harms explaining what's wrong with moral transgressions? Perhaps harms cause sympathy and distress. Why do children consider moral rules independent of authority? Perhaps thoughts about moral transgressions stir up negative emotions, and these remain in place even when children imagine prohibitions being lifted.

Support for this interpretation can be found in the responses that children give to questions about moral rules. For example, in one series of studies, Nucci (2001) asked children if stealing would still be wrong if God said that stealing was permitted. The overwhelming majority of children answered affirmatively. They insisted that stealing would be wrong regardless of what God says. When Nucci asked the children to justify their answers, they tended to appeal to emotions. Here's what an eleven-year-old boy tells us: 'if people would steal, then the world wouldn't be a happy place . . . it would still make everybody unhappy . . . Like when my sister stole my batteries, it really irritated me. If everybody's stuff kept getting stolen, everyone would be mad' (Nucci, 2001: 36). This response is typical. A nine-year-old girl explains that stealing is wrong because, "the one who got stealed from would get real angry" (p. 38). A ten-year-old girl echoes this justification: "You're taking another person's stuff and they would probably get upset" (p. 47). There is considerable evidence that, when people attribute emotions, they also experience them (Goldman and Sripada, 2005). It is likely, then, that the children in Nucci's study feel vicarious anger on the part of crime victims. The very idea of stealing makes them feel mad because they imagine the anger of others.

There is evidence that children begin to appreciate the emotional consequences of bad behavior considerably earlier. By the time they are two years old, children show signs of guilt and shame when they do something wrong (Barrett et al., 1993; Zahn-Waxler and Robinson, 1995; Kochanska et al., 1995). In one experimental paradigm, experimenters give toddlers a toy doll that is rigged to fall apart when they play with it. Two-year-olds show signs of self-conscious distress when such "mishaps" occur. For example, they avoid eye-contact, they squirm, they hang their heads down, and they cover their faces. Such negative feelings may help children acquire mastery of the moral/conventional distinction, which begins to appear shortly before the third birthday. Smetana and Braeges (1990) found that children at that age regard moral rules differently from conventional rules, judging that the former are more generalizable than the latter (e.g., more likely to be followed at other schools). By early childhood, the moral/conventional distinction is very well entrenched. Children come to recognize that moral wrongs are more authority-independent and more serious than conventional wrongs.

At slightly older ages, children become very sensitive to the effects that bad behavior has on others. Arsenio and Lover (1995) described a series of bad behaviors to kindergarteners, and then asked them to pick facial expressions that capture what the victims and observers of those behaviors would feel. Kindergarteners reliably choose facial expressions of negative emotions, such as fear, anger, and sadness. Interestingly, kindergarteners expect that the perpetrators of moral transgressions will feel happy. This is called the happy victimizer effect. Presumably, they think victimizers are happy because their misdeeds achieve intended goals. For example, a person who steals some candy will be happy to have obtained the candy. Kindergarteners do not judge happy victimizers to be any more reprehensible than victimizers who show remorse. They begin to regard happy victimizers as worse than remorseful victimizers by the time they are eight years old. This is an important developmental milestone. It indicates that eight-year-olds do not merely have norms about how people ought to behave; they have norms about how people ought to feel. Happy victimizers commit two wrongs: one in their conduct and the other in their attitude.

This developmental trajectory is probably the product of both nature and nurture. Children are naturally prone to empathetic distress, fear, and personal attachments. When they do bad things, they discover emotional costs. The costs are likely to be especially bad in the case of moral wrongs, since violations of social conventions tend to produce weaker reactions in others, and caregivers respond with more severe forms of discipline (Smetana, 1989; Grusec and Goodnow, 1994; Nucci and Weber, 1995). In this way, children are conditioned to associate moral wrongs with strong negative emotions. This explains why moral rules are psychologically distinct from conventional rules, and it explains why moral rules are regarded as more serious and less dependent on authority. The systematic relationship between emotions and moral comprehension in children supports the hypothesis that moral concepts are emotionally implemented. This story contradicts Kohlberg's claim that people tend to understand morality conventionally. The fact that people appeal to rules in justifying moral judgments is better explained in emotionist terms.

1.2.5 Moral Mary

After reviewing the literature on moral development, one might concede that emotions play a central role in acquiring moral competence, while insisting that this role is merely contingent. Children are too unsophisticated to understand complex philosophical arguments, so they must be emotionally conditioned to behave in accordance with moral rules. But adults are different. We are responsive to reason. To explore this possibility, I want to construct a thought experiment that describes an individual who learns about morality without the benefit of emotional conditioning.

Imagine a woman named Mary who was never exposed to any moral education while she was growing up, but her other cognitive capacities developed normally. She is now an intelligent adult. Imagine that Mary has no intact innate moral attitudes. She doesn't feel guilty or indignant about anything. But she decides that she wants to learn what morality is all about, so she coops herself up in a room with masterworks by Kant, Mill, and other normative ethicists. She learns their theories, and she becomes very adept at identifying the kinds of considerations that they bring to bear. For any action that she considers, Mary is able to determine (a) whether it would maximize utility and (b) whether it would lead to any practical contradictions if it were pursued by all agents. Indeed, she can discern any of the facts emphasized by leading normative theories. Now here's the crucial question. Suppose Mary discovers that doing X will in fact maximize utility. Is that sufficient for her knowing that doing X is morally right? Can she wonder whether X is morally required even though she knows that it maximizes utility? The answer is obvious. Mary can wonder. She may be totally unsure about whether X is an action that *morality* demands. Suppose Mary also contemplates another course of action Y. She knows that doing Y would lead to a practical contradiction if everyone did it; perhaps it requires using another person as a means rather than as an end. Kant would say Y is morally wrong, but Mary can wonder. She knows that Y is practically irrational, but she doesn't know whether it is *immoral*. Suppose the Kantian and Millian recommendations for action come into conflict. Can Mary decide which option is morally superior? Certainly not. Mary began her training wondering what people are talking about when they moralize, and she is still in the dark; reading normative ethics books proved fruitless. Intuitively, Mary can be a perfect detector of the features that normative ethicists identify as the basis of morality, and she can have no idea whether those features have any moral significance.

Indeed, moral Mary might not even be able to pose the relevant questions. She could not ask herself whether maximizing utility is morally required, because the concept of moral requirement would elude her. She would have no understanding, given her deviant development, of what people mean when they refer to something as "right" or "wrong." At best, she could ask whether these words, used by members of her community, designate the properties discussed by Kant and Mill. She can mouth the words "right" and "wrong," but she cannot understand them. This strongly suggests that the concepts of right and wrong (or good and bad) are not explicable in terms of the concepts introduced by Kant, Mill, and other normative ethicists.

This thought experiment is just a version of G. E. Moore's "open-question argument." Moore (1903) tried to refute the thesis that morality can be reductively analyzed, by showing that, for any "natural" property P, it is an open question whether possessing P is good (though what Moore meant by "natural" isn't exactly clear, see Dreier, 2006). In a similar spirit, I am using Moral Mary to argue that it is unlikely that moral concepts can be analyzed in terms of the constructs used in familiar normative ethical theories. Despite this resemblance, I want to distinguish my argument from Moore's because his argument trades on a mistake. Moore was arguing for a metaphysical conclusion. He took the fact that it was an open question whether any property P was good as support for the conclusion that the property of being good is not constituted by any such property. This is certainly a mistake. Since Moore's time, philosophers have come to recognize the existence of a posteriori identities—metaphysical facts that cannot be discovered through conceptual analysis. Before modern chemistry, no one knew that alcohol is a hydroxyl compound, with a molecular structure $C_nH_{2n+1}OH$. The claim that alcohol is a hydroxyl compound is certainly not an obvious truth, because one can possess the concept of alcohol without knowing any chemistry. But it would be a mistake to challenge this identity by pointing out that one can intelligibly wonder whether it is true. Likewise, it was a mistake for Moore to infer that moral properties are non-natural, and it would be a mistake to infer from the thought experiment about Moral Mary that moral properties do not refer to the kinds of properties discussed in the normative ethical theories of Kant and Mill.

Open-question arguments cannot establish metaphysical conclusions, but they can establish conceptual conclusions. If it is an open question whether some natural property N is good, then the concept of N cannot be part of the concept of goodness. Were there a conceptual link between the two, the question would be closed. For example, it might be part of the ordinary concept of alcohol (i.e., the concept used by most adults when thinking about alcohol on most occasions) that drinking alcohol can result in intoxication. If that is part of the ordinary concept, then no one who grasps that concept could intelligibly wonder whether drinking can result in intoxication. Where there is a conceptual link there is no open question. Likewise in the case of Moral Mary. If Moral Mary cannot acquire the ordinary concepts of good and bad or right and wrong by reading about the properties described in normative ethical theories, then it cannot be the case that those properties are constitutive of our ordinary moral concepts. Moral concepts may, for all I have argued so far, refer to Kantian or Millian properties, but it is not a conceptual truth that the right is that which maximizes utility or that it is wrong to do that which cannot be universalized.

The Moral Mary thought experiment can also be compared and contrasted with Frank Jackson's celebrated argument against materialism. Jackson has us imagine a brilliant neuroscientist named Mary, who is trapped in a black and white room. Mental Mary knows everything about what happens in the brain when people see red, but this does not help her understand what it would be like to have a red experience. Like Moore, Jackson tries to draw a metaphysical conclusion. He says that the experience of seeing red cannot be identical to a brain state. That conclusion is very controversial. Many commentators think that it is fallacious to infer a metaphysical conclusion about the basis of red experience from epistemological or semantic premises about whether we can infer what red is like from knowledge of the brain. But just about everyone is willing to grant that Jackson's argument establishes an epistemological conclusion. The concepts involved in knowing what experiences are like differ from the concepts involved in knowing about brain states as such: one cannot infer one class of concepts from the other.

Likewise, the Moral Mary argument firmly establishes an epistemological conclusion. The concepts invoked in normative ethical theories differ from the concepts of right and wrong. One cannot infer that an action is morally right or wrong from a Kantian or Millian description of that action. This is enough to establish that Kant, Mill, and other normative ethicists fail to explain moral concepts. That does not prove that metaphysical emotionism is right. We cannot infer that Kant and Mill are wrong about moral properties from the fact that they are wrong about moral concepts. It is possible (though, for reasons given in chapters 3 and 4, implausible) that moral concepts designate Kantian or Millian properties. But conceiving these properties is not sufficient for grasping moral concepts. Mary understands what it is to maximize utility and what it is to universalize a behavioral maxim, but she does not understand what people ordinarily grasp when they use the words "right" and "wrong."

Unlike Jackson and Moore, I am not trying to establish a metaphysical conclusion; that must be argued for independently. So far, I have tried to establish only a negative thesis about ordinary moral concepts: those concepts are not bound to the properties emphasized by normative ethicists. If moral concepts refer to such properties that would be an a posteriori discovery. I now want to extend the Moral Mary thought experiment to establish a positive thesis. Moore thought that no analysis of moral concepts would lead to a closed question, and he concluded that moral concepts are conceptually primitive. Here too I think Moore was mistaken. Suppose Mary develops the capacity for human empathy. Suppose she starts to feel spontaneously happy when others are happy, and sad when others are sad. Suppose, now, she takes special delight in maximizing the good because she knows it will bring happiness to others. Suppose she feels terribly guilty when she doesn't maximize the good because she knows that she failed to bring pleasure to someone who could have been made happier. Suppose she experiences rage at other people when they fail to maximize utility. At this point, it seems perfectly okay to say that Mary believes it is wrong not to maximize utility and right to maximize utility. We can attribute the moral belief to her, once she starts to have an emotional attitude toward utility maximization. Had she instead developed emotional attitudes toward the actions that Kantian ethics deem morally compulsory, we would attribute moral attitudes toward those actions. This is an important positive thesis. We attribute moral attitudes to Mary once she has emotional attitudes. Once certain actions lead her to feel guilty and outraged, we say she has a moral point of view. The intuitions about the moral Mary case suggest that there is a conceptual link between moral judgments and emotional responses. We attribute moral attitudes if and only if a person has certain emotional responses.

This positive thesis can be expressed by saying that, once Mary acquires emotional attitudes, certain questions become closed. But one needs to be careful in stating what the closed question is. Suppose Mary would feel guilty if she were to steal and outraged if someone else were to steal. There seems to be no question about whether Mary has a moral attitude toward stealing. Clearly she regards stealing as wrong. The question of Mary's attitude is closed. If I am right, Moore was mistaken when he claimed that moral concepts admit of no analysis. Ordinary moral concepts are conceptually linked to emotions, and this allows us to say that someone who harbors guilt and anger is taking a moral stance.

In response, one might object that the link between moral concepts and emotions leaves us with open questions. Suppose Mary feels outrage at those who steal. She can still wonder whether stealing is *really* wrong; she can wonder whether the attitude is justified. Doesn't *this* open question undermine my claim that there is a conceptual link between wrongness and certain emotions? Absolutely not. The reason why Mary can wonder whether stealing is really wrong has to do with a gap between sense and reference. Many of our concepts are grasped by means of features that are neither necessary nor sufficient for category membership (see e.g., Prinz, 2002). We think of birds as creatures with wings and feathers, but there could be a wingless featherless bird. As a result, we can usually wonder whether a concept that we are applying, on any given occasion, *really* does apply. Mary knows that she *regards* stealing as wrong, but she can wonder whether stealing really falls under her concept. Because sense and can come apart, there are often open questions about what a given concept refers to, even if we know that the sense by which we grasp the concept has been satisfied. The open question in the present case is a question about what moral concepts refer to, not about their sense. The fact that we can say Mary is moralizing simply in virtue of her emotional attitudes suggests that there is a conceptual link between moral concepts and emotions.

At this stage, I don't want to rule out the possibility that one can think about morality without possessing emotions. If moral concepts refer to Kantian properties or Millian properties, then surely one can. But I think the argument establishes that our ordinary way of thinking about morality depends on the emotions. Above, I introduced the term "standard" concept to refer to an ordinary way of conceptualizing something. The standard concept for a property is the concept that is most commonly used within a community; it is usually the concept that we learned first, and it is the concept we would try to convey if we were teaching someone a corresponding term. We standardly construe birds as feathered, we standardly construe alcohol as intoxicating, and we standardly conceive of colors by imagining the phenomenal qualities that they cause. The intuitions behind the thought experiment here suggest that Mary does not have standard moral concepts until she develops moral emotions. Without moral emotions, she cannot form moral judgments in the ordinary sense. She cannot take the moral stance.

1.2.6 Psychopaths

The Moral Mary thought experiment suggests that emotions are necessary for making moral judgments in a standard way. This is a conceptual argument for epistemic emotionism. Parallel conclusions can be drawn from empirical research. Mary is someone who fails to grasp moral concepts, despite her high level of intelligence. There are people who have this profile in the real world. There are people who can learn everything there is to know about the consequences of an action without understanding that it is immoral. The people I have in mind are psychopaths.

Psychopaths present an important test case for ethical theory. Epistemic emotionists are committed to motivational internalism: the view that moral judgments are intrinsically motivating. Internalism faces a serious challenge. Critics believe that a person could form a moral judgment without being motivated to act. They call such hypothetical individuals "amoralists" (Brink, 1989). When this challenge is offered, internalists and externalists tend to get embroiled in a battle of intuition-mongering. Internalists insist that a person who was unmoved by moral judgments would not really comprehend morality. Externalists disagree. If we use emotional or motivational criteria as the litmus test for moral competence, that would beg the question against externalists. If we reject these criteria, internalists will cry foul. I think psychopaths offer a very promising way out of this quagmire.

Psychopaths seem to be the closest thing we have to real-world amoralists. They are perfectly intelligent and articulate. They seem to comprehend moral values, but they are utterly indifferent to them. They engage in chronic antisocial behavior, from lying and stealing to torturing and killing, and they commit these crimes without emotional cost. When psychopathic killers hear words pertaining to violence, they do not have a normal emotional response (Gray et al. 2003). They also show little empathy, guilt, shame, or remorse (Hare, 1998). Hare

(1993) and Cleckley (1941) catalogue many examples of psychopaths showing an astonishing indifference to the harm that they cause. For example, one psychopathic murderer insisted that he was blameless because he made a clean wound when he killed his victim.

On the face of it, psychopathy seems to demonstrate that amoralism is not only possible, but actual. Closer examination, however, reveals a very different story. Psychopaths *seem* to comprehend morality, but they really don't. They use moral terms in a way that deviates strikingly from the way non-psychopaths use those terms. These deviations suggest that they do not possess moral concepts; or at least that their moral concepts are fundamentally different from ours. Here's a passage from Cleckley:

The [psychopath] is unfamiliar with the primary facts or data of what might be called personal values.... Beauty and ugliness, except in a very superficial sense, goodness, evil, love, horror, and humor have no actual meaning, no power to move him.... It is as though he were colorblind, despite his sharp intelligence, to this aspect of human existence. It cannot be explained to him because there is nothing in his orbit of awareness that can bridge the gap with comparison. He can repeat the words and say glibly that he understands, and there is no way for him to realize that he does not understand. (Cleckley 1941: 40)

Externalists might resist Cleckley's assessment because he seems to *presuppose* that emotional states are required for comprehension. Cleckley says that values have "no actual meaning, no power to move" the psychopath. If Cleckley is using observations about moral motivation to support the thesis that psychopaths cannot understand moral concepts, then he is begging the question against externalists. Fortunately for the internalist, the evidence for moral retardation in psychopaths is not restricted to evidence pertaining to their motivational states. Crucially, psychopaths' incomprehension of moral concepts can be established using criteria that *both* externalists and internalists should agree to. Let me explain.

Both externalists and internalists should agree that moral rules differ from other kinds of rules. "Morally right" and "morally wrong" mean something different from "conventionally right" and "conventionally wrong" (for a discussion of how this can be reconciled with relativism, see chapter 5). Anyone who grasps moral concepts should be able to draw this distinction. As we saw already, healthy children have begun to master the moral/conventional distinction by the time they are three years old. If psychopaths fail to grasp the distinction, then they cannot be said to understand what healthy people mean by morality. Concepts are individuated by sense and reference. If psychopaths place moral wrongs and conventional wrongs in the same category, then their concept of "moral wrongs" has different reference and, presumably, different sense from the concept we ordinarily express when we talk about moral wrongs.

Blair (1995) demonstrates that psychopaths fail to grasp the moral/conventional distinction. Using the methods of Turiel, Smetana, and Nucci, he asked criminals who had been diagnosed as psychopaths to consider various scenarios in which rules had been violated. Some of the rules were moral and some were conventional, but the psychopaths were not alerted to this fact. They were simply asked to rate the wrongness and seriousness of the violations, and to justify their answers. They were also asked whether the described behavior would have been wrong if an authority had allowed it. The results were striking. Psychopaths did not treat moral and conventional wrongs significantly differently. Unlike a control group of non-psychopathic criminals, they tended to ignore victim's welfare when justifying their answers about moral wrongs.

There was an unexpected finding in Blair's study. Psychopaths tended to treat both moral and conventional wrongs as if they were authority-independent. It's wrong to speak out in class no matter what the teacher says. On the face of it, this seems to suggest that psychopaths are interpreting conventional as moral, rather than the other way around. But Blair offers another, more plausible explanation. He speculates that his subjects were trying to sound as if they were sensitive to moral rules. Inmates have great motivation to do that, because moral sensitivity can hasten release. Psychopaths tended to treat all rules as inviolable in an effort to convince the experimenter that they were mentally healthy. The plan backfired. Non-psychopathic criminals in the control group who were equally motivated to impress the experimenter answered in line with normal subjects. They treated conventional transgressions as authority-dependent. If psychopaths understood the difference between moral and conventional wrongs, they would have treated the transgression-types differently, in order to convey their moral health. The compensatory strategy of feigning moral rectitude actually revealed the profundity of their deficit. This interpretation finds confirmation in another study. Instead of looking at incarcerated adults, who have strong motivation to lie, Blair (1997) administered the moral/conventional test on children with psychopathic tendencies, and they found that these children tend to treat moral transgressions as if they were conventional. Blair concludes that psychopaths fail to grasp the difference between moral and conventional wrongs, and they tend to regard all wrongs as merely conventional. For them, morality is like etiquette, like conventions about which side of the road to drive on, or like chess: a group of more or less arbitrary conventions that place demands on us only because they have been adopted by a social group. Psychopaths can give lip service to morality, but their comprehension is superficial at best.

Psychopaths are not real-world amoralists, so they cannot be used as evidence against internalism. In fact, they seem to furnish internalists with a useful piece of supporting evidence. In psychopathy, a deficit in moral motivation co-occurs with a deficit in moral competence. This suggests that the two are linked. In fact, leading explanations of psychopathy maintain that the deficit in moral comprehension is a direct result of the emotional deficit.

First, consider the explanation offered by Blair (1995). Blair speculates that psychopaths suffer from an abnormality in a psychological system designed to inhibit violence. The idea of a violence-inhibition mechanism (VIM) is inspired by work in ethology. Dogs and other animals withdraw during acts of aggression when a victim displays a submission cue, such as bearing the throat. This response could be mediated by a VIM. An homologous mechanism might be responsible for the well-established fact that healthy humans are emotionally disturbed when they see others in distress. The vicarious distress response is even present in infants, but it is seriously impaired in psychopaths (House and Milligan, 1976; Blair et al. 1997). Blair takes this as evidence for a VIM dysfunction. He thinks that psychopaths never master the moral emotions, because they lack the mechanism that makes them sensitive to others in distress. Antisocial behavior is a consequence of impaired violence inhibition and also a secondary by-product of a more general lack of emotional concern for others, brought on by that impairment.

I think Blair's explanation is partially right and partially wrong. Psychopathy involves impaired inhibition, but it is not restricted to violence inhibition. The VIM story explains why psychopaths may lack moral emotions, but it leaves other symptoms unexplained. First, the focus on violence inhibition seems a bit narrow, given that psychopaths engage in all manner of crime, not just violence. This is confirmed by the two diagnostic tools that are most frequently used to identify psychopaths: Hare's (1991) Psychopathy Checklist includes an item labeled criminal versatility, and the DSM-IV criteria for antisocial personality disorder includes items for deceitfulness and failure to meet financial obligations (American Psychiatric Association, 1994). More seriously, Blair's account does not explain a general pattern of general *cognitive* abnormalities found in psychopaths. For example, psychopaths make numerous errors when completing mazes of increasing difficulty (Schalling and Rosen, 1968). They are tempted to go down paths that will not succeed. And finally, the VIM story does not explain the full range of emotional deficits in psychopathy. Another diagnostic criterion is flattened affect (Hare, 1991). Psychopaths lack moral emotions, but they are also alarmingly deficient in non-moral emotions. Psychopaths show deficits in fear, as evidence by a diminished capacity for electric-shock conditioning and distress-induced increases in startle response (Davies and Maliphant, 1971; Patrick et al., 1993). They also show a deficit in sadness. Cleckley (1941) discusses a teenage psychopath who showed only superficial concern when her pet dog was run over by a car (p. 71), and he also describes a man who shows no sorrow after murdering his mother and numerous others without provocation (p. 266). It has also been shown that psychopaths have difficulty recognizing facial and vocal expressions of sadness (Blair et al., 2001; Stevens et al., 2001).

The pattern of cognitive and emotional deficits in psychopathy suggests that the dysfunction cannot be restricted to violence inhibition. Instead, there seems to be a dysfunction in a more global and rudimentary affective system that underlies numerous emotions and inhibitory processes in cognition. Gray (1987) has postulated a Behavioral Inhibition System (BIS) that fits this profile perfectly. It is a core component of negative emotions such as fear and sadness, as well as moral emotions, and it also plays a role in cognitive tasks that require a change or cessation in behavior. Some authors have suggested that BIS deficiencies could explain the core symptoms of psychopathy (Fowles, 1980).

The main difference between Blair's VIM theory and the BIS theory has to do with the extent of the initial defect. Blair attributes psychopathy to a specific kind of inhibition impairment, rather than a general inhibition impairment. Both theories agree on the point of central interest here. They entail that moral retardation results from emotional retardation. Poor performance on the moral/conventional distinction derives from a deficit in moral emotions caused by a deficiency in inhibition. The key point is that both accounts see psychopathy as an emotional disorder. The moral blindness of psychopaths issues from an emotional blindness. If this is right, psychopathy provides positive evidence for internalism. Internalism, I have said, is entailed by epistemic emotionism. If moral judgments are intrinsically motivating, it may be due to the fact that standard moral concepts are essentially emotion-laden. That is precisely what research on psychopathy seems to confirm.

This account of psychopathy is primarily intended as an account of moral concepts, but it may have a metaphysical upshot. If moral properties were not essentially emotion-involving, then there should be a way of drawing the moral/conventional distinction without appeal to emotions. Psychopaths should be able to learn the difference. After all, psychopaths generally have intelligence quotients within the normal range. Some are extremely bright. They are often articulate and cunning. They have a great interest in learning to distinguish right from wrong. Most psychopaths have long histories of misconduct (that is actually a diagnostic criterion of the DSM-IV). These histories put them into contact with people who take special care in helping them grasp morality. They often encounter concerned parents, teachers, lawyers, and law enforcers. Given this combination of exposure and motivation to learn, psychopaths should be more likely than others to develop ways of reliably identifying moral properties. The fact that they fail to master the moral/conventional distinction suggests that there may be no way to draw that distinction without adverting to or experiencing emotional responses. The distinction may be emotional to the core. Rightness and wrongness may be constituted by emotional reactions in us. Subtract these reactions and the distinction becomes as invisible as the color spectrum is to the blind. Psychopaths can carefully monitor the moral judgments of healthy individuals. They can sort familiar examples of good conduct into one bin and bad conduct into another, but they lack insight into the very essence of this division. They would have difficulty reasoning about morality in modal contexts ("would it remain wrong if . . . ?"), and they would have difficulty extending the category to unusual cases. Epistemic emotionism predicts that emotionally deficient individuals will not develop normal moral concepts. Metaphysical emotionism predicts that it will be difficult to compensate for that deficiency by acquiring concepts that have the same referents but different senses. Like color concepts, moral concepts may be a case where sense and reference are intimately linked.

1.2.7 The Disunity of Morality

I will conclude with a further argument for metaphysical emotionism, since most of my arguments pertain to the epistemic thesis. Epistemic emotionism does not entail metaphysical emotionism. Moral judgments could be essentially tied to emotional responses even if moral properties were not. The good might have an essence that is independent of our emotions. Compare Litmus paper. It tests for acids by changing color. Litmus paper detects acid by the effect that acid has on it. But acid is not defined by its effect on Litmus paper. Acid has an essence that can be independently characterized. By parity of reasoning, we might detect good and evil by measuring our emotional responses even if good and evil have some independent essence.

Epistemic emotionism would support metaphysical emotionism if there were no mind-independent way to characterize the essence of good and evil. Suppose that good things don't have anything in common other than the fact that they cause positive emotions in us. Suppose evil things share nothing but their capacity to excite our negative emotions. If that is how things are, then metaphysical emotionism is a plausible thesis. Good and evil are essentially response-dependent; they are defined by their effects on us. Compare poisons. There is no intrinsic unity in the class of things that are poisonous. They have wildly diverse chemical constitutions, and their actual effects on the body are varied. Poisons are defined by the fact that they cause illness and death in us. Moral properties could be like that.

How do we decide between these two options? The evidence from psychopathy is suggestive, because psychopaths do not succeed in finding an emotion-independent way to identify moral rules, even though it is in their interest to do so. But the case for metaphysical emotionism should not rest with psychopaths. Their failure to find a mind-independent essence of good and evil might derive from the fact that they don't care enough about values or they don't have enough philosophical training. To prove that morality lacks a mind-independent essence, one would really need to examine philosophical theories. One would need to show that philosophers have been unable to identify a mind-independent essence for morality. I examine some of those attempts in chapters 3 and 4. Here I want to advance the case for metaphysical emotionism by doing some burden-shifting. I want to argue that, *on the face of it*, morality is more like the poison case than the acid case. The class of moralized behaviors *seems* to be disunified. If good and evil deeds appear disunified, then opponents of metaphysical emotionism have the burden of proof; they must show that appearances deceive. They must establish that good and evil have unifying essences that are independent of human emotional responses.

I will focus on the class of evils. Do immoral acts have anything in common? Ostensibly, the answer is no. Immoral acts comprise a hodgepodge: lying, stealing, hoarding, hurting, killing, neglecting, harassing, polluting, insulting, molesting, vandalizing, disrespecting, and so forth. What do these things have in common *other than the fact that we frown on all of them*? It is tempting to reply that they are all harmful. Perhaps harm is the essence of iniquity. There are three fatal objections to this proposal. First, the notion of harm is itself response-dependent. There are many things that are difficult or painful, but not regarded as harms: writing term papers, exercizing, spending eight hours at work, venturing out in the cold, saying "goodbye" to a loved one before a business trip, eating spicy food, going to the dentist, and so on. Harms seem to be those psychological and physical ordeals that we regard as candidates for moral concern. Second, some harms are not considered morally bad. Many cultures have harmful initiation rights, and most consider it morally acceptable to harm people in self-defense or retribution. Third, and most importantly, some of the things that we morally condemn do not cause harm; some wrongs lack victims. Consensual incest strikes many people as immoral even though no one seems to be harmed in any obvious way. Consider Murphy et al.'s (2000) scenario in which a brother and sister have consensual sex using contraception. They do it only once, they enjoy it, and they keep it a secret. People tend to regard this as morally wrong, even though no one is harmed.

Victimless wrongs present a serious problem for other attempts to find unity in the class of iniquities. When there is no victim, there is no violation of rights, and no reduction in net happiness. Victimless crimes are also a problem for Kant, who tried to show that all wrongs are unified by a particular kind of irrationality. In particular, Kant suggested that wrongs are those actions that cannot be coherently universalized. The difficulty is that there is no contradiction in wanting consensual incest to be a universal law. No contradiction arises in a world where all siblings have protected sex with each other when they want to. In such a world, sibling sex is like play fighting between siblings. Play fighting is morally acceptable because it is good practice and no one gets seriously hurt. Sex is a central human activity, and a bit of practice does some good. Still, consensual incest strikes us as very wrong. This is not a refutation of Kant. Kant could argue that there is a hidden irrationality in consensual incest, or he could say that it is not really wrong. But, on the face of it, Kant's proposal and other normative ethical theories don't seem to get the pretheoretical taxonomy right. There are things that ordinary people consider wrong, but are not wrong on leading philosophical accounts. Those accounts tend to focus in on categories that are narrower that the class of things that are regarded as wrong pretheoretically. When we consider the full class of things that we ordinarily regard as wrong, prospects for finding a unified theory begin to look grim.

I will briefly discuss Kant again in chapter 3, and in chapters 4 and 5, I will dwell further on the theme of disunity. My present goal is to show that there is no obvious intrinsic property that unifies the class of wrongs, and that suggests that the wrongness of an act *might* have more to do with our reaction than with the act itself. Consensual incest and stealing might belong to the same category in virtue of offending our sensibilities. Sentiment could be the thread that binds together all vices and virtues. Those who believe in the intrinsic unity of wrongs have the burden of proof. On the face of it, we moralize a heterogeneous class of things. The only thing that items in this class seem to have in common is our moral attitudes toward them.

1.2.8 The Emotionist Upshot

I have offered a battery of arguments in favor of emotionism. I intermingled philosophical arguments with evidence from experimental psychology, neuroscience, child development, and psychopathology. Emotionism enjoys convergent support from armchair intuitions and empirical work. Moral concepts seem to be bound up with emotional responses. Those who lack moral emotions lack moral concepts as well. This supports epistemic emotionism. Furthermore, there is little evidence that anyone can successfully pick out moral properties without the help of emotions, and moral properties seem to lack any unifying characteristics independent of our reactions to them. This supports metaphysical emotionism. There may be other ways to make sense of all the evidence that I have been discussing, but emotionism emerges as the most obvious explanation.

The case that I have been presenting is not intended to be a demonstrative proof. A knock-down argument for emotionism may be too much to hope for. For now, I will settle for prima facie support. If emotionism has prima facie support, then it is worth exploring. In the following chapters I will present an emotionist theory in more detail, and I will argue that it can withstand objections. I will also present objections to non-emotionist ethical theories, such as Kant's, and weak emotionist theories, such as utilitarianism and expressivism. I will conclude that the case for strong emotionism is compelling. Emotions are implicated essentially in both the ontology and epistemology of morals.

2

Emotions: Non-moral and Moral

In chapter 1, I presented preliminary support for a strong form of emotionism. There are reasons for thinking that moral ontology and moral judgments both involve emotions essentially. The nature of that involvement remains to be worked out, but there is an important hurdle to face before the project can even begin. Historically, philosophers who invoked emotions in their moral theories also provided detailed, independently motivated accounts of the emotions. Spinoza developed an influential theory of the emotions in his *Ethics*, and Hume dedicated Book Two of his *Treatise* to the passions before proposing his emotionist theory of morals in Book Three. Twentieth-century emotionists have been less thorough. All too often, we are told that emotions are central to morality without being told what the emotions really are. Emotionists cannot afford to be silent on this question, because some theories of emotion are difficult to reconcile with their approach to morality. In this chapter, I defend a non-cognitive theory of emotions, which can be reconciled with emotionism. I then present an overview of the moral emotions, and I argue that different moral emotions play different functional roles. I also argue that the moral emotions are not basic. Rather, they are derived from non-moral emotions.

2.1 A THEORY OF EMOTION

2.1.1 Two Views

The history of emotion research can be regarded as a battle between two opposing sides. Some authors argue that emotions are cognitive. According to this approach, emotions essentially involve judgments or thoughts. Other authors deny this, arguing that emotions are fundamentally non-cognitive. The divide between cognitive and non-cognitive theories is the most conspicuous and volatile fault line within emotion research, and most theories line up neatly on one side or the other. The problem is that neither approach sits well with emotionism. Both views raise a problem for the epistemic thesis that moral judgments necessarily involve emotions. To make the problems explicit, it will be useful to describe cognitive and non-cognitive theories in more detail.

Consider cognitive theories first. Spinoza (1677) says emotions are judgments accompanied by pain or pleasure. Pain and pleasure are feelings, devoid of meaning on their own. So Spinoza's theory is really part cognitive and part non-cognitive. Most cognitive theories are like this, because without a non-cognitive element, it is hard to account for the heat of passions. While some cognitive theorists think emotions are nothing but judgments (Solomon, 1976; Nussbaum, 2001), most are not so bold. What sets cognitive theorists apart is the claim that emotions contain cognitive elements essentially. A mere feeling, for example, would not be enough.

In contemporary psychology, the prevailing cognitive theories emphasize a particular class of cognitive states called appraisals (e.g., Arnold, 1960; Lazarus, 1991; Scherer, 1993). An appraisal is a representation of an organism/environment relation that bears on well-being. Call such a relation a "concern." Anger, for instance, involves an appraisal of threat or offense. Fear involves an appraisal of danger. Sadness involves an appraisal of loss. Offenses, dangers, and losses are all matters of concern. On standard cognitive theories, emotions are felt responses to appraisal judgments, and appraisal judgments are explicit, though perhaps unconscious, assessments of one's relation to the world. These judgments are usually thought to be highly structured and complex. They fall along several fixed dimensions. We constantly ask ourselves questions about how things are faring. Are my goals being achieved? Who if anyone is responsible for my current situation? What options are available for coping? Scherer (1993) calls these judgments stimulus evaluation checks. Each emotion corresponds to a different set of answers. Anger involves not just a judgment that I have been offended, but also a judgment that my goals have been threatened, that the source of the threat is another person, and that aggression is an available option for coping with the situation. If my stimulus evaluation checks lead to this pattern of answers the resulting state is anger. That state may be a feeling; it may be a pain, or a pleasure or a feeling of arousal. Had the same feeling come about in some other way, it would not have been anger. Appraisals are essential to an emotion's identity.

Detractors find this approach, and its philosophical precursors, overly intellectual. They insist that emotions can occur and retain their identity without any judgments or thoughts. They find implausible the demand that emotions require mastery of concepts or propositional attitudes. Instead, they prefer non-cognitive theories. The simplest non-cognitive theories identify emotions with pure feelings. A pure feeling would be a feeling whose identity is exhausted by its felt aspect or phenomenal character. Folk psychology has some sympathy for this suggestion. It seems intuitively plausible for a person to say, "I know that I am angry because I feel angry—I recognize the feeling." But one should be cautious about inferring that emotions are pure feelings from the fact that they are known by their feelings. By analogy, consider pain. I know that I am in pain by feeling my pain, but pain is more than a feeling. Pain has a particular function. It occurs, ordinarily, when the body suffers from some injury or malady. It is coherent to say that pains are feelings and that they are recognized by the way they feel while insisting that there is more to their identity. Suppose we found a creature that experienced states that were qualitatively like our pains but had no correlation with injury. Would we call those pains? Or, to use another analogy, suppose we found a creature that had experiences that were qualitatively like our color sensations, but had no connection to light. Would we call those color sensations? These cases are fanciful in the extreme, and I don't pretend to have decisive intuitions about them. But they highlight an important difference between identification procedures and identity conditions: states that can be identified by their phenomenal character may have further unfelt attributes that are necessary for their identity.

One reason for doubting that emotions are pure feelings is that there are not enough feelings to go around. Anger feels a certain way, and that feeling is different from sadness or fear, but some emotions feel alike. Can I tell anger from indignation by feeling alone? Can I distinguish joy from pride? Or mourning from remorse? It is likely that emotions attain their identity in part from the context in which they arise.

This point was already implicit in the presentation of appraisal theories. On such an account, emotions are differentiated by their cognitive causes, and are, thus, ineliminably linked to cognition. A non-cognitive theorist might admit that emotions get their identity, in part, from the conditions under which they arise while denying that those cognitions need be cognitive.

Hume can be interpreted as holding a theory like this. He says that emotions are impressions. Impressions come in two forms. There are sensations and impressions of reflection. Sensations are caused when the senses are stimulated, and reflections are caused by sensations or other mental states. Reflections are like inward-directed sensations: they are immediate responses to events in the mental world. Every impression of reflection has a mental cause, and many have mental effects. Emotions get their identity from these causes and effects. They are impressions caused by other impressions or by ideas. Fear is an impression that arises when we have an impression of pain joined to an impression of uncertainty. Joy can arise from, say, recognizing a friend. Some emotions get their identity from the impressions or ideas that they cause, rather than from the impressions or ideas that cause them. Pride, for example, causes one to think about the self. In some cases, Hume's story is indistinguishable from a modern cognitive account. Emotions are individuated by the mental states with which they interact, and these include ideas pertaining to how we are faring in life. But Hume's account is non-cognitive, because emotions can be caused directly by sensory experiences without any explicit evaluative judgments. When joy is caused by sensory pleasure or by glimpsing the visage of a dear friend, there is no cognitive mediation. Percept triggers affect. Hume also says that emotions are constituted by feelings, regardless of their causes and effects. Emotions are neither constituted by judgments nor necessarily caused by them. The story is somewhat complicated by the fact that Hume identified a class of emotions, called the indirect passions, which essentially involve ideas of an object: pride and humility are directed at oneself, while love and hate are directed at another. Hume says that these emotions bring to mind the idea of the self or of another person, and that implies that they have a conceptual component, unlike other emotions, which he calls direct passions. It could be that Hume has a cognitive theory of the indirect passions and a non-cognitive theory of the direct passions, Alternatively, Hume may be interpreted as saying that the indirect passions are non-cognitive feeling states that just happen to, as a matter of contingent fact, reliably cause us to think of self or other. Either way, Hume is committed to the view that many emotions (the direct passions) can arise without any thoughts or concepts.

Hume's approach is also non-cognitive in another sense. He maintains that emotions lack meaning or intentionality. They are not representations. Sensory impressions represent features of the world. Emotions represent nothing. They are just feelings of a particular kind. One can get an idea of why Hume makes this claim by considering the fact that representation was closely linked to resemblance in the eighteenth century. The sensation caused by seeing a friend's face resembles that face, one might argue: there is an isomorphism between the inner image and its external cause. The joy triggered by that sensation, however, does not resemble the sensation in any way.

The claim that emotions lack intentionality is closely associated with non-cognitive theories, but it is not essential to them. Consider the theory advanced by William James (1884) and Carl Lange (1885). They argue that emotions are feelings of patterned changes in the body. Lange emphasizes changes in blood vasculature. James is more inclusive. He mentions facial expressions, musculoskeletal changes, activity in visceral organs, and even stereotyped behaviors. In *The Principles of Psychology* James quotes from the detailed observations of Darwin and others who took note of the intimate link and steady correlation between affect and bodily response—the pallor of fear, the clenched fists of anger, the throat lump of grief, and the toothy grin of joy. These responses, from flush to phlegm and fiber, are ordinarily thought to arise after an emotion is elicited. We say that sadness makes us cry, and not the reverse. According to James and Lange, folk psychology gets things backward. Emotions are internal states that register bodily changes. The central argument for both of them involves an exercise in mental subtraction. Imagine an intense emotion and then systematically eliminate every bodily feeling associated with that state. When the last bodily feeling is removed, there will be nothing left to the state that one would call an emotion. Emotions are felt perceptions of bodily changes.

The James–Lange theory shares something important with Hume's theory. According to both, emotions can occur without judgments or other cognitions. Emotions have no essential connection to cognition. But the James–Lange theory also contrasts with Hume's in several respects. Most obviously, James and

Lange emphasize the bodily concomitants of emotions. Second, they do not say that emotions are individuated by their causal links to other mental states. Third, they implicitly reject the sensation/reflection distinction, treating emotions as a class of sensations. And finally, they imply that emotions are representations; they represent states of the body.

The links between emotions and bodily changes are not arbitrary. Emotions correlate with bodily changes that serve useful ends. The somatic changes associated with fear can be understood as preparations for behavioral responses to danger; we flee, freeze, and fight in fear. The erection of bodily hair follicles is a vestige from earlier mammalian ancestors; when hairs stand on end in hairier creatures, apparent body size is increased and predators are deterred. The racing heart sends blood to the extremities to facilitate flight. Strained breathing makes us quieter and harder to detect. Open eyes and mouth take in visual and olfactory information. For James and Lange, fear is the perception of these behaviorally useful changes.

Another possibility is that fear is a set of bodily commands. Some psychologists have suggested that emotions are action tendencies. They orchestrate the bodily changes that facilitate action, and they dispose us to act. The action tendency theory preserves the folk psychological assumption that emotions cause bodily response, rather than the reverse. This theory can actually be reconciled with the James–Lange view if we loosen the distinction between inputs and outputs. That distinction is sometimes blurred in the nervous system. Consider the recent flurry of research on "mirror neurons" (Rizzolatti and Craighero, 2004). These are cells in premotor areas of the frontal cortex that respond when a creature (monkey or man) executes a manual action or when that same action is visually perceived. This seems to be a relatively common strategy in the brain. Cells that cause actions sometimes also detect actions. In addition, there might be neural networks in which some neurons generate outputs and others register inputs, but all are so tightly coupled that it makes little sense to describe any as part of an input system or an output system. The best we could say of such a network is that it is an input–output system—a unified consortium of cells contributing to perception and action. If the neural networks that underlie emotions have this character, then emotions are both perceptions of bodily changes and causes of bodily changes. This would collapse the distinction between somatic sensations and action tendencies. On this approach, we could say that emotions are "somatic signals," because the term "signal" is neutral between an effect and a cause.

2.1.2 What's at Stake for Emotionism

We have seen that there are two main approaches to explaining emotions. Defenders of cognitive theories either equate emotions with cognitive states, such as judgments, or claim that emotions necessarily include such cognitive states. For Spinoza emotions are judgments coupled with pain or pleasure, and for many contemporary psychologists, emotions are states of arousal or feelings caused by appraisal judgments. Non-cognitive theorists deny that emotion requires cognition. For Hume emotions are a class of *sui generis* feelings, individuated by the impressions and ideas with which they causally interact. For James and Lange, they are sensations of bodily changes. For others, they are action tendencies, or bodily commands. Before adjudicating this debate, I want to indicate what's at stake for emotionist theories of morality. I want to argue that emotionists should favor non-cognitivism.

Cognitivist theories of emotion may be difficult to reconcile with emotionism. If such theories are right, emotions contain thoughts or judgments. If emotionism is right, then moral judgments contain moral emotions. These two hypotheses are difficult to reconcile. If cognitive theories of emotion are right, then moral emotions contain judgments. But what sort of judgments might they contain? The natural answer is that they contain moral judgments. For example, guilt might be defined as containing the judgments that I have done something morally wrong. If this proposal were right, emotionists would be ensnared in a circle. They would have the infelicitous view that moral judgments contain moral emotions, and moral emotions contain moral judgments.

To avoid this circle, emotionists who are drawn to cognitive theories of emotion might try to argue that moral emotions contain *non-moral judgments*. For example, guilt might contain the judgment that I harmed someone, rather than the judgment that I have done something morally wrong. There is nothing circular about supposing that moral judgments contain the judgment that I have harmed someone. But this proposal faces another difficulty. It falls prey to a version of Moore's open-question argument. Someone can coherently wonder whether it's wrong to cause harm. If the concept wrong contains guilt, and guilt contains the judgments that I have harmed someone, then "harming is wrong" amounts to the tautology that harming is harming. Therefore, on this approach, no one could wonder whether harming is wrong. The argument works for *any* analysis of the judgments underlying moral emotions. Every cognitive analysis of moral emotions, when combined with emotionism, entails that the concept WRONG can be decomposed into a judgment of some kind. For any such judgment, it should be impossible to consistently believe that something is wrong while wondering whether the judgment also applies. But that is difficult to reconcile with the fact that analyses of WRONG in non-moral terms always seem to sound surprising or informative. If there were a non-moral judgment that constituted the judgment that something is wrong, then it should not feel like an open question whether something is wrong when that judgment applies. But it seems that, for any non-moral judgment, there could be such an open question.

In sum cognitive theories of emotion present a dilemma for the emotionist about morality. If cognitive theories are true, then moral emotions either contain moral judgments or they contain non-moral judgments. If they contain moral judgments, then the emotionist account of moral concepts is circular. If they contain non-moral judgments, then emotionists would face a version of the open question argument. There are undoubtedly ways that a cognitivist about the emotions might try to wiggle out of the dilemma. But it does look like there is a tension between emotionism and cognitive theories of the emotions. Rather than wiggling, the emotionist might be better off looking for a non-cognitive theory of the emotions. Fortunately, I think non-cognitive theories are independently more plausible.

2.1.3 The Case for Embodiment

I will now present a case against cognitivism and in favor of a non-cognitive theory. To begin, let's ask whether cognitive states, such as judgments, are necessary or sufficient for being in an emotional state. Pure cognitive theorists are alone in maintaining that cognitions are sufficient for emotion, and I find their accounts singularly implausible. Take whatever thought you like and ask, "Could I have this thought without having an emotion?" Consider a person who thinks she has been insulted. Could she have this thought without being angry? I submit that the answer is an obvious yes. It may happen that most of us become angry when we entertain that thought, but we need not. The following individuals are likely to deflect insults without agitation: a person with an especially strong ego, a recipient of frequent insults, a person with a stoic disposition, a person just about to fall asleep and unable to muster arousal, a glutton for punishment, and a person engaged in a game of exchanging clever verbal slights. Perhaps we need a different judgment to make the pure cognitive theory plausible. Perhaps no ordinary judgment will do the trick; one must have instead an *evaluative* judgment. A pure cognitive theorist might maintain that anger involves the judgment that I have been insulted and that being insulted is a bad thing because it poses a threat to my well-being. I think this proposal provides little improvement. A well-trained stoic could make this judgment dispassionately. Of course, a person who really took this judgment to heart, who really felt threatened by an insult, would feel angry. The point is that the anger cannot be fully constituted by the judgment. A machine could detect threatening insults without getting miffed. When we think about threats to our well-being, we experience emotions, but that is because we react to those thoughts in a particular way.

If not sufficient, might thoughts at least be necessary for emotions? Most philosophers would answer affirmatively. The answer depends on what one takes a thought to be. At a minimum, I take thoughts to be mental representations that contain concepts. The thought that I have been insulted contains the concept INSULT. A concept is a mental representation that can be combined with other mental representations by the person (or creature) who possesses it. To say that emotions are necessarily cognitive is to say that one cannot have an emotion without possessing and tokening certain concepts. How plausible is this? How plausible is it to say that one cannot be angry without being able to think about insults (or threats or some other form of provocation)?

I think cognitive requirements are too demanding. They put emotions too high up on the phylogenetic and ontogenetic scales. Cognitive requirements also seem to fly in the face of emotional immediacy. We often emote under time pressure with little time to reflect. Anger can be provoked by a glare, someone cutting you off on the highway, or someone bumping into you in a supermarket aisle. The emotion seems to occur before one has had time to evaluate or even classify the situation.

There is a long-standing empirical debate about whether emotions have cognitive prerequisites. In a classic discussion, Zajonc (1984) cites a number of lines of evidence against cognitive theories. His most impressive examples involve cases in which emotions are induced by direct physical means. Studies on facial feedback show that changing one's facial expression can unwittingly trigger the corresponding affective state (Strack et al., 1988). Studies of opponent-processing suggest that intense positive emotions cause a negative emotional after-affect, as in drug withdrawal, and conversely (Solomon, 1980). And, of course, emotions can be altered by drugs, sex, and rock and roll.

Zajonc also cites anatomical evidence. His citations are a bit out of date, but recent work confirms his suspicion. LeDoux (1996) has shown that a visual stimulus can trigger an emotional response before the involvement of the neocortex. There is a subcortical pathway from the eyes into the amygdala, mediated by the thalamus. The amygdala is a structure located deep within the temporal lobe that associates perceptual signals with other subcortical structures that regulate bodily responses. When the amygdala triggers a bodily change, that change is experienced as an emotion. The thalamus is a sensory hub where sense organs send signals en route to the neocortex, where object recognition is achieved. Thalamic representations of visual stimuli are relatively unprocessed but they are sufficient for identifying certain emotionally salient objects. LeDoux gives the example of a coiled snake. This is such a distinctive visual cue that it can trigger a fear reaction before the cortex has time to allow for a perceptual judgment. Morris et al. (1999) present evidence that the thalamo-amygdala pathway also underwrites emotional responses to rapidly presented facial expressions. This pathway even allows for emotional responses to faces in blindsight. Individuals with blindsight have lesions in visual cortex. They react emotionally to faces presented in their blind field even though they have no visual experience of those faces (de Gelder et al., 1999). It would be totally untenable to claim that the thalamus or the amygdala harbor concepts. They do not seem to contain anything like freely re-combinable representations of insult, or danger, or loss, or ego as would be required by a cognitive theory. These findings strongly suggest that emotions can arise without judgments, thoughts, or other cognitive mediators.

The argument that I just presented goes like this: evidence from neuroscience shows that we don't need the neocortex to trigger a bodily response that, when experienced, would be identified as an emotion. Defenders of cognitive theories may try to object as follows. LeDoux's work shows that judgments are not needed to *initiate* a state that we experience as an emotion, but perhaps judgments are involved at a later stage of processing. Perhaps a perpetual stimulus that is processed subcortically triggers a bodily response, and that bodily response is then both perceived in the central nervous system *and* assigned meaning by a cognitive appraisal process: the snake sets our hairs on end, and we interpret that response as a reaction to danger. The cognitive theorist may say that fear arises when, and only when, this cognitive appraisal is added to our experience of the somatic response.

The best way to respond to this objection is to show that somatic signals are sufficient for emotions. Demonstrative proof of this claim is not easy to come by, but the empirical evidence is suggestive. Consider, again, facial feedback. Levenson et al. (1990) have shown that making an emotional facial expression causes two things to occur. It causes a pattern of bodily changes (e.g., changes in heart rate) associated with the emotion expressed, and it causes one to report experiencing that emotion. The distinctive bodily pattern suggests that at least some emotions can be distinguished somatically. The self-report suggests that one is in an induced emotional state. But there is no evidence for appraisal in this process. I invite you to perform the following experiment. Smile and see if you feel a little bit happier. Now, assuming that you do, ask, are you entertaining the thought that your goals have been satisfied? Next scowl as if you are very angry, and see if you feel the anger. Then ask yourself whether you are entertaining the thought that you have been insulted. I suspect that you will answer these questions negatively. Of course unconscious evaluations *might* be occurring, but to suppose they are is ad hoc and unnecessary. We can recognize our emotions introspectively in these feedback cases, and we seem to do so by introspecting our bodily states. If we can recognize an emotion by a bodily state, there is no reason to think non-introspectable evaluative judgments are contributing to our self-reports. I conclude that somatic signals are sufficient for certain emotions.

But are they necessary? Defenders of pure cognitive theories would have us believe that an emotion can exist without any disruption of the body, real or imagined (e.g., Solomon, 1976). They would have us believe that some emotions are disembodied, in this sense. Consider emotions that endure over extended periods of time. Love can last for a lifetime, as can fear of spiders. One can be sad for months, and ceaselessly angry about the current state of the world. It would be ludicrous to assume that the body sustains a disrupted state for the duration of these standing emotions. On the other hand, each of these carries a disposition to undergo a bodily change. We would question the sincerity of a self-proclaimed spider phobic who never shuddered in the presence of her eight-legged foes. Emotional terms, like many mental terms, have a dispositional use. By comparison, the claim that Jones thinks that God exists does not imply that Jones compulsively entertains that thought through every waking minute. We can distinguish state emotions and trait emotions, and reserve the somatic account for the former, provided we recognize that traits are dispositions to states. This concession is no victory for the opponent of the James–Lange view.

Opponents of the James–Lange view must defend the dubious claim that an occurrent emotional state can be disembodied. In this context, we might consider the calm passions, discussed by Hume. Aesthetic appreciation, for example, is not regularly associated with bodily changes. Should we say it is a disembodied emotion? I don't think so. First, it's not clear that aesthetic appreciation is an emotion; it certainly isn't a paradigm case. Second, aesthetic appreciation may have a bodily component. We find artworks breathtaking. They make our eyes widen and send shivers down our spines. Artworks can also cause garden-variety emotions such as sadness and delight. These are not just armchair speculations. Neuroimaging studies have confirmed that emotions are engaged when people look at art, and the brain areas involved include the anterior cingulate, which is known to be involved in bodily regulation (Kawabata and Zeki, 2004; Vartanian and Goel, 2004).

The opponent of James and Lange must look beyond aesthetic appreciation to find disembodied emotions. It is tempting to look for those emotions that seem most phylogentically advanced. Aesthetic appreciation falls into this category, but there are other examples. One especially pertinent emotion is guilt. It is often said that guilt lacks a characteristic bodily pattern. There is no expression of guilt, no telltale sign. Guilt stands out as a plausible candidate for a disembodied emotion.

Plausibility diminishes on reflection. We often speak of guilt pangs. One can be wracked by guilt, haunted by guilt, and driven to despair by guilt. Guilt makes us avoid the eyes of those we've betrayed, and it prods us to seek forgiveness. None of these familiar observations prove that guilt is embodied, but they are suggestive. Imagine the killer who testifies to feeling guilty but seems totally unstirred. If every autonomic response were at baseline levels, we would be suspicious. The suspicion derives from the fact that we tacitly recognize a bodily disruption when we ourselves feel guilty.

More direct tests for the embodiment of guilt are also available. In an informal study, I presented subjects with the following story:

> After a few months at college, you have met some great people and have been involved in many activities. High school seems like a distant memory. One of your best friends from high school has written you several long letters, but you have been so caught up in college life that you haven't gotten around to responding. Months have gone by since the first letter was received. Think about the feeling you have when you think about the fact that you haven't written back.

Subjects were then asked to rate the appropriateness of six facial expressions. All subjects gave significantly high ratings to a frowning face. Subjects also identified the feeling in question as guilt. More careful studies would have to be done to draw strong conclusions from this, but I think it does raise doubts about the assumption that guilt has no expression. Further evidence for the embodied nature of guilt comes from a neuroimaging study. Shin et al. (2000) took positron emission tomography images of subjects as they recalled the episodes of guilt from their own lives. The results showed activation in areas that have become very familiar to neuroscientists studying emotion: anterior cingulate cortex, insular cortex, and the temporal poles. As I have already noted, anterior cingulate and the insula are also implicated in regulation and perception of the body. Their appearance in this study is strong evidence for the hypothesis that guilt is an embodied emotion. I submit that no bona fide emotion is disembodied. Every apparent candidate proves visceral to the core.

I have been arguing that somatic signals are both necessary and sufficient for emotions. This tells against cognitive theorists, who insist on the necessity of judgments, thoughts, or concepts. It also tells against Hume, who identifies emotions with *sui generis* impressions, rather than impressions of bodily changes. It appears to be a solid victory for James and Lange. The story isn't quite that simple, however. Their somatic theory falls prey to a pair of serious objections. I will discuss these in the next two sections.

2.1.4 Rational Assessment and Intentionality

The first objection to the James–Lange theory stems from a simple observation. We often talk about emotions using rational terms. We say that emotions are justified or unjustified, warranted or unwarranted, appropriate or inappropriate. Fear of free roaming copperheads is sensible, fear of captive corn snakes is not. As Pitcher (1965) notes, these evaluative categories do not apply to ordinary bodily sensations, such as tickles, or itches or stomach cramps. An emotion can be rational or irrational, while a mere pang or twinge is always *a*rational. Call this the Rational Assessment Problem.

Notice that a cognitive theory has no trouble with either of these Problems. If every emotion is partially comprised of a judgment of thought, then each emotion can be distinguished even if their somatic symptoms are similar. Anger and indignation implicate different judgments: one involves a judgment about a threat or offense, and the other involves a judgment about an injustice. The rational assessability of emotions can be pinned on these judgments as well. Unwarranted anger is anger that arises when no offense has taken place or when the offense is itself the result of a prior provocation. It is anger that contains a judgment that is wrong or unjustified.

This leaves us in a quagmire. The Rational Assessment Problem points us toward a cognitive theory, but there is strong evidence that cognition is not necessary for emotion. Emotions seem to be meaningful but not cognitive. There is evidence that they represent, but equally good evidence that they do not require the deployment of concepts.

Fortunately, there is a way out of this quagmire. Representation does not require cognition. We can have meaningful mental states without deploying any concepts. Cognitive theories overlook this possibility. They assume that each emotion must come along with an explicit thought and describe some relationship between organism and environment. Anger comes with the thought that I have been insulted. But another possibility is that anger itself is a non-conceptual state that has representational content.

To get this proposal off the ground, we need a theory of representation. It's best to call on the theories of representation that were not developed to explain emotions. Such theories have the virtue of being independently motivated. We should figure out how emotions represent by figuring out how representation works in general. We should ask how, in general, do mental states come to represent anything?

There are a number of answers to this question in the literature. One of the most popular approaches was developed by Fred Dretske (1988; see also Fodor, 1990 and Millikan, 1984). According to Dretske, a mental representation, M, represents that which it has the function of reliably detecting. Roughly, M represents that which it was set up to be set off by. Smoke alarms are a good example of this kind of representation outside of the mind. A beep represents smoke, because it is reliably caused by smoke and it was engineered so as to be caused by smoke. Mental representations are presumed to work the same way. A concept of water represents water because it is reliably activated when water is encountered and it was acquired for that purpose. Pain represents physical maladies because it is reliably caused by them, and was evolved for that purpose. Dretske's approach to representation is widely regarded as among the most promising in the literature. Elsewhere I have defended a version of it (Prinz, 2000). I have also argued that this general-purpose theory of representation applies equally well to emotions (Prinz, 2004).

To see how this would work, we need to ask two questions. What reliably causes emotions to occur? And, of all the things that cause emotions, what do they have the function of detecting? Consider sadness. Sadness can be induced by a wide range of things. The death of a loved one, the loss of a favorite sweater, a rejection letter from a journal, a cruel glance from a lover. Sadness can also be caused by bad weather, by Mozart's *Requiem*, by alcohol, and by frowning or other bodily changes. Each of these is a reliable cause. But which of these many things does sadness have the function of detecting? To answer this question, let's make the plausible assumption that sadness is an innate emotional capacity—the product of natural selection. If that's right, then the question of function is a biological question: of the many things that cause sadness, which of its causes allowed sadness to increase our ancestors' fitness and pass the capacity onto later generations? If sadness were a culturally constructed emotion or a learned response, we would ask a parallel question: which cause of sadness was responsible for its acquisition and social transmission? Questions about biological function are difficult to answer, because we don't have a record of the conditions that led to the propagation of many phenotypes among our ancestors. But we can make an educated guess. Suppose sadness detected bodily changes and nothing else. Would it have conferred a survival advantage? Probably not. There is no advantage in detecting the bodily changes associated with sadness if those changes do not themselves have any biological significance. If frowns had no import, frown detection would be relatively useless. Might sadness have the function of detecting certain kinds of music? Unlikely, because music may have emerged more recently than sadness in evolutionary history. It's more likely that music makes us sad in virtue of resembling a more fundamental sadness elicitor, such as the sound of crying (Panksepp, 1995).

Might sadness have evolved as a response to bad weather? Here, we're getting warmer. Bad weather signals a potential reduction in the accessibility of essential resources, so it is advantageous to detect bad weather. But, if this is a function of sadness, it's not the sole function. It's equally advantageous to detect the loss of a loved one, failures of achievement, and cool treatment from a lover. All these pose a threat to well-being, and the person who is saddened by them will seek out coping strategies. So, intuitively, sadness is likely to have been selected for a range of different things, including bad weather, deaths, failures, marital break-ups, and misplaced articles. Notice that this seemingly arbitrary collection of elicitors is actually unified by a single coherent principle. Each item on the list is a kind of loss. Loss of life, loss of resources, loss of lovers, loss of things—all these losses induce sadness. Thus, we can say that sadness evolved as a response to losses writ large. Sadness is a loss detector. It's also a detector of bodily changes and D-minor chords, but it does not have the function of detecting these things. Sadness probably evolved as a response to loss.

In sum, Dretske's independently motivated theory of representation delivers a very satisfying answer to the question about what sadness represents. It simply falls out of Dretske's theory that sadness represents loss. The important thing about this outcome is that Dretske's theory does not depend on any assumptions about the form or format of representations. There is no condition in his theory requiring that the mental states to which it applies be proposition, conceptual, or cognitive. Dretske's theory applies to highly conceptual representations, but can also be applied to pains, sensory images, and even antibodies in the immune system. It can apply to emotions, even if emotions are identified with states that regulate and register bodily changes.

Think of it this way. The brain's somatosensory systems have internal states that are evolved to detect and regulate systems in the body. Such states evolved to detect stimuli impacting on or in our bodies, to identify muscle positions for behavioral control, and to maintain homeostasis and adaptive changes in our organs. But, in addition to each discrete change in each individual organ or muscle, the brain can detect patterns of bodily changes. Some of those patterns have evolved as preparations for behavioral responses, such as flight or aggression. The patterns that serve those behavioral ends are also evolved to occur under specific conditions. One of these patterns—the one we experience as sadness—is triggered by thoughts about loss, failed efforts, cool glances from lovers, and gray skies overhead. The bodily states that occur probably prepare us for withdrawal and diminished activity, so we can store up energy, end fruitless pursuits, and identify other ways to cope. The perception of this pattern is, for the reasons I have been spelling out, a representation of loss, even though each part of the pattern is also a sensation of some specific bodily change. Likewise for other emotions. The flight response is triggered by sudden noises, approaching predators, and other hazards; when we perceive this pattern, the bodily perception is a representation of danger. The aggression response is triggered by attacks from non-specifics, and other threats and provocations; the bodily perception of aggression is a representation of an affront. We call one state fear and the other anger. Both are bodily perceptions that have come to represent specific relationships between organism and environment.

James and Lange imply that emotions are sensations of bodily states, and hence representations of those states. Dretske's theory, and others like it, suggests that James and Lange were wrong. Emotions are reliably caused by bodily changes but they represent things such as loss and danger, the organism/environment relations that induce these changes in us. James and Lange were right about the form that emotions take, but wrong about their content. In a word, emotions represent concerns.

Cognitive theorists assume that non-cognitivists have no way of explaining how emotions come to be caused by concerns. If emotions contain judgments, we can easily explain how fear is caused by danger. Fear contains the judgments "I am in danger," and that judgment tends to occur when I am in danger. Non-cognitivists do not deny that judgments can trigger emotions; they simply deny that such judgments are the only possible triggers. Fear can be triggered by hearing a loud noise, feeling a sudden loss of support, seeing a snake, *or* judging that I am in danger. Each of these inner states can be regarded as items in a mental file. They are functionally unified by their capacity to cause the bodily pattern that we experience as fear. Fear represents danger in virtue of the fact that it has the function of detecting danger, and that function is sustained by this file. The file calibrates fear to danger. It can be called a calibration file. Calibration files contain a wide range of representations, both cognitive and non-cognitive, and these representations can change over the course of cognitive development. There is no reason to think that calibration files are component parts of emotions. As Hume might say, they are too contingent and variable. Moreover, when a representation from a calibration file triggers an emotion (e.g., when hearing a loud sound triggers fear), that representation occurs prior to the onset of the emotion, and may endure for a briefer period than the emotion. Representations in calibration files are causes of emotions, not components. They are the mechanisms that get emotions to serve as meaningful detectors of our relationship to the world.

In sum, we can explain how emotions represent concerns without supposing that emotions are, contain, or essentially involve judgments. This conclusion falls out of Dretske's theory of representation and others like it. Emotions represent things such as losses and dangers because they are set up to be set off by such things. They represent these things even if they have no constituent concepts or ideas. Like the beep of a smoke detector, emotions can represent without describing.

This saves the James–Lange theory from refutation, by furnishing a response to the Rational Assessment Problem. Non-cognitivists have had difficulty explaining the intuition that emotions can be reasonable or unreasonable. Hume says that emotions are arational. Hume said that emotions can be caused by reasonable or unreasonable ideas, but they cannot be reasonable or unreasonable themselves. This is unsatisfying because we can assess emotions as reasonable or unreasonable even when they are not associated with judgments or ideas. Fear caused by seeing a caged snake is unreasonable, even if no ideas precede or follow the emotion. James and Lange do no better. Emotions represent bodily changes on their approach, and nothing else. I have offered an amendment to the James–Lange theory that can address this problem. If emotions represent concerns, they can be correct or incorrect. If Jones fears the captive snake, she is literally representing the snake as dangerous. That is an error. But it is perfectly warranted for her to fear the venomous viper coiled around her leg.

The issue is actually a bit more complicated. If emotions are passive, or outside of our direct control, then epistemic norms may be weaker than they would be for judgments. We can be blamed for reasoning badly, but it's hard to blame someone for getting depressed. We can say that a thought is unreasonable *and* that a thinker is unreasonable for having that thought. With emotions, it's harder to criticize the person, because we exercise less control over how we feel than over what inferences we draw. To say that an emotion is irrational is not always an indictment of its bearer. The fear we experience on roller coasters is irrational, given their relative safety, but we, as agents, are not irrational for having the fear. Irrational emotions entail irrational agents only when agents can exert some control over those emotions, as when the emotions are triggered by beliefs rather than low-level perceptions. Fear of flying entails irrationality on the part of an agent in a way that fear experienced on a roller coaster does not. The latter entails irrational agency only if it is used to ground certain decisions or beliefs ("I refuse to go on roller coasters because they are dangerous"). Here the agentive fault lies with the inference from the emotion, not the emotion itself.

In sum, I have been arguing that the James–Lange theory can be modified to address the Rational Assessment Problem. Like Hume, James and Lange never explained how emotions could represent concerns. Consequently, their theory fails to explain the rational assessability of emotions. By supplementing the James–Lange theory with an account of how emotions represent, this problem can be solved. I call this the *embodied appraisal theory*. Emotions are embodied, because they are somatic signals, just as James and Lange maintained. But emotions are also appraisals, insofar as they represent concerns, as standard cognitive theories maintain (Prinz, 2004).

2.1.5 Somatic Similarity, Basic Emotions, and Calibration

I said that the James–Lange theory faces two serious objections. I have just offered an answer to the first of these. Emotions can be rationally assessed because they represent concerns. And they represent concerns even though they do not contain conceptual constituents. This means that the Jamesian equation of emotions with somatic signals can be preserved. The remaining problem with this view is that there simply aren't enough bodily states to go around.

Strictly speaking, the body has an unbounded number of distinct states. Every minute of our lives, our bodies are probably in a slightly different state than they've ever been in before. Each arrangement of muscles, rate of blood flow, and sequence of breaths is unique. But, all these variations can be classified into repeatable patterns. The problem for the James–Lange approach is not that there are too many bodily patterns, but that there are too few. If we group similar patterns together, the array of bodily patterns associated with emotions seems quite limited. Different emotions are associated with the same or similar somatic changes. Consider guilt again. Above, I said that guilt is associated with frowning. It is a low-energy, downtrodden emotion. This should sound familiar. The same would be said about sadness. If we study the bodily expressions of guilt, we may find that they overlap with the expressions of sadness considerably. Or, to take a more obvious example, consider anger and righteous indignation. These are distinct emotions. One can be angry without being indignant (though, interestingly, the converse is less plausible). If there were a unique bodily pattern for every emotion, then we would expect anger and indignation to be somatically distinguishable. This is unlikely to be the case. Sometimes different emotions correspond to the same bodily patterns. Call this the Somatic Similarity Problem.

This problem poses a serious threat to the James–Lange theory as originally formulated. That theory is in danger of misrepresenting the number of emotions that we have. It implies that anger and indignation are a single emotion, and likewise for numerous other seemingly distinct pairs of emotions: sadness and guilt, physical revulsion and moral disgust, joy and pride. Fortunately, there is a way out. The amended James–Lange theory that I am recommending has a simple solution to the Somatic Similarity Problem.

On the embodied appraisal theory, emotions represent concerns, such as losses, dangers, and offenses. Using the kinds of analogies that Dretske has made popular, I likened emotions to smoke alarms. More accurately, they are like the tones emitted by smoke alarms. Tones, it turns out, can do double duty. Acoustically identical tones can be emitted by different devices. Imagine a house that has both a smoke alarm and a carbon monoxide alarm, and imagine that both emit very similar tones. When one goes off, the homeowners may not know which alarm is sounding, but there is a fact of the matter which tone it is. Each tone has one meaning, as determined by the mechanism to which it is attached.

By analogy, I want to claim that a somatic signal of the same bodily pattern can have distinct meanings on different occasions depending on the mental mechanisms that caused that pattern to form. Imagine that a smoke-detecting mechanism and a carbon-detecting mechanism are wired to the same beeper. What are we to say about the meaning of a tone on any given occasion? There is a strong temptation to say it has a disjunctive meaning, smoke-or-carbon-monoxide. I think this is wrong. Upon hearing the tone, the homeowners might indeed say, "That tone means there is either a fire or gas," but they would also say, "That tone is probably indicating the presence of just one of these two hazards, and we'd better find out which." I think the tone has a univocal meaning when it occurs, in exactly the same way an ambiguous word has just one meaning when it is uttered in a speech act. The word "bat" refers to an animal if it issues from one lexical entry in the mind's language system, and to a piece of sporting equipment if it issues from another lexical entry. Put in terms of Dretske's theory, each token of the sound "bat" is actually a token of a different type. The sounds issue from separate mental files, one of which has the function of tracking flying rodents and the other of which tracks baseball players.

Let us see what follows for the emotions. Suppose that anger and indignation have the same bodily symptoms. Suppose further that these bodily symptoms can be produced via two different mechanisms. One mechanism is a collection of impressions and ideas pertaining to insults and threats, and the other mechanism is a collection of impressions and ideas pertaining to injustice. And, finally, suppose that cognitive systems in which these mechanisms reside can sometimes determine which of these two mechanisms has recently been operative. The system can recall whether it has recently tokened thoughts of insult or of injustice. Imagine a case where the experience of reading a newsletter from Amnesty International causes a bodily perturbation. The representation of that perturbation is type-ambiguous, but this particular token is easy to diagnose. It has been caused by thoughts of injustice; it is a case of indignation. If someone with amnesia could not recall what thoughts had triggered the emotional response, there would still be a fact of the matter. The response counts as anger if it has one kind of cause, and indignation if it has the other. We sometimes don't recall the conditions that triggered our emotions, and, when that happens, we can be unsure what emotion we're feeling. A psychotherapist might help a patient recognize that the unidentified emotion she is experiencing is guilt.

The calibration proposal provides a solution to the Somatic Similarity Problem. Two tokens of the same somatic signal type can constitute distinct emotions, because they can be under the control of different calibration files, and represent different concerns. In this way, a small group of bodily patterns can underwrite a large group of emotions.

This raises a question. Why all the duplication? Why are the same bodily patterns used over and over again? Why are there so few stable patterns of bodily change and so many emotions? The answer to this question has something to do with where emotions come from. I think we are innately furnished with a small emotional repertoire. Our "basic" emotions get reused in novel ways to create new emotions. Through experience, mechanisms are set up to correlate an existing bodily response with a new set of eliciting conditions, a new concern.

The idea of basic emotions is not new. Descartes believed in basic emotions, and so did Spinoza. Basic emotions have been a common theme in modern empirical research as well. McDougall (1908) postulated a set in his pioneering work in social psychology. Another list was advanced by Magda Arnold in her seminal appraisal theory (Arnold 1960). The most widely researched list of basic emotions owes to Paul Ekman and his collaborators, who used them in his seminal studies of cross-cultural emotion recognition (Ekman, 1972). Ekman's classic list contains six items: happiness, sadness, anger, fear, surprise, and disgust. I think this may need a bit of revision, but it is a good first approximation, especially if we regard these emotion labels as referring to broad families of emotions, which may have subtly different manifestations across cultures. The idea is that we have a universal emotional vocabulary, which is quickly co-opted by experience and tuned to culturally specific eliciting conditions.

There are two ways a basic emotion can be used to create new emotions. First, it can be combined with another basic emotion, to create an emotional blend. Contempt may be a blend of anger and disgust. Exhilaration may be a blend of joy and fear. Second, a basic emotion can be assigned a new set of eliciting conditions. In the standard case, these will be a subset of the initial eliciting conditions that have been elaborated, through experience, to form an independent elicitation mechanism. I call this recalibration. Above, I said that emotions are associated with mental files that calibrate them to concerns. In recalibration, a new mental file is established, which establishes an existing emotion with a new set of eliciting conditions. For example, pride may be joy recalibrated to one's own successes.

In many cases, blending and calibration conspire together. Nostalgia may be a blend of joy and sadness directed at the past. Pity may be a sad disgust directed at another individual, who is deemed inferior. Jealousy may be a blend of anger, sadness, fear, and disgust tuned to situations of suspected sexual infidelity.

These methods of generating new emotions are crucial for explaining moral emotions. For example, indignation may be anger calibrated to injustice, and guilt may be sadness calibrated to self-caused harm. I will develop and defend these proposals in the next section, but first I want to point out that this approach can be used to overcome a worry raised in section 2.1.2. There I argued that emotionism is difficult to reconcile with cognitive theories of emotion. One reason for this had to do with Moore's open-question argument. Suppose that we defined indignation as the judgment that there has been in inequitable distribution of resources. And suppose that indignation is part of the concept WRONG. In other words, suppose that some token instances of the concept WRONG literally contain a state of indignation. If that were the case, then, when using such a token, it would be incoherent to wonder whether inequity was wrong, because the answer to this question would be a conceptual truth. The calibration approach circumvents this difficulty because calibration files are not components of the emotions they calibrate. Indignation does not contain a calibration file. Indignation is just a somatic signal. Its occurrence is caused by a calibration file and that file presumably contains judgments about inequity and various other kinds of injustice. The calibration file may also contain stored perceptual records of events that are unjust. For example, if you ever saw or imagined someone stealing from a homeless person, an image of that event might get stored in the calibration file that triggers indignation. The items in this file are causes of indignation, not components. Therefore, tokens of the concept WRONG that contain indignation do not contain any of the images or ideas in the file that calibrates indignation. No instance of the concept WRONG contains the concept INEQUITY, for example. Thus, it is never a tautology to wonder whether inequity is wrong.

Before turning to a more thorough discussion of moral emotions, let's take stock. I have been developing a theory of the emotions that builds on the somatic approach of James and Lange. The original James–Lange theory faces two serious objections: the Rational Assessment Problem and the Somatic Similarity Problem. The embodied appraisal theory is capable of solving both of these problems. This theory follows the James–Lange theory in saying that emotions are somatic signals. Emotions are not cognitive states. But the theory departs from James and Lange in a crucial respect: emotions represent concerns. This means that an emotion can be unwarranted or warranted, and it also allows that two emotions can have different content despite being somatically indistinguishable. In short, I have argued that cognitive theories are right about the content of emotions, but non-cognitivists are right about the form.

2.2 THE MORAL EMOTIONS

As a rough definition, I will say that moral emotions are emotions that arise in the context of morally relevant conduct. More specifically, moral emotions promote or detect conduct that violates or conforms to a moral rule. Reading the pages of early British moralists, one might get the impression that there are only two moral emotions. Hutcheson talks about approbation and condemnation.

He says these "are probably simple ideas, which cannot be farther explained" (1738: 67). Hume suggests a similar view when he refers to approbation and disapprobation. Adam Smith criticizes Hutcheson for failing to appreciate that moral sentiments derive from more basic emotions (1759: 7.III.iii). I think Smith is right. Approbation and disapprobation are not the names of simple feelings; they involve a variety of different emotions. Smith says that approbations involve such things as sympathy and gratitude, while disapprobation involves antipathy and resentment. My analysis is a bit different. I will begin with a distinction between reactive and reflexive emotions. These correspond, roughly, to what some authors call "other-blame" and "self-blame" emotions (Ben-Ze'ev, 2000), but they also include emotions of praise. I will then turn to various kinds or moral caring, including sympathy.

2.2.1 Reactive Moral Emotions

I define reactive moral emotions as emotions that arise when another person (or group) is interpreted as conforming to or violating a moral rule. Reactive moral emotions divide into two classes: blame and praise or, in Humean terms, approbation and disapprobation. I begin with blame.

I mentioned one example of an other-directed blame emotion earlier. That was indignation. Indignation is not a basic emotion; it derives from anger. Indignation is anger calibrated to injustice. We feel indignation when the government fails to take care of the governed. At a more local level, we may feel something similar when minor injustices are committed against us personally. If someone does not reciprocate or acknowledge a favor (saying "thank you"), we may feel indignant. We use the adjectival form of the word rather than the nominal form, perhaps because the nominal signifies grander or loftier injustices.

Anger is also the source of another moral emotion. When a person inflicts physical harm on us, we sometimes experience a kind of rage that does not require any thoughts about injustice. We feel wronged, in a moral sense. A similar anger is felt when someone takes something from us. In both cases, we feel that our rights have been violated. There is no precise name for this anger in English. I will call it righteous anger to emphasize the link to rights. Righteous anger differs from indignation because some violations of rights are not violations of justice. As I intend the term, justice involves principles having to with fairness, equity, and proportion. When someone steals something, we do not necessarily think about fairness. A greedy person, unconcerned with fairness or justice, might feel violated when someone steals from her. She might say, "How dare you!" but not "How could you!" In many cases, however, rights and justice coincide. The thief who takes from a needy person has done something unjust. In these cases, violations evoke righteous *indignation*. In the case of minor violations, we feel righteously *indignant*, as when someone cuts us off on the road or knocks into us, without apology, on the street. I will refer to this entire class of emotions as moral anger.

Righteous anger and indignation are different because they represent different concerns. But they both derive from the same basic emotion. Why is that? The answer is that their concerns overlap with the concern that elicits anger in its more basic form. Ordinary anger is a response to insults or threats. Likewise for moral anger. Moral anger arises when there has been an injustice or when someone's rights are violated. In both cases, there is typically a victim: someone has been harmed or insulted, by being treated in a way that indicates he lacks entitlement or worth. When we react emotionally to victimization, the anger response is natural because it evolved to cope with threats, and it disposes us to aggression. If you have an innate capacity for anger, it's likely that it will recruited when you become sensitive to injustice and rights violations.

Some philosophers suppose that anger is always a moral emotion. I don't agree. Anger arises when someone glares at you, or picks a fight, or belittles you. All of these things can be regarded as immoral, but they need not be. Two boxers in a bout might experience anger, even though they don't think it wrong for the other to hit them in that context. Or consider this example from Baier (1967). A married couple have saved up money for their son's education, but now they decide to take that money and spend it on an extravagant vacation. The son is peeved about this, but he is also morally munificent; he says to his parents, "You have no moral obligation to pay for my education, but I am angry at you for your choice." The son feels that his parents have selfishly deprived him of something, but he does not think it was immoral for them to do so; they had no moral obligation. Baier thinks that this example poses a threat to emotivism (and by extension to epistemic emotionism). If moral judgments were merely a matter of having emotions such as anger, then the son in this scenario could not say consistently that he is angry without also saying that his parents have done something immoral. But this worry can be addressed if we distinguish ordinary anger from moral anger. The son's anger in this case does not arise from a calibration file containing ideas pertaining to injustice or rights violations.

Moral anger is central to morality because many of our moral rules are prohibitions against rights violations and injustice. Such rules concern victims; they always involve threats or harms to people. But there are also moral rules that have little to do with justice and rights. Consider, for example, sexual taboos. We morally condemn those who engage in certain sexual practices: bestiality, incest, adultery, and, in earlier times, premarital sex, homosexual sex, and masturbation. In some cases these acts involve a violation of rights (father–daughter incest is an especially disturbing example), but in other cases there is neither slight nor threat. Consensual sibling incest, mentioned in chapter 1, is an example. The intuition that this is morally wrong cannot depend on construing it as a slight or a threat. No one is harmed by consensual incest, if the offending parties enjoy the experience and don't tell anyone about it. Consequently, the emotion felt toward the offending parties cannot be moral anger. Instead, as noted in chapter 1, the emotion elicited is a form of disgust.

Moral disgust is not a basic emotion. It is an outgrowth of ordinary disgust. Ordinary disgust concerns physical contamination. Paul Rozin has done extensive empirical research demonstrating that disgust arises in situations where there is ordinarily a risk of harm due to germs or other hidden dangers (Rozin et al., 1993). Its primitive elicitors include bodily fluids (all except tears), non-human creatures, dead things, refuse, or objects that have come into contact with any of these things. The contact principle is important. Germs posed a threat before we had any conception of them. To ensure our safety, evolution furnished us with a negative response to things that might harbor germs including certain biological materials and things that have touched those materials. Disgust is a digestive emotion. Its bodily basis involves a pattern associated with digestive rejection in the mouth, nose, and gut.

Rozin et al. (1993) have demonstrated that moral disgust derives from physical disgust by showing that it has the same bodily basis and the same logic of contamination. We do not like to have physical contact with objects that have touched a person we deem morally disgusting. For example, we would not like to live in the former home of a condemned pedophile.

Sexual mores are obvious candidates for moral disgust because sex is a carnal act that saliently involves the transfer of bodily fluids. Since these things can elicit disgust on their own, it is unsurprising that violations of sexual rules are regarded as disgusting. Moral disgust is also directed at mass murderers, perhaps because they are associated with mutilation and death, which are primitive elicitors of disgust. In an experiment, Rozin et al. (1993) found that subjects were unwilling to try on a sweater that he said had belonged to Hitler. Their refusal continued even after monetary offers were made, and they expressed disgust. Rozin and Singh (1999) also found that disgust is associated with moral taboos against smoking. Smoke is a pollutant, so it can easily elicit disgust.

Pollution is often metaphorically extended in the moral domain. For example, certain religious traditions think the soul will become polluted if you act in ways that violate divine laws. Shweder et al. (1997) have shown that theologically construed ideals of purity are central to the moral system in Orissa, India, where they have done extensive fieldwork. There are moral rules pertaining to what you can eat, to whom you can talk, what you can wear in temples, where you can go if you are a woman menstruating, and what psychological states you can have. In all of these cases, violators are regarded as impure or polluted. For example, it's a form of moral impurity to have hatred in your heart. In some of these cases, there is a direct link to elicitors of physical disgust, but in most the impurity is metaphorical. Physical purity is transformed into spiritual purity. Shweder et al. (1997) refer to moral systems that emphasize purity as "ethics of divinity," because they often play a central role in non-secular societies, and purity is typically conceptualized in a supernatural way: immoral acts contaminate the soul. When your soul is contaminated you are not necessarily in any physical danger (at least in this world), but you are corrupted in the eyes of God or gods. In secular societies, emphasis tends to be placed elsewhere: on justice and rights. Shweder et al. call this the "ethics of autonomy." The concern for justice and rights stems from the view that individuals are entitled to certain things, and immoral acts are construed as crimes against persons. Within an ethics of autonomy, the core moral concept is harm, rather than purity. Behaviors that don't cause harms (such as consensual sex acts, diet, or dress) are less likely to be moralized in societies that have an ethics of autonomy.

Shweder et al. (1997) also identify a third kind of ethical system, which is very central in some cultures. They call it an "ethics of community," and its rules govern personal relationships with social groups. Rules governing rank, respect for the family, and treatment of communal resources fall into this category. Collectivist societies tend to emphasize rules of this kind. They place special value on each individual's place in society, and failure to play the roles associated with that place are morally prohibited. When people step out of line, they disrupt the social order. In such societies, disrespect is a cardinal transgression, and it is often more heavily emphasized than impurity and harm. Shweder and his collaborators do not think that societies operate under a single moral system: divinity, autonomy, or community. Rather, all communities tend to have norms in each category. The cross-cultural differences manifest themselves in the degree to which any category is stressed, and, in some case, the very same form of conduct will be construed under different categories. For example, in our society we tend to think of incest as harmful, whereas in a non-secular society, it is more likely to be seen as impure, and in a collectivist society it might be construed as a threat to the family structure. Of course, in most societies, all three conceptualizations play some role. When we are presented with cases of consensual incest, in which no one is harmed, we fall back on thinking of incest as kind of contamination.

In a very important study, Rozin et al. (1999) show that these three classes of rules are associated with different emotions. They presented Japanese and American subjects with a series of vignettes and asked them to identify the appropriate emotional response. They devised examples in which there was either a clear harm (e.g., murder), a clear instance of disrespect (e.g., a teenager eating dinner before others are served), or a clear case of something we tend regard as polluting the body (e.g., a teenage girl having sex with a seventy-year-old man). Rozin et al. found that autonomy violations tend to be associated with anger, purity violations with disgust, and community violations with contempt (an emotion I will discuss shortly). They call this the CAD model, for contempt, anger, and disgust. They note, coincidently that CAD is also an acronym formed from community, autonomy, and divinity. The CAD model is one of the most elegant achievements in recent moral psychology. But it is not entirely new. The idea that different emotions might be elicited by different kinds of transgression has been suggested before. Hume (1739: III.iii.iv) explicitly argues that different kinds of acts elicit different moral emotions, and, in another prescient remark, he writes:

[I]n moral deliberations we must be acquainted beforehand with all the objects, and all their relations to each other; and from a comparison of the whole, fix our choice or approbation.... The approbation or blame which then ensues, cannot be the work of the judgment but of the heart; and is not a speculative proposition or affirmation, but an active feeling or sentiment.... [T]he mind, from the contemplation of the whole, feels some new impression of affection or disgust, esteem or contempt, approbation or blame. (Hume, 1751: Appendix I, ii)

Here Hume seems to anticipate specific features of the CAD model: if we replace the word "blame" with "anger," we can see that he assumes that anger, contempt, and disgust are the primary moral emotions, and each arises after deliberation about the nature of the transgression under consideration.

I endorse the CAD model, but I want to offer a few suggestions about how it should be understood. My first point is terminological. Following Shweder, Rozin et al. refer to purity violations as belonging to the ethics of divinity, but, ironically, none of their vignettes in this category involve religious violations. This suggests that Shweder's label for the category is too narrow. Disgust can arise in response to mass murderers, especially when bodies are mutilated, and to violations of sexual mores, even among people with secular values. Thus, moral disgust does not belong exclusively to the domain of spiritual purity. It belongs, instead, to what might be called "the natural order." Within religious cosmology, nature is subsumed by the divine; the natural order is the order that has been established by the gods. Violations of divine nature elicit disgust because they are violations against nature, not conversely. Such violations are first, and foremost, unnatural acts. Therefore, I will say that moral anger is directed at transgressions against autonomy and moral disgust is directed at transgressions against the perceived natural order.

The next point I want to make concerns contempt. Rozin et al. discovered that this is the dominant emotional response to violations of community norms. People feel contempt toward the teenager who eats before others are served. People also feel contempt for those who disrespect the elderly, or who destroy public property, or who fail to act in accordance with their prescribed place in society. There is a close relationship between contempt and class. The wealthy have contempt for the poor and the poor have contempt for the wealthy. When discussing moral anger and moral disgust, I argued that both are extensions of non-moral emotions. Now I want to ask about the origins of contempt. Is it a basic emotion or does it emerge from emotions that are not initially linked to morality?

My answer to this question was already indicated in my discussion of blended emotions. There I suggested that contempt is a blend of anger and disgust. On the face of it, that is difficult to reconcile with Rozin et al.'s discovery that contempt is elicited by a fundamentally different kind of moral transgression from anger and disgust. On closer analysis, however, the blending story actually finds confirmation in their model. Anger is directed at transgressions committed against persons; disgust is directed at transgressions committed against nature; and contempt is directed at transgressions against community. Community can be thought of as an organized dynamic system of individuals. Within a community, each person has a particular place and makes certain kinds of contributions to the organic whole. In this respect, community is like nature. The communal order is the natural order of a human collective. If this interpretation is right, a violation against community should elicit anger, because it is a violation against persons, and disgust because it is a violation against a natural order. The hypothesis that contempt is an anger–disgust blend explains why contempt is elicited by violations against community.

The blending proposal faces three objections. First, one might argue that contempt seems to be more than a blend of anger and disgust. A central feature of contempt is a feeling of superiority. We look down on people whom we hold in contempt. Feelings of superiority are not typically associated with anger or disgust. If contempt were a blend, it should not have emergent features.

This objection can be answered by reflecting further on the nature of anger and disgust. We regard disgusting people as defective, or animalistic. We do not necessarily feel superior, but we feel repelled. Those who provoke our anger are regarded as insensitive to us as individuals. Now consider what happens when disgusting people disrespect you. It is no longer possible just to shun them. They have entered your space. To be threatened by a disgusting person is different from being threatened by an equal. It draws our attention to the difference in social status and instills a feeling of superiority. When a person merely disgusts us, we look away; but when they disgust and anger us, we cannot look away, so we look down on them, repelled, as we are, by their animality. I am not suggesting that we explicitly think this way. Moral arrogance is contemptuous in its own right. The suggestion is that violations against community typically involve factors that automatically promote a kind of smugness. Anyone who makes us both angry and disgusted is likely to make us feel superior as well. In light of this, it might be best to describe contempt as a blend of all anger, disgust, and superiority (assuming there is an emotion of superiority).

A second reason for resisting the blending analysis is that contempt seems to have its own facial expression. Ekman and Friesen (1986) have argued that contempt is associated with a unilateral lip curl, and that this expression is recognized across cultures. If contempt has a universal facial expression, then it is likely to be a basic emotion. Or so Ekman and Friesen would have us believe.

This objection can be countered. For one thing, existing research on the expression of contempt is very controversial. Wagner (2000) has argued that the studies in which contempt is recognized are flawed. In those studies, subjects are given a forced choice of emotion labels, including the word "contempt" or its synonyms. When given an open choice instead of a forced choice, subjects do not label the face "contempt." For another thing, if there is an expression of contempt it might be a blended expression that derives from the expressions of more basic components. Contempt is associated with a fixed stare and a straight or lowered brow, both of which are consistent with anger. The unilateral lip-curl may derive from the disgust expression: disgust involves an upward wrinkling of the nose, which typically pulls the lips upward as well. But why is the lip-curl unilateral? One possibility is that disgust and anger place different demands on the mouth. In anger, lips are typically either closed, with the upper lip puffed outwards, or open in a "box-like" grimace to reveal the teeth. Perhaps the co-occurrence of the disgust facial display with these anger displays leads to a partial curling of the lip. The asymmetry of the lip-curl in contempt could derive from the fact that the facial expressions of anger and disgust are under control of different hemispheres of the brain. There is some evidence that approach emotions are more associated with the right hemisphere, while withdrawal emotions are more associated with the left (Davidson and Irwin, 1999). If anger is an approach emotion (aggression is a kind of approach behavior), and disgust is a withdrawal emotion, one might expect the co-occurrence of these emotions to manifest themselves asymmetrically on the face. Another possibility is that the unilateral lip-curl involves the introduction of a third expression over and above anger and disgust. In particular, the lip-curl could suggest an interaction with the same muscle groups using in smiling. Why smiling? We often think of smiling as a signal for happiness, but smiling and laughter are also known to signal dominance (Provine, 2000). Notice too that there is a close relationship between contempt and ridicule or derision, which use laughter in a demeaning way. The unilateral lip-curl is a kind of sneer, and sneers are associated with feelings of superiority. It is possible that the combination of anger and disgust tends to co-occur with dominance, because, when we feel disgusted by someone we view them as an animal, and when we feel angry we want to aggress against them. In addition, many community norms involve rank, so feelings of superiority will naturally arise. If this is right, then the contempt blend may ordinarily involve an emotion of dominance, and that emotion may contribute to the expression. The smile that signals dominance may be asymmetric because it may be controlled by the hemisphere that houses negative emotions. All of this is highly speculative, of course. The main point is that a universal facial expression for contempt is compatible with the hypothesis that contempt is a blended emotion.

The blending analysis of contempt might be challenged in a third way. Contempt is frequently associated with violations of rank in hierarchically organized societies. Rank is not original to our species, however. Most social mammals live in hierarchically organized groups. Any emotion associated with rank violations is likely to be quite old. The suggestion that contempt is a blend of more basic emotions seems to conflict with the observation that rank has a long phylogenetic history. There might well have been selection pressure for the emergence of a distinctive moral emotion for keeping people stratified.

Three remarks in response. First, if contempt is a blend of anger and disgust, we might expect it to arise in any species that has those two more basic emotions.

Rank doesn't require the evolution of any new emotions if previously evolved emotions can do the job. Second, the suggestion that contempt is a blend of anger and disgust is consistent with the suggestion that contempt is evolved. We might have evolved mechanisms that facilitate and promote the blending of certain emotions. Third, there is no reason to assume that rank violations elicit the same emotion in us as they do in other mammals. When an animal vies for rank, the dominant animal reacts with anger (or, at any rate, a feeling of aggression) rather than contempt. If the animal vies unsuccessfully, it may experience fear and submission. I suspect that non-human animals do not have a sufficiently rich conception of the social order to construe rank violations as disgusting in the manner that I suggested. Non-human animals have rules concerning rank, but they are enforced using a more restricted emotional repertoire. Putting this differently, for non-human animals, rank violations are more akin to autonomy violations.

I conclude that there are two fundamental classes of other-directed moral emotions (moral anger and moral disgust) and one derived class (moral contempt). All of these emotions, I submit, are non-basic. They are natural extensions of basic emotions that arise in contexts of transgression. The emotion elicited by a transgression will be determined by the overlap between that transgression and situations that elicit emotions in non-moral contexts. Rights violations are threats to persons. Sexual mores involve threats to the natural order. Rank violations are threats to the natural order of persons.

2.2.2 Reflexive Moral Emotions

Contempt, anger, and disgust are other-blame emotions. When we blame ourselves, different emotions follow. Shweder's three ethical systems and the CAD model suggest that there may be different kinds of self-blame. The emotions we experience when we violate rules may depend on the nature of those rules.

Consider what happens when we violate a rule pertaining to justice or rights. You've just stolen something. You've just hurt someone. You took more than your fair share. I hypothesize that the default emotional response in these cases is guilt, especially when the victim is a member of a group with which you affiliate. If you take something from a group with whom you have no relation or harm an enemy, you may not feel any kind of self-blame. But when you harm a member of the in-group, guilt is likely to follow; Baumeister et al. (1994) have shown that guilt is most frequently associated with actions that threaten individuals to whom one has an attachment relationship. Guilt may represent the concern expressed by: I have violated an autonomy rule against a member of a group with which I feel a connection.

A different emotion is felt when we violate rules having to do with the natural order. Violators of sexual taboos and rules of religious purity are more likely, I would predict, to feel shame. It is sometimes suggested that guilt is act-directed while shame is person-directed. A guilty person can feel that her actions were wrong without feeling like a bad person. A person who feels shame will typically feel dirty, unworthy, or corrupt. This makes perfect sense in the context of transgressions against nature. The person who engages in reviled sexual acts or the person who mutilates another human being may feel subhuman. The ashamed person feels hideous and impure.

The model that I have been proposing predicts that people who transgress against community will feel a blend of guilt and shame. We have no word for that emotion, but I suspect it exists. Consider how you might feel if you mistreated an elderly person (one of the community norms left in our very autonomous culture). Both shame and guilt seem appropriate. If someone discovered your crime, you would want to conceal yourself, as if in shame. But you would also dwell on the harm you caused in an act-directed way, as if guilty.

To test this extension of the CAD model, I conducted a study in which subjects read moral scenarios in the second-person. The scenarios includes crimes against persons ("Suppose you take something from someone and never return it"), crimes against nature ("Suppose, in a moment of weakness, you allow a person who is really old to kiss you romantically"), and crimes against community ("Suppose you unthinkingly start to eat your dinner at a family gathering before everyone has sat down at the table"). In each case, subjects are asked whether they would be more likely to experience guilt or shame. For the crimes against nature subjects overwhelmingly chose shame, and for the crimes against persons, they overwhelmingly chose guilt. There was no statistically significant difference, however, between guilt and shame for the crimes against community.

I said that moral other-blame emotions are not basic. The same is true of moral self-blame emotions. As mentioned above, I think guilt is an extension of sadness. Both are associated with frowning and feeling downtrodden. It's noteworthy that excessive guilt is a diagnostic symptom of clinical depression (American Psychiatric Association, 1994). Conversely, as noted in chapter 1, psychopaths have a sadness deficiency *and* a guilt deficiency. The hypothesis that guilt is an extension of sadness predicts these co-morbidities. But now we need an explanation of why guilt emerges from sadness and not another emotion. The answer emerges from my extension of the CAD model. Guilt is associated with violations of moral rules concerning rights and justice. It is especially associated with self-caused harm. More specifically, it is associated with harms against people for whom one feels a sense of attachment. Attachment is intimately related to sadness. The most powerful elicitor of sadness is the loss of a loved one. We generally feel a sense of loss or sadness when others are harmed, regardless of how the harm occurred. Thus, if I harm someone I care about, I will probably feel sad about that person's suffering. Moreover, if I harm someone in my in-group, other members of my in-group will be angry at me or disappointed; they will withdraw affection from me. In chapter 1, I suggested this may play an important role in moral development. If caregivers withdraw love from children who behave badly, those children will feel sad, because withdrawal of love is a kind of loss. This sad feeling, originally associated with the lost affection of caregivers, becomes associated with the kinds of conduct that bring about such a loss. If refusing to share with your sister makes your parents mad, then you will become sad. The sadness will be compounded if your parents draw your attention to the fact that your behavior made your sister cry. Initially, the sadness is a response to lost affection and vicarious distress, but eventually it is transferred to the actions that lead to these consequences. The very thought of hurting or stealing or refusing to share makes us sad, not the supposed harm or punishment it will bring about. Once this transfer takes place, we can be said to have the emotion of guilt, as opposed to mere regret, which is feeling badly about an action in light of its consequences. Guilt is sadness that has been calibrated to acts that harm people about whom we care.

I think that shame derives from embarrassment. Embarrassment arises when we receive unwanted attention from others. It is a negative feeling, but often negative in a lighthearted way. We giggle with embarrassment. Shame is more serious. Giggling is a way of saving face when there has been a minor *faux pas* or a prophylactic strategy against harsh judgment in a public forum. Shame arises when we have done something more serious, something from which no giggle can rescue us. Moral shame is a species of aversive embarrassment that has been calibrated to norms having to do with the natural order. Violations of such norms reliably trigger intense embarrassment, because they make others view us as repugnant. The reaction triggered by a minor faux pas is magnified when we engage in behaviors that are regarded as bestial or unnatural. We are embarrassed when we break wind, but ashamed when we fantasize about disfavored sexual acts. Embarrassment may be a basic emotion (Miller, 1996). Shame is probably non-basic, because it is a form of embarrassment that could arise only after our species began metaphorically to extend the class of physical impurities into the social and behavioral domain. Shame arises inevitably once a culture starts to label certain acts as unnatural or deviant. Shame also arises when cultures develop rigid systems of social stratification. Members of such cultures sometimes feel intense and aversive embarrassment in the presence of higher-ranking individuals, because such encounters draw attention to their inferiority.

On the story that I have been telling, reactive and reflexive moral emotions divide into two fundamental categories and one blended category. All of these moral emotions are non-basic. There is also a class of moral emotions that lies somewhere between the reactive and the reflexive. Consider cases in which a transgression has been committed by someone extremely close to you, such as a parent or a child. In this case, the moral response is other-directed, but also self-directed. You see that person's conduct as reflecting on you. When this occurs, I think we often experience emotions that are similar to emotions of self-blame. If your child commits a crime against justice or rights, you may feel

Table 2.1. Emotions of blame as function of transgression and transgressor

| | | Transgressor | | |
		Stranger	Self	A loved one
Transgression	Against Persons	Anger	Guilt	Hurt
	Against Community	Contempt	Guilt/Shame	Hurt/Ashamed
	Against Nature	Disgust	Shame	Ashamed

hurt. Hurt and guilt overlap, because they are both derived from sadness. If your child commits an unnatural act, you may feel ashamed. If your child commits a violation against the community you may feel a combination of hurt and shame—a wistful sense of disgrace. The parent of a gang member whose child has destroyed public property might feel a biting ache of disappointment, while blushing before the disgruntled neighbors. All of these amplifications of the CAD model are summarized in Table 2.1.

2.2.3 Positive Emotions and Morality

It will not have escaped notice that I have been focusing on negative emotions. Every emotion in Table 2.1 is negative. Positive emotions are important for morality as well. We have positive reactive emotions directed at those who do good deeds, and we experience self-directed positive emotions when we do good deeds ourselves. In contrast to emotions of blame, these good feelings can be described as emotions of praise.

Emotions of praise have not been extensively studied, and they seem to behave somewhat differently from emotions of blame. There does not seem to be a distinctive positive emotion for each of the three kinds of ethical rules that I have been discussing. One reason for this is the simple fact that these ethical domains are defined by transgression-types, and it's not clear what role positive emotions would have in enforcing them. We blame someone for stealing, but we don't issue a medal when he refrains from stealing. We don't lavish the non-pedophile with praise for good conduct. In other words, we tend to *expect* people to behave morally.

This suggests a general asymmetry between positive and negative emotions in morality. Desirable behavior is more likely to be shaped through negative emotions than positive, and, as a result we are more generous with blame than praise. This can be demonstrated experimentally. For example, Malle and Bennett (2002) found that people were more likely to blame bad intentions than they were to praise good intentions, and Knobe (2003) found that subjects were more likely to regard actions as intentional when they produced foreseen bad side-effects than when they produced foreseen good side-effects. The origin of these asymmetries has not been well established. One possibility is that societies have a greater interest in eliminating bad behavior than in promoting especially good behavior. And, when it comes to eliminating bad behavior, punishment can be more effective that praise. It's not entirely clear why punishment should be more effective than praise. It may be a brute fact about us that good feelings are fleeting (especially in the face of bad temptations), while bad feelings are more likely to leave an enduring mark on memory and motivation.

If this is right, ordinary decency or conformity to moral rules depends much more on negative emotions than on positive emotions. But positive emotions may play a role in promoting behavior that goes above and beyond ordinary decency. Positive emotions may lead us to do things that are generous, noble, or kind. It has been demonstrated that positive affect can lead to pro-social behavior. Isen and Levin (1972) found that subjects are vastly more helpful if a good mood is induced prior to having an opportunity to help. One possible explanation is that positive emotions make us more outgoing, and that increases our awareness of others' needs. Another intriguing explanation is that once a positive emotion is induced, we want to maintain it, and helping behavior can do the trick. On this explanation, helping is construed as a source of positive affect. We feel good when we do good. This may play an important role in moral education. Imagine a scenario where you have an opportunity to save someone in need. One motive for doing so is that we would feel guilty if we didn't, but the huge literature on "bystander effects" suggests that people are all too willing to watch passively as people cry for help. But those who do intervene may do so because of the anticipated reward of noble behavior. They may anticipate feeling happy when they help. Support for this comes from a study by Valdesolo and DeSteno (2006). They asked subjects to consider a standard trolley case, in which a trolley is speeding toward five people, but they can save those lives by pushing someone into the trolley's path. Like most subjects in trolley experiments, the overwhelming majority thought it was wrong to push the person, killing one and saving five. But some subjects considered this scenario after watching a ridiculous film clip from *Saturday Night Live*. Those subjects were three times as likely to judge that it was appropriate to push the person. The positive emotions may have altered the response in two ways: they may have reduced the negative emotions associated with killing someone, and they may have increased the positive emotions associated with the anticipated reward of saving five lives. This interpretation is speculative, but, if it's right, it suggests that positive emotions may play a dominant role in helping, while negative emotions play a dominant role in not harming.

Table 2.2. Emotions of praise as a function
of who is the agent and patient

Agent	Patient	Emotion
Other	Other	Admiration
Other	Self	Gratitude
Self	Other	Gratification
Self	Self	Dignity

So far, I have been speaking quite generically about positive emotions. I have said little about which specific emotions are involved. The field of moral psychology needs a taxonomy of positive passions. I will attempt only a speculative first stab at that here. I have already noted that positive emotions may not vary across the three ethical domains discussed by proponents of the CAD model. But one dimension that I discussed above—self vs. other—may be important. In the case of good deeds, it matters who is doing the deed. It also seems to matter who benefits from the deed. For this reason, I think it is useful to sort positive moral emotions along the dimensions of agent and patient: who is acting and who is being acted upon.

Imagine reading about someone who performed an altruistic act, such as giving generously to charity or helping someone in need. My guess is that the default emotional response would be admiration. Now suppose that this kind soul does something nice for you. When someone does you a good turn, you probably feel gratitude. Thus, other-directed emotions of moral praise include admiration and gratitude, and the difference depends on who benefits from the act. Now consider cases in which you are the author of a good deed. If you do something very kind, you might feel a kind of gratification. It feels good to do good. Or consider a case in which your good actions are directed not toward someone else, but toward yourself. Perhaps you resist an especially strong temptation, or perhaps you pull yourself out of addiction or work your way up from poverty or acquire a skill that improves yourself as a person. In such cases, you might feel a kind of self-respect or dignity. These emotions are summarized in Table 2.2.

I am not suggesting that these are the only positive emotions that contribute to morality. There may be others. Haidt (2003) has proposed the existence of an emotion that he calls elevation, which he describes as a positive response to moral beauty. When a noble deed occurs, we feel elevated by it. I think elevation is an intriguing emotion, and it deserves further investigation. In my framework, however, elevation may just refer to intense admiration. Haidt implies that we can feel elevated by our own good deeds and the good deeds of others. I am inclined to think that self and other tend to be objects of subtly different emotions. If that is the case, self-directed elevation may be an intense form of moral gratification, or perhaps a blend of gratification and dignity (we feel good about doing good, and that makes us feel better about ourselves).

In addition to the positive emotions that I have been discussing, moral conduct may also benefit from the positive feelings that we get through social affiliation. Such emotions promote kindness and conformity. Good behavior ingratiates us to members of the community, and the desire to feel connected may be a source of motivation. In the next section, I will discuss some affective constructs related to affiliation: caring, sympathy, and concern. As we will see, some of these constructs are not positively valenced.

The foregoing suggestions need more experimental support to get any traction. Hopefully, positive moral emotions will begin to receive more attention (see, for example, McCullough et al., 2001 on gratitude). The very fact that they have been neglected may support the conjecture that negative emotions play a disproportionate role in moral conduct. In what follows, I will continue to focus on negative emotions, but the positive emotions should not be forgotten.

2.2.4 Caring, Sympathy, and Concern

Misbehavior is easy to explain. People act badly because bad behavior often carries an immediate reward. We attain goods through stealing and pleasure through condemned sexual acts. The deeper mystery is good behavior. Why do we ever obey moral rules? One answer has to do with the emotional price of bad behavior. Guilt and shame are unpleasant. Well-being is threatened when we incur others' wrath or evoke their disgust. Another answer, mentioned above, is that good behavior forges valuable affiliations. It is beneficial to be trusted. But both of these answers are limited because they presume that we behave in accordance with self-interest. Sometimes we do good things because we care about other people, even when there are no foreseen rewards. This insight is at the heart of Hume's moral philosophy, and it also figures prominently in the work of Adam Smith (1759).

Hume emphasized sympathy. Sympathy leads us to look after those in need or distress. Sympathy can be defined as a negative emotional response to the suffering of others. A sympathetic person feels bad that you feel bad. It's not clear empirically whether sympathy always refers to the same underlying emotion. If so, it's probably a species of sadness. In this respect, sympathy differs from empathy, which manifests itself differently from context to context (compare Darwall, 1998). In empathy, we feel the same emotion that someone else is feeling; we put ourselves in another person's shoes. If you are afraid, an empathetic person will experience fear too. Empathetic responses can be measured by, for example, comparing brain activation in people while they observe others in distress. In empathetic responses, the brain areas that activate in the observer are the areas that correspond to the kind of distress being observed. For example, during empathetic responses to observed pain, pain centers of the brain are active (Singer et al., 2004). Interestingly, in these studies, the observer seems to acquire the affective component of pain but not the sensory component; she acquires the distress of pain, without necessarily imagining the sensation that produces that distress. Sympathy has not been studied with neuroimaging, because most people tend to empathize, but we would expect a sympathetic person to show signs of negative affect, when witnessing pain, but not necessarily the same kind of negative affect that arises during the experience of pain. A person who congenitally lacks pain, owing to a genetic disorder, could sympathize with someone in pain, but couldn't empathize. Or, to change examples, parents might sympathize with their child's fear that there is a monster in the closet, but they may not feel any fear themselves.

Sympathy and empathy should both be distinguished from vicarious distress. Infants will sometimes cry when they hear other infants cry. This does not mean that they sympathize or empathize. They are distressed *by* the crying of other infants, but not distressed *about* that crying or *about* the events that led the other infant to cry. When we sympathize or empathize, our unhappiness is locked to the knowledge that another person is suffering. In cases of vicarious distress, our unhappiness is locked to the symptoms of another person suffering, not to the suffering itself. An adult experiencing vicarious distress will leave the room to avoid contact with a person who is suffering, and the distress will subside. An adult experiencing sympathy or empathy is more likely to offer help. Leaving the room does not eliminate the source of unhappiness; it just makes the source less salient. Psychologically this means that sympathetic and empathetic responses require an attribution of suffering rather than just an observation of suffering. In acknowledging that another person is suffering, empathetic or sympathetic people feel compelled to engage in pro-social behavior.

Sympathy and empathy interact in important ways with caring. The term "care" is ambiguous. It can name an attitude or a behavior ("taking care"). These two meanings are related to each other: if you care about a person, you are likely to care for them. This link may typically be mediated by sympathy or empathy. If you care about a person, you will pay attention to her needs. If she is needy, you will sympathize or empathize, and these feelings will impel you to help. Care does not always induce sympathy or empathy. You can care about art or care about the environment. Caring is a disposition to pay attention to something in a way that motivates both interaction with that thing and behaviors that promote the flourishing of that thing. Sympathy and empathy happen to be a vehicle for care when care is directed at other human beings. Sympathy and empathy can also promote care. Feeling distressed about another's distress can orient you toward that person in a way that makes you care about her well-being.

Like empathy, care is not any specific emotion. It manifests itself differently on different occasions, depending on the object you care about and the current condition of that object. In this respect, care may differ from concern. I think concern is a species of fear. To be concerned about someone is to worry about his or her well-being. Care is related to concern, because we are concerned for those we care about. Concern arises when something or someone we care about is in jeopardy. Like sympathy and empathy, concern may also help bind caring-about with caring-for. If you care about someone, and that person is in danger, you will become concerned; and if you become concerned, you may try to take care of that person. But unlike sympathy and empathy, we can be concerned for someone who is not herself experiencing any negative emotions. If your friend is a happy drug addict, you cannot sympathize or empathize with her, but you can be concerned.

In sum, there are a number of ways we can react negatively when bad things befall other people. We can experience vicarious distress, in which case we merely catch their feelings in the way that one might catch a cold (no attribution is necessary). We can experience sympathy, in which case we feel bad that they are going through a hard time. We can experience empathy, in which case we feel bad for them by putting ourselves in their emotional shoes. Or we can experience concern, in which case we will worry about their well-being even if they fail to appreciate that anything bad has happened. All distresses except vicarious ones are both promoted by care, and promote caring behavior.

2.2.5 Moral Sentiments

I said that care is not an emotion, but rather a disposition to experience different emotions. If you care about someone, you will be delighted by her achievements and distressed by her suffering. I will use the term "sentiment" to refer to an emotional disposition (see Prinz, 2004). Care is a sentiment. Other examples include liking, disliking, loving, and hating. If you like something, you will be happy when it is attained or near and sad when it is lost or far away. Liking may also make you envious (she has what I like!), frightened (I may lose what I like!), or hopeful (I may get what I like!).

In saying that sentiments are dispositions, I don't mean to imply that they are not real, physically implemented states of the mind. As I will use the term, a psychological disposition is a standing state of an organism that can manifest itself as an occurrent state. The standing/occurrent distinction is commonly used in philosophy. In psychological jargon, psychological dispositions can usually be identified with encodings in long-term memory that can be retrieved by working memory and maintained there during explicit mental processing. In neurocomputational terms, dispositions are usually identified with weighted connections between neurons that can activate the assemblies of neurons that they connect. All these ways of talking capture the basic idea that dispositions are internal states that do not always participate in information-processing, but can become active contributors under the right circumstances. A sentiment is a disposition whose occurrent manifestations (or working memory encodings, or neural activation patterns) are emotions.

Sentiments often manifest themselves as different emotions on different occasions. If you love tiramisu, you will be happy when you find it on the dinner menu and devastated when you learn that the restaurant has just run out. On any occasion, the specific emotion that you experience is a manifestation of your sentiment. Some other sentiments manifest themselves via the same or similar emotions on every occasion. Consider phobias. If you fear flying, you will not experience that fear every moment of your life. The fear is a standing state that will become an occurrent experience when, for example, you board an airplane.

The semantics of sentiments is somewhat different from the semantics of their constituent emotions. Emotions, I argued, represent concerns. Concerns are organism—environment relations that bear on well-being. Such relations can be characterized without mentioning the emotions that they cause in us. In other words, concerns are not secondary qualities (Prinz, 2004). Anger represents offense, not the property of being irksome. Fear represents danger, not the property of being scary. Sadness represents loss, not the property of being depressing. Happiness represents achievement or attainment, not the property of being enjoyable. Something could be offensive, dangerous, a loss, or an achievement without making us angry, fearful, sad, or happy. Emotions are defined by the concerns they have the function of detecting, and those concerns can be defined in non-emotional terms.

Now contrast this with sentiments. Liking provides a good example. Liking is partially constituted by a disposition to happiness, but liking does not represent achievement or attainment. Liking is also a disposition to sadness, as when you lose the object you like. But it doesn't represent loss. Because liking does not manifest itself as any single emotion, it cannot represent any single concern. Rather it locks onto the things that happen to instill these different emotions in you. In a word, liking represents the property of being likeable. Likeability is, plausibly, a secondary quality. It can be defined with reference to the sentiment of liking. The traits that count as likeable depend on what we are disposed to like. Thus, sentiments may represent secondary qualities even if their component emotions do not. This may even be true for sentiments that manifest themselves via the same emotion on every occasion. Consider phobias again. If you have a flying phobia, your phobia will probably always manifest itself as fear; we call it a fear of flying. Fear represents danger, but, arguably, the phobia itself represents scariness. Scariness is a secondary property. Something is scary if it causes fear. If you tell someone you have a fear of flying, you are telling them that you find flying scary; flying has the secondary quality of scaring you. I mention this point about phobias as an aside; when I talk about sentiments I will usually focus on cases where the emotional manifestations vary across contexts.

So far, I have been focusing on non-moral sentiments. A moral sentiment is one that manifests itself in moral emotions. Liking and disliking are not moral sentiments. Caring is not a moral sentiment either, as I define the term, though it can promote pro-social behavior, and pro-social behavior is morally valued.

Caring does not typically manifest itself in moral emotions, and we can care for things and people that lack moral significance.

There are a variety of different moral sentiments. Some of them are directed at persons. Consider resentment. Resentment is not an emotion. It is a sentiment. It is a disposition to feel something like bitterness, anger, or contempt. Resentment may be specific to the moral domain. We typically resent those who violate moral rules. On the face of it, there may seem to be non-moral instances of resentment. We may resent those who have more than us. But here, resentment can be understood as pertaining to injustice. We resent that there is an inequitable distribution of goods. We resent people for having what they do not deserve, and desert is a moral concept.

Another person-directed moral sentiment underlies the phenomenon of holding a grudge. Grudges are more linked to action than resentment. We hold grudges for what people have done, not for what they have. Grudges are typically directed against those who have violated rules of autonomy. Grudges are a kind of dispositional moral anger.

Some moral sentiments are broader in scope. They apply not just to persons, but to forms of conduct. One can have a negative moral sentiment toward lying, for example. In the next chapter, I will argue that such sentiments are the backbone of morality. Some emotionists call themselves sentimentalists, but few distinguish between emotions and sentiments. I think sentiments are essential for understanding moral concepts. My goal in this chapter has been to lay a foundation for a sentimentalist theory. Now it's time to lay out the bricks and mortar.

3

Sensibility Saved

3.1 SENSIBILITY THEORIES

In chapter 1, I began to present a case for emotionism. I argued that moral properties and moral concepts essentially involve emotion. In this chapter, I will present and defend an emotionist theory that accommodates the data in chapter 1 and draws on the approach to emotions developed in chapter 2. The theory that I will defend here is sensibility theory. It is a cousin of other theories in the literature (Dreier 1990; Johnston 1989; D. Lewis, 1989; McDowell 1985; McNaughton 1988; Wiggins 1987; Wright 1992). I will argue that sensibility theories can explain some central folk intuitions about the nature of morality. But sensibility theories face a number of serious objections. In the second part of this chapter, I will address ten objections that can be found in the literature. I argue that a properly formulated sensibility theory has resources to overcome each of these.

3.1.1 Standard Sensibility Theories

In chapter 1, I defined sensibility theories by the following schema:

(S1) *Metaphysical Thesis:* An action has the property of being morally right (wrong) just in case it causes feelings of approbation (disapprobation) in normal observers under certain conditions.

(S2) *Epistemic Thesis:* The disposition to feel the emotions mentioned in S1 is a possession condition on the normal concept RIGHT (WRONG).

Sensibility theory offers one way of accommodating the evidence that moral judgment is affect-laden. This is one of its main advantages. But, it's not the only approach that ties moral judgments to emotions. Emotivism, for example, can boast the same. To motivate the adoption of sensibility theory, we need to show that it has other advantages.

One attraction is that sensibility theory accommodates the evidence used to support moral intuitionism without taking on any of the baggage. Intuitionists typically make three claims (see Ross, 1930; Audi, 2004): there are a plurality of basic moral values, rather than one single moral principle; these values can be discovered by intuition without drawing any inferences; and when we intuit a moral value in this way, it is self-justifying (i.e., the way we grasp a moral judgment also counts as justification for that judgment). These claims are all phenomenologically plausible. We seem to intuit moral facts. The problem is that intuitionism is usually saddled with weird metaphysics and weird epistemology. If moral facts are not known by inference or observation, then they must be accessed in a mysterious way, and they must be very unusual facts.

Sensibility theory accommodates the core claims of intuitionism without the baggage. There is a plurality of basic values because we can develop each of our emotional attitudes individually: we can acquire a distaste for killing in one way and a distaste for incest in another. Sensibility explains the intuitive character of basic values because the emotions that constitute those values can be known non-inferentially; killing just feels wrong. Moral judgments are self-justifying because the emotions that we experience when we grasp those judgments are also responsible for making the judgments true: moral facts are consequences of our emotional reactions. Thus, sensibility theory can be viewed as a form of intuitionism, but it is metaphysically and epistemologically innocuous. Intuition is not a mysterious faculty on this approach, but rather an instance of the mundane capacity to introspect on our emotional states, or gut reactions. Moral facts are generated by such feelings, and they are no more metaphysically peculiar than facts involving properties such as funny or scary or irksome.

Sensibility theory also offers an attractive answer to a challenge put forward by J. L. Mackie (1977). Mackie claims that moral concepts are hopelessly confused. On the one hand, we act as if moral facts are part of the fabric of the world. On the other hand, we tend to think that moral facts are action-guiding. But these two assumptions are difficult to reconcile. How can a fact about the world be prescriptive in this way? In Mackie's terminology, moral concepts purport to designate properties that are utterly queer. We have no reason to think that such properties exist. Therefore, moral concepts are really vacuous. Ethical judgments are false or meaningless because they ascribe properties that are no more real than fairies or phlogiston.

Sensibility theorists respond to Mackie by demonstrating that moral properties are not so queer after all. Compare the following puzzle about colors: colors seem to be in the world, located on the surfaces of things, and yet they also seem to be experiences, because they can vary even when surfaces have not undergone any physical transformations. A Lockean account of color can explain this. Locke (1690) defines colors as secondary qualities. This may be captured by the following definition:

(C) The property of being blue (red, yellow, etc.) is that which causes blue (red, yellow, etc.) sensations in normal observers under certain conditions.

In other words, the Lockean account says that colors are powers that certain surfaces and media have to cause experiences in us. Powers are relational properties of physical things. In one respect, colors are located in the world, because the powers in question are possessed by things outside the mind (bananas and daffodils, for example). But colors are also constituted by experience, because these powers are individuated by effects on us. A banana would not be yellow if it were not disposed to cause certain experiences in us. Colors are, therefore, external things, but they are individuated by subjective states.

Now consider moral properties. Instead of appealing to visual experiences, we can define moral properties as powers to cause emotions in us. Emotions have motivational force, so something that causes emotions is motivating. If moral properties are powers to cause emotions, then moral properties are motivating. In one sense, moral properties are constituted by motivating states in us, but moral properties are also features of the world. Certain situations have the power to cause the relevant emotions. Those situations exist outside the mind, and they elicit emotional responses in us. On this view, there are moral facts, just as there are color facts. We can say truly that an action was right or wrong. But when we say these things, we deploy moral concepts that have emotional components. The emotional components are action-guiding. We cannot recognize moral facts as such without being disposed to act, just as we cannot recognize colors (in a standard way) without having visual experiences of a particular kind.

Emotions bring in something else that is essential to morality: they carry prescriptive power. If I judge your actions to be wrong, I will experience a form of disapprobation that is directed at you. My disapprobation does not merely describe what you have done; it prescribes that you act otherwise. Disapprobation directed at another person poses a threat to that person, which can promote compensatory behaviors, apologies, and better conduct in the future.

Sensibility theorists respond to Mackie by building a conceptual bridge between metaphysics and motivation (see McDowell, 1985). S1 tells us about moral properties, and S2 tells us about moral motivation. Here's how the story goes. A concept is a representation of a property. Concepts represent by being reliably or lawfully caused by property instances. Moral properties are powers to cause emotions in us. How do we mentally represent such properties? The obvious answer is that we represent them emotionally. We represent colors by means of the color experiences that colors cause in us. By analogy, we represent moral properties by the emotions they cause. Moral concepts incorporate the emotions that are caused by moral properties, and thereby serve as reliable detectors for those properties. Emotions are motivating. Therefore, tokening a moral concept disposes us to act. Moral judgments dispose us to act because they contain moral concepts. We get from metaphysics to motivation via concepts. *Pace* Mackie, an analysis of folk intuitions does not force us to conclude that moral concepts are vacuous. They are affectively infused, not fatally confused.

3.1.2 Approbation and Disapprobation

The schematic definition of sensibility theory needs some refinements. One problem with (S1) is that it makes reference to the Humean emotions of approbation and disapprobation. In chapter 2, I noted that these are not the names of individual emotions. "Approbation" names a range of positive emotions and "disapprobation" names a range of negative emotions. The British moralists of the seventeenth century did develop plausible theories of approbation and disapprobation. We are now in a position to fill in that gap with substantive, empirically supported proposals.

Let's begin with disapprobation. The negative emotions underlying moral disapproval vary across moral contexts. As we saw in chapter 2, there is a coarse division to draw between self-blame and other-blame. If I perpetrate a moral transgression, I will feel emotions of self-blame, notably shame or guilt. If you perpetrate the transgression, I will feel emotions of other-blame. The other-blame emotion that I feel will depend on whether you are a friend (disappointment) or a stranger (moral anger, contempt, or disgust). Different self-blame and other-blame emotions correspond to different kinds of transgressions, as outlined in my extension of Rozin et al.'s (1999) CAD model (see Figure 2.1). Given these complexities, we should say the following about moral wrongness:

> (S1'-W) An action has the property of being morally wrong just in case it causes feelings in the spectrum of both self-blame and other-blame emotions in normal observers under certain conditions.

To simplify, I will refer to this as the "disapprobation spectrum." It will be important to bear in mind that, to qualify as wrong, something must be disposed to cause both self-blame and other-blame emotions. It's not the case that anything that merely disgusts or irritates us is wrong. We are repelled by the idea of eating grubs, but we don't regard such a meal as a moral transgression. We are irritated by children crying on airplanes, but we don't condemn their conduct as morally wrong. Moralizing requires the disposition to have both self-directed and other-directed emotions in the disapprobation spectrum. Some of the actions that disgust us when we observe others performing them would also make us feel ashamed if we were to perform them ourselves (consider cannibalism). And some of the actions that anger us when performed by others would also make us feel guilty (imagine an adult making a huge ruckus on an airplane). When I refer to actions that cause emotions in the disapprobation spectrum, I mean to designate actions that would elicit both self-blame and other-blame. These are the actions that are morally wrong on my view.

In addition to the disapprobation spectrum, there is also an "approbation spectrum." This encompasses the emotions of praise listed in Table 2.2 in chapter 2. The phrase "morally right" is used in different ways. Sometimes it functions as a synonym for "ought," as when we say, "the right thing to do in this situation is . . ." When used in that way, "right" doesn't necessarily express anything positive. We rarely praise people for doing what morality demands of them. A person who abstains from shoplifting is doing the right thing, but we wouldn't usually feel grateful to that person. For present purposes, I will ignore this notion of "right" because it can be defined in terms of "wrong" (see the remarks on "ought" below). In addition to this notion, we sometimes use the phrase "morally right" to express a positive attitude. When we judge a good deed to be morally right, we are praising that deed, not claiming that it was obligatory. In these cases, the following definition can be used:

(S1′-R) An action has the property of being morally right just in case performing it causes an emotion in the approbation spectrum in normal observers under certain conditions.

In what follows, I will focus almost entirely on cases of moral wrongs rather than moral rights. My hunch, unexamined here, is that the concept WRONG plays a more important role in morality than the concept RIGHT: we condemn more often then we praise.

Both (S1′-R) and (S1′-W) need further explication. These definitions refer to "normal observers" and "certain conditions." But which observers are normal and which conditions matter? Let's begin with the conditions. As a first approximation, one might be tempted to say the conditions that matter are those in which observers have knowledge of relevant facts, and are not under emotional or cognitive influences that are not relevant to the case at hand. This isn't a bad starting place, but it isn't fully satisfying. For one thing, it uses the tricky notion of relevance, and for another it may prove difficult (as I will later argue) to distinguish factual knowledge from evaluative beliefs in some cases. But rather than fine-tuning the characterization of ideal conditions, one can simply alter the definition so as to avoid any appeal to conditions whatsoever. The trick is to invoke sentiments.

In chapter 2, I said that the term "sentiment" designates an emotional disposition. I think of psychological dispositions as physically realized states of the mind. If realism about the mind is true, then there is a fact of the matter whether someone has a sentiment; there is a thing in the brain that is the realization of that disposition. Suppose I have a negative sentiment toward killing. Never mind how frequently thoughts about killing cause me to get angry, and never mind what conditions I need to be in for thoughts about killing to elicit this reaction. The crucial thing is that somewhere in my brain there is something that disposes me to have this negative reaction to killing. We can define moral properties by appeal to the existence of such sentiments and bypass any need to specify when those sentiments can actually be relied on to produce the emotions that they dispose us to produce. So rather than saying that moral properties exist in virtue of causing certain emotions under certain conditions, we can say they exist in virtue of the fact that some observers have sentiments that dispose them to have those emotions.

But which observers? The term "normal observers" is troublesome because normality is an evaluative term. Typically, someone who makes a moral judgment considers herself and others like her to be normal. It is, I will later argue, up to the judge who counts as normal, and, for most of us, a normal observer is just "me." So the appeal to normality may turn out to be empty when thinking about the moral domain. We can define moral properties in terms of observers, and drop the normal bit. Integrating these points, I propose the following formulation:

> (S1′) An action has the property of being morally wrong (right) just in case there is an observer who has a sentiment of disapprobation (approbation) toward it.

Here approbation and disapprobation are to be understood as the disposition to feel emotions in the approbation and disapprobation range. (S1′) gives a good working definition of the view I will be defending in this chapter. This formulation is consistent with the view that moral properties are powers to cause emotional states. If an observer has sentiments toward certain actions, and sentiments dispose that observer to have emotions, then the actions in question have the power to cause emotions. (S1′) can be regarded as a notational variant of the secondary quality view; it simply bypasses the need to specify the conditions under which emotion elicitation can be taken as evidence for the instantiation of a moral property. These features of (S1′) obviously introduce a strong form of relativism that is sometimes underestimated by other sensibility theorists (though see Wiggins, 1987: n. 24). Let me note at the outset, however that many observers may converge on the same sentiments. The formulation is strictly consistent with there being one single morality, because, in principle, it could turn out that all people agree. And if that doesn't happen in practice, it might still be that large numbers of people within a culture or subculture agree. I think that is quite likely, and there are good reasons to expect such convergence (see chapter 5).

3.1.3 Moral Concepts

The refinements of (S1) point to a refinement of (S2). Sensibility theorists need an account of moral concepts. I have been suggesting that moral concepts incorporate emotions. More must be said about what that incorporation consists in. A full account of moral concepts should be developed against the background of an independently motivated theory of concepts. I have defended a theory of concepts elsewhere, but a full explication and defense would be well beyond the scope of this project (Prinz, 2002). I will restrict myself to a few brief comments.

Following the mainstream in cognitive science, I regard concepts as mental representations. Mental representations can be individuated by what they represent and by what might be called their vehicular properties. Vehicular properties are the properties that mental representations have as mental particulars. They include representational format and structure. On some theories, concepts are couched in a language-like format. They are amodal symbols in the head. To say a concept is amodal is to say that it is not in a format that is specific to an input or output system. To say a concept is symbolic is to say that its vehicular properties are arbitrarily related to what that concept represents. Those who favor the language analogy for concepts sometimes claim that many of our concepts are unstructured; they are not constitutively related to any other concepts. Fodor (1975) is most associated with this view. He says that most of the concepts that we would express using a single word of English (lexical concepts) are themselves word-like: they do not decompose into meaningful parts. The concept representing dogs, for example, would be a primitive symbol in the language of thought.

A contrasting view would say that most lexical concepts are structured entities couched in modality specific formats. This is the view that the British empiricists endorsed, and I think they were right (Prinz, 2002). On this view, the concept representing dogs would be an assembly of perceptual features garnered from our various encounters with dogs. One might wonder, how can a perceptual representation of dog represent dogs and only dogs? After all, the very same perceptual features might be observed in wolves and well-disguised cats, and there may be dogs that are so unusual in appearance that they are difficult to recognize perceptually. Of course, one might ask a parallel question about the language of thought account. How does an arbitrary symbol represent dogs? As it turns out, both theories can provide the same answer. A mental symbol and an assembly of perceptual features can represent dogs in the same way. In particular, they can represent dogs by entering into reliable (but imperfect) causal relationships with doghood. More accurately, dog images can, as much as dog symbols, refer by having the function of detecting dogs. This is the Dretskian (1988) approach to semantics that I endorse in chapter 2. Fodor (1990) offers a closely related theory for his mental symbols, and my point here is that empiricist theories of concepts can avail themselves of the same theories of references that their opponents endorse. Empiricist theories and language of thought theories are semantically on all fours (so to speak).

This point of similarity can also be used to bring out an important distinction. In order for an arbitrary mental symbol to enter into a reliable causal relation with a property in the world, we must be able to detect that property. In order to detect a property that is, at least partially, outside our skin, we need to perceive it or perceive something that regularly correlates with it. In other words, an arbitrary mental symbol comes under the causal control of something out there by means of perceptual features. So assemblies of perceptual features are needed on both accounts. The empiricist identifies concepts with those features, and the language of thought defenders regard those features as middlemen between symbols and world. Defenders of the language of thought could express their view by saying that assemblies of perceptual features are *conceptions*, rather than concepts. A conception is a contingent and variable way of thinking about something. Two people can have the same concepts (e.g., symbols representing doghood) and different conceptions (e.g., mental images of what dogs typically look like). The empiricist may say that these conceptions *are* concepts, and deny that we have any need for symbols in a language of thought.

I favor the empiricist side of this debate, but what I say about moral concepts can be recast as a theory of moral conceptions. Moral conceptions are a central aspect of moral cognition, whether or not conceptions are concepts. When we form moral judgments, we form a conception of how things are, and that conception will have an impact on subsequent judgments and actions.

This digression allows us to address the question of interest. If concepts are perceptually-based detectors of moral properties, then what are moral concepts? If (S1′) is right, the answer is simple. S1 says that moral properties are those things toward which some observer has sentiments of approbation and disapprobation. Sentiments are emotional dispositions and, if the theory of emotions defended in chapter 2 is right, then emotions qualify as perceptual states; on the embodied appraisal theory, emotions are perceptions of patterned changes in the body that carry information about our relationship to the world. Thus, we can capture the idea that moral concepts are perceptually based detectors of moral properties by postulating that moral concepts are constituted by sentiments. So, for example, the concept WRONG could be characterized as follows:

> (S2′-W) The standard concept WRONG is a detector for the property of wrongness that comprises a sentiment that disposes its possessor to experience emotions in the disapprobation range.

Notice that (S2′-W) used the phrase "standard concept." This refers to concepts that ordinary people ordinarily use, leaving open the possibility that one might be able to designate the same property via unorthodox means (see chapter 1). For example, psychopaths might track the property of wrongness deferentially by applying the word "wrong" to all and only those things that some non-psychopath labeled with these words. That would not be a standard concept. My conjecture is that people who do not have mental disorders ordinarily think about wrongness by means of sentiments. To believe that something is wrong in a non-deferential way is to have a sentiment of disapprobation toward it.

Other moral concepts can be analyzed in similar ways. The concept RIGHT will be defined with reference to both approbation and disapprobation. The concepts MORALLY BAD and MORALLY GOOD may be akin to WRONG and RIGHT, but whereas the latter two are used to refer to actions, the former two can apply to actions, persons, and traits. This is a departure from the way some consequentialists deal with these concepts. They say we must define GOOD and BAD prior to RIGHT and WRONG, by appeal to some intrinsically good quality. The RIGHT is then usually defined in terms of maximizing the good. I think this is a departure from ordinary usage. We often praise actions as right regardless of whether they maximize anything, and, I suspect, people use these pairs of moral terms interchangeably in many contexts. A bad action is a wrong action, for example. As suggested, I think the main difference is that GOOD and BAD are broader notions, which can be applied to things other than actions. But, I don't want to be overly rigid about this. Conceptual analysis is a tricky business, and we probably use moral terms in a variety of different ways. I am content here to capture roughly one of the central ways in which we understand moral terms, allowing that there may be others.

The only other concept that I will mention here is OUGHT. As a starting place, consider an analysis offered by Westermarck (1900), another epistemic emotionist. He suggested that we ought to do what it would be wrong not to do. This is an elegant proposal, because it reduces the concept OUGHT to the concept WRONG. It therefore has the interesting consequence that ought judgments are not commands, because it is not a command to say that it is wrong not to do something. Westermarck argues that this is a virtue of his account. It makes sense of the idea that we can make ought judgments about the past ("I ought to have given more to Oxfam last year"). When we make such judgments we cannot be issuing commands, because it is impossible to change the past. Of course, our judgments about the past do have motivational implications. When I judge that I ought to have given more to Oxfam, I feel guilty, and that guilt may influence my current behavior.

I think Westermarck's analysis of ought is almost right, but needs a minor amendment. It is a consequence of his view that there is a simple equation between certain ought judgments and certain wrongness judgments. If I say you ought not to beat your dog, then I am saying nothing more than it's wrong to beat your dog. But these two claims seem slightly different. The first is a comment on the moral status of dog beating. It has motivational impact, but it is not overtly a claim about what you should do. Our claims are overtly about action. When we infer that you ought not ϕ from the premise that ϕ is wrong, we seem to be making a substantive inference not a notational variant. Putting it differently, a wrongness judgment may put you in a motivational state, but an ought judgment says those motivational impulses should be heeded. In effect, an ought judgment conveys the fact that a norm *has authority* over the behavior of the person addressed by that judgment. In chapter 5, I will come back to this idea of authority and explain it further. I will also return to the issue of motivation below.

According to (S2'-W), moral concepts dispose us to feel other-blame emotions when we are victims of transgressions and self-blame emotions when we transgress. If you believe that ϕ-ing is wrong, on this approach, you have a long-term memory representation that disposes you to feel guilt or shame if you ϕ, and anger, contempt, or disgust if someone else ϕs. On any given occasion, when you have the occurrent thought that ϕ-ing is wrong, only one of these emotions will manifest itself. If I catch you ϕ-ing, and I say "That's wrong!" the word "wrong" may express my current state of anger, which is a manifestation of my complex emotional disposition. We can think of the sentiment in long-term memory as standing belief, and the emotion in working memory as an occurrent belief. Or, to introduce a useful piece of terminology, we can call the sentiment a *moral rule*, and we can call a particular emotional manifestation of that sentiment a *moral judgment*.

This proposal is illustrated in Figure 3.1. The picture shows a person observing a pickpocket in action. After that there is a series of mental events. First, the observer interprets pickpocketing as an instance of stealing. This is a categorization stage; it involves drawing on prior knowledge to classify an observed action. Stealing is something toward which the observer has a moral sentiment in long-term memory. His sentiment toward stealing constitutes a rule. When the idea of stealing enters his mind, the rule causes the sentiment to become active. This is a rule retrieval stage. At this stage, the sentiment is not yet experienced as an emotion. Sentiments are dispositional. Once a sentiment is activated, contextual factors are used to determine which emotion will be elicited. Because the observer is not the author of the action, and because stealing is an autonomy norm, the elicited emotion is anger. This is an emotion elicitation stage. The anger that arises in the observer is not simply free-floating rage. The anger was triggered by the experience of pickpocketing, and it gets bound to the representation of pickpocketing. The result is a compound state: anger at pickpocketing. This compound constitutes the judgment that pickpocketing is wrong, because the emotion it contains was generated from a moral sentiment. This is the judgment stage. In sum, there is a progression from categorization, to rule retrieval, to emotion elicitation, to judgment. Moral rules usher the transition labeled 1 in the Figure, and moral judgments come into existence with the transition labeled 4, in which an active emotion is applied to an action that is under consideration.

The model depicted here has several nice features which bear mention. First, it helps to diagnose cases in which moral judgments can be said to be erroneous. Consider Wheatley and Haidt's (2005) study described in chapter 1. They found that some people who were hypnotized to feel disgust ended up morally condemning a perfectly innocent individual. I think such condemnations qualify as errors because they were not caused by sentiments in long-term memory, but rather by extraneous facts; they do not qualify as legitimate expressions of the subjects' moral attitudes. In short, a wrong action is an action against which an observer has a moral rule. If an action is condemned because of hypnotically induced disgust, it does not qualify as wrong.

A second advantage of the model is that it immediately overcomes a common objection to emotionist theories. Critics like to point out that our emotions

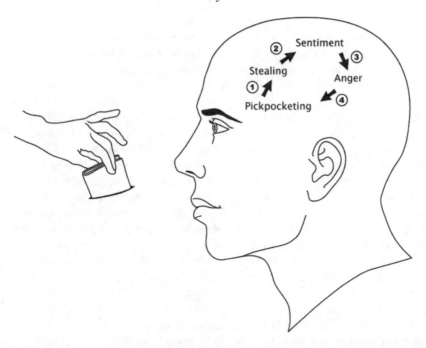

Figure 3.1. Information-processing stages that lead to a moral judgment. (1) A perceived event is categorized; (2) a rule is retrieved from memory, which activates a sentiment; (3) the sentiment elicits an emotion in a contextually sensitive way; (4) the emotion is associated with the perceived action

fluctuate in a way that our moral values do not. For example, Mele (1996) points out that people who are listless or depressed may not get very aroused when they think about moral matters, but it would be uncharitable to suggest that they no longer find murder wrong. He argues that this shows that there is no essential link between motivation and moral belief. But the model I am recommending is a dispositional one, and it does not require that our moral convictions always manifest themselves emotionally (compare Dreier, 1990). I can recognize that I have a negative sentiment without feeling that sentiment (as when I say, without disgust, that I dislike chopped liver). The model I am recommending also has resources to deal with a related objection put forward by Millgram (1999). He notices that emotional reactions diminish after multiple exposures. A joke is less inclined to make us laugh the tenth time we hear it, and when this happens we say the joke is less funny. Similarly, repeated exposure to, say, people who are homeless will lead to a reduction in our feelings of outrage, but, in this case, we do not say that homelessness is less wrong than it was when we encountered a homeless person for the first time. As a first line of response, I am tempted to bite the bullet here and say that over-exposure (or, for that matter, under-exposure) can alter our sentiments and thereby alter our views about what's right and wrong. It would be interesting to track how people's attitudes toward homelessness change over repeated encounters. But my model can also explain what Millgram thinks any theory must explain: it can allow continuity of morals across fluctuations in affect. In some cases, repeated exposure leaves our sentiments intact and simply diminishes their likelihood of generating intense emotions. Repeated exposure diminishes deep processing; when I see the a homeless person for the thousandth time, I am not startled into reflecting on the fact that a wealthy society should never allow such extreme destitution, but, were I so to reflect, emotions would be elicited. I should note that I think a similar analysis is available for humor. Is a joke really less funny after repeated exposure? We sometimes say that, but we go on to tell the joke to all our friends. It would be better to say the joke remains funny, but it no longer makes me laugh. Why does it remain funny? Because it continues to have properties (a clever play on words for example) that dispose me to laugh.

My account of moral judgment is similar to other empirically supported proposals in the literature. It is related to ideas that have been developed by Haidt (2001) and Nichols (2004*a*), but there are important differences. Haidt defends a "social intuitionist" model of moral judgment. An intuition is an affectively valenced mental state that appears suddenly in thought without any awareness of going through a deliberative process. Certain things just feel wrong or just feel right. Haidt does not equate moral judgments with these intuitions. He says, instead, that moral judgments are ordinarily caused by intuitions (Haidt, 2001: 814). Nichols equates moral values with "sentimental rules." He says that senti-mental rules involve two mechanisms: a "Normative Theory" and an emotional response system. Normative Theories are lists of prescriptions about what one should and shouldn't do. These prescriptions have no emotional content. They become "affect-backed" when conjoined with the emotion response system, and Nichols places special emphasis on emotions that are triggered by the perceived suffering of another person — emotions of concern. So, roughly, a sentimental rule is an affect-free prescription combined with a disposition to feel concerned when that prescription is violated. One can think of this as a bidirectional causal model: when a norm prohibiting harm is violated, we feel concern, and when we see someone in pain, the resultant concern can cause us to retrieve a relevant norm from memory. These two components are dissociable; psychopaths have Normative Theories without emotional concern, and very young children have concern without Normative Theories (Nichols, 2004*a*: 18 ff.).

My approach differs from the Haidt and Nichols models. Unlike Haidt, I do not want to insist that moral attitudes typically arise in the absence of deliberative reasoning; it may take a lot of inference before we see an action in a way that triggers an emotional response (see below). Unlike Nichols, I don't think concern is the most fundamental moral emotion; the emotions that figure in moral judgments express blame for the wrongdoer, not sympathy for the victim.

Hume (1739) thinks that blame and sympathy are closely linked. He says that we judge that some action is wrong by first feeling sympathy for a person who has been harmed by the action. Our sympathetic distress, which might be likened to Nichols's feelings of concern, then causes a feeling of disapprobation in us. I think Nichols and Hume place too much emphasis on sympathetic responses. We can morally condemn an action without thinking about a victim (consider consensual incest), and oftentimes we think about victims only after an action has been condemned (consider tax fraud).

These are minor differences. Haidt sometimes admits that we need to reason before we experience a moral intuition, and Nichols sometimes discusses emotions of blame (especially disgust) and downplays the role of concern. There is, however, a more important difference between these models and the approach that I favor. Both Haidt and Nichols think that there is a *causal* relationship between moral judgments and emotions. Moral judgments do not contain emotions as parts; they are merely causally backed up by emotions. Thus, these models allow that one could form a moral judgment without emotions. On my approach, emotions are *constituents* of moral judgments, because emotions constitute token-instances of concepts such as right and wrong. Here my view echoes Hume (1739: III.i.ii): "We do not infer a character to be virtuous, because it pleases: But in feeling that it pleases after such a particular manner, we in effect feel that it is virtuous."

My reasons for preferring a constitution model over a causal model were already sketched in chapter 1. A causal model implies that emotions and moral judgments are two separate things that can come apart. This seems implausible given that emotions co-occur with moral judgments and seem to be developmentally necessary for moral judgments. Here let me add one further piece of evidence. In an unpublished study, I asked subjects to consider two scenarios in which emotions are pitted against verbal behavior. In one scenario, a student in a fraternity insists that there is nothing morally wrong with smoking marijuana, but he feels disgusted when he sees his fraternity brothers smoke and ashamed when he himself smokes. In the other scenario, a student in a fraternity tells his brothers that smoking marijuana is morally wrong, but he never gets disgusted at them when they smoke, and he would not feel ashamed if he smoked. In each case, subjects are asked whether the student's moral values are reflected by what he says or what he feels. Subjects in both conditions were much more likely to say that the value corresponded to the emotions: the student who feels ashamed of smoking marijuana is morally opposed to it, and the shameless student is not. This suggests that folk morality draws a conceptual link between values and emotions. If a causal model were correct, then a moral value could be constituted by an affect-free propositional attitude. If this possibility were consistent with folk morality, then responses to these scenarios should be less clear cut.

I don't deny that our emotional attitudes are often *accompanied* by affect-free propositional representations. When we judge that something is wrong, we tend to verbally express that judgment out loud or in inner speech. On seeing a pickpocket, we may think to ourselves, "That's wrong!" Such verbalized thoughts can occur in the absence of emotions. This is probably how people think about morality when they are listless or over-exposed. People may also deploy verbalized thoughts in casual conversation when we are not directly experiencing immoral acts. If you have thought about pickpocketing before, you will have stored a verbal representation of the form, "Pickpocketing is wrong," which you can retrieve without getting agitated. But, empirical evidence suggests that emotions are ordinarily elicited even in casual reflection (e.g., Moll et al., 2002). Moreover, I want to insist that these verbalizations get their meaning from the underlying emotional states. We often talk as if verbalizations of moral judgments were moral judgments in their own right. I will refer to sentences, such as "Pickpocketing is wrong" as a verbalized moral judgment. But this label is really shorthand. "Pickpocketing is wrong" is not a judgment; it's a string of words. In calling it a verbalized moral judgment, I mean it is a verbal form that might be used to express a moral judgment.

Verbalized moral judgments are very useful, because they allow us to reason about moral values that we don't actually hold. For example, we can reflect on conditionals such as, "If murder is good, then Stalin was a saint." When we entertain this conditional, we use the verbalized judgment rather than forming a genuine moral judgment, because it is psychologically difficult for us to entertain a positive attitude toward murder. But the word "good" would have no meaning to us in conditionalized contexts if we did not assign emotional significance to it in unconditionalized contexts. We understand the meaning of "right" and "wrong" or "good" and "bad" in unconditionalized contexts by means of underlying moral emotions. By analogy, I can comprehend the sentence, "If murder is funny, then Stalin is a comedian" without feeling amused. But, to understand what "funny" means, there must be sentences in which I utter the word outside of a conditional context, and, when I do so, the word expresses my amusement. Likewise, I can understand conditional moral talk only if moral terms express emotions for me when used in unconditionalized contexts.

I just said that unconditionalized verbal moral judgments are *expressions* of emotion. They convey how we feel about things. In this respect, my account is closely related to expressivist theories, such as emotivism, which emphasize the expressive character or moral discourse. But expressivists argue that verbalized moral judgments are *mere* expressions of feeling; they don't have representational content. On my view verbalized moral judgments simultaneously express how we feel and represent things. When we say, "That's wrong!" we convey our feelings and also aim to assert a fact. "Pickpocketing is wrong" represents the fact that pickpocketing has the property of wrongness. Moral wrongness, I have suggested, is the property of being the object of disapprobation. That is equivalent, I noted, to saying that wrongness is a secondary quality.

Expressivists say that moral concepts don't refer, and I say they refer to secondary qualities. It is important to note that, when using moral concepts, we do not necessarily have any explicit beliefs about what kind of properties they pick out. The concept WRONG is not a description of a secondary quality as such. It represents a secondary quality in virtue of its causal relation to the world. Concepts that refer causally do not need to describe their referents.

I think that moral concepts have an additional layer of representational content that hasn't been noticed by other sensibility theorists. As I just noted, sentiments represent secondary qualities, but sentiments also dispose us to experience emotions, and emotions do not represent secondary qualities; they represent concerns (see chapter 2). Thus, when an emotional state is generated from a sentiment, it represents both the secondary quality tracked by the sentiment *and* a concern. Consider phobias. Phobias are sentiments that represent the secondary quality scariness, but phobias manifest themselves in the emotion fear. When you have a phobic reaction to something you are simultaneously attributing to that thing the property of being scary *and* the property of being dangerous, which is the representational content of fear. Moral sentiments comprise moral emotions, and, following Rozin et al. (1999), I argued that different moral emotions correspond to different domains: personal order, social order, and natural order. Therefore, the judgment that some action is wrong conveys two things about it. The judgment conveys the view that the action causes certain emotional responses in me, and that it is a transgression of a certain kind. Moral concepts evaluate and classify.

If I am right about the semantics of moral judgments, then Bernard Williams (1985) is mistaken when he says that concepts such as RIGHT and WRONG are "thin." According to Williams, a "thick" moral concept does two things: it expresses an evaluative attitude and it classifies. Examples include generous, heroic, and cruel. When we call some action "generous" we simultaneously classify the action as an instance of giving things to others and we evaluate the action as positive. Williams argues that concepts such as RIGHT and WRONG or GOOD and BAD are comparatively thin: they express attitudes without classifying. I think Williams is mistaken. On most occasions, when we judge that something is bad, for example, we are experiencing a specific emotion and that emotion serves to classify the action under consideration. If I experience contempt when I assert that a corrupt politician is "bad" then my contempt serves to classify his conduct as a harm against the community. The concept BAD on this occasion represents both a response-dependent evaluative property and a specific category of moral transgression. Likewise, when I judge that incest is wrong, I do not merely condemn it; I experience disgust, which serves to classify incest as a violation of a rule that pertains to the natural order. I don't mean to suggest that we explicitly think about the community when we feel contempt or about the natural order when we feel disgust. Emotions represent concerns in virtue of their causal relations to the world. When we judge that something is wrong, the only thing that is directly available to us in consciousness is that it makes us feel a certain way. These feelings have two layers of semantic content, but we typically are not explicitly aware of either.

This discussion of moral concepts can be summarized as follows. If you have internalized a moral rule against, say, incest, you have a moral sentiment toward incest in long-term memory. That sentiment represents the secondary quality of causing disapprobation in you (and others like you) under good epistemic conditions. That rule is a standing attitude toward incest. It becomes an occurrent moral judgment when you think about someone committing an act of incest. When that occurs, you experience disgust and this feeling, applied to your current thought about an act of incest, constitutes your judgment that the act in question is wrong. The disgust is caused by the sentiment in long-term memory, and, as such, it represents the property of wrongness (i.e., the secondary quality of causing disapprobation). But disgust also represents violations of the natural order, which is a specific subset of wrongs. When you judge that incest is wrong, you experience disgust, but you may not realize that this feeling represents a secondary quality or anything having to do with the natural order. All you know from the feeling is that you think incest is wrong. You don't know what wrongness consists in.

3.1.4 Moral Motivation

I have been arguing that moral concepts are constituted by sentiments, and these sentiments manifest themselves in different emotions on different occasions, depending, for example, on the domain of the rule that has been violated. The appeal to sentiments has important implications for the link between moral judgment and motivation. I said that one big attraction of sensibilities theory is that it can account for the observation that moral judgments tend to motivate. If moral judgments contain moral concepts, and moral concepts have an emotional composition, then moral judgments motivate action, because emotions are motivational states. Sensibility theory entails internalism, which, I argued in chapter 1, is a desirable outcome. Here I want to say something about how the particular brand of sensibility theory that I favor contributes to motivation

The first thing to note is that my theory makes the generic internalist prediction that, barring listlessness and other impediments, people will be motivated to behave in accordance with their moral values. If you contemplate doing something that you regard as immoral, you will anticipate the negative emotional consequences, and avoid that behavior. During deliberation about action, the concept WRONG functions as what Damasio (1994) calls a somatic marker: it allows us to experience the emotional, and hence bodily, feelings that would arise if we pursued immoral actions. If you contemplate doing something morally good, you may anticipate a positive affective response, and you may act accordingly.

My brand of sensibility theory also goes farther. Most philosophical discussions of internalism discuss only two kinds of behavior: doing the good and avoiding the bad. But, once we have identified the specific emotions that constitute our moral concepts, we can begin to make other highly specific behavioral predictions. Different emotions have different motivational consequences, and a token of the concept WRONG will motivate us differently depending on which emotion it happens to manifest on a particular occasion.

To illustrate, let me focus on four of the emotions that are crucial for the CAD model: anger, disgust, guilt, and shame. These emotions are associated in the psychology literature with different motivational states. On the model that I am defending, the concept WRONG will typically manifest itself through the emotion anger, when we catch another person stealing, or harming, or acting unjustly. These are crimes against persons, and anger is the dominant response. Anger is associated with aggression, so the current model predicts that moralizers would be motivated to aggress against those who commit crimes against persons. For example, the model might predict that people will have retributive attitudes toward those who harm others. This is consistent with empirical findings. For example, Carlsmith et al. (2002) report that people tend to favor "just deserts" over deterrence when selecting punishments for violent criminal offenders.

Now suppose that you yourself have perpetrated a crime against another person. The model predicts that you will feel guilty. Behaviorally, guilt is associated with reconciliation behavior. Guilt compels us to repair threatened attachments (Baumeister et al. 1994). There are two ways to achieve reconciliation if you have caused harm: one is to confess your misdeed and the other is to make amends by doing something good. Strictly speaking, these coping strategies are not incompatible, but there is some evidence that, if you confess, you'll feel less obliged to make amends. To show this, Harris et al. (1975) set up a donation stand for the March of Dimes near a confession booth in a Catholic church. They found that people were twice as likely to donate if they were on their way to confess than if they had just finished confessing.

Anger and guilt are responses to crimes against persons. Disgust and shame are responses to violations of rules having to do with the natural order, and they have different effects on motivation. Disgust is behaviorally associated with rejection and withdrawal. We don't want to have contact with anyone who disgusts us. This suggests that people will have strong withdrawal tendencies when they judge, for example, that another person has engaged in immoral sexual behavior. If someone is accused of bestiality, we won't want to go near them, and we might urge the court system to keep that person locked away and far from our neighborhoods on release. Ironically, this model predicts that people might prefer living next to a thief than a person who has sex with animals, even though the thief poses more of a threat. The emotion shame arises when you yourself commit a crime against nature. Behaviorally, shame is associated with gaze avoidance, head lowering, and other efforts to hide oneself in the eyes of others. One might expect to see such bodily changes in a person who deemed his or her own sexual conduct to be immoral. Such a person would be more likely to avoid others than to seek reconciliation by confession or making amends.

This discussion highlights the explanatory mileage that we can get out of exploring the specific emotions that contribute to moral judgment. The central feature of my approach is that I distinguish emotions from sentiments, and I argue that our moral values are based on sentiments in long-term memory, which manifest themselves through different emotions in a context-sensitive way. My approach is a sensibility theory, but other sensibility theorists do not distinguish emotions and sentiments, and they are often vague about which emotions our moral judgments comprise (expressivists are often more specific; see especially Gibbard, 1990). Wiggins (1987) follows Hume in talking about sentiments of approbation, without saying what such sentiments consistent in. McDowell (1985; 1987) compares the relationship between moral judgments and moral facts to the relationship between amusement and the property of being amusing and between fear and the property of being fearsome, but, like Wiggins, he doesn't specify which emotions underwrite morality. McDowell and Wiggins may suppose that moral emotions are *sui generis*, whereas I think the moral emotions have a non-moral foundation. As we will see below, McDowell and Wiggins also favor a metacognitive approach, according to which valuing is a matter of *believing that emotions are appropriate*. My approach is first order. There are other dispositional theories of value in the literature, but recent defenders of dispositionalism do not tend to define values in terms of emotional responses. Firth (1952) invokes approval (which may or may not be an emotion), David Lewis (1989) invokes second-order desires, Dreier (1990) refers to "motivational states," and Smith (1994) equates the good with the rationally advisable.

My view shares much in common with the theories developed by the British moralists, or, more accurately, the Scottish moralists, such as Hutcheson, Hume, and Smith. Of course there are many differences in detail. One important difference is that I place less emphasis on sympathy and benevolence. For Hutcheson, benevolence is the source of all virtue; feelings of benevolence are what motivate us to treat others well, and such benevolent behaviors are the ones that we find morally good. Hume departs from Hutcheson by making sympathy more fundamental. For Hume, sympathy is the cause of benevolence (we are motivated to help those in need because we sympathize with their suffering), and sympathy also engenders virtues that do not involve benevolence. For example, Hume regards wit as a virtue because we sympathize with the pleasure it causes. Hume also argues that sympathy, but not benevolence, grounds the virtue of justice (by which Hume usually has in mind property rights); we take sympathetic pleasure in the feelings of those whose property rights are protected and displeasure in the pain of those whose rights are violated, and those sympathetic feelings motivate us to behave justly and condemn injustice.

I think that Hume is right to accuse Hutcheson of inflating the role of benevolence as a moral motivator, but he errs equally in inflating the role of sympathy. The empirical evidence suggests that sympathy is only a weak moral motivator. In a meta-analysis, Neuberg et al. (1997) found that sympathy correlates only modestly with helping, and is unlikely to motivate us to help when helping carries significant costs. In contrast, consider guilt. In one study, Carlsmith and Gross (1969) showed that subjects who have administered electric shocks to another person were more than three times as helpful in a subsequent environmental fundraising campaign than subjects who had not administered shocks, suggesting that guilt significantly boosts altruistic behavior. In another study, Zhong and Liljenquist (2006) asked subjects to recall an event in which they had behaved unethically, as a means of inducing guilt and shame. Afterwards, they had some subjects wash their hands with a moist towelette, and others were not given that opportunity. All subjects were then asked to help voluntarily with another study, and 73.9 percent of the cleansed subjects agreed, as compared to 40.9 percent of the uncleansed subjects. This suggests that guilt is a strong moral motivator, and that eliminating guilt (in this case, literally cleaning it away) can reduce helpfulness dramatically.

Anger is also a great moral motivator. In chapter 1, I noted that Lerner et al. (1998) were able to increase punitive desires by showing subjects anger-inducing film clips. This has been corroborated in other studies. Using a public goods game, Fehr and Gächter (2002) showed that stingy players incur anger from cooperative players, and, when angry, cooperative players are willing to incur significant monetary costs to punish stinginess, even if there was no opportunity to be compensated for those costs. Such findings suggest that sympathy is a less important motivator than other emotions.

Moreover, emotions such as guilt and anger seem to be sufficient for moral motivation in the absence of sympathy. Indeed, there are many kinds of moral judgments that do not seem to depend on sympathy at all. Consider cases where the person making the judgment has been the victim of a crime (you cannot sympathize with yourself). Or consider cases where the victim is not salient, but the crime is (e.g., actions that will cause environmental harm in the distant future). Or consider cases in which a morally questionable act does not cause suffering to a victim (e.g., consensual incest and cannibalizing the bodies of people who died of natural causes). I also question Hume's suggestion that sympathy is the foundation of our concern for justice. Sympathy can be an impediment to justice because, as Hume observed, we often sympathize most with those who are near and dear. To overcome bias, Hume encouraged us to take up a general point of view, but this may be very hard to do. It may be comparatively easy to condition people directly to feel outrage at inequality itself without their having also to feel any sense of emotional resonance with the victims of injustice. Moreover, Hume may have gotten the direction of causation wrong: in many cases, thinking about injustice may cause sympathy, rather than the other way around.

In sum, I think that an adequate understanding of moral motivation requires a careful, empirically informed investigation of the specific emotions that contribute to moral judgment. I think the British moralists may have placed too much emphasis on sympathy and benevolence, and not enough emphasis on anger or guilt. In later chapters, I will depart from the British moralists in other ways, by rejecting virtue ethics (in chapter 4), defending relativism (chapter 5), and denying Hutcheson's claim that there is an innate moral sense (in chapter 7). For the moment, I want to bracket the differences, and underscore the similarities. Like the British moralists, I think that moral judgments have an emotional basis, and moral motivation derives from those underlying emotions. I take this to be the most important contribution of British moral philosophy, and sensibility theorists are heirs to that tradition.

The remainder of this chapter is dedicated to defense. Sensibility theories have been widely criticized. I want to show that my version can withstand critique. I consider ten objections here. Some other objections will be addressed in the chapters that follow. Along the way, I will offer some refinements to the theory that I outlined in this section.

3.2 DEFENDING SENSIBILITY

3.2.1 The Expressivist Objection

Sensibility theories are similar, in some respects, to expressivist theories, so in arguing for a sensibility theory, it is important to see whether expressivism is a better alternative. The main difference between the approaches is semantic: expressivism is the view that moral concepts do not refer to anything; they merely express the attitudes of those who use them. Emotivism is a version of this approach (Stevenson, 1937; Ayer, 1952). Emotivists say that sentences such as "Killing is wrong" should be interpreted as something like "boo to killing!" This expletive cannot be true or false; it merely expresses a feeling. In recent decades, more sophisticated forms of expressivism have come on the scene (Blackburn, 1984, Gibbard, 1990). Gibbard, for example, would analyze "Killing is wrong" as something like, "I accept a norm that prescribes or permits guilt or outrage if I or someone else were to kill without sufficient motivation." Expressivist theories and sensibility theories are close cousins, because they both implicate emotions in moral concepts; they are both forms of epistemic emotionism. The sensibility theory that I favor is also committed to the view that ordinary moral talk is expressive. Tokens of moral concepts are normally constituted by emotions, so, when I say, "Killing is wrong," I am typically having an emotional response, and that emotion is expressed, in some sense, by my utterance. The most important difference between the sensibility theory and expressivism is that expressivists traditionally deny the existence of moral properties and facts. They do not think that moral judgments are truth apt (Gibbard, 2003, may be an exception, but his view is a departure from traditional expressivism in this respect). As we saw in chapter 1, Hume harbored such doubts. In contrast, sensibility theorists are realists. More accurately, they are internal realists: moral properties exist, but they depend on us. Expressivists challenge sensibility theorists to defend this claim. If moral judgments express how we feel about things, what does it add to say there are moral facts? Doesn't this complicate our ontology by adding a level of reality that is fundamentally different from rivers, rhinos, and railroads? Why multiply properties beyond necessity?

The answer is that moral properties come for free. Our best theories of intentionality say that any mental representation represents their reliable causes. If moral sentiments are reliably engaged by murders, muggings, and molestations, then those things fall within the extension of moral concepts. One doesn't need to introduce any extra semantic machinery to get this result. It just falls out of the semantic theory that has been independently motivated to explain mental representation in general. There is no offense against Occam here. Some things cause our moral sentiments to be engaged. That is a fact no expressivists would deny. Thus, there is a property of causing us to engage our moral sentiments. Certain forms of conduct have that property. They have the power to make us guilty or angry or ashamed. Given that expressivists are equally committed to the existence of this property, the difference between their view and the sensibility theory is not a difference in parsimony. It is a difference in semantics. Sensibility theorists claim that moral concepts represent these real properties, and expressivists disagree. Sensibility theorists win this skirmish, because prevailing semantic theories favor their position.

Expressivists might reply by arguing that prevailing semantic theories are designed to explain how concepts refer to natural kinds, not how concepts refer to response-dependent properties. They might claim that sensibility theorists cannot avail themselves of prevailing semantic theories, and must instead recruit *ad hoc* semantic theories to explain how moral concepts refer.

I don't find this reply compelling. First of all, there must be a workable theory of how concepts refer to response-dependent properties, because such concepts clearly exist. Examples include LIKABLE, SCARY, and perhaps FUNNY, and RED. Sensibility theorists can say that moral concepts refer in the same way that these concepts refer, however that may be. Second of all, the Dretskian theory of reference that I endorsed is sufficiently general to encompass concepts that refer to response-dependent properties. On that theory, concepts refer to what they have the function of reliably detecting. Arguably, the only property that murders, muggings, and molestations share in common is their capacity to cause certain emotions in us. Thus, it is plausible that moral concepts refer to this response-dependent property, because it is the most reliable cause of our moral concepts (for more discussion, see chapter 4). There is no obvious barrier to applying the Dretskian semantic theory to moral concepts.

In addition, it's important to remember that the expressivist alternative is unattractive. If moral concepts did not refer, then it would be hard to make sense of moral discourse. After all, we talk as if there were moral facts, and we use assertoric moral statements in conjunction with non-moral statements. Consider this argument: If killing is bad, then Jack the Ripper was bad; if Jack the ripper was bad, he is in hell; if he is in hell, he is suffering right now; therefore, if killing is bad, Jack the Ripper is suffering right now. To make the argument work, all of these sentences need to be treated as standard indicative conditionals. Geach (1965) famously argued that expressivists cannot deliver on this requirement. If expressivism is right, moral sentences stated in the indicative are covertly expletive: they really express their speaker's convictions. If we translate moral sentences into expletives, arguments like the one just presented will collapse. Sentences that appear to be ordinary indicative conditionals turn into grammatical monstrosities. Expressivists have tried to meet this challenge by devising logical systems that treat moral sentences as if they were indicative even though they are not (Blackburn, 1984, 1988; Gibbard, 1990). Some of these logics can get around the technical problem, but one wants to ask, what right expressivists have to help themselves to indicative logics that treat moral sentences as pseudo-indicatives. And, more pointedly, if we can find a theory according to which moral sentences really are indicatives, rather than pseudo-indicatives, shouldn't it be preferred? Sensibility theories offer exactly that. They come very close to expressivism in emphasizing the emotional nature of moral judgments, but they say that emotional judgments refer to real facts. When expressivists question the semantic commitments underlying sensibility theories, they are casting stones from a glass house. Sensibility theorists can rely on independently motivated semantic theories, while expressivists are forced to construct arcane new logical systems to explain away the seemingly referential character of moral discourse.

3.2.2 The Color Objections

Expressivists are not going to take these complaints lying down. They think that sensibility theories have fatal flaws. If they are right, then perhaps we should go the expressivist route after all, along with the drastic program of logical revision. But, what are these fatal flaws? One family of worries concerns the thesis that moral properties are secondary qualities (McDowell, 1985; Wiggins, 1987). This is the core insight of the sensibility theory, and it rests on the claim that the moral properties seem to behave in ways that are suggestively similar to properties that are widely believed to be secondary qualities, especially colors. The color analogy is instructive, as we have seen, but also risky. Critics have identified various ways in which morals are quite unlike colors, and those contrasts can be used to raise doubts about the whole program. I agree that the color analogy is defective. But analogies are often defective, and sensibility theorists are aware of that. I think the differences between morals and colors would actually be predicted by the sensibility theory that I have been defending. To make this case, I want to consider six disanalogies that are emphasized by Blackburn (1985) in a critique of Wiggins and McDowell. I will focus on alleged disanalogies between morals and colors.

First, Blackburn claims that moral properties supervene on natural or primary qualities in a very different way than colors supervene. The relationship between colors and their bases in physical objects is a scientific truth, not a conceptual one. Suppose yellow is the power to cause yellow experiences in us and that power is possessed by certain wavelengths in the electromagnetic spectrum. Someone could possess the concept YELLOW without knowing that yellow supervenes on these wavelengths (together with facts about our visual systems); someone could conceive of a world in which the very same wavelengths exist (and our very same visual systems exist), but those wavelengths are not yellow. But no one who possesses the concept WRONG could conceive of a world in which, say, recreational killing isn't wrong.

This is an intriguing asymmetry, but it does not undermine the secondary quality view. Rather, it suggests colors may not be a perfect analogy for morals. But colors are not the only plausible examples of secondary qualities. Consider disgustingness. Arguably, disgustingness is a secondary quality. It is the power to cause a certain feeling in us. Indeed, it is exactly the kind of secondary quality that sensibility theorists should appeal to when defending their theory. If moral properties are dependent on emotional responses, they should behave in the way that other emotion-dependent properties behave. Now, consider how disgustingness supervenes on the world. We don't look to science to tell us what's disgusting. And we assume that the things that disgust us in this world would be disgusting in every world. Can we imagine that maggot soup is anything but disgusting? In these respects disgustingness seems to behave like wrongness.

I also want to point out that Blackburn exaggerates the extent to which people believe that morality supervenes on the world. He says we cannot imagine that, say, recreational killing isn't wrong in some worlds. This is partially true and partially false. The case of disgustingness is, once again, illuminating. Someone might, after exposure to cultural variation, come to recognize that the very same thing (even maggot soup) can be disgusting for some people and not others. A person who had this insight would come to recognize that disgustingness does not supervene on the external world alone, but also on us. Such a person could, in some sense, conceive of a world in which maggot soup was tasty. The same might be said of morality. After surveying the anthropological record, one might come to realize that some cultural groups (perhaps the Ilongot headhunters of Luzon) do not think recreational killing is wrong. This might lead one to adopt the view that morality does not supervene on external facts alone, but also depends on us. But in both the maggot case and the murder case, there is a limit to what we can imagine. We can recognize, in some cool and intellectual way, that there are worlds in which no one is repelled by maggot soup or murder, but we cannot conceive of this possibility imaginatively through first-person simulation. If maggot soup repels you, you will not be able to imagine having the thought that maggot soup is delicious (though you might imagine saying those words). Likewise, you may not be able to imagine finding it acceptable to go on a killing spree. In both cases, the fixity of your own emotional responses limits the extent to which you can really imagine possible worlds in which the very same external things change their evaluative status. This limit on imagination promotes the impression that evaluative facts supervene on the external world. Blackburn would agree, I think, but he fails to appreciate that this point about the apparent supervenience of moral properties is consistent with a secondary quality view.

Now let's turn to Blackburn's second contrast. He says colors require special receptive mechanisms that can be selectively impaired. Colors are seen through the eyes. There is no organ of moral sensation, and so the analogy breaks down.

As with supervenience, the analogy to colors breaks down at this point, but not the comparison to emotions. Is there a receptive mechanism for the emotions? Yes and no. On the one hand, if the embodied appraisal theory is right, emotions are sensations of patterned bodily changes, and they involve the receptors that monitor somatic events. On the other hand, the concerns that trigger our emotional responses can be represented in various different ways. We can discover a danger by sight, sound, smell, or the light of reason. In that respect, there is no sensory organ of the passions. Exactly the same can be said about morals. No single sense is dedicated to perceiving matters of moral concern, but once those matters have been identified, they stir us up in ways that can be perceived through our bodily senses.

Blackburn's third contrast involves the conditions under which colors would disappear. He says that blue would cease to exist if our minds changed in such a way that all things that once struck us as blue now appeared red. In contrast, he says maltreatment of animals would remain wrong even if we began to regard it as permissible. As I understand it, this contrast is very closely related to Blackburn's first point about supervenience. My reply here echoes my reply to that objection. According to *untutored* intuitions, we actually think blue could survive any mutation in our visual systems. Likewise, untutored intuitions lead us to think that animal cruelty would be wrong regardless of our inclinations. These latter intuitions are recalcitrant because we find it difficult to imagine animal cruelty without feeling a pang of horror.

Next, Blackburn contrasts the ways in which colors and morals might be culturally relative. People raised in different cultures might come to classify colors somewhat differently, but no one would argue that the color terms used in another culture are wrong. There are many compatible ways of organizing color space. In contrast, when morals vary across cultures, the divergent values are seen as incompatible, and moral debates are impossible to resolve. To use a popular phrase in philosophy, moral debates are "essentially contestable" (see Wiggins, 1987: n. 19).

Blackburn's assumptions about color relativism and moral relativism are both highly contentious, but I am prepared to grant both. This is a genuine disanalogy between colors and morals, but notice that a strong analogy can be drawn between moral debates and debates that arise from divergent sentiments. If a phobic person insists that insects are scary, there is little anyone can do to persuade her otherwise. Likewise, if you enjoy country music, and I do not, you will be hard pressed to get me to agree with you that country music is enjoyable. Being scary and being enjoyable are secondary qualities. The fact that moral debates are essentially contestable does not threaten the claim that moral concepts represent secondary qualities. It shows only that moral concepts behave like the concepts SCARY and ENJOYABLE, which is just what the sensibility theory predicts.

In a fifth point of contrast, Blackburn argues that we can be indifferent to colors, but we cannot be indifferent to morals. He is quite right to emphasize this point, but it plays into the hands of the sensibility theorist. If morals are constituted by our emotional responses, then it should be very difficult to be indifferent to them.

Blackburn's final contrast is that evaluative predicates, unlike color predicates, are typically attributive. In other words, "x is good" implicitly mean "x is a good for such-and-such category." Thus, someone can be a good president and a bad father. In contrast, Blackburn claims, nothing can be a red tomato without being a red object. I do not agree with this analysis. I think color predicates are attributive. Red hair is not a red thing, and likewise for red tides, red granite, red gold, red clay, and red sand. Blackburn cherry-picks his example (so to speak) by choosing red tomatoes. Tomatoes can exhibit colors that are so saturated that they would qualify as red under any object category to which they belong.

I conclude that the alleged disanalogies between colors and morals pose no threat to sensibility theories. Some of the apparent contrasts disappear on close examination, and others can be explained. When the color analogy breaks down, there is still a strong analogy between moral concepts and concepts that refer to secondary qualities such as scary or enjoyable. Sensibility theorists should not rely too heavily on the comparison between moral properties and colors. Instead they should compare moral properties to emotion-dependent properties. That, after all, is what moral properties are supposed to be on a sensibility theory.

3.2.3 The Merit Objection

There is another apparent disanalogy between colors and morals, which deserves special attention. It is usually assumed that something has a certain color if it causes a certain kind of color experience. But a causal model of moral properties seems problematic. It seems that causing disapprobation is neither necessary not sufficient for being wrong. Imagine a mob hit man who is going through a process of reform. He may not experience any sentiment of disapproval toward killing, but he nevertheless judges that killing is wrong. That suggests that sentiments are not necessary. Or consider a person who was raised to think homosexuality is wrong, but now rejects that view. She may still harbor irrepressible negative sentiments when she thinks about homosexuality even though she insists that homosexuality is morally acceptable. That suggests that sentiments are not sufficient for moral judgments.

It is tempting to accommodate these counterexamples by shifting away from a merely causal model of the relationship between moral properties and moral sentiments. McDowell (1985) writes:

The disanalogy, now, is that a virtue (say) is conceived to be not merely such as to elicit the appropriate attitude (as a colour is merely such as to cause the appropriate experiences), but rather such as to merit it.

A parallel point is made by Wiggins (1987), and some kind of appeal to meriting is now considered a central feature of contemporary sensibility theories (Darwall, et al. 1992; D'Arms and Jacobson, 2000). But what are we to make of the contrast between eliciting and meriting? The most popular suggestion is that morality does not require actual emotional responses but rather norms about which moral responses we should have. More specifically, contemporary sensibility theorists have been inclined to replace (S1) with this metacognitive alternative:

> (S1-M) An action has the property of being morally right (wrong) just in case observers *deem it appropriate* to have feelings of approbation (disapprobation).

Correspondingly, a moral judgment on this view is not itself an emotional response, but is rather a judgment to the effect that an emotional response would be appropriate. In other words, tokens of moral concepts *mention* emotions rather than *use* them. McDowell and Wiggins seem to favor views of this kind, and Gibbard (1990) has defended a related proposal. The metacognitive accommodates the former hit man and the former homophobe. The former hit man feels no disapprobation toward killing, but he deems disapprobation appropriate. The former homophobe feels disapprobation toward homosexuality, but does not deem that disapprobation appropriate.

(S1-M) might be a tolerable revision of the theory if it weren't for an annoying problem with appropriateness. We can deem something appropriate in many different ways. For example, something can be appropriate because it gets the job done, or appropriate because it will avoid embarrassment, or appropriate because it's what others have done in the past, and so on. What kind of appropriateness is required for (S1-M)? The natural answer is moral appropriateness: stealing renders disapprobation *morally* appropriate. But that introduces a vicious circle.

Moral concepts cannot be defined as beliefs about what emotions are morally appropriate.

D'Arms and Jacobson (2000) have developed a version of this objection. They come up with cases where different kinds of appropriateness come apart. Consider an offensive joke. The joke may be good as a joke. It may be clever and funny. In that sense, it may merit amusement. But the joke may be so offensive that we deem it inappropriate to be amused in another sense. What is the difference between these two kinds of appropriateness? Well we might say amusement is socially inappropriate and comically appropriate. The appeal to comic appropriateness seems innocuous enough, but it gets us into trouble if we define "amusing" as that which makes amusement comically appropriate. This definition gets us nowhere, because "comical" and "amusing" are near synonyms. We seem to be in a similar situation when we define the moral as that which merits certain emotional responses. Suppose I want to stand my ground in a dispute where I know that I am in the wrong. Guilt would be deemed morally appropriate in this situation, but tactically inappropriate. The relevant sense of appropriateness is difficult to capture without circularity.

I think this difficulty should be nipped in the bud. There is no reason to introduce a metacognitive component into the definition of moral properties. (S1-M) should be rejected. On the view I favor, (S1′), something is wrong if there is a sentiment of disapprobation toward it. This is an improvement over a very simple causal model, because it implies that something can be wrong without, on some occasion, actually causing negative emotions. If I am depressed, I may not get outraged at the atrocities reported on the nightly news, even though I have a sentiment that, in less depressed moods, would dispose me to outrage. There may also be times, like the hypnotically induced disgust case, in which I am driven to outrage in the absence of a sentiment. So the actual elicitation of an emotion is neither necessary nor sufficient for moral wrongness on my view. But things get a little more complicated with the former hit man and the former homophobe. I think that these cases require a bit of scrutiny.

With respect to the hit man, I am tempted to say that if he really has no negative sentiment toward killing, he doesn't really think that killing is wrong. He is merely giving lip service to thinking so. By comparison, if I think I should like opera, but opera doesn't really elicit a response in me, then I don't really like it. But the former hit man may have something that comes close to the moral judgment that killing is wrong. He may have a moral judgment to the effect that it is wrong to approve of killing. He might feel guilty when he doesn't feel guilty about killing. Thus, he doesn't really believe that killing is wrong yet, but he believes he is wrong not to have that belief, and this metacognitive moral judgment might ultimately lead him to acquire the sentiments needed for the first-order judgment. My version of (S1) allows me to draw the distinction between first-order and second-order moralizing. That distinction is lost on the metacognitive version of (S1).

The former homophobe invites a similar analysis. Maybe the person who is rejecting her homophobic upbringing is, during this period of transition, still homophobic; if she feels disgusted by homosexual behavior, we would be entitled to say she harbors a negative moral attitude toward homosexuality. But, she may believe that this attitude is unwarranted, and she may be working hard to change it. In this respect, we can say that she is a recovering homophobe (like a recovering alcoholic). She condemns the fact that she condemns homosexuality, and that metacognitive attitude will, we can hope, ultimately erode her first-order dispositions. This strikes me as the right way to describe the case, and the metacognivie version of (S1) is less equipped to describe it accurately.

I conclude that there is no reason to adopt the metacognitive view, and plenty of reason against it. The view falls prey to the worries raised by D'Arms and Jacobson, and it blurs the distinction between first- and second-order moralizing.

This line of response leaves one question unanswered. I have not yet explained McDowell's intuition that wrongness *merits* disapprobation. Notice that seeing a banana does not merit a yellow experience. Moral responses, unlike color responses, have more than a merely causal relationship to things they represent.

How can I accommodate this difference between colors and moral sentiments? Where does this intuition about meriting come from? It may have something to do with the fact that the link between emotions and their causes is less direct than the link between colors and their causes. In the color case, the causal connection is fixed by our biology. We experience colors in the way that we do because we are built in a certain way, and it would be difficult or impossible to change that through training. In the case of emotions, we can exercise more control. In some cases, emotions require a fair amount of deliberation before they arise. We may have to think about a foreign policy decision for hours before it elicits condemnation or praise. In cases where emotions occur more spontaneously, they are still amenable to alteration through training. We can train ourselves to be fearless when skydiving or unperturbed by insults. When we say that something merits an emotion, we imply that a person who failed to have the emotion could be held accountable. We cannot hold a color-blind person accountable for failing to distinguish red and green, but we can hold an emotionally healthy person accountable for being afraid of foreigners or for failing to fear the effects of cigarette smoke.

If this analysis is right, then an emotional response can be merited, as opposed to *merely* caused, without being deemed appropriate. A psychological response is merited by its cause if (a) it applies to its cause, and (b) if the agent can be held responsible to some degree for having or failing to have that response. Colors do not merit color experiences because they satisfy only the first condition. Emotion elicitors merit emotions because they characteristically satisfy the second condition as well. Hard-wired emotional responses may be exceptions to this (does a loud sudden noise warrant being startled?), but many emotional responses have a degree of plasticity. This is true, a fortiori, for sentiments.

Likes and dislikes can change over time, through training and experience. Moral emotions are merited by their causes to the extent that they apply to their causes and to the extent that we hold some responsibility for our moral responses. We can deliberate more, acquire more facts, expose ourselves to more experiences, and undergo more training. I think we can explain our intuitions that merit is involved in moral response without embracing a metacognitive version of (S1). The fact that actions merit emotions does not entail that we have any metacognitive thoughts about which emotions are appropriate; it derives merely from the fact that emotional responses can be controlled to some degree. To think of something as wrong is not to deem negative emotions appropriate; it is to be disposed to have such emotions. It just so happens that such dispositions are relatively plastic.

The D'Arms and Jacobson objection still leaves us with a puzzle. Even if deeming emotions appropriate is not built into the definition of right and wrong, it is still a phenomenon that needs to be explained. People clearly distinguish between different kinds of appropriateness. They distinguish between cases where guilt is demanded by morality and when it is tactically inconvenient. How is it that we draw that distinction?

I think the sensibility theory that I favor can offer a natural answer to this question without any vicious circularity. To deem guilt morally appropriate is to have a moral sentiment toward guilt. It is to have a meta-sentiment. We sometimes feel guilty about not feeling guilty. If we repress guilt in order to save face in an argument, we may feel guilty about the repression. Moral emotions are often implemented by a second layer of moral emotions. This fits with my analysis of the former hit man and the recovering homophobe. Meta-sentiments can be used to change moral values over time. Meta-sentiments may also play an important role in sustaining norms. If our first-order norms are backed up by meta-norms, they will be harder to lose.

This digression reveals a genuine contrast between the case of colors and the case of morals. Moral emotions are not merely caused; they are merited by their causes and they are regulated by meta-emotions. There is a sense in which we deem our moral emotions appropriate, but that is not essential to those emotions, or to our concept of morality. It is, instead, a powerful mechanism for sustaining our sentiments. In this respect, thinking about merit reveals limitations of the color analogy. But it does nothing to undermine the kind of sensibility theory that I have been defending.

3.2.4 The Developmental Objection

The account presented in section 3.1 makes appeal to moral sentiments. A moral sentiment is a disposition to experience moral emotions. Nichols (2004*a*: ch. 4) has recently developed an empirical critique of accounts that appeal to some of these emotions. He focuses on guilt. The major thrust of his critique is that guilt develops later than moral competence, where moral competence is measured by the ability to distinguish moral and conventional norms. Children can determine which norms are moral before they master guilt, and disorders that impair guilt development do not necessarily impair the development of morality.

Nichols' main target is Gibbard (1990). According to Gibbard's theory, to regard an action as wrong is to accept a norm that permits or obligates us to feel guilt when we perform that action (and anger or resentment when someone else does). Gibbard's theory is metacognitive. Moralizers need to have attitudes about guilt and other moral emotions. If they do not comprehend these emotions, then they cannot have those attitudes. Nichols tries to show that some people, including young children, moralize before they comprehend these emotions.

Nichols uses sensitivity to the moral/conventional distinction as a measure of moral competence. Smetana and Braeges (1990) have shown that children of two years and ten months already distinguish moral and conventional wrongs. They regard moral wrongs as comparatively independent of authorities. Children do not seem to understand guilt until they are older. Nichols cites a study by Nunner-Winkler and Sodian (1988) that seems to support this conclusion. In one of their experiments, they ask children how a child would feel if he pushed another child off a swing. Children younger than six said that the offending child would feel happy. Nichols and the authors conclude that children younger than six do not comprehend guilt. If they are right, comprehension of guilt comes several years after the emergence of basic moral competence.

Nichols also argues for a dissociation between guilt comprehension and moral competence in autistic adults. People with autism are sensitive to the moral/conventional distinction (Blair, 1995), but they are known to have deficiencies in their comprehension of certain emotions. Studies have shown that people with autism do not fully comprehend pride and embarrassment, and Nichols infers from this that they probably also have difficulty comprehending guilt. This is a reasonable inference. Guilt is a fundamentally interpersonal emotion; it arises in contexts when we believe we have harmed another person, and it promotes efforts to repair the relationship with the harmed person. People with autism have difficulty understanding the interpersonal domain, and this may limit their ability to recognize and reason about guilt.

Nichols poses a serious challenge to Gibbard and others who think that possession of moral concepts requires the ability to form beliefs about moral emotions. Gibbard could reply by saying that people with autism and young children really don't possess moral concepts. He could say that the moral/conventional distinction is not a sufficient test for mastery of moral concepts. But this reply is *ad hoc*. People with autism and young children are relatively good at identifying moral transgressions, and they tend to behave in accordance with moral rules.

Fortunately, Nichols's arguments do not threaten the kind of sensibility theory that I endorse. As I insisted in section 3.2.3, my theory is not metacognitive. Something is wrong if there is a first-order sentiment against it. A person can have moral attitudes without grasping concepts that refer to moral emotions. The crucial thing is not emotion concepts, but the emotions themselves. Moralizers must be disposed to feel guilty when they transgress. There is no requirement that they have the belief that guilt is appropriate.

The experimental evidence that Nichols discusses does not demonstrate a lack of moral emotions in children and people with autism. There is comparatively little data available on moral emotions in autism, but there are many studies of moral emotions in children. Those studies confirm, again and again, that children have emotions that resemble the moral emotions of adults (see Eisenberg, 2000, for a review). They feel badly when they do bad things to others, for example. Michael Lewis (1998) has argued that guilt emerges around the third birthday, but it may actually be present earlier. Reparative behaviors are already present in the second year, especially when a child causes distress in a caregiver (Hoffman, 1998). In chapter 1, I described experiments that probe early guilt using a mishap paradigm (Barrett et al., 1993; Kochanska et al., 2002). Children are given an object (a doll or T-shirt) that is said to have special value to its owner. The children are warned to be careful with the object, but the situation is rigged for a mishap (the doll breaks or ink spills on the T-shirt). Kochanska et al. (2002) found that children as young as twenty-two months show signs of guilt when the mishap occurs; they squirm, avoid gaze, cover their faces, and so on. Barrett et al. (1993) distinguish signs for guilt and for shame, and find evidence for both in two-year-olds. Some children exhibit avoidance behavior, indicative of shame, and others attempt reparation and apology, which is indicative of guilt. This suggests that guilt and shame (or precursors to those emotions) are available early in life.

One could quibble about whether the emotional responses just described qualify as *bona fide* instances of guilt. I don't think it matters. The emotions in the disapprobation spectrum should actually be defined broadly. These emotions may vary a bit from culture to culture, and across different age groups. They are bound together by a family resemblance. In all cultures, there seem to be self-blame emotions and other-blame emotions. The character and scope of these may differ in subtle ways. For example, in so-called cultures of shame, shame-like reactions may be more prevalent, and the semantic content of that response may be more inclusive than the species of shame we have in our culture (see Prinz, 2004). But, we can still identify these emotions as belonging to a family of shame-like emotions, characterized by an aversive response to attention from others. There may also be a family of subtly varied guilt-like emotions, each of which can be characterized as distress associated with causing harm to another person. Children with autism do not exhibit the characteristic signs of guilt, but they do exhibit aversive emotions when they violate rules (Peter Hobson, personal communication). It is as if they have an analogue of guilt that has been stripped of its interpersonal character. Where a normally developing child may try to emotionally engage a person she has harmed, an autistic child might withdraw or become upset without trying to re-establish the threatened social connection. We might be reluctant to call this aversive response guilt, but it bears a family resemblance. There is no evidence that I am aware of for moral competence in an individual who has no analogue whatsoever of guilt or shame.

3.2.5 The Euthyphro Objection

Sensibility theories are subjectivist theories. The moral value of an action depends on subjective responses in us. It is sometimes argued that subjectivism gets things backwards. Recall Plato's *Euthyphro*. Socrates asks Euthyphro whether the actions are pious because the gods approve of them or whether the gods approve of certain actions because they are pious. Socrates argues for the latter option. Similar considerations can be brought to bear against subjectivism. Consider the questions: Is an action wrong because we disapprove of it, or do we disapprove of it because it's wrong? The latter option seems more intuitively appealing.

There is a sense in which sensibility theorists can accommodate the Euthyphro intuition, at least half way. Subjectivists say that moral properties are created by our attitudes, but they can also say that our attitudes are created by moral properties. Here's how. The wrong is that which elicits emotions of a certain kind. What kind of emotions? Well, moral emotions of course. A moral emotion is an emotion that occurs in response to something that conforms or fails to conform to a moral rule. And thus we have a circle. It is not a vicious circle, but rather a circle of co-creation. Moral emotions create moral norms, which simultaneously create moral emotions. Wiggins (1987: 195) and McDowell (1985: 219) defend a related idea, but they go a bit farther. They say that there is no way to individuate the emotions that constitute our moral sentiments without reference to what those emotions designate. This "no-priority thesis" introduces a degree of circularity that I don't want to accept. We have many different kinds of sentiments (loving, hating, caring, morally disapproving, and so on). If each of these could be individuated only by the properties to which they refer, and those properties could be individuated only by the sentiments that they elicit, then it's hard to see how we could ever distinguish one class of sentimental secondary qualities from another. We couldn't distinguish the quality of being lovable from the quality of being morally reprehensible if we could not distinguish the emotions involved in love and moral blame. To avoid this, we need some way of referring to moral emotions without referring to that which we moralize. At the same time, we need a way to capture the co-dependency of moral emotions and moral facts.

One can think about this process as a ratchet effect. Here's an origin myth. Imagine that certain behaviors cause emotions that are not yet specific to the moral domain. An act of cruelty might cause anger on the part of the victim, and sympathy among others. The perpetrator may be ostracized, criticized, and punished. This may cause the perpetrator to feel sad. If these responses are stable, then cruelty is governed by a kind of rule. The rule consists in the fact that cruelty is discouraged as a result of these emotional responses. The emotions guarantee a predictable pattern of behavior. Cruelty is less likely to occur, and when it does, certain emotions and corresponding behaviors will follow. After this pattern is established, the emotions that once had no moral significance take on new meaning. Sadness is not just a generic loss-response, but a feeling associated with violating a rule. Anger is not a generic response to a threat, but a feeling directed at rule violators. Guilt and righteous anger are born. At the very moment these emotions are born, the rule takes on new meaning. It is now a rule enforced by moral emotions. It is a moral rule.

This circle of co-dependency avoids the problem that faces Wiggins and McDowell's no-priority thesis, but it allows me to make a more benign no-priority claim in response to the Euthyphro intuition. If you ask, "Why does cruelty infuriate you?" I can answer, because it is immoral. If you ask, "Why is cruelty immoral?" I can answer correctly by saying it violates a moral rule. It is wrong because there is a special kind of rule in place that prohibits it. We can say that cruelty infuriates us because it is wrong. We can even specify what kind of wrong it is, capitalizing on the fact that morality divides into different kinds of transgressions. Wrongs that make us very angry involve autonomy violations. When you ask why cruelty infuriates me, I can answer that it violates the victim's autonomy. Of course, there is a further question you might ask: "Where does that rule come from?" Here, the subjectivism comes to the fore. The rule comes from us; it is our rule; the rule exists because there are certain things that incur our outrage. The Euthyphro question asks, is something wrong because we find it morally outrageous or morally outrageous because it is wrong? The correct answer is both.

The objector might complain that this halfway solution is unsatisfying. It does not go far enough. The Euthyphro intuition demands that we have no hand in making the moral. To this the sensibility theorist has two options: deny the intuition or admit that folk intuitions about morality are confused. I prefer the first option. Is it intuitively obvious that morality doesn't depend on us? I don't think so. It's easy to muster the intuition that morality is a human construction. Some people worry that such a view would undercut the force of moral claims. I will discuss this concern at length in a later chapter, but let me offer a brief reply here. It would not undercut morality to say that moral rules issue from human preferences. Indeed, if morality comes from us, then morality is fundamentally important. We can be neutral about things that do not depend on our responses, but we can't be neutral about morality. Morality is, by its very nature, something we care about.

In short, sensibility theorists can have it both ways. They can say that we condemn bad things because they are bad, and they can say that things are bad because we disvalue them. Both of these claims have intuitive support. Theories that deliver only the first claim unfasten morality from human interests. They give morality a kind of priority that we have no reason to embrace. Indeed, if morality had such priority over our concerns, there would be a question about why we were concerned about it at all.

3.2.6 Moral Debate

The sensibility theory that I am defending is overtly relativist in formulation. Moral properties are defined relative to observers, and it seems plausible that two observers may have conflicting sentiments. If so, then there will be no single fact of the matter to decide who is right, but rather two facts corresponding to each observer's value system. I will have much more to say about relativism in chapter 5, but I want to address one obvious objection, which poses a threat to sensibility theories. If morality is defined relative to individual observers, then it's not at all clear why individuals should ever engage in moral debates. Suppose an abolitionist says to a slave owner, "Slavery is wrong." If morality is relative to observers, the slave owner should respond, "Perhaps to you its wrong, but to me slavery is just fine, so there is no disagreement between us." But this is not what happens. We engage in moral debates incessantly. If your moral outlook differs from mine, I will want to bring you over to my side. By contrast, if I discover that you and I like different kinds of music, I may not try to persuade you to like what I like. The sensibility theory needs to explain this difference. If moral values are sentiments, why do we debate morality when we don't debate other matters that depend on sentiments, such as musical taste?

I think the sensibility theorist has many resources for dealing with this question. First, some people may have the false belief that moral absolutism is true. Those individuals will engage in debate because they think their opponents' moral judgments have no claim to truth. A moral debate between two absolutists with conflicting values is, I believe, confused, but the confusion may be perfectly innocent. People do not necessarily have direct conscious access to their concepts, and, thus, even if it is a conceptual truth that morals are relative to observers, ordinary users of moral concepts fail to recognize that fact.

Second, we very often engage in moral debates with individuals who share our basic moral values. It is possible for people to be mistaken about what their values entail. Bad faith, misunderstanding of facts, competing interests, and various other factors may prevent us from experiencing moral outrage at something that is morally outrageous *by our own standards*. When this happens, a moral reformer can show us the error of our ways. When William Lloyd Garrison denounced American slavery, he was not suggesting that slave owners change their moral values. Rather, he was saying that slave owners are hypocrites because they engage in behavior that is wrong according to values that they endorse in other contexts.

Third, moral values are implemented by other-directed emotions. If I think you are morally wrong, I will feel anger (or some other emotion of blame) toward you, and that emotion may lead me into conflict with you. My anger may cause me to start an argument with you, or some other kind of dispute, even if the dispute can't be decided rationally. Consider how emotions lead to lovers' quarrels. In some cases, an emotionally instigated fight may have a rational resolution, but this isn't always the case. Nevertheless, our emotions lead us into conflict.

Fourth, moral sentiments are backed up by meta-emotions, so we don't just value actions; we also value the valuing of those actions. If your values disagree with mine, I will have a negative response to both your behavior and your values. The former may lead me to try to alter your behavior directly, but my distaste for your values will require that I try to alter how you feel. Moral debate is one tool for affecting the psychological states of others.

Fifth, even if we recognize that moral values are relative to observers, we may have a stake in carrying out moral debates. By analogy, consider relativism about taste. If you love country music and I don't, then I normally wouldn't try to alter your taste. But suppose I know that you are going to select the music for an upcoming party. In that case, I would try to persuade you to alter your taste. In the case of morality, we are often in this kind of position. Moral values are used to guide policies or social practices. If your values differ from mine, you will try to support policies that conflict with my values, and these policies will have an impact on me. Consequently, I will be motivated to try to change your views. In general, we don't tolerate other people's values (moral, aesthetic, or otherwise) when those values affect us. Moral matters are often matters of life and death, so we have an especially strong interest in getting those with conflicting values to change their minds.

Sixth, there is a flipside of point five. Just as I have an interest in changing your views, you have an interest in changing mine. That means you will try to alter my values by any means available, including moral debate.

Seventh, we regard morality as deeply reflective of who we are. A person with different values is alien and off-putting. Alternative values threaten us, because they can lead us to reconsider the things we care about most, and such reconsideration could lead to a loss of identity. In general, we resist conversion and feel more comfortable when the people around us have a similar outlook on life. These facts about the psychology of identity give us a further reason to engage in moral debate.

3.2.7 Distant Others

There is still a puzzle here. I have just been arguing that we have ample reason to care about the moral values of those nearby. People in our community have an impact on our lives. We have motivation to persuade anyone who is shaping policies that can affect us. But what about more distant places? The moral values of people in foreign lands should be of less concern if what I have been saying is right. This prediction turns out to be true. Most people are somewhat indifferent to the moral values of people in distant lands. But we are not entirely indifferent. When we hear about practices that we deem reprehensible (e.g., "female genital mutilation" or torture), we tend to feel moral outrage.

There are at least three ways to explain this fact. First, we may be erroneously over-extending in our values. If moral values are dispositions to react emotionally to certain forms of conduct, then any example of such conduct might elicit those reactions. This generality of response may be, in part, a simple solution to an engineering problem. How do we construct a system that morally chastises immoral actions within the community? One solution is to build a system that first establishes community membership and then chastises. A simpler system would skip the first step and chastise no matter what.

Second, we sometimes chastise distant others, because, despite the distance, they may pose a threat to us. When we have occasion to consider activities in other communities, it is often because we are interacting with those communities. Such interactions can have an influence on things here at home. So we have a stake in making sure other communities are doing as we do. In some circumstances, we learn of distant others whom we are very unlikely ever to encounter. Suppose we are considering an anthropologist's ethnography of a remote people whose customs would be strongly prohibited at home: Amazonian cannibalism, for example. In these cases, the sensibility theory correctly predicts, that we may not get very upset. We can regard their activities with a kind of moral detachment, because we see them as utterly separated from us.

Still, it must be admitted that some people are morally outraged even when harm comes to people in very remote cultures. This may be a case of erroneous over-extension, but there is also a third story to tell about why we care about distant others. As Hume pointed out, people are naturally prone to sympathy (or perhaps empathy). Hume thought that sympathy was very parochial: we naturally sympathize only with people who are similar to us or close to us. But he may have been wrong about this. We may be disposed to sympathize with all (or almost all human beings) as research on the neural mechanisms of sympathy might suggest. When we see another person suffer, it makes us suffer (Singer et al., 2004). We condemn actions that lead to the suffering of others, because we sympathize with the victims. This is true even if the victims are far away. A person who is outraged by Amazonian cannibalism may be driven by sympathy. Of course, that sympathy may be misplaced; perhaps the victims feel genuinely honored to be eaten. The point is not that we are right to sympathize, but that we may do so automatically, and this can lead us to be morally concerned about people who are incredibly unlikely to have any direct impact on our lives.

3.2.8 The Reasoning Objection

Sensibility theories emerged out of the Humean tradition. Hume is (in)famous for saying that moral reasoning is subordinate to our emotional responses—reason is slave to the passions. Some critics think that this picture is incompatible with the common observation that we often arrive at moral conclusions through a process of rational deliberation. We try to alter each others' moral judgments by presenting arguments. In private ethical reflection, we take special care to think about all of the relevant facts and weigh evidence. If emotions were driving morality, rational means of moral deliberation would be poorly suited for arriving at moral judgments.

To address this objection, I want to consider the role of reasoning in non-moral sentiments. Consider the sentiment of liking. Suppose I want to persuade you to like someone. To do that, I must convince you that she is likeable. At the outset you are unconvinced. You have been put off by her arrogant and boorish manner. I may try to diminish these traits. Perhaps her arrogance is just a defense for insecurity. I tell you that she is a smart and engaging conversationalist and has a sardonic sense of humor. I explain that she is passionate about social causes and an avid reader with broad interests. At this point you may concede that you were too quick to judge. You may conclude that, if I am right and no other negative traits are found, then she is likeable. This does not mean you instantly start liking her, but equipped with the new interpretation of her arrogance and new information about other traits, you are disposed to begin liking her.

This is an example of rational debate. I present reasons for a conclusion and those reasons support the conclusion. If you accept my reasons, you are prepared to accept my conclusion. Nevertheless, there are two respects in which this debate departs from paradigm examples of rational discourse. First, you may conclude that the person in question is likeable without thereby coming to like her. In this respect, the debate is more like practical reasoning than theoretical reasoning. In practical reasoning, you may arrive at a conclusion about a course of action that is reasonable without acting.

Second, the debate about liking presupposes that certain traits are likeable. A sense of humor is a likeable trait. Intelligence and social conscience are likeable. Arrogance is unlikeable. Suppose we were to shift attention to these traits. Suppose my interlocutor denied that having a sardonic sense of humor was likeable. Sardonic wit, he might maintain, shows a kind cynicism that indicates elitist and pessimistic tendencies. We could have a debate about that. But now suppose my interlocutor says he does not like people with a sense of humor in general. He might give reasons for this ("life is too serious for jokes"). We might have a debate about whether a sense of humor entails a lack of care or seriousness about world affairs. But if my interlocutor just declares a personal distaste for humor, I would conclude that he and I like different things. I would conclude that what is likeable for me is not likeable for him. I would not be able to persuade him rationally. It would be a bit like trying to persuade a peanut hater to enjoy peanut butter.

Debates about liking work by trying to establish that something or someone has traits that are likeable. What counts as a likeable trait depends on what is actually liked. One can rationally demonstrate that someone has likeable traits, but it is much harder to show rationally that a trait is likeable. In some cases one can do so by showing that a trait T1 is an instance of another trait T2 that is liked. Is joke-telling a sign of callousness or of *joie de vivre*? Eventually, we hit rock bottom. At a certain point, the traits we like are not liked for any reasons. They have to do with how we are constituted. Perhaps I could come up with a reason for liking people with a sense of humor. That reason would be *post hoc*. It's not my reason for liking such people; I just like them. Humor is likeable to me. If you dislike humor, we are constituted differently.

I think moral disagreements are often like this. There is plenty of room for rational debate. We often need to use reason to demonstrate that an action falls under a moral category (recall the categorization stage in Figure 3.1). Suppose I say that prayer in school is wrong. I might add a reason: it is wrong because it discriminates against atheists and members of minority religions. You might reply that it does not discriminate. Or you might reply that prohibitions against school prayer discriminate against members of majority religion, and hence discriminate against more people than if the prohibitions were lifted. This is a rational debate. We could settle on a prior definition of discrimination, and provide evidence for our respective views. If I persuade you of my view, your emotional attitude toward prayer in school would not change instantly, but it would be disposed to change. But now suppose you are not persuaded. Suppose, instead, that you say discrimination is not morally wrong. The best I can do is stare at you incredulously. If you think discrimination is not wrong, then we are constituted differently.

Some authors who emphasize the role of emotions underestimate the role of reasoning in moral judgment. For example, Haidt (2001) says that reasoning typically enters the process only as a *post hoc* justification of these intuitions. I agree with Haidt that reasoning often plays this role, but reasoning can also play an important role in determining whether a certain event falls under a category about which we have a moral sentiment. We often have to reason to determine whether something is a case of discrimination, for example. Haidt's model allows for this but he doesn't emphasize it. That's an important oversight, because a lot of moral debate may involve rational disagreements about how to categorize things. But once we've categorized something as a case of discrimination, reasoning stops. There is an immediate emotional reaction. This is the bit that Haidt emphasizes, and it is essential to my version of the sensibility theory as well.

In chapter 1, I said we can think about moral debates as being arranged in a series of why-questions (compare Anscombe, 1957, on intentions). Why is ϕ-ing wrong? It is an instance of ψ-ing. Why is ψ-ing wrong? Well, it just is. If ψ-ing is rock bottom for me, I will be baffled by someone who asks why it is wrong. Why is tax evasion wrong? Because we reap benefits from taxes, and it is wrong to reap benefits from other people's contributions if you have contributed nothing; that would be free riding. Why is it wrong to be a free rider? This question is hard to answer. It is fundamental to our moral outlook. It is like asking why it is wrong to kill innocent people. Well it just is. Someone who doubts that has a different conception of what it is to be wrong. I call these rock bottom values "grounding norms."

We can now put the role of reasoning in moral discourse as follows. When two people disagree about whether something is wrong, they can have a rational debate about whether it falls under a category about which they have a grounding norm. Is letting someone die the same as killing? Are tax shelters a form of legally sanctioned free riding? But when it comes to grounding norms, rational debate is impossible. If two people have different grounding norms, they must resort to other means of persuasion.

If I am right about grounding norms, then a lot of philosophical work in ethics is based on a false assumption. Philosophers are preoccupied with the idea that moral judgments can serve as practical *reasons*. Invocation of a moral judgment is supposed to provide us with a reason for action, and reasons are supposed to be justifying. I think there is a thin notion of reason according to which this approach is right. If you have a grounding norm that demands certain behavior, then you have a reason to behave that way. But this is analogous to saying that, if you like chocolate, then you have a reason to eat chocolate. Grounding norms cannot serve as reasons in a more robust sense. My grounding norms would not be seen as reasons for someone who did not share them. Philosophers who want to show that moral norms provide robust reasons for action are embarking on a fool's errand. For one thing, if there are preference-independent demands on action, there is absolutely no reason to think that our moral vocabulary refers to those demands. For another thing, moral discourse does not seem to presuppose that grounding norms have this status. If grounding norms were construed as preference-independent, moral interlocutors should feel some compulsion to justify them in purely rational terms. But, I would guess that such attempts at justification have no significant role in ordinary moral discourse. It's not the case that I value human life because of some well worked out rational argument, and I don't feel any obligation to generate such an argument (just as I don't have to argue for the deliciousness of chocolate). If I encounter someone who baldly states that human life has no value, I assume that the person is depraved, not dumb. I respond, not with reason, but with the fist.

3.2.9 The Manners Monger Objection

Some people really care about etiquette. Those people get annoyed when people put their elbows on the table, or chew with an open mouth. They may feel ashamed when they fail to pass salt in the right direction or say the proper words of excuse after a sneeze. But surely these are not moral rules. Surely these are not moral values. Sensibility theories seem too liberal. They entail that intuitively non-moral rules are moral, and this leaves us with no good way to distinguish between the moral and the conventional. Sensibility theorists can draw a moral/conventional distinction only in those cases where conventional rules are not enforced by the moral emotions, but this leaves out cases in which people get indignant over etiquette.

There are several things one can say in response to cases like this. The first is that people who express strong moral emotions about etiquette may be moralizing. They may be treating manners as if they were morals. People often moralize things that others regard as merely conventional. Examples may include the parent who makes her child feel guilty or ashamed for not practicing the piano. Sometime people merely pretend to moralize in order to achieve a desired effect. For example, feigning indignation can be a way to gain complicity or achieve the upper hand. Consider the disgruntled customer who complains to a store manager that she has been cheated (Greenspan, 2000). These cases are not a concern to the sensibility theorist.

In every culture, there are probably some manners that are frequently moralized. In contemporary American culture, we tend to have a moral attitude toward leaving the dinner table while everyone else is still eating and toward obscene language. These are behaviors that people outside the culture would immediately recognize as conventional, but there is a tendency for us to have full-fledged moral sentiments toward them. In Victorian England, the list of moralized manners might have been much longer, and other cultures at other times have had their own lists.

Breaches of manners can be taken quite seriously, but, even when we get outraged, we can sometimes recognize a difference between bad manners and moral wrongs. Is saying "bless you" really a demand of morality? There is a tension in our intuitions that needs to be resolved. On the one hand, we morally chastise those with bad manners, and, on the other hand, many of our manners are arbitrary conventions.

I think the tension can be handled by the sensibility theorist. The trick is to deploy the notion of grounding norms, which I introduced above. Grounding norms are the norms that we tend to regard as not needing any explanation. In our value system, examples include prohibitions against killing, stealing, and incest. When someone asks "Why is killing wrong?" we respond with an incredulous stare or fumble through a *post hoc* explanation. Only lunatics and philosophers ask such questions. But other norms are not as fundamental. If we declare that tax evasion in wrong, we need to make it clear why, and the answer will involve showing that tax evasion is an instance of a grounding norm. Perhaps it violates a norm of fairness. Perhaps it is a kind of stealing. Perhaps it is a kind of disrespect for others. Or all of these things.

Now consider etiquette. It may be that having good manners is a grounding norm. Or perhaps manners derive from a more basic norm having to do with respect. If you don't obey etiquette rules, you disrespect those who care about such rules. Thus, it can be immoral to have bad manners, but only in a derivative sense. Specific etiquette violations are immoral to the extent that they are violations of some more fundamental moral norm.

This explains why manners strike us as moral in some sense, and why they also strike us as non-moral—as mere conventions. Etiquette violations are explicitly recognized as depending on local customs. There may be a grounding norm prohibiting bad manners, but that norm gives us little guidance in determining which behaviors should be frowned upon. The inference from a general prohibition against bad manners to some specific etiquette norm requires an auxiliary premise about which behaviors are locally regarded as bad. For example, you need to know that, in the local culture, people say "bless you" when someone sneezes, and people take off their hats when eating. People who abide by these manners usually recognize that they are contingent on local customs. When they fail to recognize this (consider attitudes toward spitting in public), they take the behavior in question to be morally reprehensible, not just uncouth. This gives a straightforward analysis of the moral/conventional distinction. A norm is moral if it is a grounding norm or if it is derived from a grounding norm without necessary appeal to a premise about customs. A norm is conventional if it depends on appeal to customs. We may get miffed about bad manners sometimes, but our response depends on the belief that certain behaviors are customarily prohibited. If we changed our beliefs about the local customs, the anger would subside. Sensibility theorists need not be embarrassed by the fact that we sometimes get emotional about conventional wrongs.

Before leaving this topic, it must be noted that the moral/conventional distinction is not without critics. Kelly et al. (2007) have recently advanced a powerful empirical critique. According to Turiel, Nucci, Smetana, and other psychologists who study the distinction, moral rules are supposed to be authority-independent. Moral violations should remain wrong even when local customs allow them. Kelly et al. found that this is not the case. Their subjects were willing to tolerate core moral wrongs (physical harms) in different cultural contexts. For example, subjects were asked to consider the captain of a ship who whipped a drunken sailor. In one version, the vignette takes place in the present, and, in another it takes place 300 years ago, when corporal punishment was widely tolerated. Subjects were inclined to say that whipping was okay for a captain back then, but not now. This suggests that moral norms are not authority-independent. It also suggests a worry about my analysis of the distinction, because it implies that beliefs about local customs factor into judgments about paradigmatically moral cases. Kelly et al. think that there will be no secure way to draw a distinction between moral and conventional norms.

I think these results are intriguing, and they do raise worries about the way in which the moral/conventional distinction has been operationalized in the literature. But I do not think the results undermine the moral/conventional distinction as I've drawn it. First, prohibitions against corporal punishment may be regarded as a conventional norm for many people. Second, when subjects judge that it is okay for a captain to whip a sailor a few centuries ago, they may not be suggesting that it is morally acceptable behavior; rather they may be suggesting that we should forgive the captain for his conduct because people were less enlightened back then. Third, subjects may believe that there were factors back then that made it morally acceptable to whip; for example, they may imagine sailors from past eras as being more unruly and prone to mutiny than the highly professionalized sailors of contemporary sea commerce.

The key test for the way I've drawn the distinction would be to ask subjects why it is wrong to whip someone. If I am right (and the literature on the moral/conventional distinction bears this out), people do not ordinarily appeal to local customs when justifying harm norms. They don't say that it's wrong to whip because people don't whip around here. In contrast, if you asked people why it's wrong to wear a hat while eating, they would be more likely to mention local customs. If beliefs about customs enter into deliberations about the two sea captains, those beliefs do not play a role in deriving the judgment that certain behavior is wrong. Rather they serve as an excuse when deciding that a dubious form of behavior may be tolerated under certain conditions. The fact that considerations about customs can override moral judgments is consistent with the claim that moral norms are ones that people do not justify by appeal to customs.

3.2.10 The Categorical Imperative

Morality places demands on us. That would be hard to deny. The interesting question concerns the nature of these demands. Kantians insist that they are categorical. This is said to present a serious challenge for anyone who grounds morality in emotions. Categorical imperatives are thought to have three noteworthy features. First, they are said to govern us regardless of our inclinations, passions, and desires. That is what it means to say they are categorical. Second, they are said to be commands of reason. That is the best explanation of how they could govern us independently of our passions. Third, they are said to be universal. A command of reason must apply to all rational persons. Universality is at the heart of Kant's conception. He thinks there is but one categorical imperative, from which more specific demands derive. We should do that which we would will as a universal law. If moral imperatives are categorical, sensibility theories are not going to fly. This is the major point of contention between Kantians and descendants of Hume.

It would be impossible to develop a complete argument against Kantian ethics here. I can only raise some familiar worries. Kantians will not be convinced. My goal is not to refute Kant, but to remind readers that the Kantian program remains highly contentious, and I will point out that some of the strategies for patching holes in Kantian arguments bring passions back into the picture. I also have a more important goal. I want to explain how a Humean view can account for core aspects of the intuition that there is something categorical about moral imperatives. Indeed, I will argue that Humeans may do a better job than Kantians at capturing the distinctive normative status of moral claims. Thus, even if there is a way to derive imperatives from reason, this would not obviate the need for a Humean story about moral concepts.

Sensibility theory can go reasonably far toward giving morals a categorical flavor, but not all the way. Let's begin with passion-independence. The sensibility theorist has at least two different strategies for showing that an action is wrong even if people do not happen to react negatively to it. First, on the kind of sensibility theory I favor, moral values are constituted by sentiments and sentiments are dispositions. On some occasions, the disposition to have a negative emotion is not actualized. If I am distracted, tired, depressed, ecstatic, or drunk, I may witness a crime with total indifference. That does not mean the crime is permissible in that case. Its being wrong depends on what I am disposed to feel, not on the feelings I happen to have. Second, passions will not be elicited when I fail to realize that a particular action is incompatible with my grounding norms. Consider slavery again. Imagine that everyone in a community of slave owners has a grounding norm that prohibits slavery, but they do not deploy that norm properly. Members of that society fall under the norm that prohibits slavery even if they fail to see that. Because they don't see it, slavery does not instill a sense of outrage. The norm holds even though they do not, as a matter of fact, find slavery abhorrent. Thus, there is a sense in which the norm is passion-independent.

Passion-independence has its limits. Sensibility theorists cannot say that something would be wrong even if people were not disposed to disapprove of it. Is this a problem? I don't think so. Intuitions about passion-independence derive from cases in which people ignore morality in favor of other concerns. A wealthy person who gives nothing to the needy may be morally obligated to give, even if she has strong desire to keep her cash. Moral demands don't vanish every time something more enjoyable comes along. Sensibility theorists can accommodate this kind of passion-independence easily. Paradoxically, even affect-dependent properties are passion-independent in this sense. Something can be fearsome even if, on a particular occasion we do not fear it. Something can be depressing, even if we are not saddened by it. The same is true for likeable things. I like sushi, and thus, sushi is likeable to me. But there are occasions when I do not want sushi. I do not enjoy eating sushi while eating chocolate ice cream, and I would not want sushi after a big meal. But sushi is likeable to me at all times. Likeability is a dispositional property. It is independent of transient desires, but not passion-independent *tout court*.

A stronger form of passion-independence would entail that an action could be wrong even if no one had a psychology that promoted disapprobation of it under conditions of full information and no competing emotional demands. Imagine an isolated community of psychopaths, living in a world with no other intelligent beings. They may lie, cheat, and kill on a regular basis. They recognize conventional rules, and they set up many laws to discourage these kinds of behaviors. The laws confer a kind of stability, like the Hobbesian state, but no one regards law violations as immoral. Punishments are valued as prudential (and perhaps entertaining) but not morally justified. The category of moral justification does not exist. What are we to say about murder in this community? Is it morally wrong? I don't think so. It's no more immoral for a psychopath to kill, in this horrible world, than it is for a lioness to kill a wildebeest on the African savanna.

I will consider such cases in more detail in chapter 4. Here I just want to register an intuition. I think our moral rules do not encompass those who are not disposed to moral sentiments. The Kantian might agree by arguing that the community of psychopaths is not a community of persons. They are not constituted in a way that allows them to see each other as ends. They are not human, in the relevant sense. That may be so. But this concession might be a victory for the sensibility theorist. The main thing that distinguishes psychopaths from us (paradigm cases of persons) is their emotional indifference. To place them outside of morality is to concede that passion-independence can be taken only so far.

Turn now to the second feature of categorical imperatives. According to Kant, they are demands of reason. Reason requires us to avoid immoral conduct. Immoral conduct is irrational. Humeans can accommodate this intuition to some degree. They can say that immoral behavior is incompatible with *practical* reason, where practical reason is defined with reference to our desires. Immoral conduct may be like weakness of the will. It may involve acting on desires that conflict with other desires that we would have if we had all the relevant information. But Humeans deny that morality issues from *pure* reason. The idea of a "sufficient reason" is an oxymoron for Hume. Just as concepts are blind without percepts, practical reasoning is aimless without passion. Kant says that reason can provide ends, as well as means, without any contribution from passion. Humeans disagree.

How could reason provide sufficient grounds for action? Kant's most famous argument rests on the very shaky assumption that some courses of action are literally incoherent or contradictory when they are followed by everyone. His classic example, mentioned in chapter 1, is the lying promise. If everyone were to make promises with no intention of keeping them, then the practice of promising would collapse. Promises cannot exist if they are not kept some proportion of the time. If everyone told lying promises, there could be no promising, and hence no lying promises. We cannot will that all others make lying promises without a contradiction, and, Kant says, we cannot rationally do what we cannot consistently will all others to do. So we cannot rationally make a lying promise. Perhaps all moral wrongs are wrong in virtue of being contradictory in this sense.

But this cannot be right. First, there are many apparent wrongs that yield no contradiction when universalized. If everyone were to kick children whenever they saw children on the street, the practice of child-kicking would not be rendered incoherent. Second, some paradigmatically good actions become contradictory when universalized. Suppose that there are sufficient resources to feed all the needy people in the world. Now consider the moral command: give food to those in need. If everyone did this, to the extent that they were able, neediness would disappear, and the practice of giving to the needy would be rendered empty. Does that mean giving to the needy is wrong? Or, to take another example, consider the command: work to abolish slavery. If everyone did this, slavery would be gone, and abolitionism would be impossible. Or consider the command: "boycott Jim Crow laws." A successful boycott would undermine future boycotting. A Kantian might protest that the commands to give food to the needy, to fight slavery, and to protest discriminatory laws remain in place even if there are no needy people, no slaves, and no discrimination. But this violates the stricture that ought implies can. Granted, one could universalize a maxim that said, "fight slavery if there is any," but one could probably also universalize a maxim that said, "lie if it serves you." Once we conditionalize our maxims, the universalization test fails to filter out bad behavior.

One can also take issue with the derivation of the categorical imperative. Here is one interpretation. According to Kant, the only thing that is intrinsically good is a good will. A good will is a will that acts from duty. We humans alone can act from duty, because we alone can represent ourselves as acting on the basis of reasons; non-human animals simply follow their inclinations. For duty to control the will, and liberate us from inclinations, it must supply the will with reasons that are sufficient for action. But what kind of reason can be sufficient for action? Kant's answer is that we can achieve freedom only by acting from reasons that we could will as universal laws. To discover commands of reason, we need to ask whether a given command would govern all rational creatures. That is the basis of the good.

There is plenty of room for doubt here, but I restrict myself to two points. First, Kant draws a highly questionable link between our concept of freedom and the concept of acting from the universal rules of reason. Such rules seem neither conceptually necessary nor sufficient for freedom. Phenomenologically, we can feel a sense of freedom when we can act on our desires, so acting from reason is not necessary. Doubts about sufficiency arise when we consider the fact that Kant takes reason to demand a single course of action. But, if reason gives us only one option, then acting from reason can be said to deprive us of freedom rather than endowing us with freedom. The fact that we can construe our wills as free does not commit us to construing our wills as bound by reason. Thus, if we necessarily seek freedom, it doesn't follow that we necessarily want to heed the demands of reason.

My second complaint about Kant concerns his first premise: the claim that good will (construed as acting from duty) really is an intrinsic good. The whole idea of intrinsic goodness is a little puzzling. I find it bizarre to suppose that something can be good without being good for an agent, or regarded as good. Let me put that worry to one side. The more pressing worry is that, if there are intrinsic goods, then good will doesn't look like an especially compelling example, much less the sole example. Arguably, good will is valuable only in virtue of the fact that it is disposed to bring about good effects. More intuitively plausible examples of intrinsic goods include happiness, friendship, courage, health, and knowledge. These look like ends that we might seek in their own sake. Kantians may protest that these goods lack intrinsic value because we despise them when they are possessed by the wicked. But, if we are to take the idea of intrinsic value seriously, we must focus on these goods in isolation from who happens to have them. Considered in isolation, health might seem like a good thing. Indeed, it is bad that the wicked be healthy precisely because health is good and we don't want the wicked to have good things. At this point, Kantians may object that health and happiness are not *moral* goods. But how are they to demonstrate that good will, construed as acting from reason, is a moral good? Should we morally value devotion to rational duties? Is Mr Spock our moral paragon? The answer is far from obvious. If good will has moral value it may be derivative. It may stem from the fact that good will brings about other ends that we value morally. If so, rational duty cannot be the foundation of morals.

Many contemporary devotees of Kant would admit that the argument in the *Groundwork* is multiply flawed. But rather than giving up his program, some have offered improved arguments that do not depend on dubious claims about the nature of freedom or the goodness of duty. One of the best of these improved Kantian arguments is put forward by Gewirth (1994). Here is a reconstruction:

P1. I am an agent.
P2. If I am an agent, I accept that freedom and well-being are necessary for me.
C1. Therefore, I accept that I must have freedom and well-being. (From P1 and P2.)
C2. Therefore, I accept that it is impermissible to not have freedom and well-being. (From C1, because its denial is the contradiction of that premise.)
C3. Therefore, I accept that it is impermissible for others to remove or interfere with my freedom and well-being. (From C2.)
C4. Therefore, I accept that others ought to refrain from removing or interfering with my freedom and well-being. (From C3.)
C5. Therefore, I accept that I have a right to freedom and well-being. (From C4 because of the correlativity of oughts and rights.)
C6. The same argument applies to all agents. (Universal generalization of P1.)
C7. Therefore, all agents accept that they have the right to freedom and well-being. (From P3.)
C8. Therefore, I accept that all agents have the right to freedom and well-being. (From P1 and C7.)

If this argument is sound, then we have a sufficient reason to respect the freedom and well-being of others.

But the argument hinges on an equivocation. The necessity invoked in P2 is conceptual. To view myself as agent, I must view myself as having freedom and well-being. This is already a highly contentious claim, which I find implausible, but let's grant that it's true for the sake of argument, and hence that C1 is true. But now consider C2. Does it follow from the fact that I must view myself as free that I must also believe others are *not permitted* to harm me? Absolutely not. It follows only that if they happen to harm me, I will no longer be able to view myself as an agent. Gewirth illicitly shifts from conceptual to moral necessity. To escape this problem, the necessity in P2 has to be construed normatively. It has to be the case that I think I have my freedom and well-being by moral necessity. On this interpretation, P2 is question-begging and probably false. It doesn't seem to follow from being an agent that I see myself as being morally entitled to anything. In principle, I could see myself, in a Hobbesian way, as an agent in a dog-eat-dog world. Others are entitled to trample on me, and I am entitled to trample on them. Let the best trampler win.

One might try to patch up the argument by pointing out that, *as a matter of fact*, we do feel that we are entitled to freedom and well-being. P2 happens to be true. Nagel (1986: 63) makes such an argument by appeal to the fact that we *resent* those who trespass against us. The emotion of resentment reveals that we think others have no right to harm us. This suggests that C1 is true, and, indeed, that Gewith's premise C5 is true. We take ourselves to have rights. If I take myself to have rights then I cannot, on pain of contradiction, deny that others have rights. Or so Nagel argues. Does this prove that moral requirements can be derived from pure reason? I think the answer is negative, and obviously so.

Nagel's argument is based on emotions, not reason. It is not a conceptual truth about agency that agents have rights. Rather, it is an emotional truth about me and other agents that we assume we have rights. We could (as in the Hobbesian scenario) give up this assumption and continue to construe ourselves as agents. Nagel's point about resentment shows that we have internalized a norm that allows us to hold others accountable for harming us. Once this norm is internalized, it follows that we are also committed to respecting the well-being of others, but the norm itself is grounded in our emotions. Nagel's point about resentment undermines Gewirth's argument by pinning our sense of entitlement on emotional norms. If our sense of entitlement is emotionally based, and not derived from purely rational premises, then Gewirth does not have the resources to show that pure reason is sufficient for moral concern. Gewirth's argument is representative of attempts to update the Kantian program, and its shortcomings suggest that we may never be able to derive moral requirements from reason alone.

I think there is an even more serious problem with the Kantian program. Kant's chilly rationalism cannot do justice to the main intuitions underlying the hypothesis that moral commands are categorical. That hypothesis derives, I suspect, from the intuition that moral requirements answer a fundamental normative question. When we are told that an action is required by morality, we don't feel that we need any further fact for that action to have normative status. We feel like we *ought* to perform the action. The normative question asks why this is the case. After all, when presented with rules outside of morality, we sometimes feel compelled to say, "I understand that this is the rule, but why on Earth should I follow it?" Non-moral rules leave a gap between rule and action. Moral rules do not seem to leave a gap. Korsgaard (1996) thinks that Kant has an explanation. If moral rules are rules of reason, then whenever there is a moral rule we have sufficient reason to act. The gap between rule and action closes. With non-moral rules, the rule is insufficient on its own. I think this Kantian solution fails on its own terms. Kant cannot answer the normative question. Here's why.

Kant's whole enterprise is designed to liberate moral rules from the passions. I think such liberation would come at a terrible price. If morality were purely rational, we would actually risk placing ourselves back at the mercy of whim. A purely rational rule cannot have motivational effect on us. It would leave us cold. And if we could be emotionally indifferent to morality, we might fail to act morally. "Why obey the rules of morality?" asks the sensible knave. Kant's reply is that it would be irrational not to. To which the knave has a simple reply, "Why be rational?" Or, more exactly, the knave might say, "I recognize that it is inconsistent to value myself while treating others poorly, but I simply don't mind being inconsistent in this respect. After all, by favoring myself I have so much to gain!" Here, Kant must fall silent.

Hume has a more satisfying analysis of the knave case. He says that no person who is *constituted like us* can disobey morality without incurring an emotional cost. Ordinary people, thankfully, don't raise knavish questions. This response parallels Hume's response to skepticism. Ordinary people don't ask skeptical questions. We cannot help believing in an external world. Likewise, some of us cannot help being swayed by sympathy and moral indignation. Hume's reply explains why moral rules seem to have power over us. He closes the gap between moral rule and action by arguing that, whenever we see a rule as moral we are thereby moved to act on it. That's why rules seem categorical. Kant's approach suggests that we can be indifferent to the demands of morality. Therefore, he fails to answer the normative question.

In response, the Kantian will contend that moral commands would have greater weight if they issued from reason. For Hume, moral commands are commands of passion, and, as such, they can be trumped by other affective states. For Kant, moral commands are reasons no matter what we desire. This makes moral commands seem more powerful. They hold no matter what. But this move backfires. First, Kant's view has the same practical limitation as Hume's. Morality can be trumped by desire. Someone can ignore a moral imperative because she desires something else. A moral command can fail to have any impact. Second,

Hume's view has the same advantage as Kant's. Moral commands remain in place when we fail to heed them. When a moral command fails in its battle for control, it does not vanish into oblivion. It waits eagerly in its corner for the next round in the ring. Third, Hume has an advantage over Kant. For Hume, moral commands directly bid for the attention of the will. For Kant, they can exist without any inclination to follow them. The Humean view gives moral commands more weight, not less.

I have been trying to raise doubts about the rational character of moral imperatives, but there is a final dimension of the Kantian view that I have not squarely addressed. Kantians claim that morality is universal. Moral truths hold for all rational beings. On sensibility theories, morality need not be universal. But there is a sense of universality that it would be unfortunate to lose. This has to do with the prescriptive nature of the moral. Modulo societies of psychopaths, we take our moral rules to apply to others. If we learn that someone has been tortured in a far-off land, we condemn the action as wrong, no matter what moral judgments the person doing the torturing might make. Can sensibility theories allow this?

Of course they can. According to sensibility theories wrongness is constituted by our emotional reactions, and those reactions may be directed toward events in far-off lands. Sensibility theories even predict that this will be the case. As Hume observed, some of our strongest sentiments of disapprobation derive from our deep capacity for sympathy. We feel for the victim of torturing, and those feelings fuel indignation. Hume noted that our sympathies diminish with distance, but this is partially an effect of salience. When the suffering of distant others becomes salient to us, our sympathies awaken. Moral judgments are encompassing, by virtue of their passionate nature. They are prescriptive, and we prescribe them to people outside of our communities. But moral judgments fall short of being universal, or so I will argue in chapters 4 and 5. The fact that we apply our moral rules to others does not entail that they are always applicable.

In sum, I have argued that a moral rule can hold for me, even if I have no inclination to follow it, at a particular moment in time, because I am distracted or tired or unaware that the rule is entailed by one of my grounding norms. This gives moral rules a categorical character. But moral rules are only weakly categorical; I would have no obligation to follow a rule that was not grounded in my sentimental dispositions. Does this mean that moral rules are hypothetical? Moral rules are certainly not overtly conditional; "Stealing is wrong" does not mean "Don't steal if refraining from stealing satisfies some desire of yours." Hypothetical imperatives have two parts: the imperative (Don't steal!) which has no intrinsic motivating force, and the conditional clause that gives it force. On my view, moral norms are intrinsically action-guiding. I don't refrain from stealing in virtue of recognizing an end that refraining from stealing will help me meet; rather, refraining from stealing is one of my ends. But moral rules are not action-guiding or authoritative in any other way for those who have not internalized them. Like hypothetical imperatives, moral rules depend on ends, and those ends are entirely contingent. One might say that moral rules are neither strongly categorical, nor strictly hypothetical. They are psychologically categorical (we see them as intrinsic ends), and metaphysically hypothetical (if we didn't have those ends, they would have no authority). Kantians who insist on a strong categorical status for morality sever the link between moral demands and human wants. In trying to free moral rules from inclinations, Kantians deprive moral rules of the motivational force that makes them act as imperatives in the psychological sense. Moral rules become categorical, but far less imperative.

I will conclude with one parting objection to the Kantian program. According to Kant, we should avoid actions that we cannot will as a universal law. Perhaps he is right. My closing complaint is that there is little reason to think that *this* requirement, if it is one, is a moral requirement. Kant's universalization procedure places demands on us that do not align with pretheoretical intuitions about the requirements of morality. His brand of universality is neither necessary nor sufficient. It is not necessary for the moral, because some moral wrongs pose no threat of logical or practical contradiction when universalized. In chapter 1, I mentioned the consensual sibling incest taboo as a possible example. Kant's law is not sufficient for the moral, because it places demands on us that fall outside of the moral domain. Some authors have noted that Kant's universalization procedure may entail a categorical law pertaining to hypothetical imperatives (Hill, 1973). While no *particular* hypothetical imperative is categorical, there may be a categorical imperative pertaining to hypothetical imperatives in general: If you fully will an end, you also will the necessary means to that end that are within your power. If this is a categorical imperative, and categorical imperatives define morality, then every time we will the means to ends that we happen to have, we are doing what morality demands. Willing a trip to the pub when you desire a beer becomes a moral act. Some authors argue that Kant has no way to distinguish these imperatives from bona fide moral imperatives (Frei, 2005). If so, Kant's method of obtaining universality extends the moral domain beyond recognition. If we construe Kant as offering an analysis of moral concepts (rather than an analysis of some other class of obligations), then he can be accused of woefully missing his target. Kant's theory renders the moral domain both larger and narrower than it ought to be. Passions provide the procrustean rack and saw.

3.3 CONCLUSION

I began this chapter with an overview of a sensibility theory, and then I surveyed ten objections. I tried to show that these objections can be answered. Sensibility theories are more resilient than critics presume. But I would not want to rest my case yet. Sensibility theories face two serious objections that require more detailed discussion than I have offered in this chapter. First, there is a persistent intuition that morals are objective. Sensibility theories tend to stumble on this intuition, because they are committed to a rather strong form of subjectivism. In the next chapter, I address this concern. Second, sensibility theories seem to be committed to relativism. I have mentioned that throughout this chapter. Relativism is sometimes regarded as a vile doctrine. It is said to be reprehensible, mistaken, and even incoherent. I will argue otherwise in chapter 5.

4

Against Objectivity

The sensibility theory of morals is a subjectivist theory. To some, this is a sufficient reason for rejection. Morality is objective, they insist. It is an objective fact that killing innocent people is wrong. Subjectivism loses sight of this. It makes morality too dependent on us.

Subjectivists can respond to this objection in one of two ways. One strategy is to deny that objectivity and subjectivity are incompatible. Another is to deny that morality is objective. The former strategy has been more popular, but the latter is more viable. Objectivity and subjectivity are compatible, but morality is not objective. That's what I intend to argue.

I will begin by laying out several broad definitions of objectivity. Then I will survey leading ethical theories that have defended objectivism in one or another sense. Some of these objectivist theories are compatible with subjectivism, and others are not. All of them, I contend, have insurmountable flaws. If I am right, it may be time to abandon hope for ethical objectivism. I will conclude by pointing out that a flight from objectivism need not be a flight from realism. There are moral facts; they are just purely subjective facts.

4.1 SPECIES OF OBJECTIVITY

In chapter 3, I showed how sensibility theorists can satisfy the pretheoretical intuition that moral judgments can be true or false. A form of conduct is truly wrong for someone if that person has a sentiment of disapprobation toward it. I said that this captures an intuition that morality has something to do with how things really are in the world, without forfeiting the intuition that moral judgments derive from us. These two things appear to be incompatible, and the allegation of incompatibility lies at the heart of Mackie's argument that moral concepts are incoherent. In proving that moral judgments can be both true and intrinsically motivating, sensibility theorists undermine Mackie's argument (McDowell, 1985). But a defender of Mackie might complain that this is insufficient. According to Mackie (1977: 94), our intuitions demand not only that moral judgments can be true, but that they can be objectively true: "[O]rdinary moral judgments include a claim to 'objectivity,' . . . And I do not think it is going too far to say that this assumption has been incorporated into the basic, conventional meanings of moral terms." McDowell (1985) thinks that Mackie is right, and he tries to show that sensibility theories can allow for moral objectivity. I think Mackie is wrong.

Before making this case, we need to get clear on what objectivity is and why moral discourse might seem to be committed to the hypothesis that moral truths are objective. The term "objectivity" gets used in a variety of different ways. I will consider several.

According to the first definition, objectivity is tied to impartiality. An objective fact is one that is ascertained by an objective judgment, and an objective judgment is one that a person would make if she had all the evidence, no biases, and a good capacity for reasoning. Leiter (2001) calls freedom from bias "epistemic objectivity." It has something to do with the process by which we obtain knowledge. Nagel (1986) invokes the view from nowhere.

Impartiality is clearly compatible with subjectivity. Subjectivity can be defined in terms of mind-dependence, and an impartial judgment can be a judgment about something that depends on the mind. Indeed, impartiality always makes reference to the mind, insofar as it is an epistemic appellation. Judges, judgments, or opinions are impartial; facts are not. So when we say that a fact is objective, on the present definition, we are saying that it is ascertained by an impartial method of fixing beliefs. This means that objective facts can depend on us. For example, it might be an objective fact that Bach's Mass in B-minor is evocative, because beings like us would react emotionally to it, if we rid ourselves of any biases that would prevent us from appreciating the music (e.g., a dismissive distaste for baroque composition or Christian themes in art). Being evocative is quite plausibly a subjective property. So this feature of the Mass is objectively subjective. I will call this subjective impartiality.

Some impartial truths are not subjective. The term "impartiality" is sometimes used to designate judgments that are free from subjective responses. Or, more specifically, it is used to designate judgments that are dispassionate. Dispassionate judgments derive, not from subjective feelings, but from universal rules of reason. Call such judgments rationally impartial. Such judgments are objective, insofar as they are impartial, and rational, insofar as they are defined with reference to certain kinds of procedures for ascertaining knowledge. But rationally impartial judgments are not subjective in the sense that I have just been considering. They do not designate facts that obtain in virtue of our dispositions to have any responses. Rational judgments represent facts that would be true even if we failed to appreciate them. They are demanded by the rules of reason, which are strictures governing truth-preserving inference—strictures that we often fail to obey.

Impartiality is an epistemic construct. Leiter contrasts epistemic objectivity with a non-epistemic variety, which he calls metaphysical objectivity. He characterizes metaphysical objectivity in terms of mind-independence. The notion of mind-independence is itself ambiguous, however. On the one hand, mind-independence might mean existing independently of any mental states.

An objective fact, in this sense, is one that could obtain in a world without any minds. It would obtain even if minds never came to be and never could come to be. Call this transcendental objectivity. The fact that elms are deciduous is transcendentally objective. Internal realists or radical constructivists might disagree, arguing that the category of "elms" depends on human systems of classification, but we need not be distracted by such views here. The claim that elms are deciduous is made true at least in part by something that would be the case in a world without minds.

On the other hand, mind-independence might mean something like unrepresented. Something has a property objectively, in this sense, if having that property does not depend on being represented as having that property. Call this representation independence. I use the term "representation independence" instead of "response independence," because the word "response" is often used more narrowly, to refer to perceptual or affective states. I think responses are representations, but some representations are not responses, so I will stick with the broader term. A property can be strongly or weakly representation independent. A strongly representation-independent property is one that can be instantiated even if no one was ever disposed to represent that property. Transcendentally objective properties are strongly representation-independent, but strong representation-independence is a weaker notion. Facts about human psychology are often representation-independent but not transcendental. Trivially, they could not exist in a world without minds. To take an arbitrary example, consider the fact that human beings can recognize objects within 100 milliseconds of visual presentation. This is not a transcendental fact. It is a psychological fact. But it is representation-independent because our recognition speed would be the same even if we had never been able to measure it or think about it. Call facts that are strongly representation-independent but not mind-independent "psychological facts." These are facts about the mind, not facts created by the mind.

Psychological facts can be contrasted with weakly representation-independent facts. These are facts that *are* created by the mind. Dennett (1991) gives the example of being a suspect. Someone can be a suspect only as a result of being suspected. When Hercule Poirot considers the possibility that the butler committed the murder, the butler's metaphysical status changes. He becomes a suspect. His being a suspect requires that he be represented as such. But there is a sense in which being a suspect is perfectly objective. Once the butler has come under suspicion, he continues to be a suspect until that suspicion is officially discharged (e.g., as when the real culprit is identified). In fact, he may continue to be a suspect even if Hercule stops actively suspecting him. Suppose Hercule suddenly dies, and the case is not taken up by anyone else. The butler remains a suspect. Being a suspect does not depend on there being anyone who is currently harboring suspicions. It depends on a one-time intentional action of suspecting made by a person in an official investigative capacity. The property of being a suspect may be termed an "intentional product."

There are many different kinds of intentional products. Suppose a Viking explorer dubs his ship the *Skålbåd*. When we find this ship centuries later, there is no record of its name. It is an objective fact that this ship is the *Skålbåd* even though that fact is the result of an intentional action. This is true in the case of artifacts more generally. If someone crafts an object intending it as a paperweight, but forgets its function later on, it remains a paperweight. The class of intentional products also includes some institutional facts. If Fred and Wilma get married, but forget their vows later on due to senility, they remain married. Marriage is not established by intentions alone. Other institutional factors are necessary, but those factors depend ultimately on the past intentions and practices of a human population. They are, at least partially, intentional products.

I have identified several kinds of objective facts. They are based on different sorts of things. Subjectively impartial facts are based on subjective responses; rationally impartial facts are based on rules of reason; transcendental facts are based on how things are in the mind-external world; psychological facts are based on human psychology; and intentional products are based on human intentions and intentional acts. Some of these are compatible. Facts that are ascertained impartially can be intentional products or transcendental truths. Some are incompatible. Transcendental facts cannot be psychological facts, subjectively impartial facts, or intentionally produced facts. And something can be an objective fact of any one of these species, without being an objective fact in any of the other species. So ethical theorists who claim that moral facts are objective ought to be very specific about what kind of objectivity they have in mind. Differences between leading objectivist ethical theories can be characterized in terms of the taxonomy that I have offered here. For example, Kant is committed to the rational impartiality of moral judgment, but not committed to the idea that morality is independent of human psychology. The authority that moral rules have over us has something to do with human freedom and the structure of the will. If we did not act from laws, then we would not need to universalize in seeking reasons, and if we didn't universalize, reason would not lead us to pursue the good and avoid the bad. Having examined the Kantian program in chapter 3, I will not discuss rational impartiality again. But some ethical theorists push for other kinds of objectivity. I survey some leading examples in the next section. I don't think any of these theories succeed in finding an objective foundation for morality.

4.2 ARE MORAL TRUTHS OBJECTIVE?

4.2.1 Impartiality: Ideal Observers

The idea that morality might be both objective and subjective has appealed to a number of authors. Folk intuitions about morality seem to push in both directions. In defending sensibility theories, I invoked the intuition that moral judgments are inextricably bound to emotional reactions. Heeding this link promotes a kind of subjectivism. On the other hand, we tend to think that people are capable of being wrong in their moral reactions. Moral truths are not dictated by knee-jerk responses. If our judgments change after considering a situation in greater depth, we say that our earlier judgments were false. This gives the impression that moral judgments are objective.

To accommodate both of these intuitions, some philosophers have endorsed ideal observer theories. On this approach, something is right (or wrong) if it causes approbation (disapprobation) under ideal observation conditions. Hume (1757) is interpreted as defending a theory of this kind for aesthetic judgment. He says an artwork is good if it is favorably regarded by a good critic. A good critic is someone who has delicacy of taste, good sense, practice in making aesthetic judgments, and freedom from prejudice. Hume implies that all good critics will agree on their aesthetic evaluations. Baille (2000) suggests that Hume's moral theory can be interpreted along similar lines. Perhaps there are ideal moral critics (see Sayre-McCord, 1994, for a different interpretation of Hume). Francis Hutcheson (1738) may have held a view like this. In more recent times, the view has been defended by Firth (1952). He says that an ideal moral observer is omniscient, omnipercipient, disinterested, and dispassionate. Of course, no actual observers can achieve these things. The best we can do is approach the ideal. In so doing, Firth suggests, we have a greater chance of making moral judgments that are true.

If ideal observer theories are right, then morality is objective in one of the senses discussed above. Morality is subjectively impartial. But are ideal observer theories right? Before addressing this question, I want to note that ideal observer theories do not guarantee universality (see Brandt, 1954). It is quite possible that two people who have access to all the facts and no personal investments might form different moral assessments of the same situation. Our emotional reactions are influenced by biography, personality, core values, and other non-cognitive individual differences. Such variability is obvious when we shift from matters of value to matters of taste. Two fully informed observers might disagree about whether good Bordeaux is better than good Burgundy. As a sentimentalist, the defender of ideal observer theory must concede that values are not logically entailed by factual knowledge, so idealized information access underdetermines the ideal observer's evaluative judgments. If other factors bear on those judgments, and those factors are variable, ideal observers will not reach consensus. Ideal observers are impartial, hence objective in one sense, but divergent.

On the face of it, this observation does not undermine ideal observer theory. It merely illustrates the surprising compatibility of objectivism and relativism. On closer analysis, however, it exposes a serious problem. In presenting the ideal observer theory, I simply assumed that popular characterizations of ideal observers qualify as characterizations of impartial observers. This assumption may be false. For, if an observer has a set of basic values, and those values reflect her moral education, enculturation, or personality, then she cannot be said to be free from bias. Indeed, the idea of an unbiased evaluator may be incoherent. To evaluate is to express one's biases. Biases are personal preferences. The best one can do is try to liberate one's personal preferences from idiosyncratic features of one's biography. But how impersonal can an observer get? Can an observer bracket off preferences imparted by culture? Perhaps not. In practice, ignoring culturally imposed preferences is very difficult, because preferences are built into our affective responses and these are not amenable to direct or deliberative control.

The ideal observer theory might reply that such practical limitations are irrelevant. Ideal observation conditions are ideal, and they can only be approached asymptotically. What matters is principle, not practice. But there may be principled worries here too. Why suppose that a person who could, *per impossibile*, bracket culturally imparted preference would have any moral preference left. Moral responses require moral emotions, and moral emotions may emerge through enculturation. A person liberated from culture might be angered by certain things and saddened by others, but there is no guarantee that she would have full-fledged moral sentiments, since these, I have suggested, are acquired through a regimen of punishment, love withdrawal, and induction during moral development (see chapter 1). Once a person has developed a mature capacity for moral sentiments, there is no guarantee that she will have any opinion about how to apply those sentiments without taking cultural cues. The view from nowhere may be confused and morally indifferent. If we free ourselves from culture, we may free ourselves from morality as well.

Another worry is that severing ties to cultural bias may leave us with responses that are repugnant by cultural standards. To recover preferences that are not biased by culture, we must return to a precultural state. The thought of such a return awakens quaint Romantic fantasies, but Rousseau's dream may be a nightmare. Preference schemes that are not culturally informed may license impropriety, brutality, and rape. If the behavior of great apes is any indication of what human values would be like without the edifice of cultural history, the values of the unenculturated mind are hardly worthy of deference. Moreover, the unenculturated mind is not an unbiased mind. It is just a mind whose biases reflect more nature than nurture.

I have been suggesting that it is imprudent to strive for true impartiality. But the most important issue in assessing ideal observer theory is descriptive. Do people really, as a matter fact, regard impartial moral judgments to be authoritative? This question would have to be investigated empirically, but I am willing to bet that strong forms of impartiality do not play a prominent role in moral thought. Admittedly, we do value careful reflection, full factual knowledge, and disinterest when deciding what is right. Legal systems are a testament to that. But we also have a stake in the values of the groups to which we belong. Consider moral rules regulating kinship relations. When asked whether monogamous relationships are right, I would predict that most people have little tendency to consider the issue from a transcendental stance. They would not defer to someone who said that, in other cultural settings, monogamy is not always valued. They would say instead that "we value monogamy," and that's what really matters. Putting the point more generally, in making moral judgments, we don't try to accommodate what just anyone would value; we try to accommodate what *we* value, where "we" refers to evaluator and the evaluator's cultural group. If we value democracy and people in another cultural setting don't, we have little interest in making moral judgments from their point of view, and little hope of finding a helpful common ground.

In sum, I suspect that ideal observer theories, when taken to demand total impartiality, are not accurate descriptions of our goals in moral reasoning. Complete impartiality is not our ideal, and partial impartiality is not fully objective. If I am right, we seek good observation conditions because we want to discern what conforms best to our biases, not because we want freedom from bias.

4.2.2 Transcendentalism: Natural Kinds

The idea that moral truths are transcendental in the full sense seems peculiar at first. Morality governs the lives of intelligent creatures. It has no place in a universe without minds. The idea that moral rules can exist mind-independently sounds very implausible. On further reflection, however, this idea actually has a long and distinguished history. Many people believe that morality is handed down by a supernatural being. Morality is a divine command. On this view morality has important connections to the mind: it is intended for creatures with a faculty for understanding, it is intended to regulate human affairs, and it is imposed by a being with supreme intelligence. But, in a more restricted sense, a divine command morality is transcendental. To see this, let me distinguish between two kinds of mind-dependence. First, something may be mind-dependent in that it supervenes on psychological facts; if it were different, psychology would have to be different too. Psychological supervenience subsumes cases of what I called representation-dependence above. Facts that are representation-dependent cannot change without us changing what we represent (or what we are disposed to represent). Second, something may be mind-dependent in that it is *applicable* only to psychological agencies without supervening on them; for example, if something is a "lesson," it must be a lesson for a mind. Divine commands are mind-dependent in this second sense. They are applicable only to minds. But divine command theory is not fully mind-dependent in the first sense. A supernatural being could change the moral rules without changing our psychology. Of course, divine commands do supervene on psychological facts about the divine commanders, but they do not necessarily supervene on the minds of those whom they govern. So, divine commands transcend human minds in this sense. If we restrict transcendentalism in this way (morals are not generally supervenient on human psychology), then transcendentalist theories of morality begin to look possible.

Divine command theories do not enjoy the popularity that they once did. Many moralists have given up gods, and many others have been convinced by the kind of reasoning in Plato's *Euthyphro* that morality must have a non-theological foundation even if gods exist. On the divine command theory, the claim that God is good just means that God acts in accordance with his own wishes. That is faint praise. Morality must have another source. It turns out that the Euthyphro insight is widely, though implicitly, recognized by people with strong religious faith. Nucci (2001) conducted a series of experiments (mentioned in chapter 1) to probe the moral values of young people from different religious groups: Catholics, Orthodox and Conservative Jews, and Mennonites. He wanted to know whether they would regard an immoral act, such as hurting or stealing, as wrong even if there were no divine prescription against it. He asked them whether these things would still be wrong if God has not prohibited them. The response was overwhelming. Between 80 and 100 percent of the religious children in his studies said "yes": stealing and hurting are wrong regardless of divine command. This suggests that divine command theories do not fully capture the moral concepts of believers. The major fault with divine command theories isn't the theological premises upon which they are based. The problem is that most people do not really believe that morality depends on divine command, even if they are religious, and even if they would assent to such a claim. Divine command theory is not a good analysis of ordinary moral concepts.

Does this prove that transcendental theories of morality are all wrong? Perhaps not. Transcendentalism need not be theologically based. Kant's reason-based morality comes close to being transcendental, but it does not go all the way, because normativity depends for Kant on aspects of human nature (especially our capacity to act from duty). To see what a non-theological transcendental theory might look like, imagine a program that tried to defend moral truths by appeal to features that are intrinsic to the situations that we hold in moral regard. One might try to argue that cruelty is wrong in virtue of its intrinsic properties, not in virtue of how we are constituted. On this view, wrongness and rightness would be natural properties, rather than supernatural properties. Indeed they would be like natural kinds insofar as their existence did not depend on facts about us. Wrong and right would be like uranium and elephants.

My goal here is not to flesh out a theory along these lines. I will address a prior question. Do we take our moral concepts to refer to natural kinds? Do moral concepts aim to pick out mind-independent features of the world? The brief discussion of divine command theory already hints at the answer. If the Mennonite boy is representative of the rest of us, then moral concepts do not presuppose a transcendental foundation.

The idea that moral concepts are natural kind concepts faces some difficulties. We generally assume that the essences of natural kinds are unknown to us and that we discover them using scientific instruments. Even when we don't have those instruments at our disposal, we often have a sense of what kinds of instruments are necessary and where we should look. This contrasts with the moral case. We do not presume that moral properties have hidden essences in the same sense. What tools would we use to discover the good? Where should we begin to look? What sort of essences does wrongness have?

Moral concepts and natural kind concepts also exhibit different patterns of deference. With natural kind concepts, we assume that there are experts who have special access to the essences of things. We defer to chemists, biologists, geologists, and others who are in the business of discovering hidden essences. With moral concepts, we are less likely to defer. We may listen carefully to family members, or community leaders, or religious authorities, but we also presume that we personally have access to moral truths. Moral authorities can help guide us to the good, but when they do so, it is as if they are helping us see things that we already have the capacity to discern on our own. We take ourselves to be moral authorities. When our own moral intuitions diverge from alleged moral experts, we tend to think that the experts are wrong. We do not claim to have such authority with tigers or titanium.

In addition, there is an important semantic contrast between natural kind concepts and moral concepts. With natural kind concepts, we can construct Twin-Earth cases (Putnam, 1975). Two people who are exact duplicates of each other in all of their intrinsic properties could have concepts that referred to different things if they lived on different worlds. In a parallel universe where the stuff that looks like gold has a different chemical constitution, the word "gold" and the corresponding concept refer to something other than gold. This does not seem to be the case with moral concepts (see Horgan and Timmons, 1990–1). If we consider two people who are exact duplicates and situate them in different worlds, it seems that their moral concepts will be the *same*; their concepts of right and wrong will refer to the same properties. This is not to deny the fact that some moral judgments would change truth values if the world were different. For example, factory farming might be okay if cows were not sentient. But no facts about the world seem to bear on core moral values. If it is a basic value for you that sentient creatures should not be tortured, then the same value is held by your duplicate on Twin Earth and, intuitively, the concepts that enter into this value have the same referents, and no facts about the world could render your value true while his is false. For it's not at all clear how we would go about settling a moral dispute between counterparts on Earth and Twin Earth: what fact about the world could settle which side of the debate was right? Intuitions about such cases suggest that we do not construe moral concepts in the same way that we construe natural kind concepts.

Together, these observations suggest that we do not take moral concepts to refer to properties with deeply hidden essences. But this does not exhaust the options available to the transcendental objectivist. Perhaps moral concepts refer to aspects of the mind-independent world that are not hidden in any deep way. Consider concepts that refer to Lockean primary qualities, such as shape concepts. Shapes are readily discerned. All of us can be shape experts. Perhaps moral concepts aim to refer to something like that.

To test for mind-independence, what really matters are not hidden essences, but moral properties. We assume that mind-independent entities can exist without us. Uranium and gold would exist if we didn't. Likewise for shapes. We assume that shapes would exist without us. Of course, they have existed without us already. The world had shapes before it had minds. Things were round or angular or oblong before there were any sentient creatures around to appreciate these things.

But what about moral properties? Do we presume that they could exist without us? In a certain sense, obviously not. A world without highly intelligent beings has no place for morality. Unlike shapes, moral properties, such as wrongness or rightness seem to be instantiated only when there are creatures who can appreciate them. When a lioness kills a wildebeest, we do not say that she did something immoral. Immorality requires the capacity to comprehend moral rules. This makes immorality quite unlike the property of being round or square.

The defender of mind-independence might concede that moral properties are unlike shapes while still holding out hope for a kind of objectivism. Recall my earlier example of a lesson. Lessons couldn't exist unless there were learners, but being a lesson does not supervene on psychological facts. Perhaps moral properties are like that. They are properties that relate to minds without supervening on minds.

This response will not help, however, because lessons differ from morals in a crucial respect. Arguably, to be a lesson, something just needs to be directed at a learner. The learner need not have the capacity to understand the lesson; lessons can be poorly designed. Their connection to the mind has to do with their purpose, not their content, though, in successful cases, the content is well-designed for its purpose. Moral rules seem to be different. They must be understandable if they are to apply. When a lioness fails to comply with strictures against killing innocent creatures, we do not say that she committed an iniquity unwittingly. If moral rules were the products of divine command, we might say that they were like lessons. We might say that they could exist even without a comprehending audience. But we do not seem to regard moral rules this way. We do not assume that moral rules can exist in a world without intelligent creatures. That assumption is at best non-compulsory and at worst incoherent. If our moral concepts were committed to a strong form of mind-independence, we should embrace the assumption without hesitation.

Defenders of mind-independence can try to stand their ground by invoking further modal intuitions. Rather than imagining a world without intelligent creatures, let's imagine a world where intelligent creatures simply fail to appreciate moral rules. Intuitively, killing innocent people would be wrong even if no one recognized that it was wrong. In fact, killing innocent people would be wrong even if the human race became so corrupted that we were not even disposed to recognize the wrongness of such acts. That gives the impression that wrongness enjoys a kind of independence from psychology. The intuition just invoked is especially embarrassing for sensibility theories. Wrongness is not conceptually bound to response dispositions.

I am not sure that we really do have the modal intuitions just invoked. Some people might be happy to say that killing innocent people would be fine if people were not disposed to think otherwise. In a post-apocalyptic, dog-eat-dog world, present morality might not apply. Morality may have no place in the Hobbesian state of nature. The intelligibility of this supposition can be empirically investigated. We can ask subjects whether moral rules apply in a community of mass corruption. As far as I know, no one has performed an experiment asking that particular question, but there are some empirical results that cast doubt on the question of whether ordinary users of moral concepts are committed to objectivism. For example, Kelly et al. (2007) found that subjects are willing to say that certain actions (such as a sea captain beating a drunken sailor) are not okay for us, but okay when done by members of other cultures. They use this result to criticize the moral/conventional distinction, and, in chapter 3, I suggested that their conclusion may be premature. But their results do raise the possibility that people may be open to a certain degree of relativism about morality. (Further studies will have to determine whether subjects think that behaviors performed in other cultures are morally okay or just excusable for some reason.)

Shaun Nichols (2004*b*) performed a more direct test of whether people are moral objectivists. In a series of studies, subjects were first told to imagine an argument between a person in our culture and a person in a culture that tolerates hitting or shoving innocent people "just for the fun of it." They were then asked whether one party to this debate was objectively right or whether there is no objective fact of the matter about who is right. In every study, a sizable portion (as many as 66 percent) gave the non-objectivist answer. This finding is consistent with other research that suggests individual differences in moral ideology. Forsyth (1980) developed a scale for measuring moral personality types, and that scale has been used in a considerable number of studies that classify people as having a relativist outlook or an absolutist outlook. He found a split between those who postulated universal moral values and those who deny such values. This suggests that intuitions about objectivity are divided. If so, there are two possibilities. Either people in these groups have different concepts of morality, objectivist for some and non-objectivist for others. Or, alternatively, objectivism is not a conceptual truth but is rather an independent belief about morality. This latter alternative is a bit more attractive because it seems that moral objectivists can coherently wonder whether morality is objective. If objectivism were a conceptual truth, this would be impossible. Perhaps moral concepts are ordinarily silent on the question of objectivism, and beliefs about objectivism are option add-ons, which may arise late in moral development, if at all.

Let's put this point to one side, and assume the objectivists are right about the intuitions. Let's assume that people ordinarily take moral rules to apply even when no one is disposed to recognize them. Can the sensibility theorist accommodate intuitions about unrecognized wrongs? I think so. One move is to rigidify. Let "wrong" refer to whatever people are *currently* disposed to condemn on reflection. People are currently disposed to condemn killing. So when we say that killing would be wrong even if we became corrupted, we are grounding the word in current usage. The sentence is perfectly true. If we become corrupted in the future, killing is still such that we (now) are disposed to condemn it. Rigidification gives moral truths a kind of tenacity under counterfactual conditions. The modal intuitions can be captured in this way. They pose no threat to sensibility theories.

This last point shows that sensibility theories can explain modal intuitions just as well as transcendental objectivist theories. Thus, we have a stalemate. Sensibility theories inch ahead of transcendentalism when we consider the independent arguments for subjectivism in chapter 1, and the doubts about transcendentalism raised earlier in this section. For example, I have suggested that we tend to think morals exist only in a world of beings who can appreciate them. That intuition supports sensibility theories. Of course, that intuition clashes with the intuition that moral rules would exist if we all became corrupted. The rigidification proposal reconciles these two intuitions, and sensibility theories edge out ahead of transcendentalism, because they can easily handle both intuitions.

I want to conclude this section by raising one final point that echoes a lesson from chapter 1. Thus far, I have been arguing against the hypothesis that moral concepts aim to pick out mind-independent properties. Contra transcendentalism, we do not ordinarily assume that moral concepts designate properties that are objective in that sense. My final observation is that arguments against transcendentalism would still be possible if moral concepts *did* aim to pick out mind-independent properties. A concept can aim to pick out such properties and fail.

Consider color again. It is very plausible that color concepts aim for transcendental objectivity. That is to say that we assume our color concepts designate real features of the mind-external world. We locate colors in the surfaces of things, and we assume that the world was colored before we came on the scene. But suppose that the world doesn't comply. Suppose that there are no features of surfaces out there that systematically correspond to our color concepts. Suppose that there is no way to group the properties that cause us to have particular color experiences into tidy classes without mentioning the fact that they cause those experiences. Do we conclude that colors do not exist? Some philosophers go this route (Hardin, 1993a), but it is not the only option. We can conclude instead that colors are just different from what we had initially believed. We can conclude that colors are response-dependent properties. For each color concept, there is a highly heterogeneous set of surface properties that are unified by their capacity to cause certain responses in us.

I think the second option is better than the first. It's extremely useful to believe that colors exist, because they play systematic roles in our lives, and few of our color-oriented practices depend on the assumption that colors are mind-independent. In this respect, color is unlike "phlogiston," which is postulated in theoretical contexts and plays no role in daily life, or "witch," which could not play its intended role in daily life if we abandoned the assumption that witches have supernatural powers. Consider some ordinary cases in which we make reference to the color blue. The manager of a clothing boutique might hang all the blue items together on a single rack. A woman might decide she is pregnant when a thin blue line appears on her pregnancy test. After an eyewitness tip, police might stop all people driving blue sedans. Picasso created a series of paintings in shades of blue. "Blue" is a projectable predicate, at least at the macro-level. If we know that Otto likes blue blazers, shirts, and slacks, we can safely buy him a blue necktie. All of these practices effectively reify blue; they are a sufficient condition for saying that blue exists. But notice that none of these practices depends on the claim that blue is mind-independent. The category of blue things may have no intrinsic unity. Its boundaries may be entirely determined by us. We call certain things "blue" in virtue of the fact that they have similar effects on our trichromatic visual systems. But even those effects underdetermine color boundaries. In Russian there is no word for blue. There are words for light blue (*goluboy*) and dark blue (*siniy*) but no word for blue in general. They draw a categorical boundary between shades that English speakers group together (compare our red and pink). If an English speaker likes dark blue, she probably likes light blue, but, if a Russian speaker likes *goluboy*, she may not like *siniy* (again, compare red and pink). Examples like this underscore the mind-dependence of color space. The categories depend on our responses. This is an interesting discovery about colors, but it does not force us to be color anti-realists. Given the robustness of human color practices, it's more plausible to say that colors are real but mind-dependent. When Russians classify things as *goluboy* or *siniy*, they engender two properties, which can be used to make generalizations, to guide behavior, and to organize items in the world.

The ordinary concept of blue aims to pick out a mind-independent property and fails. But that failure does not entail failed reference. Think about BLUE as a concept with a fallback plan. It would refer to a property that is mind-independent if such a property were reliably tuned to our blue experiences. If there is no such property, it refers to the property of causing blue in us, regardless of whether that property has any greater integrity. I suspect that many concepts have fallback plans. The concept DOG aims to pick out a natural kind, but, if no natural kind is reliably linked to our use of this concept, it refers instead to a class of creatures that share similar morphological and behavioral properties. If oceans and lakes had been filled with a great variety of chemicals, WATER would not pick out a natural kind, but it would still refer. Or, to take actual examples, the concept WEED may refer to the things we take to be weeds and PNEUMONIA may refer to several conditions that are alike in symptoms, despite differences in etiology (bacteria, fungi, viruses, mycoplasmas, etc.).

I submit that even if moral concepts aim to pick out properties that are mind-independent, they may fail, and, if they fail, they fall back on mind-dependent properties. This observation supplements the reply to Mackie, begun in chapter 3. There I recited McDowell's point that the sensibility theorist makes moral judgments both intrinsically motivating and capable of being true. We can correctly say that cruelty is wrong, and, in so saying, be disposed to act. But, Mackie might respond that the species of truth available to the sensibility theorist does not capture pretheoretical intuitions. Folk thinking about morality demands that moral truth be mind-independent. Since something cannot be both mind-independent and mind-dependent (i.e., essentially motivating), moral concepts must be incoherent, hence vacuous. In response, I say two things. Moral concepts do not aim to pick out mind-independent properties, as Mackie claims, and, even if they did, they would not be vacuous.

Mackie assumes that if moral concepts fail to latch onto objective properties, they are vacuous. This assumption rests on an overly strict semantic theory. Mackie fails to realize that concepts can contain mistakes. Putnam (1975) gives the example of the GORILLA concept, which, for many people, contains the feature FEROCIOUS. (Putnam used this example in the early 1970s. It may be less true now that Dianne Fossey's research has trickled down into folk wisdom. We no longer derive all gorilla knowledge from King Kong.) If ferocity is a feature in our GORILLA concepts, then those concepts contain an error. Gorillas are docile. Nevertheless, our GORILLA concepts manage to denote gorillas, because they contain a number of other features, and those features allow the concept to become reliably correlated with gorillas. If moral concepts contain errors, it does not follow that they are vacuous. If they aim to pick out objective properties (which I doubt), and those objective properties do not exist, then they can revert to representing properties that accord with other features. They refer to properties that are essentially motivating, even if not objective. The utility and projectability of moral categories, like colors and gorillas, testifies to their non-vacuity.

4.2.3 Psychological Facts 1: Virtue Theory

Transcendental objectivists claim that moral properties are strongly independent of us. They claim that moral properties are representation-independent *and* that morality does not depend on any psychological facts. Some ethical theorists drop the second claim, while retaining the first. They say that moral properties supervene on facts about psychology, to a significant degree, but that moral truths would obtain even if we were not disposed to recognize them. I have already argued that we are not conceptually committed to response-independence. There is, however, a class of ethical theories that makes response-independence sound plausible. These are virtue theories. They say that moral truths derive from truths about virtues, and the virtues derive from facts about human nature, including our psychological nature. Virtue theories assume that there is a link, therefore, between morality and psychology. The virtues are typically taken to be traits of character that allow or constitute human flourishing (cf. Aristotle, 350 BCE). So one cannot change morality, on a virtue theory, without changing something about character or flourishing—something psychological. This means that morality is mind-dependent for the virtue theorist, but not response-dependent. Virtue theories are objectivist theories insofar as they ground morality in psychological facts that could obtain without our taking notice of them.

Virtue theories have become increasingly popular in recent years, and they have also come under empirical attack. Critics argue that character traits are empirically indefensible. I believe that this attack is ultimately unsuccessful, but virtue theory suffers from other fatal flaws.

Virtue theories are normative theories, but unlike other normative theories, they are not primarily in the business of prescribing actions. Virtue theories tell us what kind of people we should be, not how we should act. Action, of course, comes for the ride. We should do as virtuous people would do, but we should do so by cultivating the virtues in ourselves. But what exactly are virtues? According to prevailing theories, they are laudable traits of character. A character trait is an enduring aspect of personality that disposes one to act or react in particular ways. Aristotle, who developed an especially seminal virtue theory, emphasized such traits as courage, magnanimousness, truthfulness, temperance, liberality with finances, patience, wittiness, and friendliness. He claimed that each of these lies between undesirable extremes. Courage lies between cowardice and rashness; liberality lies between extravagance and thriftiness; friendliness lies between obsequiousness and cantankerousness. Each of these triads belongs to a different domain. Courage pertains to confidence in the face of danger; friendliness pertains to social interactions; and liberality pertains to spending.

Virtue ethics is generally supposed to be grounded in human nature. The traits are supposed to capture something about how we are, or rather, how we are ideally. Humans flourish most, when they express their humanity most fully and fruitfully, when they posses virtuous character traits. Strictly speaking, one can be a virtue ethicist without invoking such character traits (Thomson, 1997; Harman, 2001). One can talk, instead, of courageous, friendly, or magnanimous actions. But theories that talk about actions rather than traits give up on the tie between morality and human nature, which is so important on more orthodox virtue theories. The mandates that we should act honestly, courageously, generously, and so on, sound more like mandates of mainstream normative ethical theories. It is a return to the view that ethics should tell us how to act, not what kind of people we should be. I will focus on character-based virtue ethics.

Character-based virtue ethics has recently come under attack on empirical grounds. The virtues are traditionally conceived of as character traits, but many social psychologists regard character traits as a defective construct. Behavior is not determined by character, these psychologists claim, but by external features of the situations that we happen to find ourselves in (e.g., Mischel, 1968; Ross and Nisbett, 1991). Doris (1998; 2002) and Harman (1999) argue that the empirical findings that support this situationist approach are fatal to character-based virtue ethics (see also Flanagan, 1991; Merritt, 2000; and Vranas, 2005). Virtue ethicists define traits as broad, enduring, and efficacious: they influence behavior in a consistent way over a wide range of situations. Evidence from social psychology raises doubts about whether such traits exist. In reality, behavior is strongly influenced by circumstances. Minor features of a situation can sway behavior, and people who claim to have different character traits will be equally swayed. If traits don't exist, then a moral theory that asks us to cultivate traits is asking for the impossible.

Let's look at some of the examples used by Harman and Doris. They both cite one of Stanley Milgram's classic obedience studies (described in Milgram, 1974). Subjects in this experiment were instructed to ask another volunteer, located in an adjacent room, a series of questions. Each time the second volunteer failed to answer a question correctly, the subject asking the questions was asked to administer an electric shock using a dial with increasing voltages. Unbeknownst to the subject the second volunteer was really a stooge working with the experimenter, and the voltage dial was a harmless prop. The stooges were instructed to make errors so that the subjects would have to administer shocks. At preplanned stages, the stooges would express pain, voice concerns about safety, make sounds of agony, pound on the wall, or, ultimately, stop making any noise at all. If a subject conveyed reluctance to continue increasing the voltage, the experimenter would reply that it was crucial for the experiment to continue. The experiment ended if and when a subject persistently refused to continue.

Surprisingly, all of Milgram's subjects turned the dial to 300 volts, which was labeled "intense shock," or farther. Even more disturbingly, 65 percent of Milgram's subjects turned the dial to the maximum level of 450 volts, which was simply labeled "XXX." By that point, the stooge was totally silent, indicating unconsciousness or even worse. Milgram did not find significant individual differences in his subjects, and all seemed to be very susceptible to blind obedience when coaxed by an authority figure.

Harman and Doris also discuss a study by Darley and Batson (1973). They invited seminary students to deliver a sermon on the biblical parable of the Good

Samaritan. All subjects filled out personality questionnaires and questionnaires about their religious convictions. The experimenters made sure that some of the subjects would run late for the sermon, some would have just enough time, and some would have more than enough time. On the road leading to the locale of the sermon, they had a stooge lie, slumped over, coughing, and groaning in pain. 63 percent of the students who were running early helped out, whereas only 10 percent who were running late offered help. Personality and religiosity variables had no impact.

Doris discusses another study, which shows that the situational factors influencing behavior can be remarkably trivial. Isen and Levin (1972) had a stooge drop a stack of papers to see whether bystanders would help. Beforehand, they set things up so that some bystanders would find a dime in a public phone just before. Eighty-eight percent of those who found a dime helped out, and only 4 percent of those who didn't find a dime helped out. Dramatic differences in behavior can be driven by a tiny unexpected reward. Doris concludes that character cannot have much impact on behavior, if such minimal circumstantial factors can drive the difference between human decency and selfish indifference.

These findings are just a few well-publicized examples from a large literature showing similar effects. They seem to show that the best predictor of behavior is not character, but predicament. Character-based virtue ethics is based on bad folk psychology.

Defenders of virtue ethics have replied to this critique in various ways (Kupperman, 2001; Sreenivasan, 2002; Annas, 2003; Kamtekar, 2004). I will not review this growing literature, but I want to mention three recurring themes. One response is that the virtues are supposed to be hard to achieve. Of course, this reply is an expression of faith in the absence of empirical evidence. It would be easier to believe that virtuous traits are possible if there were good evidence for vicious traits. But if the situationists are right, there is no good evidence for broad, efficacious character traits. If so, achieving virtue would require the cultivation of psychological mechanisms that depart radically from how human minds usually operate. This would seem to make virtue not just hard, but almost impossible.

Another common objection to Doris and Harman is that they misrepresent the nature of traits, as understood within the virtue theory tradition. Virtue theorists define traits as practical reasoning skills, not as inflexible automatic reactions; thus, the fact that people respond differently across situations does not threaten the relevant conception of traits. The problem with this objection is that situationist experiments raise doubts about robust practical reasoning skills. For example, Milgram's (1974) subjects engage in extensive practical reasoning during his obedience experiment, but the situational factors determine how they reason, and lead them to make bad choices.

A third objection to Doris and Harman is that the experiments may introduce factors that can be rationally regarded as good reasons for behaving in otherwise unscrupulous ways. For example, Milgrim's subjects may form the rational belief that a scientist in a lab coat would not lead them into evil, and Darley and Bateson's subjects may form the rational belief that it would be wrong to keep their professor and audience waiting, when they have been asked to give a lecture. On this explanation, subjects in these experiments are not blindly swamped by extraneous situational factors, but rather presented with relevant facts that are used to make rational, perhaps even virtuous, decisions. I find this response especially insidious, because it implies that we should let the subjects in these experiments off the hook. Surely, fear of tardiness is not a good reason to abandon someone who is groaning in pain; the audience and professor would forgive—even applaud—the student for arriving late under these circumstances. And surely faith in scientists is not a good reason to ignore a person who is begging for mercy; subjects in Milgrim's experiment reported afterwards that they thought that their shocks might be fatal. Furthermore, the suggestion that the situationist experiments introduce variables that can be used to rationally support the observed behavior does not explain the Isen and Levin results. Finding a dime is not a *reason* to be helpful to others.

To undermine Doris and Harman's critique, one would need to find experimental evidence that contradicts the bleak assessment of character traits found in the situationist literature. Such research is not hard to find. Situationism is not the dominant view in personality psychology. Many psychologists believe in traits, and they base their faith on scores of studies that show certain aspects of personality to be highly stable and predicatively valid. Certain traits seem to remain constant over years, and they seem to have a measurable and reliable impact on behavior. For example, personality psychologists have identified five trait dimensions that are highly robust (Costa and McCrae, 1992). One dimension, Neuroticism, includes traits that span from high anxiety, on the one end, to high stability on the other. Another dimension, Extroversion, spans from high gregariousness to total introversion. The third dimension is Openness, which includes traits such as imaginativeness, at one pole, and rigid lack of imagination on the other. Agreeableness, the fourth dimension, spans from trustworthiness and altruism to unpleasantly egoistic personality types. The final dimension, Conscientiousness, spans from order, discipline, and dutifulness, to their disorderly, irresponsible opposites. In a meta-analysis, Roberts and DelVecchio (2000) found that these traits are highly consistent across the lifespan. In childhood, correlations range from 0.35 to 0.51, and, in adulthood, correlations range from 0.57 to 0.75. These traits are also known to correlate with a variety of behavioral variables, including job performance (Ones et al., 1993), marital relationships (Caughlin et al., 2000), risk-taking (Krueger et al., 2000), and antisocial behavior (Lynam et al., 2005). Traits are not the only factor, of course, but they make a measurable contribution.

These findings contradict strong forms of situationism, but they can be reconciled with situationist results. It is evident that situational factors can override the behavior dispositions of character. An adequate theory of behavior would allow for interactions between situation and traits, and it would specify the conditions under which each factor is most likely to dominate. Buss (1989) offers a useful overview of the conditions that make a difference. Situational factors tend to influence behavior in tasks when context is novel, instructions are detailed, choice is diminished, duration is brief, or response is narrowly defined. Traits tend to influence behavior in tasks where context is familiar, instructions are not given, considerable choice is available, duration is long, and responses are broadly defined. In the Milgram obedience studies, subjects are given little choice and their instructions are detailed; in the Darley and Bateson Good Samaritan study, instructions are also detailed, because subjects are supposed to be delivering a lecture. In the Isen and Levin study, the situation is novel and brief. Thus, apparent conflicts between situationists and their opponents can be resolved by paying close attention to task demands. Since traits seem to play a big role in some tasks, it is safe to conclude that trait-based theories are potentially relevant to those tasks. Cultivating good character for situations where character can have an impact may be worthwhile. Situationist findings expose limits on the scope and efficacy of character but they do not render trait constructs null and void.

Doris and Harman might complain that the character traits emphasized in personality psychology bear little resemblance to the traits emphasized in the virtue ethics tradition. Traits such as neuroticism and extroversion are difficult to fit into Aristotle's list, and they may have limited moral relevance. If the five trait dimensions that I have been discussing were the only robust elements of character, virtue theory would still be in trouble. This rejoinder can be answered by looking at research that goes beyond the so-called "big five" dimensions of personality. For example, Paunonen and Jackson (2000) found evidence for nine other dimensions. Altering their labels slightly, they found evidence for: Religiosity, Cunning, Honesty, Sensuality, Thriftiness, Conservativeness, Gender (masculinity or femininity), Arrogance, and Wittiness. Some of these coincide with Aristotle's virtues. Thriftiness, Arrogance, Honesty, and Wittiness are all discussed in his work.

As an interim moral, then, I conclude that character traits may be in good standing and may encompass traits that are of interest to virtue ethicists. The Doris and Harman critique fails because it is based on a denial of these claims. Given the existence of morally relevant traits, they would need to provide further arguments for the inefficacy of those traits and, at this point, the evidence simply isn't available.

In spite of all this, I do not want to conclude that virtue theories are true. I think they suffer from another flaw, and that flaw relates, in part, to the findings that I have been discussing. The real issue is not the reality of character traits, but rather, their place in the foundations of morality. Virtue theorists would have us believe that moral goodness and badness derive from facts about virtues and that the virtues have their moral standing in some non-derivative way. The virtues are supposed to be moral rock-bottom. The problem is that this conclusion cannot be sustained.

The word "virtue" refers to a character trait that is good. But what makes a trait good? The standard response in virtue theory is that good traits are more natural then bad traits. It is part of the human design, part of our natural teleology to have certain traits and not others. Someone who lacks virtue is not fulfilling the proper function of human beings.

I can identify two strategies for cashing out the idea that virtues are grounded in human nature. On an indirect strategy, one could argue that certain traits are conducive to or constitutive of what we would naturally regard as well-being. Those who lack the virtues won't flourish. On the direct approach, one could argue that certain traits are themselves more natural. Let me consider these options in turn.

The problem with the first approach is that there is little evidence supporting the claim that well-being is a natural construct. There is significant cross-cultural variation in what counts as the good life (for reviews, see Diener et al., 2003; Tiberius, 2003). For example, in Western populations, well-being is highly correlated with such things as self-satisfaction, freedom, positive emotions, and goal achievement. These factors tend to be less important for well-being in Far Eastern cultures. There people are more likely to emphasize acceptance by others, making others happy, and driving toward goals. Neither of these conceptions of well-being has a claim to being more natural; they simply reflect cultural differences in values. If conceptions of well-being are shaped by culture, then no set of character traits can said to be more naturally constitutive of well-being.

Turn now to the idea that virtues are just more natural than other traits. Aristotle presents his virtues as middle-points, between unlikable extremes. This elegant framework makes his traits appear like natural equilibria. Because they lie in the middle, virtues appear healthy and natural, just as satiety lies between starvation and overindulgence. But this is all an illusion. While some of Aristotle's traits probably exist, his dimensions may not. The traits that he placed in the middle of two extremes may actually reside at the poles. For example, Aristotle puts truthfulness in the middle of a range that extends from self-aggrandizing boastfulness to self-effacing bashfulness. But truthfulness might actually be an extreme in a dimension that extends from honesty to dishonesty. The traits we value may be inelegantly distributed across the dimensions of personality. Some might be in the middle, and some might be near the ends. Once we realize that the virtues have a messy distribution along dimensions of character, this seductive story begins to sound like a Siren call, beckoning us onto the rocks.

One might abandon Aristotle's elegant taxonomy and argue that the virtues are more natural in another sense: they are the traits that we are evolved to possess. This Darwinian alternative is not very promising, however. Human personalities vary, and that variation is perfectly natural. Some of the variation in basic traits seems to have a genetic basis (Jang et al. 1996), and all traits within the normal range are compatible with productive lives and reproductive success. There may even be benefit to our species in individual differences. A variety of traits may allow people to play different roles (suppose everyone wanted to be the alpha male or the alpha female). Even traits that we strongly disvalue may be highly adaptive. Antisocial personalities reproduce, on average, more than other people, and game theoretic models suggest that having a small percentage of them around may help us maintain good skills for detecting cheaters and wrongdoers (see Mealey, 1995). The cruel and the cunning can thrive, and we can thrive better in virtue of having a few of them around. So, when we turn to questions about human nature, we find only human natures, in the plural (Ehrlich, 2000). We find that a variety of very different traits with a different moral status are adaptive. We have many different bioprograms. Grounding virtue in human nature is dubious biology.

I conclude with one final objection. Suppose, against all evidence, that human nature did favor one suite of character traits over the others. Suppose, against all the evidence, that those traits happen to coincide with the traits that we pretheoretically regard as virtuous. We can still ask why these traits are *morally* good. Certainly being natural is not sufficient for being morally good. Defecation is not a noble act. Something else must give the virtues their moral status. Sensibility theories can provide an answer. The difference between a virtuous trait and a trait that lacks moral significance is determined by our sentiments. We *value* certain traits. Valuing them consists in emotional dispositions. So far I have focused on moral values pertaining to how people should act. But we can also have sentiments directed toward character traits. We detest greediness and feel ashamed of cowardliness. It is sentiments that make these traits good, not nature, though nature may exert some influence on our sentiments. If I am right, then virtue theory is not a path to moral objectivism. The virtues attain high station because of the reactions they arouse in us.

4.2.4 Psychological Facts 2: Consequentialism

Virtue ethicists attempt to secure response-independence without divorcing morality from psychology. In this, they are not alone. There is another celebrated tradition within ethical theory that has similar goals. That, of course, is consequentialism. Consequentialists say that the moral merit depends on outcome. More exactly, they offer a theory of what is good, and a theory of what is right. In giving a theory of the good, consequentialists try to identify things that have intrinsic value. Classical utilitarians, such as Bentham and Mill, are consequentialists who identify pleasure or happiness as the most fundamental good. Consequentialists define the right as that which maximizes that which they define as good. Utilitarians mandate maximizing happiness. Happiness, of course, is a psychological state. But, utilitarians do not say that happiness is rendered morally good in virtue of our representing it as such. Happiness would be good regardless of our moral convictions. Thus, maximizing happiness is not morally right in virtue of our taking it to be right. Maximizing inherits its moral merit from the good of that which is maximized. If happiness is good, more happiness is better. If we have to choose between two courses of action, and one leads to something better, then it is the course of action we should pursue. Utilitarianism is, thus, a psychologically based theory of morality, but not a response-dependent theory. If utilitarianism is correct, things have moral merit (they are good or right) objectively, in one sense of that term. Likewise for other forms of consequentialism; things can be good or right without being represented as such.

I think consequentialist theories are untenable, but this is not the place for a full assessment. The literature on that topic is vast. Rather than developing a detailed critique, I want to suggest that consequentialism is not really in competition with the kind of theory I am proposing. My thesis in this chapter is that morality is not objective. By that I mean that moral concepts, *as they currently exist*, do not refer to objective properties. In this respect, my project is descriptive. In contrast, consequentialism is a normative theory, and it is a revisionist one at that. Rather than capturing the moral values that ordinary people actually endorse, consequentialists offer a new system of values. Thus, if consequentialism could identify an objective source for values, it wouldn't follow that *our* values are objective—it wouldn't follow that our moral concepts refer to the features that consequentialists define as the foundations of right action. Put more pointedly, if moral vocabulary is fixed by how we use moral terms, then consequentialism is best construed, not as an account of morality, but as an alternative to it. (I think Kantian ethics should be construed in the same way.)

There are many reasons for thinking consequentialism is a revisionist theory, rather than an account of what we are already committed to morally. One can see this by noticing that the recommendations of consequentialist theories often depart from untutored intuitions about good behavior. Consider some examples. First, consequentialism is difficult to reconcile with the intuition that we should not harm one person in order to save others. For example, only 8.3 percent of subjects think it's permissible to push a person in the path of a trolley that is speeding toward five people (Mikhail, 2002). Second, consequentialist theories typically imply that it would be good to distribute material resources on the basis of need, but many people are uncomfortable with that idea. For example, Kluegel and Smith (1986) found that 81 percent of Americans prefer a scheme according to which income is determined by skills and training, while only 13 percent favor distribution on the basis of need. There is little consensus about such questions. In general, liberals are more supportive of distributive justice than conservatives, even when asked to make this assessment from behind a veil of ignorance (Mitchell et al., 2003). There are also huge cultural differences in attitudes toward redistribution programs. For example, 69.5 percent of Austrians think that the government should work to achieve economic equity, and 38.3 percent of Americans agree (Svallfors, 1997). Third, people often morally condemn bad intentions even when they do not lead to bad consequences, which is inconsistent with most consequentialist theories. Interestingly, there are group differences in the tendency to condemn bad intentions; for example, Protestants are more likely to do this than Jews (Cohen and Rozin, 2001). Fourth, some versions of consequentialism (especially utilitarianism) seem to imply that people who have higher degrees of subjective well-being have greater moral worth. For example, extroverts are happier than introverts, depressives, and people who score high on neuroticism scales (e.g., Diener et al., 2004); Scandinavians and South Americans are happier than Asians (Diener and Oishi, 2003); and religious people are a bit happier than the non-religious (Witter et al., 1985). Does this mean that, say, atheist introverts should be placed on the front lines during warfare, rather than religious extroverts, because their lives have less value?

Consequentialist theories seem to place demands on us that go against our current values. Of course, the consequentialist literature is flush with attempts to accommodate ordinary moral intuitions. But these efforts sometimes involve significant departures from consequentialist principles. For example, the badness of bad intentions is accommodated by Adams's (1976) motive utilitarianism, but, strictly speaking, this is a departure from the view that consequences have normative priority. More generally, the pervasive pattern of discrepancies between the demands of consequentialism and ordinary values suggests that consequentialism can never be made to match our intuitions perfectly. Indeed, the diversity of moral intuitions suggests that even if some complex and impure consequentialist theory can be constructed to match some people's intuitions about what counts as good and right, no theory can accommodate everyone's intuitions. If a consequentialist makes motives matter morally, the theory may do a better job of capturing the moral intuitions of a Protestant, but it might do a worse job of accommodating the intuitions of a Jew. If the theory places limits on redistribution, conservatives will be happy, but liberals may balk.

I don't think most consequentialists would disagree with my assessment. Consequentialists do not try to capture folk moral values, at least not in detail. Most consequentialists would probably say that ordinary moral values should be abandoned and replaced with consequentialist values. Perhaps they're right. But that undermines any argument from the truth of consequentialism to the conclusion that morality is objective. Consequentialism is not a good account of what we mean by our moral terms, and therefore it adds no support to the claim that moral values have an objective foundation. At best, consequentialists might argue that morality *should* have an objective foundation.

4.2.5 Intentional Products: Conventionalism

I want to consider one more way in which one might try to argue that morality is objective. The strategy that I have in mind begins with the supposition that morality might be closely related to law. Laws are rules of conduct, they have normative force, and they are objective, in one important sense of the word. It is an objective fact that drivers in the United States must drive on the right side of the street, and that jaywalking is illegal. These facts do not depend on our opinions and attitudes. They do not even depend on being enforced. Legal facts count in virtue of their etiology. A rule is a law if it was produced in accordance with certain procedures. In this respect, laws are like artifacts. Their status as laws depends on the way they come about. They are, in the terminology introduced above, intentional products. They are created through an intentional process, but once created, they enjoy a degree of autonomy.

One might think that moral rules are like legal rules. Philippa Foot (1972) for example, has argued for an analogy between moral rules and the rules of etiquette. Rules of etiquette remain in place even if we don't care about them. They are, in that respect, categorical. But, unlike Kant's categorical imperatives, they are created by us, and they carry little rational force for the person who has no regard for operative conventions. This view of morality is also in harmony with certain kinds of contractualism. The kind of contractualism I have in mind differs from the contractualist theories inspired by Kant. Kantian contractualists argue that moral rules are those that we *would* devise if we generated social policies from an ideal epistemic position (such as reflective equilibrium). This becomes a kind of ideal observer theory, and it is vulnerable to the worries about ideal observers that I raised above. The kind of contractualism I want to consider here focuses on the social policies that we have *actually* created, not those that we would create. The idea is that we have an obligation to follow the law, because the law is a special kind of social product. It came about through procedures that make it authoritative, even if we become lazy, jaded, critical, or criminal.

Conventionalist contractualism opens the door to a strong form of relativism, and it would therefore fail to attract many philosophers with objectivist leanings. Nevertheless, it does seem to be compatible with one form of objectivism, which I have yet to assess. Contracts are like artifacts. They must be created with certain intentions, but they are not themselves subjective. A rule of law, for example, does not count as a rule in virtue of the fact that we are disposed to represent it or respond to it in a certain way. It counts as a rule in virtue of the way it was created, but once created it enjoys a degree of autonomy. Laws are intentional products, and we might say the same about social contracts more generally. If laws have moral standing in virtue of how they were created, then morality has a kind of objectivity.

Conventionalist theories, such as conventualist contractualism, allege that there is a connection between moral rules and conventional rules that have been created by members of social groups. The key feature of these theories, for our purposes, is that they regard moral rules as intentional products; once rules have been created in the right way, they have normative force regardless of our attitudes and dispositions. If a theory of this kind can be defended, then morality will be objective in the way that artifacts have their function objectively.

I think conventionalism has a kernel of truth, but only if we jettison the objectivism. The problem with conventionalism is that it incorrectly assumes that moral rules depend solely on prior events and not current practices. I think that moral rules become binding only relative to current response dispositions. Morally significant social conventions are not *mere* intentional products. Unlike hammers and nails, they must be sustained by human responses after their initial creation. Once those responses wane, social conventions fail to have moral authority.

To make this point, I want to distinguish two kinds of "social facts." A social fact is, roughly, a fact that cannot be characterized without reference to a social practice. Social practices are constituted by behaviors or coordinated mental states of members of a social group. The first class of social facts that I want to consider can be called etiological social facts. They are facts that depend etiologically on social processes. An etiological social fact is one that would not have occurred were it not for some social process in the past. Once a social fact of this kind has come to pass, the relevant social processes need not continue. The fact can hold without any sustaining mental states or social practices. Marriage is an example. Two people would not count as married unless they got married, and once married, they remain married regardless of their intentions and practices. The couple would have to go through a socially prescribed procedure to end their marriage. If the couple became senile together and forgot that they were married, and no one else remembered either, then they would remain married, nevertheless. Facts about who is married are etiological social facts. Facts involving names are etiological social facts as well. Consider the fact that this island is Fiji. It is Fiji in virtue of having been dubbed "Fiji" in the past. The fact that certain borders circumscribe Canada may be another etiological fact, as is the fact that a particular person is president.

Contrast this kind of social fact with those that must be continually sustained by the mental practices of a social group. Facts about monetary value are classic examples. The monetary value of a piece of currency depends on social practices. Some of those practices must be etiological. A piece of paper can only count as a dollar if it was created under certain conditions. But the monetary value of a dollar also depends on *current* practices. If everyone collectively decided to regard dollar bills as valueless, they would be valueless. Dollars have value only if they are regarded and treated as valuable. Call this an immanent social fact. Immanent social facts must be sustained by social practices. The fact that a particular baboon is the alpha male in a troop of baboons is another example of an immanent social fact. So is the fact that the Democratic Party is more liberal than the Republican Party.

Equipped with this distinction, we can now ask whether moral rules get their normative force immanently or etiologically. Social conventions seem to have etiological normativity. Laws and rules of etiquette are binding even if we don't care about them. It is wrong, in some sense, to eat with an open mouth or to jaywalk across a quiet street. But is moral wrongness like this? I don't think so. The conventionalist about morality concedes that moral rules are human products, rather than, say, divine commands or demands of reason. So the question can be put in conditional form: if moral rules are social facts, then are they etiological? To answer "yes" would be to take the analogy between law and morality literally. The idea would be that we created moral rules, and now we are morally obligated to obey them. If that is the case, there must be something about the way they are created that gives them normative force. But now the conventionalist faces a problem. The mere fact that a rule was devised in the past does not seem sufficient to give that rule force. So the conventionalist must admit that the normative force of a moral rule derives from something about the conditions under which it was devised.

To meet this requirement, conventionalists can stipulate that a rule is good because it was created by a morally authoritative process. Here, two possibilities come to mind. Rules might be created by a process of consensus, or they might be created from a position of reflective equilibrium. I have already dismissed the latter option as a version of ideal observer theory, so let me focus on consensus. If consensus can confer moral force, then a lack of consensus should undermine moral force. In a society where people stopped caring about earlier moral rules, those rules would cease to have force. So, if conventions get their moral force from consensus, their moral force is contingent on current dispositions of the population; it is immanent, not etiological. Rules exist immanently, only as long as they are regarded as rules. For this reason, I conclude that conventionalism only stands a chance as a subjectivist theory.

There is, in addition, a further and deeper sense in which conventionalism depends on subjectivism. In discussing other ethical theories, I have said, again and again, that rules get their status as moral only if they are the objects of moral sentiments. This point applies here as well. Suppose we found a society that followed a set of laws, and thus had immanent conventions. It would seem a huge leap to call these conventions moral. A society of psychopaths might live in accordance with conventions too. What gives a convention moral status is not simply that people agreed to follow it. Consensus is not enough. People might insist that a rule has moral authority because others have agreed to it, but this appeal to consensus is not an analytic truth; it is a statement of value. Consensus takes on moral authority only for the person who regards consensus as a moral good. Those who take a practical attitude toward consensus (like our community of psychopaths) cannot be credited with following the dictates of morality. Consensus is not an intrinsic good in other words. It's good because we value it. Or, more typically, consensus is derived from other things we value, such as fairness. If we had no moral attitudes toward such things, we might still abide by conventional rules, but doing so would have no moral significance. Conventionalists who reject this intuition must show why conventions have moral merit without appealing to an affectively based grounding norm, and I think that deduction will prove impossible.

4.3 CONSTRUCTIVE REALISM

4.3.1 Realism without Objectivity

The foregoing survey demonstrates that many philosophers want to find an objective foundation for morality. I don't think such a foundation exists. Each of the leading theories that I have considered has serious flaws. Other objectivist theories might be devised in their wake, but I am not optimistic about their success. I have not shown that objectivism in ethics is incoherent or impossible, but I hope to have shown that faith in objectivism may be misplaced. First, objectivist intuitions, to the extent that we have them, can be explained on a subjectivist theory. Second, leading attempts to ground morality in something objective are fraught with difficulties. I am led to the conclusion that there is no strong reason for thinking that morality is objective in any sense. Indeed, I think that objectivism is a pious hope.

In conducting this survey, one theme emerged again and again. The objective facts that purport to ground morality don't seem to have moral significance on their own. An action may be imprudent if it fails to maximize utility. An act might be eschatologically risky if it goes against divine command. An action may be unhealthy if it goes against human nature. An action may be irrational if it goes against the dictates of universal reason. An action may be unpopular if it goes against consensus. For an action to be *morally* wrong, something else is required. An action can be wrong in one of these other senses, and not be immoral. Likewise, an action can be rational, prudential, satisfying, and popular without being morally good. I have tried to show that moral claims are made true—morally true—by reactions in us. Our reactions are moral truthmakers; they are that in virtue of which moral claims attain their status as moral. That means that morality is subjective. I have also argued that the relevant reactions cannot be idealized to a position free from bias, and they must remain immanent for moral truths to persist. That suggests that morality is subjective in a way that precludes objectivity. The arguments for subjectivism in chapters 1 and 3 help support these claims, as do the arguments for relativism, which I will present in the next chapter. I conclude that moral objectivism is mistaken.

What implications does this have for debates about moral realism? Realism is a cagey concept. The term has been used in different ways by different branches of philosophy. For some, realism is conceptually bound to objectivity; to be real is to be objective in some sense. For example, it is sometimes said that realism implies some kind of mind-independence (e.g., Brink, 1989). When philosophers talk about semantic realism or scientific realism, they sometimes mean the possibility of facts that could obtain without any human observers. This definition does not encompass all technical or vernacular uses of the term. Berkeley was not speaking utter nonsense when he said that a world constituted by ideas would still qualify as *reality*. A person with a headache would not find any comfort in a doctor's insistence that pains are not *real*. Roses *really* are red even if red is a secondary quality. There are, evidently, uses of the term "real" and its cognates that are not synonymous with "objective." There are alternative definitions.

According to one definition, realism has something to do with truth. A domain might be said to be real if statements about that domain can be true. Call this truthfulness. The idea is closely related to another definition of realism, which focuses on facts. A domain is real, on this definition, if it contains facts. This is factualism. Truthfulness and factualism hang together because, according to many, a statement is true just in case it corresponds to a fact. Realism of this kind is most naturally contrasted with non-factualist theories or error theories. A statement is non-factual if it is not in the business of trying to assert a fact. Expressivist theories are a case in point. Expressivism is the view that statements within a domain of interest express feelings or attitudes rather than describing facts. Error theories claim that statements within a domain aim to pick out facts and fail. They are truth-apt, but always false.

The term "realism" has also been associated with the notion of causal efficacy (Harman, 1977; Sturgeon, 1985). We might imagine that real things contribute to the causal ebb and flow of the world. If something is real, it must be capable of doing causal work. This may be a stronger condition than truth-aptness and factualism because there are, arguably, facts about things that are not causally efficacious. It is a fact, perhaps, that Superman is weakened by kryptonite. The sentence, "Unicorns have one horn" is, arguably, true. But Superman and unicorns are not part of the causal ebb and flow of the world. They are not real. One might also try to define realism in terms of existence. Superman and unicorns do not exist. If "existence" is a predicate, then this is a substantive claim. If "existence" is a quantifier, the point is that we are not entitled to objectually quantify over Superman and unicorns. That is, we cannot specify an object that is Superman or an object that is a unicorn. This raises the question of when we are entitled to quantify objectually. A plausible answer is we can quantify objectually over all and only things that are causally efficacious—things that we need to postulate in order fully to explain all the events that take place in the world. Such objects are, in an intuitive sense, real. Realism of this kind can be contrasted with fictionalism and eliminativism, as these terms are most typically used. Fictionalist theories claim that a domain of discourse presupposes the non-existence of the entities it describes. Those entities "exist" only in a fictional sense. Eliminativist theories claim that a domain of discourse aims to pick out entities that literally exist, but those entities do not actually exist. Eliminativism and error theories go hand in hand, but they can come apart if one adopts an account of truth according to which we can make true claims about non-existent entities (not limited to negative existential claims).

Now we can ask: if morals are not objective, might they nevertheless be real in some sense? Consider, first, the sense of realism associated with truth and facts. The kind of subjectivism that I outlined in chapter 3 is designed as an alternative to expressivism. It is designed to accommodate the intuition that moral claims are truth-apt. When we say that stealing is wrong, we are not merely expressing our feelings, we are implicitly saying that stealing has the property of causing certain kinds of negative reactions in us. It is *true* that stealing makes us feel angry, or guilty, or disappointed. So the statement that stealing is wrong is true. By the same token, we can say it is a fact that *stealing* causes these reactions in us, and thus the statement that stealing is wrong corresponds to a fact. Subjectivism of this kind is a realist theory, on one construal of realism.

The subjectivism I favor is also realist on the construal that emphasizes causal efficacy and existence. Moral facts impact our behavior, and they impact our behavior in virtue of being moral facts. Consider, by analogy, the causal efficacy of other emotion-inducing properties, such as scariness, disgustingness, or likeability. These properties are trivially causal insofar as they are defined by their tendency to cause emotional reactions in us. They also make causal contributions to our behavior. We might avoid watching thrillers because they are scary; we may discard rotten food because it is disgusting; we might invite someone to dinner because she is likable. In each case, the emotion-inducing property is causally implicated in our actions.

One might object that this is really an illusion. What affects our actions is not the emotion-inducing properties, but the emotions themselves. We avoid thrillers because fear causes us to; we discard rotten food because we are impelled by disgust; we invite a friend because we anticipate the pleasure of her company. Scariness, disgustingness, and likeability are epiphenomenal. They are entirely unnecessary for explaining behavior.

In response, I would point out that emotion-inducing properties are playing a different explanatory role from that played by the emotions themselves. There are situations in which one has an emotion without the emotion-inducing property. Suppose, for example, that I form the false belief that a jar of food in my refrigerator has spoiled. I might discard it because I am disgusted, or because I believe it is disgusting, but not because it actually is disgusting. To be disgusting is to reliably cause disgust under certain circumstances (e.g., knowing the relevant information). This kind of case makes it look as if disgust is the real determinant of action. But now suppose we ask where those psychological states come from.

In the current example, I might become disgusted because I misread an expiration date, or mistake a shadow for mold. But now consider the case where the food actually is spoiled. In this case, my disgust is caused by the fact that the food is disgusting. The emotion-inducing property is causally responsible for my mental state, and, thus, is implicated in my subsequent behavior. One might object by saying that my disgust was actually caused by the fact that the food is spoiled, not by the fact that spoiled food is disgusting. This move is implausible. If spoiled food were not disgusting to us, it would not induce an emotion. Take another example. Rozin et al. (1986) asked subjects in an experiment whether they would drink a glass of orange juice after a sterilized cockroach had been dipped into it. Most subjects said they would refuse. The roach is harmless. The fact that a roach has had contact with the juice is insufficient on its own to explain our response. Subjects refuse to drink because roaches have the property of causing disgust in us. Disgustingness is causally efficacious.

The same is true for moral properties on the subjectivist account. Being wrong is the property that disposes us to have certain negative reactions. The wrongness of stealing plays a causal role in preventing us from stealing and in punishing those who steal. The wrongness induces emotions in us, and those emotions impact our behavior. If stealing were not wrong, we would not avoid it.

I conclude that moral properties are perfectly real in this sense. They are part of the causal fabric of the world. We can use them to explain behavior, and we can quantify over them in our explanations.

In summary, I think we should give up on moral objectivism. Moral properties are not objective in any interesting sense. If being real entails being objective, then moral realism is false. We should be antirealists. But realism can be understood in other ways. Moral statements can be true; there are moral facts; moral properties are causally efficacious; and, therefore, we can quantify over them. For these reasons, it makes perfectly good sense to call the kind of subjectivism that I favor a form of moral realism.

There is one final question worth addressing. If moral properties are real, but they are not natural kinds, then what kind of kind are they? The answer to this question was foreshadowed above. Moral facts are like money. They are social facts that obtain in virtue of our current dispositions and practices. They are as real as monetary values and even more important, perhaps, in guiding our lives.

4.3.2 Constructive Sentimentalism

Monetary value is, in a perfectly straightforward sense, a construction. It is perfectly real, but it depends on human practices and human responses. I think morality is a construction too. In the last chapter, I defended a version of the sensibility theory, according to which moral facts depend on moral sentiments. I now propose to call this kind of sensibility theory *constructive sentimentalism*.

The term "sentimentalism" is often used as an umbrella for all theories that relate moral concepts to emotions (including both expressivism and sensibility theories). But, given my emphasis on sentiments and the distinction between emotions and sentiments, this term is especially appropriate for my view. The modifier "constructive" refers to the idea that moral properties come into being without sentiments. We, in effect, build morality; we don't discover it.

This raises a terminological issue. In chapter 1, I mentioned the distinction, drawn by D'Arms and Jacobson (2006), between perceptivist theories and projectivist theories. Sensibility theorists are supposed to be perceptivists; they compare moral properties to secondary qualities, and they imply that we use our emotions to experience the world in an evaluative way (see especially McDowell, 1987; McNaughton, 1988). Projectivists, in contrast, like to say that morality cannot be perceived, because it exists solely in us. Expressivists fall into this category (see Blackburn, 1980). On this view, when we attribute moral attributes to an action, we are simply projecting our feelings onto the world.

On the face of it, perception and projection seem to be diametrically opposed. Perception implies that we pick up on something that is outside of us, and projection implies that we take something inside of us and beam it outward. But, on closer examination, it may be hard to keep these two ideas apart. D'Arms and Jacobson argue that both metaphors are misleading: the perception metaphor implies that values are independent of valuing, and the projection metaphor threatens to undermine morality by implying that values are just "figments" of feelings. I also want to challenge the contrast between perception and projection, but not because I think both metaphors are wrong. Rather, I think both may be importantly right. There is a sense in which we perceive moral properties. In fact, one can make literal sense of this idea by noting that emotions are perceptions of changes in the body, and it is by means of our emotions that we often come to discover that something is right or something is wrong. But there is also something apt about the idea of moral projection. Morals are not objective features of the world in the way that, say, lions and tigers and bears might be. They come from us.

The idea of construction resolves the conflict between the ideas of perception and projection. Things that we construct or build come from us, but, once there, they are real entities that we can perceive. This is obviously true in the case of material constructions, such as buildings or artifacts. But it is also true of social constructions. Monetary value is created by us, but it is also a real feature of the world that has an impact on us.

I think moral facts are a special kind of construction: they are made by our sentiments, and, once made, they can be perceived. You can perceive that it's wrong to kick a dog. When someone kicks a dog, it causes an emotional response, and that response is a manifestation of a sentiment that constitutes the conviction that animal cruelty is wrong. The sentiment makes it wrong, and it also makes the wrongness palpable to us when we encounter it. Sentimental constructions reconcile projection and perception.

In the first half of this book, I have focused mostly on the perceptive side of construction. For example, I have talked about the emotions that arise in response to moral transgressions, and I have emphasized my allegiance to sensibility theories, which, in their very name, imply a comparison to perception. I have not talked much about the manufacture of morals. In particular, I have not described the ways in which cultural factors can contribute to moral truths. That is the central issue I address in the chapters ahead.

PART II
CONSTRUCTING MORALS

5

Dining with Cannibals

"I sat with Michii and with Darinimbiak, the three of us alone at the fire with the others dancing, singing around us, I took a piece of the meat that Michii held out and ate and swallowed and ate some more, and entered the circle again to dance" (Schneebaum, 1969: 106). The "meat" mentioned here, so unceremoniously, is human flesh. The author is Tobias Schneebaum, an American anthropologist, who participated in a cannibal feast with the Aka-mara people in Peru. Cannibalism tends to fill us with a sense of horror. To call cannibalism immoral is an understatement. It is morally monstrous to eat the flesh of our own species. Killers who engage in this practice are regarded as evil and deeply depraved. Yet cannibalism has been practiced by cultures all over the world. It is, by some accounts, the default cultur-al practice, rather than the exception. Cannibalism is relatively prevalent in pre-state societies (bands, tribes, or chiefdoms) and disappears with the emer-gence of agriculture, domestication of animals, and, most importantly, certain institutions associated with statehood (Harris, 1985). There is a moral gulf dividing cultures that practice cannibalism, and those that revile it. Members of different groups seem to have radically different ideas about what is right and wrong.

In this chapter, I explore moral variation. Some moral philosophers think variation has been exaggerated. Others think that variation in moral values has no implications for variation in moral facts. There can be one true morality despite significant differences in moral convictions. I will reject both of these claims. Values diverge, and that divergence matters. I will argue that moral relativism is a straightforward consequence of the sensibility theory that I favor, the theory I dubbed constructive sentimentalism. The link between sentimentalist theories and relativism has certainly been noticed by others (see especially Westermarck, 1906), but sensibility theorists have not spent much time exploring this implication. I attempt to redress that oversight here and in the chapters that follow.

Of course, one philosopher's *modus ponens* is another's *modus tollens*. If the sensibility theory that I endorse entails relativism, then many will take that as grounds for rejection. Relativism faces several powerful objections. I will address four of these in section 5.2. In chapter 7, I will critically assess the suggestion that we are biologically endowed with moral universals, and, in chapter 8, I will examine the prospects for moral progress within a relativist framework.

5.1 MORAL RELATIVISM DEFINED AND DEFENDED

5.1.1 Descriptive Relativism and Metaethical Relativism

The term "moral relativism" is notoriously ambiguous. On the one hand, it is used to label the thesis that some people have fundamentally different moral values. Following Brandt (1967), I will call this descriptive moral relativism, because it is meant to be a simple empirical fact. Descriptive moral relativism is not undisputed (as we shall see), but it is widely accepted on the basis of the anthropological record. Controversy heats up when we turn from anthropological claims to claims about moral truth. I will be defending the following thesis:

> *Metaethical Relativism*: The truth conditions of a moral judgment depend on the context in which that judgment is formed.

If this thesis is correct then a judgment that is true in one context can be false in another. Many people find this idea implausible, incoherent, and morally reprehensible. I will address such objections in due course. First, I want to ask whether there is any reason to think the thesis is true.

People often try to argue for metaethical relativism by appeal to descriptive relativism. The implied master-argument goes like this:

1. Descriptive relativism is true.
2. If descriptive relativism is true, then metaethical relativism is true.
3. Therefore, metaethical relativism is true.

The second premise is far from trivial. Differences in moral values do not entail differences in moral truths in any straightforward sense. This point is often made by drawing analogies to science. Differences in scientific beliefs do not entail that conflicting scientific judgments are equally true. The fact that cultures have varying views about the shape of the Earth, for example, does not entail that the Earth has many shapes. Indeed, scientific disputes do not have relativist implications even when those disputes are irresolvable. Suppose that there is no way to ever decisively prove that the universe has eleven dimensions rather than, say, fourteen dimensions. This would not entail that both these claims are true. There is some fact of the matter, even if debates have no resolution. We must be cautious, then, in drawing metaethical conclusions from the existence and persistence of moral debates. The metaethical relativist must offer a reason for thinking premise 2 is plausible when the parallel premise would be grossly implausible in other domains.

Premise 2 is defensible if the sensibility theory that I favor is true. Descriptive relativism is the view that people have fundamentally different moral values. It is the view that values would differ even if all the non-moral facts were in. In chapter 3, I said that moral rightness and wrongness could be defined in terms of sentiments. An action is right or wrong if there is a moral sentiment toward it. A moral sentiment is a disposition to have emotions in the approbation or disapprobation range. If descriptive moral relativism is true, then people have different moral sentiments toward the same things. If rightness and wrongness depend, metaphysically, on the sentiments people have, then the existence of differences in people's sentiments entails a difference in moral facts. Thus, metaethical relativism can be derived from descriptive relativism.

5.1.2 Appraiser and Agents

The definition of metaethical relativism that I have been working with is underdescribed. Before assessing the doctrine, I want to get a bit more precise about what I will be committing to. In particular, I want to address the question of *whose* values are relevant for determining the truth conditions of a moral judgment.

When a judgment is formed, there is a person forming the judgment, and a person (or persons) about whom the judgment is formed. If a person judges that ϕ-ing is morally wrong, she implies that it is wrong *for someone*. Sometimes that someone is the person making the judgment, but equally often, we make moral judgments about others. That means there are two potential contexts to consider. There is the context of the judger and the context of the judged. In some cases, judger and judged subscribe to different values. When that happens, we can ask whose values matter.

Lyons (1976) defines Appraiser Relativism as the view that the truth of moral judgments depends on the context of the judge, and he defines Agent Relativism as the view that the context of the judged is what matters. When a missionary tells the members of an Akamara village that cannibalism is morally wrong, should the truth conditions be fixed by the missionary's values or by the villager's values? The answer to this question may depend on the nature of the moral judgment.

Recall an observation that I made in the preamble to this book. If sentimentalism is right, one cannot make a judgment of the form "One ought to ϕ" or "One ought not ϕ" unless one is disposed to have prescriptive sentiments. Prescriptive sentiments can be identified with the forms of approbation and disapprobation described in chapter 3. A person who lacks these sentiments can come to believe that something is obligated by someone, but forming a prescriptive thought in the affect-laden sense would be impossible. I will call such prescriptive thoughts "propositional oughtitudes." In English, these thoughts are canonically expressed using the word "ought."

Suppose that a missionary forms a propositional oughtitude toward Akamara cannibalism. By definition, the oughtitude contains affect-laden moral concepts. The emotions implicit in those concepts are, of course, the missionary's emotions. It is the missionary who is disposed to feel angry or disgusted at the thought of cannibalism. Consequently, the meaning of the propositional oughtitude that the missionary forms must be fixed by his own emotions. It is the missionary's values that are being expressed. When propositional oughtitudes are formed, truth conditions are relativized to the appraiser.

Contrast propositional oughtitudes with another kind of moral judgment, which can be called a belief about obligations. Rather than forming the judgment that Akamaras ought to refrain from cannibalism, a missionary might form the thought that Akamaras are under an obligation to refrain from cannibalism. This neutral thought implicitly refers to sentiments, because obligations are determined by oughtitudes, but it does not express a sentiment. If a neutral judgment is formed, the missionary can fix the context either to his own values or to those of the Akamara. Context-fixing can even be explicit. The missionary can judge that Akamaras are under an obligation *under their value system* to engage in cannibalism, but that they have no such obligation under the missionary's values. With neutral judgments, one can relativize to agent or to appraiser. Our ability to do this explicitly provides some support for metaethical relativism.

Pragmatically, a missionary would implicate his own value system if he made a moral assertion without specifying a context. If the missionary were to say, "Akamaras are obligated to refrain from cannibalism," listeners would assume he was expressing an oughtitude or relating his own values. We do not often assert the values of others, especially when we find their values abhorrent. Similar points can be made about judgments that would be expressed using the words "right" and "wrong." These judgments can be grounded in the sentiments of the person making them, or they can be judgments about obligations. When we use the word "right" and "wrong" without specifying a context, listeners assume that we are expressing our own values.

Most relativists are Appraiser Relativists, but Gilbert Harman (1975) has argued for an ever stricter constraint on the applicability of moral judgments and terms. He suggests that we cannot have propositional oughtitudes toward members of cultures that subscribe to different values. In his terminology, moral uses of the word "ought" express "inner judgments." We assume that the word "ought," when used in a moral sense, applies only to individuals who are motivated by the kinds of moral considerations that motivate us. If Harman is right, then no gap can open up between appraiser and agent when we form propositional oughtitudes. Harman's evidence for this thesis comes from his intuition that it sounds odd when we try to extend ought judgments to those with different values. It would have sounded odd to tell Hitler that he ought not to attempt genocide. If we were being invaded by intelligent aliens from another planet, it would sound odd to tell them that they ought not to kill us. Harman argues that this oddity shows that the ought judgments are only applicable to those who share the values of the one who makes those judgments.

Harman's semantic thesis goes beyond the thesis that I endorsed above. I suggested that oughtitudes express the values of appraisers, but I did not say that those values are inapplicable to people with different values. On the form of relativism that I have been endorsing, a speaker says "you ought to φ" expresses the fact that the speaker endorses values that require φ-ing. This is a form of Appraiser Relativism. Harman's semantic thesis entails that "you ought to φ" also expresses the fact that the agent being addressed endorses values that require φ-ing. This is Agent Relativism. To see whether Agent Relativism is true, we need to examine how people use the term "ought." Harman bases his case on the intuition that we do not apply the term "ought" to people like Hitler, but this may be inadequate evidence for the thesis that he wants to defend.

Harman's argument faces two objections. First, *pace* Harman, people often seem to harbor propositional oughtitudes toward those who have different values, at least under certain circumstances. For example, missionaries might say to the Akamaras, "You ought to refrain from cannibalism." Or a parent might say to a child, "You ought not to hit your sister," even if the child clearly has a different set of values. Second, we don't need Agent Relativism Thesis to explain why we are reluctant to use the word "ought" toward someone like Hitler or invaders from outer space. As Lyons (1976) has argued, telling Hitler that he ought to refrain from genocide would be pointless. Chastising the aliens would be a waste of time. We do not bother with ought-talk when dealing with moral monsters, because we have no hope of inducing their concern. If our reluctance to form oughtitudes in these cases stems from our recognition that negotiation would be pointless, then our reluctance cannot be taken as evidence for Agent Relativism.

These objections seem to spell trouble for Harman's view, but I think they can be answered. Let's begin with the first objection, which purports to show that we often do direct ought judgments toward people with different values. This would spell trouble for the Agent Relativism if there were no other explanation for the examples under consideration. I pointed out that missionaries may use the word "ought" when talking to members of the Akamara. But this does not prove that the word "ought" actually applies in such cases. Missionaries may be making a mistake. Ordinarily, it's a bad idea to attribute conceptual errors to ordinary speakers, but I think this is an exceptional case. First of all, missionaries are likely to be moral absolutists. They are likely to have the view that there is one set of values, which issue from divine command. They may also harbor the belief that all people have epistemic access to these values. Thus, they may regard the Akamara as members of the same moral community and hence under the jurisdiction of the same moral laws. Second, missionaries are in the business of conversion, and adopting an oughtitude can be a powerful tool for influencing the values and behavior of others. Oughtitudes are constituted by moral sentiments. Those who violate our oughtitudes incur our wrath. Wrath can be very persuasive. So, by adopting an oughtitude, we can lead others to adopt our values. This may also explain why parents direct ought judgments toward their children. Parents of young children know that their kinds have not internalized adult moral values, but they tell their children what they ought to do in an effort to teach them how to behave. If Agent Relativism is true, then such directives are semantically anomalous, but tactically appropriate. I am not suggesting that missionaries and parents realize that their norms do not apply. They may or they may not. My point is that, independently of whether the norms apply, these people have good strategic reasons for making ought judgments. Even if parents realized that it was a semantic error to tell their children what they ought to do, they would continue issuing such directives because of their impact on shaping behavior. If you want to alter people's morality, it's a good strategy to treat them as if they were obligated to follow your values.

The opponent of Agent Relativism might concede these points, but notice that the concession merely leaves us with a stalemate. Casual observation suggests that we sometimes apply the word "ought" to members of another culture. I have just been arguing that Agent Relativism can explain this pattern of verbal behavior, but so can opponents of Agent Relativism. We need an argument to show which interpretation is right. This stalemate looks even worse when we consider the second objection to Harman's argument that I mentioned above. Sometimes we apply ought judgments to people with different values (as with missionaries and parents), and sometimes we don't (as with Hitler and space aliens). Harman took the latter as evidence for Agent Relativism, but Lyons offered another explanation for why we refrain from directing ought judgments to some individuals (Hitler is beyond persuasion). So there are two explanations of the verbal behavior, and we still need a way to decide which explanation is correct.

To pull out of the stalemate it will help to reflect on the concept OUGHT. In chapter 3, I pointed to a difference between ought judgments and wrongness judgments. If I say you ought not to beat your dog, I am saying something more than that beating your dog is wrong. I captured this subtle difference by saying that an ought judgment conveys the fact that a norm has authority over the behavior of the person addressed by that judgment. If I say you ought not to beat your dog, I am saying that the norm against dog-beating has authority over you, and thus your behavior should conform to it. I did not unpack this idea of authority in chapter 3, but it may be unpacked now. Missionaries presumably think that cannibalism is wrong. This thought may consist in their negative sentiments toward cannibalism. But something more is needed if they are to judge that this sentiment of wrongness has authority over that of the Akamara. Why should the Akamara heed the norm that condemns cannibalism? Why would this norm govern their actions? The answer to that question depends on the source of normativity. If norms have authority in virtue of some universal, mind-independent facts, then missionaries might be right to infer that the norm against cannibalism applies to the Akamara. But suppose that norms are local, and depend on the values that a person happens to endorse. Suppose the action-guiding quality of a norm depends on having internalized that norm. If so, then the norm against cannibalism is not in fact normative, or action-guiding, for the Akamara, and it would be a mistake to say that they are under its jurisdiction. If I am right to think that the concept OUGHT is linked to the idea of normative authority, then it seems to follow that missionaries are mistaken when they say that the Akamara ought to refrain from cannibalism, even if they are right to say that cannibalism is wrong.

This intuition is easy to motivate if we turn things around and imagine how we would respond to the moral judgments of the Akamara. If Agent Relativism were false and constructive sentimentalism is true, then when a member of another culture judges that we ought to refrain from doing something, we would be under an obligation to refrain. Suppose that the Akamara disapprove of keeping animals as pets. Does this fact mean that we have an obligation to set our pets free? Does the fact that racists oppose integration mean that we should re-segregate our schools? That would be a very troubling discovery. To avoid this conclusion, we must insist that we are obligated to follow only the values that we actually endorse. The notion of obligation, which is implied by the word "ought," seems to apply only when a norm has authority, and, if constructive sentimentalism is true, norms have authority only over those that endorse them. These observations lead me to think that Agent Relativism is true.

I conclude that our judgments are relative to the culture of moral appraisers and also to the agents who are appraised. When a speaker says "X ought to ϕ," this sentence can be true if and only if the speaker has moral values that prescribe ϕ-ing, and X has those values. As suggested above, things may be a bit more flexible with judgments that we express using words like "right" or "wrong." By default these words may refer to the speaker's values, but they do not depend on the values of agents. We can say that the Akamara are wrong to engage in cannibalism. We can say this because this judgment does not make any direct claim on the behavior of the Akamaras. It does not imply that the Akamara are under the jurisdiction of our norm.

There may also be contexts in which we can use the terms "right" and "wrong" non-prescriptively, as when we say, "For Puritans, premarital sex was wrong." But when we use "right" and "wrong" prescriptively, we relativize to our own value systems. We don't say, "Sally was wrong to have premarital sex; after all, she was a Puritan."

These lessons lead to an extension of the definition of metaethical relativism that I offered above:

Metaethical Relativism (extended definition): The truth conditions of a moral judgment depend on the context in which that judgment is formed, such that:

A judgment that X *ought* to ϕ is true if and only if it is wrong not to ϕ on the value systems of both the speaker and X.

A judgment that ϕ-ing is wrong is true if and only if ϕ-ing is the object of a sentiment of disapprobation among the contextually salient individual(s) (usually the speaker).

Further refinements could be added for other moral concepts, but this will suffice for the discussion in the remainder of this chapter.

5.1.3 Content Relativism and Truth Relativism

On the definition that I am using, the truth of a moral judgment depends on context. As stated, this formulation is underspecified. There are different forms of context sensitivity. In recent semantic theory, two forms of relativism have received considerable attention: content relativism and truth relativism. For most of this chapter, the distinction between these species of relativism does not matter, but a complete relativist theory would specify which, if either, is correct for moral terms. It would also facilitate exposition. In section 5.2, I will review objections to metaethical relativism, and the two species or relativism offer subtly different strategies for addressing some of these objections. In this section, therefore, I will offer some preliminary reasons for preferring content relativism over truth relativism. First, let me outline the distinction.

As the name suggests, a content relativist says that the content of an utterance (or judgment) is determined, in part, by context. The term "content" is a weasel word in philosophy, but the basic idea is that context plays a role in determining what an utterance means; depending on your theory of meaning, this might be further cashed out in terms of what proposition the utterance expresses. An utterance is content-relative if it expresses different propositions under different circumstances, and a term is content-relative if it makes different contributions to the proposition expressed by a sentence containing it. If propositions are structured complexes containing properties and individuals, then a term can be said to be content-relative if the property or individual that it contributes to a proposition varies across contexts.

To illustrate, consider indexicals. The word "I" in "I am a philosopher" gets its content, in part, from the context of utterance. If Gertrude were to utter this sentence, "I" would designate Gertrude. A content relativist about moral terms would say that the properties expressed by those terms depend on context. "Killing is wrong" attributes a different property to killing when different people utter it.

There are different theories about how content-relative terms and concepts work. One possibility is that uses of these terms and concepts do not internally represent the fact that they are relative. On this view, the word "wrong" means something different when spoken by different observers, but people typically do not recognize this fact because the corresponding concept or lexical entry does not contain any component corresponding to the fact that the meaning is sensitive to context. Another possibility is that this context sensitivity is internally represented. In particular, there could be a component in the lexical entry for moral terms that refers indexically to, say, the speaker and addressee, or some other salient individuals. Dreier (1990) has been a champion of this approach. His account of moral terms draws directly on Kaplan's (1989) celebrated theory of indexicals. The word "I," for example, picks out different individuals, but, in all instances, there is a common component of meaning, which can be glossed by the phrase "the speaker of this utterance." Kaplan calls this the "character" of the expression. He uses the term "content" to refer to the individual determined by this character when a sentence is uttered in a context. By analogy, "wrong" might be said to have both character and content. The character of the term "wrong" might be roughly captured by the phrase: "the property of being disapproved of by the speaker" (or some other salient appraiser). The content of the term is then determined contextually. If Gertrude utters the sentence "Killing is wrong," then that sentence ascribes to killing the property of being disapproved of by Gertrude. The term "wrong" implicitly introduces an indexical element, which determines different contents in different contexts. The character of the term "ought" might be a bit more complex; it might refer to the values of the appraiser and the agent appraised. More accurately, sentences of the form "X ought to ϕ" may mean it's wrong not to ϕ on the speaker's value system, and X falls under the authority of this norm. The value system gets determined contextually by means of a hidden indexical that points to the speaker, and there is also a hidden (non-indexical) element that implies that the agent X must fall under that value system.

Let's now turn to truth relativism. Content relativists say that judgments have different contents in different contexts, and, in contrast, truth relativists say that judgments always have the same content, but their truth varies across contexts of evaluation. To illustrate, consider the plausible suggestion that many ordinary utterances express propositions that have truth values only relative to points in time. The sentence "Gertrude is standing" has the same content whenever it is uttered, but it is true just when evaluated at times in which Gertrude is standing. A truth relativist about moral terms would say that, in addition to temporal parameters, propositions are evaluated relative to value systems. On this view, "Killing is wrong" has an invariant content, but different truth values depending on the value system relative to which its truth is assessed. In recent philosophical semantics, content relativism is called "contextualism" and truth relativism is just called "relativism" (MacFarlane, 2005), but this is unfortunate terminology, since both positions postulate a kind of relativism and a kind of context-dependency.

There is a sizable and growing literature on these two species of relativism, and little of what I have to say below depends too heavily on deciding which, if either, offers the right analysis of moral terms. Still, for the record and for ease of exposition in the remainder of this chapter, I want to convey my reason for thinking that content relativism is preferable to truth relativism.

My complaint against truth relativism is that I do not see what properties moral terms could possibly express in the absence of a context. Suppose that Gertrude says cannibalism is wrong. What is expressed by "wrong" here? A content relativist would say (roughly) that wrongness refers to the property of being the object of Gertrude's disapprobation. But the truth relativist cannot say this. That property is determined by context, and the truth relativist says that the property expressed by a truth-relative term is the same across contexts. The truth relativist might propose that "wrong" expresses the property of being the object of *someone's* disapprobation. But this can't be the right analysis. If "wrong" referred to the property of being disapproved by someone (anyone!), then I could truly utter that, say, premarital sex is wrong—something I don't believe. One might try to get around this by suggesting that moral terms refer to "unspecific properties." This term is introduced by Kompa (2002) to describe properties that are invariant across utterances of a term, but context is required to determine who has those properties. But I don't understand what properties are, such that they can be unspecific in this way. First, the proposal suggests that properties can be individuated independently of their instances, and that is a controversial claim. Second, the view seems to imply that the very same property, say wrongness, would come and go depending on who happens to be making a moral claim; if "wrong" always refers to the very same property, why should that property wax and wane as a function of linguistic context? I find the idea of unspecific properties difficult to swallow.

Those who reject content relativism in virtue of truth relativism typically do so because they think that truth relativism does a better job of explaining moral disagreements (Kölbel, 2003; Richard, 2004; Lasersohn, 2005; MacFarlane, 2005; Brogaard, forthcoming). But I don't think this is an adequate reason for preferring truth relativism. Content relativists have perfectly good strategies for explaining moral disagreement. All the strategies discussed in chapter 3 are available to the content relativist. For example, parties to a debate sometimes share basic moral values or falsely believe that they do, and even when they don't have this belief, they may conduct a debate with the hope of persuading their conversation partners to adopt a new set of values. Moreover, I reject the claim that truth relativists do a better job at explaining debates. Truth relativists like to say that, when people express a disagreement using relative terms, they succeed in referring to the same proposition, and thus there is a legitimate object of dispute. If Tobias says, "Cannibalism is wrong," and Michii says, "No; cannibalism is not wrong," then there is a proposition to which they are both referring, and the truth value of that proposition is being disputed. So far, so good. But notice that the truth relativist is also committed to saying that parties to this debate are assuming different contexts for evaluating that proposition. Michii is evaluating it relative to one value system, and Tobias is evaluating it relative to another. So, strictly speaking, there is a sense in which they are talking past each other. Both Tobias and Michii are entitled to evaluate their moral claims relative to their own value systems, so both are entitled to assign different truth values to the utterance "Cannibalism is wrong." Consequently, their debate seems to rest on some kind of confusion. It adds little to say that they express the same proposition with the utterance once it is conceded that propositions can have context-sensitive truth values. On a truth-relativist account, having a moral dispute is a bit like having a debate about whether Gertrude is standing up, in which one party insists that she is standing every time she happens to stand, and the other party insists that Gertrude is not standing, every time she happens to sit. We could not explain away this debate by pointing out that "Gertrude is standing" expresses the same proposition whenever it is uttered. Other factors would need to be introduced to make sense of why the parties to the debate failed to realize that their claims are perfectly compatible. I think that both content relativism and truth relativism are on an equal footing when it comes to moral disagreement. Both must reckon with the fact that, in some moral debates, people who make consistent claims take themselves to be disagreeing.

In sum, I think that context relativism makes more sense than truth relativism, because it has a better story about what properties our moral terms express, and truth relativism does not offer a superior account of moral disagreement. In what follows, I will assume that content relativism is correct, though the arguments I will give can be adapted in defense of truth relativism.

5.1.4 The Role of Culture

The form of relativism that I am defending relativizes moral judgments to individuals (the person who makes a judgment and, sometimes, the person or persons being addressed). But I have already had occasion to refer to the values of a *group* of people. I talked about the values of the Akamara. Relativism is sometimes presented as the view that morality varies across cultures. Strictly speaking, I think cultures are too large a unit for grounding morality, but I do think morality is deeply influenced by culture and that it sometimes makes sense to talk about the moral values of a cultural group. Moreover, much of the evidence for descriptive relativism comes from the observations of cultural differences. Before looking at objections to relativism I want to say something about what cultures are and how they contribute to morality.

Let's begin by considering a general definition of culture. The most influential early definition of culture was proposed by Edward Burnett Tylor. He defines culture as "that complex whole which includes knowledge, belief, art, law, morals, custom, and any other capabilities and habits acquired by man as a member of society" (Tylor, 1871: 1). On this definition, the components of culture are quite encompassing. Culture includes material, behavioral, and psychological components, and psychological components are wide-ranging. On the face of it, this is quite a lot of components indeed. Tylor also mentions the means by which cultures are transmitted. He says cultures are "acquired by man as a member of society." If "society" and "culture" are near synonyms, this may introduce a circularity into the definition: culture is that which is culturally acquired.

One can improve on Tylor's definition by emphasizing and elaborating his remark on transmission. Cultures consist in those things that are socially learned. Social learning is learning through the help other individuals or through things that have been created by other individuals. More specifically, cultures consist in things that are learned by a process that one might call conforming: members of a culture do things in virtue of the fact that other individuals do those things. Conformity may be conscious or unconscious. Cultures can consist in many different psychological and behavioral traits (habits, skills, ideas, values, etc.) because these things can all be transmitted socially. Material objects, such as artworks, are not component parts of a culture; rather they are cultural products. Cultures can include knowledge and attitudes pertaining to such objects, however. Cultures can include things that have both a human and a biological origin. Language skills may be an example. All things that we can learn through others depend on biological capacities for learning. But things that are acquired through genuine social learning, as I will use the term, cannot be entirely driven by biology. Things that must be socially learned are things that cannot be fully determined by a bioprogram.

By placing social learning at the center of a definition of culture, we can make some progress on the questions of cultural individuation and membership. To be a member of a cultural group is (a) to have psychological and behavioral traits that have been acquired through conformity to members of that group, and (b) to be disposed to continue to conform to that group. For simplicity of exposition, I will often leave out the second condition. An *ideal* cultural group is a group of individuals with uniform socially learned traits, each of whom gets all of her socially learned traits from other members of the group. Groups of individuals qualify as separate cultures to the extent that they do not socially learn from each other. In reality, no cultural groups are ideal. Groups blend, criss-cross, and overlap. Very often, we take cues for different aspects of our lives, from different groups. One individual can identify herself as a woman, a liberal, a Buddhist, an academic, and a Canadian. For this reason, it is often useful to talk about dimensions of culture: gender category, political party, professional group, religion, and so on. One is a member of a cultural group with respect to one of these dimensions to the extent that one's socially learned traits along that dimension are acquired by conformity to those of members of that group. In many cases we also add our own personal touch to socially transmitted traits. We adapt what we have learned to personal needs and interests. We also combine traits learned from more than one group. Cultures can evolve through such transformations.

With this general characterization of culture and cultural membership, let's turn to the question of what roles culture plays in morality. I think three roles are most important: culture can be the cause of morality, the effect of morality, and the reason for morality. Qua cause, culture is the primary source from which we get our values. We learn to be moral by undergoing a moral education, which involves being emotionally conditioned by the people around us, including caregivers, role models, and peers. The values we end up with are predominantly inherited from the values of others. Just as a culture can transmit religious beliefs, or vocational skills, it can transmit values. If we were not exposed to a culture (or cultures), we would not acquire the values we end up with, and we might not have any moral values at all. In this respect, morality can be regarded as a cultural construct.

Qua effect, cultures can be sustained, at least in part, through moral values. We affiliate with those who share our values, and shun those who do not. So morality binds individuals together. Other cultural constructs may do some binding as well, such as shared religious beliefs, but these factors often work in tandem with morality. If people who shared a religious outlook disagreed morally, they might not continue to interact, and the religious beliefs might evolve into distinct cultural traditions. Shared moral views allow for a kind of cohesion that is especially stable, because morality has an impact on behavior.

This relates to the third role of culture in morality. It is important to ask what morality is for. Why do we have moral values? The obvious answer is that morality emerges as a system of rules for getting people to function collectively in stable and productive ways. We have morality to build a coherent social group. Moral values lead us to cooperate and prevent us from harming members of our communities. Culture is the *raison d'être* for morality. Robinson Crusoe would have no need for it. In this respect, morality has a social nature (or at least a social telos).

These facts about culture are important to bear in mind when thinking about relativism. The relativist theory that I have been defending is a variant of what Dreier (1990) calls "speaker relativism." The content of a moral judgment depends on the values of the person who makes that judgment. Each of us is the ultimate arbitrator of our own values. I think speaker relativism is right, strictly speaking, but I think the label is misleading. I prefer to think of morality as intersubjective. There are two reasons for this. First, if I am right about the semantics, some moral terms actually presuppose that there are other individuals who share our moral views. In particular, I defended Agent Relativism about ought judgments, and, on this view, I cannot truly say that someone ought to do something without presupposing that this other person shared my values. Second, and more profoundly, morality is cultural in all the ways I described. If my values are informed by culture, promote culture, and came into existence to serve cultural ends, then my values are very likely to be shared by others. Moreover, when I engage in moral discourse, I do so as a member of culture in an effort to coordinate my behavior with others. Most moral debates are probably conducted between people who share basic moral values, and we typically assume shared values when we engage in debate.

For these reasons, I think we can talk about communities of moralizers, and the boundaries of such groups will often coincide with boundaries of groups which are pretheoretically regarded as cultures. This is especially likely within small-scale societies where there is greater homogeneity and less opportunity for interaction with people who have different historical backgrounds. As groups get bigger and more complex, there is often greater variation, but this does not preclude generalizations. We can even talk about the values of a nation. It would be a mistake to talk about Roman values if that means the values shared by all citizens of Rome. But it makes perfectly good sense to talk about the values promoted by those in power in Rome. There were active efforts to unify the Roman Empire through the promotion of moral values. Likewise for the Aztecs, who were ethnically diverse, but unified by a shared set of institutions and practices that probably resulted in considerable moral convergence.

Within the contemporary Western world we find similar examples. In the United States, there is a public discourse about freedom that is designed to promote the view that democracy is a basic value. Patriotism is also promoted as basic. If someone in the United States is accused of being unpatriotic, the usual response is to reject the accusation, not to reject the claim that patriotism has intrinsic value. In some European countries, there is a concerted effort to replace the ideal of patriotism with the ideal of cosmopolitanism (or at least loyalty to the European Community). Despite such homogenization campaigns, countries continue to promote distinctive values within their own borders. In France, people commonly appeal to values of the Republic: liberty, equality, and fraternity. These values are not cherished by everyone in France, and they certainly have advocates outside of France, but they may be especially likely to serve as grounding norms in moral debates among the French. We can talk of "French values" as shorthand for values that are highly promoted in France, and hence especially likely to be embraced by those who have been enculturated in France. It is simplistic to assume that any nation can be associated with a single set of values, but talk of prevalent values is unproblematic. For this reason, we can sometimes speak loosely about French morality or Aztec morality. This is not always appropriate. Moral judgments must often be relativized to groups whose boundaries fail to coincide with any particular nation. But, it would be a mistake to neglect the extent to which members of a society tend to conform. Indeed, conformity across groups (and hence group values) has a kind of priority over individual values, insofar as a given individual is likely to have acquired values from a social collective. If we neglect the morality of cultures, we will lose insight into the morality of individuals even if cultural morality is just an average across aggregated individuals.

In what follows, I will often talk about the values of a particular cultural group. I don't mean this to be a departure from the individualistic form of relativism that I endorse, but rather an indication of the fact that individuals often share moral values within cultural groups. In fact, the best way to prove that there is variation in morality is often to look at group level trends. If a moral dispute arises between two individuals, it is always possible that one of them is confused about facts, inarticulate, or insincere. But, if two groups seem to have divergent values, averaging across many individuals, the differences are harder to dismiss. Moreover, the apparent moral divergence between groups is often more dramatic than the divergence between individuals in the same group. Group disagreements are, thus, the major source of evidence for descriptive relativism and a major factor in building a case for metaethical relativism.

5.2 OBJECTIONS TO RELATIVISM

5.2.1 Descriptive Relativism

I will now survey a number of objections that have been raised against metaethical relativism. Most of these objections target relativism directly, but the first is an objection to the argument I used to defend relativism in the first place. Recall that my argument for metaethical relativism had descriptive relativism as a premise. Descriptive relativism is often taken as obvious, given the apparent diversity of moral beliefs and practices. Evidence for diversity is usually drawn from cross-cultural research. When we review the anthropological record, it seems obvious that morality varies across cultures. Alleged differences can be challenged, however, and, even if differences can be established, descriptive relativism does not necessarily follow. Before spelling out this objection, it will be useful to introduce some examples. On the face of it, many cultures engage in practices that people in contemporary Euro-American cultures would find reprehensible.

Once again, we can begin with cannibalism. Two forms of cannibalism are generally distinguished by anthropologists. Mortuary cannibalism is the practice of eating the dead. In most cases, dead bodies are burnt and then the ashes are mixed with a liquid and consumed. It is not always done this way, however. At the beginning of the twentieth century, female members of the Fore culture in New Guinea used to consume the bodies of dead relatives after burying them for a few days. This practice led to an epidemic of what the Fore call *kuru*, or the laughing death. This is a form of transmissible spongiform encephalopathy—a human form of mad cow disease (Mead et al., 2003). Mortuary cannibalism contrasts with warfare cannibalism, in which people consume the bodies of those who have been killed or captured in war. The Aztecs were responsible for the most extensive system of warfare cannibalism on record. Though estimates vary, they are believed to have sacrificed between 20,000 and 80,000 people every year (Harner, 1977). Sometimes thousands would be killed in a single festival. Victims were sacrificed on rounded alters on top of great pyramids. They would have their hearts removed by priests as they were held down. The bodies were rolled down the pyramid steps, and then distributed to their captors. Their limbs were cooked and consumed.

Massive public carnage was institutionalized at various times in European history. The blood sports of ancient Rome are an obvious example. The Colosseum could seat 45,000 eager fans, with standing room for 5,000 more (Platner and Ashby, 1929). At lunchtime, spectators at the Colosseum would see prisoners being crucified, burnt, or torn apart by animals. After that, they watched gladiators, who were almost all slaves, clash in deadly combat. If a gladiator was defeated, but not mortally wounded, the crowd could demand a finishing blow. After a gladiator was killed, his body was prodded with a hot iron and his head was smashed with a mallet. Gladiatorial bouts were not a short-lived outgrowth of the decadent years that preceded the fall of Rome. They lasted for over 500 years (264 BCE–c.404 CE). When the games were ultimately banned by the Christian emperors, it was not because they were deemed too cruel. Wiedemann (1992) argues that the games were banned because they presupposed that salvation could be achieved through military valor. This conflicted with the eschatology that Christians were trying to promote.

Let's move, for variety, from violence to sex, or at least to kinship. We tend to have moral attitudes toward marriage. We value monogamous, wedded, loving, pair bonds, and deviations from this ideal are often considered immoral. Other cultures have different arrangements. Many cultures have arranged marriages, rather than marriages out of love. Polygyny is also commonplace, in which a man has more than one wife. In societies that require monogamous marriage, there are often institutionalized systems of concubinage, which can be functionally equivalent to a polygamous system. In this arrangement, men can have multiple extramarital partners, and they can live in the man's household and inherit his wealth. Concubinage was widely practiced in Europe before being banned by the early Christian Church (Goody, 1983). Polyandry is less common than polygyny, but not unheard of. It is practiced, most famously, in Nepal and Tibet. Even without polyandry, some cultures have permissive attitudes toward female infidelity. Among the Tlingit, wives can have sex with members of the clan, but sex outside the clan is punishable by death (Oberg, 1934). Female sexual infidelity is also tolerated in some societies, especially if it remains within the in-group. Using a large cross-cultural sample, Hupka (1981; 1991) argues that there is much higher tolerance of infidelity in cultures that are sexually permissive and do not place emphasis on private property.

In almost all cultures (see below) there are prohibitions against incest, but these vary considerably. In Euro-American cultures it is considered incestuous to marry a first cousin, while in parts of India and Pakistan and the Middle East, marrying a first cousin is strongly encouraged (Bittles, 1990). In some cultures incest between siblings in punished severely, and in others it is merely discouraged. For example, among the Incas, incest is punished by gouging out the eyes, whereas among the Trumai, it is merely frowned upon (Thornhill, 1991). Kuper (2002) found evidence for a lax attitude toward sibling incest in nineteenth-century Britain. In the court record of an adultery trial only a passing mention was made of the fact that the woman accused of adultery had committed this act with her full brother.

There is cultural variation in views about what kind of sexual partners are appropriate. In some cultures, homosexuality is strongly condemned, and in others it is normal. In feudal Japan, for example, romantic relationships between Samurai and young men were encouraged (Leupp, 1995). Among the Etoro of New Guinea, all men engage in homosexual sex, and they are only allowed to have sex with women during about one hundred days of the year (Kelly, 1977). In the West, attitudes toward homosexuality have varied. In Rome and medieval Europe, it was often tolerated, but, in the thirteenth century, homosexuality went from being legal to being punishable by death (Boswell, 1980).

Sexual relations between adults and children can also be found. In parts of India, for example, daughters of poor families are given to temples to serve as *devadasi*, or wives to the gods (Marglin, 1985). These girls serve as prostitutes; they are expected to have sex with adult males from the time they are pubescent. Among the Sambia of New Guinea, boys engage in ritual fellatio with adult men (Herdt, 1987). Some cultures seem to tolerate bestiality. Among the Kuguru, there are rules prohibiting intercourse with another person's cow, but not, evidently, one's own (Davis and Whitten, 1987). In early modern England, in contrast, bestiality was often treated as a capital offense (Thomas, 1983).

Marriage is an institution designed for the production and rearing of offspring. As a final example of cultural variation, I want to consider infanticide, a fate that many offspring around the world must face. In China, infanticide was once widespread, and though now illegal, it continues to be practiced (Coale and Banister, 1994). Evidence for continued infanticide comes from gender birth rates. In some Chinese provinces, far more male births are reported than female births, suggesting that female infants are being killed. In China infanticide has been much more frequently practiced against girls, because they bring less support to the family. Traditionally, girls were especially incapable of providing support in China because they were subjected to foot binding, another practice that would be frowned upon in the West. Infanticide is much less unusual than foot binding. It has been practiced all over the world, and, as in China, the victims are usually girls. The Inuits practiced infanticide until recent times (Freeman, 1971). Ancient Greeks and Romans left unwanted babies to die of exposure to the elements. According to legend, this is just what happened to Oedipus, but, as fate would have it, he managed to survive. In contemporary American culture, infanticide is seriously condemned. In 1996, the State of New Jersey sought the death penalty when Amy Grossberg and Brian Peterson, a young couple from an affluent suburb, were charged with killing their newborn.

This survey of divergent moral values could go on and on. All the examples demonstrate that members of other cultures engage in behaviors that we find deviant, shocking, or atrocious. It is natural to infer from such examples that moral values are culturally relative. Descriptive relativism seems incontestable.

But descriptive relativism actually requires more defense. The thesis faces three related objections. First, opponents of relativism maintain that some examples of variation have been exaggerated. Take the Roman obsession with gladiatorial games. Is this so different from the contemporary obsession with football, boxing, and violent movies? Or take Inuit infanticide. In extremely harsh environments with scarce resources, population control can be necessary to save the group. Wouldn't we consider it permissible to take an infant's life if we were in such a setting? (Rachels, 1986: ch. 2) In some cases, public discourse may imply that values across two cultures differ, but observing actual practices suggests convergence.

Second, in cases where there is cultural variation in moral values, it is not clear whether the differences are intractable. Descriptive relativism can be defined as the view that people have different sentiments toward the same things. I have been suggesting that such differences exist, but they are actually difficult to establish. We have nothing like a cerebroscope for looking directly inside the brain and seeing what moral rules lurk inside. To show that people have different sentiments, we need to rely on indirect evidence, and, in particular, we need to show that there are fundamental moral disputes. A fundamental dispute is one that persists even after all the non-moral facts are in. If a moral dispute trades on different beliefs about non-moral facts, then the dispute will abate when the facts come in. A dispute that persists once all the non-moral facts are agreed upon is best explained by postulating a difference in moral sentiments. The argument from descriptive relativism to metaethical relativism depends on showing that there are moral disputes of this kind, because such disputes are the main evidence for the thesis that descriptive moral relativism is true. But the existence of such disputes has been contested.

Interestingly, Hume was not a relativist. He says that fundamental moral disputes will not arise because all human beings share the same core values in virtue of having a shared human nature. Moral disagreements stem from disputes about non-moral facts. For example, Hume (1751: Dialogue Appendix) notes that the Athenians encouraged homosexual relationships—something that he and his contemporaries in Europe violently opposed. To explain this apparent moral disagreement, Hume argues that Athenians simply had mistaken factual beliefs. In particular, they "absurdly" believed that same-sex relations could be a source of "friendship, sympathy, mutual attachment, and fidelity."

Hume's example would not sway many readers today, but the basic strategy remains popular. People challenge descriptive relativism by arguing that apparent disagreements about values turn out to be disagreements about non-moral facts. In chapter 3, I noted that American slavery was supported by claims about the racial inferiority of Africans. One could say the same about the moral opposition to women's suffrage. Opponents argued that women's physical weakness would make them vulnerable to injury at polling places. They also claimed that women had lower levels of intelligence than men, and a tendency toward hysteria (Mayor, 1974; Woloch, 2000). Once the falsity of these claims is revealed, the arguments against suffrage collapse. In other cases, moral debates hinge on religious beliefs. Some opponents of abortion believe that personhood begins at conception, and they base this on religious teachings. Aztec sacrifice might be explained along similar lines. The Aztecs believed that their universe had been created when one god threw herself in a great fire and became the sun. Then other gods sacrificed themselves to make the sun move across the sky. They believed that they needed to sacrifice human beings to these gods in order to keep the sun from stopping. If the Aztecs had the facts right, their sacrificial rituals might have been banned. In each example here moral divergence seems to derive from divergent non-moral beliefs.

Michele Moody-Adams (1997) has recently argued that there is no single established case of a fundamental moral dispute. Each apparent example can be explained in terms of differences in non-moral beliefs. And this raises a third, closely related, objection to descriptive relativism. Moody-Adams argues that there are principled barriers to establishing that moral disputes exist. If we see members of two cultural groups making different moral judgments about the same event, we cannot be sure that they assign the same "situational meaning" to that event. When we consider other cultures, it is difficult, if not impossible to understand how they construe the facts. Beliefs about the world are determined holistically against the background of cosmological theories and experiential knowledge accrued within environmental and cultural conditions that are utterly unfamiliar to us. Can we really see the world from the Aztec, Inuit, and Tlingit point of view? If not, we cannot be sure that their moral values really differ from our own.

These three objections raise serious doubts about descriptive relativism. Descriptive relativism is the first premise in the core argument for metaethical relativism. If descriptive relativism is indefensible, that argument collapses. I will address each objection in turn.

I do not think moral differences across cultures have been seriously exaggerated. Indeed, I think our inability to bracket our own values often makes it difficult to see just how different values in other cultures may be. Roman blood sports are a good example. Consider what would happen if the Italian government decided to let people kill each other in public again. There would be massive international outrage. Violent cinema is a far cry from snuff movies. And suppose, implausibly, that the outrage subsided, and people started attending the blood sports with enthusiasm. This would not mean that we shared values with the Romans. They had complex moral views that were shaped by their particular cultural situation. Romans had very short life expectancies, and they had a preoccupation with expanding their empire through military conquest. The cardinal value in Rome was *virtus*, an ideal that included courage in the face of violent death. Taking pleasure in watching violence is not equivalent to valuing violence in the way that the Roman's did.

Similar points can be made about Inuit infanticide. If a couple from the United States was trapped in the arctic tundra with their newborn child and a group of adult travelers, they might consider infanticide. But they would view this decision with horror. It would be a profound and devastating moral dilemma. The Inuits have a more casual attitude toward infanticide (Thomas, 1983). What we regard as a necessary evil, they do not regard as evil at all. We might end up with similar values if we had spent generations in arctic conditions, but, until we have, our values will be different from theirs.

What about the charge that moral debates are based on (non-moral) factual debates? Here I think it depends on the case. American slavery and the anti-suffrage movements were certainly premised on some false factual claims. But the factual arguments used to defend these practices were often *post hoc*. They were concocted to rationalize non-rational values that were already in place. The same is true of religious justifications. The Aztec religion may have emerged after cannibal sacrifices began. The anthropological record shows that cannibalism exists in cultures with varied religious beliefs.

In some cases, it is very hard to pin moral debates onto factual beliefs. The audiences at gladiatorial bouts may have had some factual beliefs that diverged from ours, but their enthusiasm for blood sports seems to have been based on their values. Likewise for diverging attitudes toward bestiality. If we were to discover that the animals involved enjoyed having sex with humans, we would find the practice no less foul. In this respect, some moral debates may be like debates about taste. The person who dislikes chocolate is not the victim of a false belief. Furthermore, there is often no easy way to draw a fact/value distinction in moral debates. If opponents of abortion claim that a fetus is a person, this is in part an evaluative claim. As Locke might put it, PERSON is a forensic concept. Who you are as a person depends on what you take to be constitutive of personhood, and that is as much a matter of decision as discovery. It may also turn out that the abortion debate does not depend on the issue of personhood or any other seemingly non-moral facts. In a pilot study, I asked people if their stance on abortion would change if they changed their view on the question of whether a fetus is a person. Fifteen percent said their stance would change, 20 percent said their stance "might be affected," and the remaining 65 percent said their stance would remain unchanged. It is as if the value precedes the reasons we give in defending it; if one reason fails, we help ourselves to another. As with studies on moral dumbfounding (Murphy et al., 2000), these results suggest that factual beliefs are often playing a post hoc role in moral justification.

This leaves us with the Moody-Adams challenge. How can we know when a debate is evaluative rather than factual? Isn't it always possible that people with different practices construe events in very different ways? I think this line of questioning actually supports relativism. Moody-Adams is willing to grant relativism about non-moral beliefs. If people have radically different beliefs, why not think they have radically different values as well? Unless we have independent reasons for thinking values are fixed and immune to cultural permeation, we should take divergence in non-moral beliefs as evidence for the possibility of moral divergence. Moreover, there is a principled reason for thinking that moralities can diverge. I have argued that moral values are based on sentiments, and sentiments can surely be influenced by cultural context. We can be conditioned to feel angry about some things and guilty about others.

One can also address the Moody-Adams challenge by finding cases of moral debates between cultural groups that are very closely related. In such cases, it is difficult to defend the claim that the groups construe the world in radically different ways. A good strategy is to look for *sub*cultures—people within the same national boundaries, who nevertheless seem to have a different moral outlook. Let me mention three possible examples. First, there are obvious moral disagreements between American conservatives and American liberals. It is sometimes suggested that liberals and conservatives have different factual beliefs (e.g., about the status of fetuses as persons, or whether supply-side economics works), but the persistence of political debates among intelligent and informed individuals suggests that there may be a value divide here. I will return to this case below. A second possible example is the gender divide. Men and women in the same community often seem to have subtly different moral values. Relevant findings include the following: men are slightly more concerned with justice than women, and women are slightly more concerned with care (Jaffee and Hyde, 2000); men tend to be more in favor of violent punishment than women, and this difference has been linked to different responses in emotional centers of the brain (Singer et al., 2006); and women are significantly more deontological than men in the their responses to trolley dilemmas (Mikhail, 2002). It could be that men and women have different beliefs about the world because of their very different experiences, but those experiences may also inculcate different moral values.

The third example that I want to consider is violence among white males in the American South (Nisbett and Cohen, 1996). The case deserves extra attention because it has been studied in some detail and it is especially hard to pin on differences in factual beliefs. White southern males are more likely than white northern males to commit acts of violence in retaliation for actions that show disrespect: e.g., one man makes a pass at another man's wife; or one man brushes into another man without apologizing; or one man belittles another man in public. Nisbett and Cohen have argued that this is due to a cultural difference. Southern whites subscribe to a culture of honor. They live by a code of conduct that licenses a strong show of force when their honor has been offended. Southern whites are more likely to judge that violent retaliation is appropriate in these cases than their northern counterparts. Southern juries give lighter sentences, for example, to violent offenders who were defending their honor.

Southerners are also more tolerant of corporal punishment, violent self-defense, gun ownership, and the death penalty. There is evidence that this value system is implemented emotionally. Nisbett and Cohen (1996) measured stress hormones in southerners and northerners just after they had been brushed into by an unapologetic stranger (artfully staged by the experimenters). Southerners showed a significant increase in stress hormones as compared to a control condition, and northerners did not. Nisbett and Cohen speculate that southerners inherited their values from Scotch-Irish settlers. The Scotch-Irish came from the Ulster province of Ireland, which was populated by Irish natives and people of Scottish decent. Ulster had a herding economy, and little protection from the central government. A herder is always vulnerable to rustlers (compare farmers, whose farms cannot be stolen). As a result, herders often develop a culture of honor, in which violent self-defense is considered appropriate, even in response to relatively minor provocations. Similar value systems have been documented among herders in other parts of the world (Edgerton, 1971).

The southern violence case gets around some of the methodological concerns about cross-cultural research. We may not know enough about the Aztecs to understand how they construe the world, but we share a tremendous amount with people within our own national borders (political systems, standardized education, entertainment, etc.). To say that northerners and southerners construe the world in radically different ways is extravagant. The differences seem to be evaluative rather than factual.

The suggestion that there can be moral disagreement within a culture gains further support from a simple thought experiment. Imagine two families of philosophers that have become proponents of different normative theories. One family might raise their child to be a staunch utilitarian, while the family next door might raise their child to be a staunch deontologist. When faced with a trolley case, the children would agree completely on the facts, but they would disagree about what course of action was right. This hypothetical case shows that descriptive relativism is possible. There is every reason, in light of the examples surveyed here, to think that descriptive relativism is also actual. It is extremely plausible that children in the southern and northern United States are raised with different values. For example, southern parents are more likely to use corporal punishment than their northern counterparts, and southerners are much more likely to judge that a ten-year-old should fight a boy who hit him (Cohen and Nisbett, 1994). Regional differences in moral education have a long history, and are documented in the antebellum South (Wyatt-Brown, 1982).

Such variation in moral education undercuts one of Hume's strategies for arguing against descriptive relativism. He suggests that apparent moral disagreements must be based on disagreements about non-moral facts because all human beings naturally have the same fundamental moral values. This claim presupposes that core values derive from human nature. I will critically examine evidence for such a view in chapter 7, but we are already in a position to refute

Hume's argument. Fundamental moral values are what I have called grounding norms—norms that do not depend psychologically on appeal to any others. Suppose, with Hume, that human nature has furnished us with a stock of shared grounding norms. It doesn't follow that these grounding norms are fixed or exhaustive. Moral education works by emotional conditioning, and conditioning can alter prior affective dispositions. Just as we can acquire new fads, fears, and fancies through conditioning, we can also acquire new grounding norms. Two people who have been conditioned differently during development will have different fundamental moral values.

Consider Hume's own example of homosexuality. He says that the Athenians supported same-sex relationships because they mistakenly believed that such relationships promote friendship and other valuable things. This is implausible. Homosexual relationships probably emerged in Athens like a fashion trend: people were conditioned to think such relationships were praiseworthy. Likewise, Hume's virulent homophobia was probably the result of conditioning, not of beliefs about non-moral facts. A community can instill negative attitudes toward just about any sexual behavior simply by expressing disgust whenever that behavior is mentioned. Hume is so repelled by homosexuality that he describes it only by allusion. My guess is that people acquire their attitudes toward homosexuality before they can articulate any reason to be in favor or opposed. Hume mentions that Athenians may have been disposed to favor homosexuality because of their affection for sports. If that's right, then moral disputes about homosexuality are clashes in grounding norms that have been culturally inculcated. If grounding norms can be acquired through conditioning, then there can be moral disputes that do not hinge on divergent factual beliefs.

I think the case for descriptive relativism is overwhelming. If fundamental values can be acquired through conditioning, as constructive sentimentalism entails, then the members of different cultures can have different fundamental values. Moral debates across such cultural boundaries cannot be resolved by appeal to non-moral facts. Such debates reflect fundamental disagreements.

5.2.2 Coherence

One of the standard objections to metaethical relativism is that the doctrine is incoherent (e.g., Lyons, 1976; Cooper, 1978). The problem is easy to see if we re-examine the definition given above. The original formulation will suffice:

> *Metaethical Relativism*: The truth conditions of a moral judgment depend on the context in which that judgment is formed.

If this thesis is correct, the same judgment can be both true and false. Take the judgment that it is morally acceptable to capture and consume a resident from your neighboring community. Call this judgment J. An Aztec can utter J truly.

I can utter "Not J" truly. Therefore, "J and Not J" is true. But "J and Not J" is a contradiction. Any theory that entails a contradiction is false (cf. Lyons, 1976).

There are obvious ways to get around this version of the coherence problem. On the version of relativism I favor, moral judgments must be assessed relative to contexts, if they have truth values at all. The judgment that it is morally acceptable to catch and consume your neighbors expresses one proposition, when uttered by an Aztec, and another proposition when expressed by me. Thus there is no contradiction when "J" and "Not J" are uttered in different contexts. Moreover, contexts are determined by speakers' values, and no speaker would assent to both "J" and "Not J"; thus, there is no context in which "J and Not J" comes out true.

The opponent of relativism might argue that this method of preserving coherence actually undermines metaethical relativism rather than saving it. If content relativism is true, then changes in context shift the meanings of moral terms. When such a shift takes place, there is no guarantee that the "moral" vocabulary still deserves to be called "moral." For example, there is nothing to guarantee that the word "good" when spoken by a member of another culture means good. And, if it doesn't mean good, then we have little reason to say that members of other cultures make moral judgments. And if they don't, then only our judgments can qualify as moral, and there is just one morality after all.

A version of this objection can be adapted from the work of Donald Davidson (1974). Davidson argues against the idea that there could be more than one conceptual scheme, i.e., two or more incommensurable conceptual systems for describing the same world. Davidson's argument is complex, because he examines a number of ways in which philosophers have thought about the scheme–world relation. Here is a very simplified rendition. Suppose there were two schemes, Schema-1 and Schema-2. Now someone utters a sentence in the vocabulary of Schema-2, and we speak the vocabulary of Schema-1. According to Davidson, a sentence can be meaningful only if it has truth conditions, and truth conditions must be specified using Tarski's T-schema. A sentence, S, is true if and only if P, where P is a translation of S into a metalanguage. Thus, a Schema-2 sentence can be deemed meaningful only if it can be translated into a language that we understand. *Ex hypothesi*, Schema-2 is not translatable into Schema-1, so we can never have grounds for thinking that Schema-2 sentences are meaningful. They are either translatable into our own language (hence commensurable) or they are mere noises.

Cooper (1978) draws on Davidson's ideas to criticize moral relativism. Adapting Cooper, we can imagine encountering a person who says that it "is morally good to break promises." We might initially think that this person has a radically different moral scheme. But this hypothesis would be difficult to maintain. The very fact that the person applies "good" to things that we find bad undermines any confidence that we might have understood what the person was saying. Either "good" means something other than good in this person's idiolect, or it means nothing at all. If Cooper is right, Davidsonian principles should lead us to doubt apparent evidence for relativism. Put more strongly, a radically different moral scheme would be unintelligible. There would be no reason to call it meaningful, let alone a theory of morality.

The Davidsonian argument against moral relativism depends on two dubious assumptions. First, it depends on the assumption that a person's utterances are meaningful only if we can translate them into our own vocabulary. In other words, an utterance is meaningful only if we can interpret it. I reject this assumption. I have already endorsed an account of how concepts get their meaning that does not depend on interpretation in Davidson's sense. On this view, a concept means whatever it was set up to be set off by. This is not the place for a full defense of Dretske over Davidson (see, e.g., Sterelny, 1990). I will point out only that Davidson's principle—if we cannot interpret an utterance, then it doesn't have any meaning—constitutes a strong form of semantic verificationism. It entails, for example, that non-human animals do not have meaningful mental states because we cannot ascribe beliefs to them using our vocabulary (Davidson, 1975). This is a bizarre claim in its own right, given the fact that animal behavior is predictable and, in some broad sense, intelligible. But, it's even more incredible when applied to the human case. Suppose we find a culture whose members use terms that closely resemble our own moral terms, but they apply these terms to different things than we would. If we cannot find any adequate translation (try to translate Roman *virtus*), we are forced to say these people are speaking nonsense. So we save ourselves from the view that there are many moralities by proposing that many cultures make meaningless noises in the situations where we would make moral evaluations. Instead of saying that these people have different conceptual schemes, Davidson would have us say they have no scheme. That's worse than bizarre; it's insulting.

The Davidsonian argument against relativism could be endorsed by someone who rejected Davidsonian semantics. Someone could maintain that any evidence for moral diversity is even stronger evidence for misunderstanding. On this approach, we wouldn't need to deny that other people in other cultures speak intelligibly; we would need only question our grasp of what they are saying. Following Davidson, Cooper says, if someone used terms such as "good" and "bad" in a surprising way, we would have no reason to think that those terms were being used to express moral beliefs. This is the second dubious assumption that I want to examine.

I have argued that moral concepts are sentimental. To believe that something is wrong is to have certain emotional dispositions toward it. These dispositions are recognizable. We can recognize anger, disgust, and shame, for example. These emotions allow us to determine, with considerable confidence, whether a member of another culture has moralized something. Suppose we find that a woman in a foreign culture shows contempt for women who do not cover their heads; suppose that she shows shame when we catch her with her head uncovered; and suppose that she shows profound disappointment when her daughter refuses to keep her head covered. Suppose, further, that these reactions are common in her culture, and that there are manuals of conduct and sacred texts that urge women to keep their heads covered. If someone of this culture uses the Farsi word "gonâkhâr" to characterize women who do not cover their heads, then we have reason to think that "gonâkhâr" is a moral term. We have reason to believe that it is semantically related to the English word "wrong." This is the kind of information that anthropologists and lexicographers go on.

Granted, it would be hard to identify moral vocabulary in a culture if sentiments there did not overlap with our sentiments to some degree. If members of the culture in question did not think that random killing was "gonâkhâr," we might wonder if that term had moral significance. But in most cases, the differences won't be that extreme. Most cultures overlap to some degree in the application of their sentiments. And even when overlap is minimal, if people in another culture use terms to express sentiments that are recognizably similar to our moral sentiments, we have reason for thinking that those terms have moral significance. We recognize moral vocabulary by telltale sentiments, and we can recognize sentiments by physiology, phenomenological reports, facial expressions, and behaviors (including punishments). When negative sentiments are expressed toward things that we value, we can conclude that some people have moral values that differ from our own.

This response to the Davidsonian argument can be explicated more precisely by invoking the distinction between content and character, which I introduced in the discussion of content relativism above. When we encounter members of other cultures who apply apparently moral terms in surprising ways, we can conclude that those terms have different content in those cultures. However, if the terms express familiar sentiments, we can also conclude that they have the same character as our moral terms. As long as the character is the same, we can safely conclude that these terms have moral significance when used by members of other cultures. If meaning were exhausted by content, the Davidsonian argument would have some merit. We would not be entitled to interpret foreign terms as moral terms if they were applied differently from our moral terms. With character, we introduce a new level for semantic comparison, and the claim that cultures have different moralities is rendered perfectly coherent. It is tantamount to the view that people in different cultures have comparable sentiments toward different things. This is no more problematic than claiming that two people can like different things.

The content/character distinction leaves us with a question. If we encounter a culture with different moral values than our own, are their moral terms *translatable* into our moral terms? The answer to this question depends on how we define translation. Let's define terms as weakly intertranslatable if they express the same functions from context to content. The word "wrong" is a function from negative sentiments and speaker's culture to content. There are words in the languages of morally diverse cultures that meet this criterion of translatability. "Gonâkhâr" may be an example. Let's define terms as strongly intertranslatable if the terms have the same character and content when spoken by speakers of the respective languages. The term "I" fails to meet this criterion quite dramatically, because it does not have the same content in any two idiolects. Moral terms fail to meet this criterion too. If we direct our moral sentiments differently from members of another culture, we cannot translate their terms into ours on this strong criterion. Our moral terms may express similar sentiments, but they have different contents. If we used our moral vocabulary to paraphrase their moral talk, the content of the sentences would change. If we paraphrased their sentences using words that had the same content, we could no longer use words that express our sentiments, so the character of the sentences would change. If we define incommensurability as the impossibility of strong translation between two schemes, then moral incommensurability is perfectly possible. There is nothing incoherent about the idea that moral vocabularies can be incommensurable.

5.2.3 Indexicality

In responding to the Davidsonian argument, I appealed to content relativism. If this analysis is right, then moral terms have meanings that must get filled in by context. There are words that clearly work this way. Examples include pronouns, such as "I," "you," and "he"; demonstratives, such as "this" and "that"; and locative terms, such as "here" and "there." No one would be surprised to hear that these words depend on context. Their indexicality is recognized by all competent language users. The claim that moral terms are indexical is, by comparison, controversial. It would be a surprising discovery to most language users. This alone is no objection. Meanings can surprise us. But, if moral terms really are indexical, then they should work like paradigm cases of indexical terms. Words like "I" and "here" have identifiable patterns of use. They leave subtle clues—often syntactic in nature—that reveal their indexical nature. We can run tests to see whether a word really is indexical. The very same tests can be applied to moral terms. When this is done, however, moral terms seem to fail. They do not behave the way that one would expect if they really were indexical. This poses a challenge to the relativist.

I will present this objection by appropriating some arguments from Cappelen and Lepore (2005). Cappelen and Lepore do not argue directly against the view that moral judgments are context-dependent. They are intent on debunking context-dependency more broadly. Consider the sentence "It's raining." A number of philosophers presume that this sentence contains an implicit reference to location. When we say, "It's raining," we invariably intend to convey that it is raining somewhere. The location is not explicitly mentioned, but it is nevertheless part of the meaning of the sentence. Some proponents of this view say that "It's raining" contains a hidden indexical. The location is represented in the underlying syntactic structure of the sentence, even though it does not appear in the surface form. Cappelen and Lepore offer a battery of arguments against hidden indexicals. They contend that the meaning of "It's raining" contains no element referring to location. Information about location is conveyed by pragmatics, and is not part of the syntax or the meaning of the sentence.

Perhaps Cappelen and Lepore are right about, "It's raining." I have no commitment on that. But their arguments seem to cause trouble for relativism. If relativism is right, the truth conditions of moral claims depend on the context in which they are uttered. I endorsed content relativism above, and content relativists sometimes assume that context-sensitive terms contain "hidden indexical" components, which make implicit reference to such things as the speaker. If such hidden indexical components exist, then one might expect them to make a contribution to the syntax of the sentences containing them, and their presence should be detectable using a variety of syntactic tests. If a sentence containing an allegedly context-sensitive term fails to show evidence of hidden indexicals using syntactic tests, then that might be taken as evidence against the claim that the term is context-sensitive. Applied to morality, one might suppose that, if moral terms really were context-sensitive, they would reveal this fact through syntactic tests. Cappelen and Lepore have proposed a variety of tests, and, at first pass, it may appear that moral terms fail. These failures might be marshaled as evidence against a relativist account of moral vocabulary.

There are two strategies one might take in response to this kind of syntactic critique. First, one might argue that the syntactic tests in question are not in fact good tests for relativism. One could propose that some context-sensitive terms, including moral terms, introduce no special syntactic elements. In introducing content relativism, I mentioned this option, and it is also available for defenders of truth relativism, who argue that context sensitivity arises at a level of semantic evaluation that occurs after meaning is assigned to terms. One of these options might work. Relativism as such is a thesis about truth and reference, not a thesis about syntax or logical form, so relativists need not endorse the hidden indexical view. But there is also a second strategy for defending relativism against syntactic arguments. One might argue that moral terms pass the tests for hidden indexicality. I want to explore this possibility. I will proceed by considering some tests that Cappelen and Lepore have discussed in their efforts to debunk context-sensitive semantics. Their tests can be adapted to the moral case, and they may appear to undermine the thesis that moral terms contain hidden indexicals. I will argue, however, that initial appearances are deceiving. Moral terms can be shown to pass the tests. If that's the case, the hidden indexical analysis may turn out to be true.

On the hidden indexical account of moral terms, saying "Cannibalism is wrong" is verbal shorthand for something like, "Cannibalism is wrong *according to the values of the appraiser or some other salient individual(s)*." "You ought not to engage in cannibalism" is shorthand for "You ought not to engage in cannibalism *according to the values of the appraiser and the addressee.*"

If the hidden indexical account were correct, the hidden syntactic component referring to context should be detectable. Cappelen and Lepore suggest some tests, based on how explicit indexicals function, and they argue that alleged cases of hidden indexicals fail these tests. I will adapt three of their arguments to the moral case. They have other tests, beyond these three, but these can be left for another occasion. The first test involves anaphoric reference. With sentences containing explicit indexicals, one can add clauses containing words that refer back anaphorically to the indexical element. Consider the following examples from Cappelen and Lepore (2005: 76):

(1a) He is a senator.
(1b) He's a senator who likes *himself.*
(2a) That's a table.
(2b) That's a table but *it* is not a book.

The word "himself" in (1b) refers back to the word "he" and picks out the same individual. In (2b), the word "it" refers back to the demonstrative, "that." If moral sentences contain hidden indexicals, it should be possible to add clauses that refer back anaphorically to them as well. But when one attempts to do this, the sentences come out as anomalous. Here is an example:

(3a) Cannibalism is wrong.
(3b) *Cannibalism is wrong, but they do eat intelligent mammals.

On the hidden indexical view, (3a) has a hidden element that can be glossed as, "according to the values of the salient individuals." The word "they" in (3b) is supposed to refer anaphorically to those individuals. The sentence, however, sounds peculiar, suggesting that this postulated hidden element doesn't really exist. Moral sentences do not pass the anaphor test.

Or so it seems. I think that the failure is merely apparent. Above, I said that moral sentences with no explicit context are taken, by default, to refer to the context of the appraiser who utters the sentence. The third-person pronoun in the second cause of (3b) sounds odd, because someone hearing the first clause of that sentence would assume that the relevant context is the context of the speaker. In other words, the anomaly here may be semantic not syntactic. Notice that that the sentence sounds perfectly fine if we switch to the first person:

(3c) Cannibalism is wrong, but we do eat intelligent mammals.

Unfortunately, (3c) does not prove that "wrong" passes the anaphora test, because first-person pronouns cannot be used anaphorically. But this observation suggests that it is actually very difficult to apply the anaphora test to moral terms. If moral terms default to the first-person when no explicit parameter is introduced, and first-person pronouns cannot be used anaphorically, the test may cut no ice. Perhaps the closest we can come is to imagine a non-linguistic context, in which it is obvious that the default of self-reference is not operative. Imagine opening an anthropologist's field book, and seeing (3b) written as an entry. In this situation, the sentence no longer sounds anomalous. It is clear that the pronoun refers to some other cultural group. Of course, it's possible that the anthropologist who wrote the sentence was observing his subjects at the time that he wrote it, and the pronoun was introduced demonstratively, not anaphorically. If that were the case, we would again have to conclude that the anaphor test is difficult to apply in the moral case. But, I want to suggest that there is an anaphorical reading of (3b) in the fieldbook case, which is perfectly intelligible. If I am right, this undercuts the contention that moral sentences fail the anaphor test.

Cappelen and Lepore have other tests, however, which may be used to challenge the hidden indexical thesis. They note that explicit indexicals can be used to produce sentences that can be known a priori. Here is an example that they borrow from Kaplan (see Cappelen and Lepore, 2005: 78):

(4) I am the person who utters this sentence.

If moral sentences contain hidden indexicals, we should be able to get comparable platitudes by making those indexicals explicit. This is not what happens. The following sentence seems paradigmatically a posteriori:

(5) If killing is wrong, then it is against my value system to kill.

Intuitively, it looks like killing might be wrong even if it is not wrong on my value system. The wrongness of killing doesn't depend on me. Suppose, for example, that I am a mob hit man, and I think killing is permissible. In this case, (5) would be false, because the antecedent would be true and the consequent false.

This looks like a powerful counterexample to the hidden indexical account of moral discourse, but the example is flawed. Recall that, on the view I am defending, "wrong" can be relativized to speaker *or* to some other salient individual. Sentence (5) may appear to be contingent, or even false, because the term "wrong" can be relativized to someone other than the speaker. If "wrong" is relativized to you, and you morally condemn killing, then the antecedent of (5) it true, and it remains true regardless of what my values happen to be. But suppose we fix the context. Suppose we stipulate that (5) is uttered in a context in which the word "wrong" is relativized to the speaker. In this case, it seems that we can derive (5) a priori. For suppose that I am the speaker, and I condemn killing; then I would say truly that killing is wrong, and it would also be true that killing is against my values. Or suppose that I am the speaker and I applaud killing; then (relative to me) it's false that killing is wrong. Either way the conditional is true. So, there is a reading of (5) on which it can be known a priori.

This example can be modified to show that the moral discourse view passes a further test for hidden indexicality. Lepore and Cappelen (forthcoming) claim that we can generate contradictions with explicit indexicals that we cannot generate with some alleged hidden indexicals. Contrast these two sentences:

(6) I am hungry, but the speaker of the sentence is not hungry.
(7) It's raining, but it is not raining in Chapel Hill.

Sentence (6) is a flagrant contradiction. On the hidden indexical account of "It's raining," sentence (7) should be a contradiction too, in contexts where the hidden location parameter is filled by "Chapel Hill." In those contexts, (7) should be equivalent to (8):

(8) It's raining in Chapel Hill, but it is not raining in Chapel Hill.

Since (7) is never contradictory, and (8) is always contradictory, they cannot be equivalent. This counts against the hidden indexical of "It's raining" (though proponents of that account may reply by arguing that (7) simply appears non-contradictory, because pragmatic factors rule out the contradictory context). Now contrast the raining case with the moral case. The following sentence, which is a counterpoint to (5), *does* have a reading on which it is contradictory:

(9) Killing is wrong, but it is not against my value system to kill.

The fact that (9) has a contradictory reading suggests that it is very much like the explicit indexical example in (6), and unlike (7) (assuming that Cappelen and Lepore are right to think (7) is never contradictory). This is just what the hidden indexical view of moral sentences would predict.

I will consider one more argument based on Cappelen and Lepore, which might be brought to bear against relativism. With explicit indexicals, sentences of the following kind are perfectly acceptable:

(10) When John said, "I am hungry," he spoke truly, but I was not hungry.

The word "I" shifts content with context, so the phrase "I am hungry" can be affirmed and denied in the same sentence, with the help of quotation (see Cappelen and Lepore, 2005: 106). Relativists assume that moral terms can also shift content with context. Therefore, it should be possible to get acceptable moral sentences that parallel (10). But such sentences come out anomalous:

(11) *When Moctezuma said, "You ought to eat prisoners," he spoke truly, but you ought not to eat prisoners.

Sentence (11) sounds very weird when compared to (10). That suggests that moral terms do not get their meaning from context, as relativism demands.

This objection is surmountable. There is an important difference between moral terms and indexical pronouns. Moral terms have what Stevenson (1937) called a "dynamic" level of meaning: they express emotions. When we use moral terms in certain contexts, we can't help but express the emotions implicated in the concepts underlying those terms. When we express those emotions, we convey endorsement. I think we can ascribe moral claims to other people without expressing our emotions or endorsing their views. But, when we say that the claims of others are true, we convey endorsement, and we cannot endorse others' moral views without feeling an emotional commitment to those views, and that reintroduces the dynamic level of meaning. When we use the word "truth" with expressive terms, we endorse their descriptive meaning and their dynamic meaning. Thus, the problem with (11) is pragmatic.

This phenomenon is not restricted to moral discourse. Consider the word "yummy," which both describes food and expresses a feeling toward food. My contention is that we cannot ascribe a sentence containing the word yummy to others without endorsing the feeling. The following example bears that out:

> (12) * When John said, "The tripe is yummy," he spoke truly, but tripe is not yummy.

To my ears, (12) sounds anomalous. It sounds as bad as (11). But this does not in any way undermine the claim that "yummy" is a relative term that gets its meaning completed contextually. I submit that (11) and (12) are pragmatically anomalous, not semantically contradictory.

To test this pragmatic interpretation, we need to find a way of canceling the emotional endorsement that arises when we praise others' expressive statements as true. Consider the following:

> (13) When Moctezuma said, "You ought to eat prisoners," what he said was true in his value system, but I think you ought not to eat prisoners.

To my ear (13), does not sound contradictory. It may be false, if relativism is false, but showing that would require a refutation of relativism; there is no glaring contradiction here. To assume that (13) is anomalous would beg the question against the relativist.

In effect, (13) makes the postulated hidden indexical components explicit. It might be objected that this move actually vitiates the hidden indexical view, because if (13) is just an explicit statement of what is implicit in (11), the two sentences should sound equally good. But this objection misses the point that I was making in my diagnosis of (11). When we do not make hidden indexical components explicit, there can be ambiguities about the context of evaluation. The use of the word "true" sounds like an endorsement and implies that the context of evaluation is the speakers' own value system. On that interpretation, (11) is contradictory. Sentence (13) does not sound contradictory, because the implicature (truth as evaluative endorsement) is cancelled. Indeed, after considering the interpretation made explicit in (13), sentence (11) no longer seems so bad. In a discussion of moral relativism, for example, (11) would be perfectly appropriate. The relativist might use (11) to express the idea that other people have values that have a claim to truth, but don't try to do those things at home. If such a reading is available, then moral terms pass this test for hidden indexicality.

The hypothesis that moral terms introduce hidden indexicals is consistent with linguistic evidence. Relativists do not need to endorse a hidden indexical view, but, as it happens, moral terms seem to pass the tests for hidden indexicality. These tests tend to confirm relativism rather than refuting it.

I do not think the hidden indexical view has been proven by anything I've said. Perhaps the syntactic tests are inadequate. But I think it enjoys enough prima facie support to be accepted as a working hypothesis. Astute readers might worry about this. The hidden indexical view makes sense of some linguistic phenomena, but it is ostensibly hard to square with a claim I have made about the psychology of moral judgment. In chapter 4, I noted that some people are moral relativists and others are moral objectivists. But how can anyone be an objectivist if the hidden indexical view is right? Hidden indexicalists build relativism into the lexical semantics of moral terms. Competent users should realize this, and they should resist objectivism as a result. The fact that some people purport to be objectivists suggests that the hidden indexical account is mistaken.

This worry can be answered in different ways. One possible response was already mentioned: we don't have explicit access to the structure of our lexical entries, so we may not immediately realize that we are all implicitly committed to relativism. Another answer is even more decisive, however. The hidden indexical view is compatible with objectivism. If "wrong" means wrong-for-me, when I say it and wrong-for-you, when you say it, there could still be a single true morality. What's wrong for me might be wrong for you; and what's wrong for both of us may even be some mind-independent feature of reality. The hidden indexical view is neutral about what our moral concepts designate in the world, and as such it is compatible with both objectivist and non-objectivist theories of morality. It is not surprising, then, that there are individual differences in response to questions about moral objectivity.

In sum, I think the hidden indexical account may be correct. Arguments that have been used against hidden indexicality in other domains do not apply in the moral case, and moral relativism cannot be debunked by syntactic tests.

5.2.4 Insidiousness

Some of the objections that are raised against relativism are technical. I have discussed the coherence of relativism and the syntactic evidence for relativism. These technical concerns can be answered, but the real resistance to relativism derives from a deeper worry. Relativism is often regarded as an insidious doctrine. If there are multiple moralities, then, it seems, there is no way to prove that one morality is any better than any other. If that is the case, then the morality that we happen to embrace is not privileged. This has two very disturbing implications. First, when we engage in moral disputes with others, there is a sense in which those disputes are spurious. Second, once we discover that our moral preferences are not privileged, our confidence in those preferences is destabilized. Why continue to embrace our moral values if they have no unique claim to truth?

To make this point vivid, think about political values. In particular, consider the contrast between liberal values or conservative values. As I mentioned earlier, I think disputes between liberals and conservatives are not merely factual. They derive from an incommensurable difference in moral values. For conservatives, traditional social roles, "family values," free markets, and faith are grounding norms. For liberals, equality of persons regardless of gender or creed, tolerance of diversity, privacy, and social welfare are grounding norms.

Lakoff (2002) has argued that the liberal/conservative contrast derives from two distinctive parenting styles. Liberals recapitulate the stereotypical maternal approach, which emphasizes interdependency and care. Conservatives mimic the stern authoritarian approach traditionally associated with fathers. Haidt and Joseph (2004) have another account of the contrast. They suggest that all people have a set of innate modules governing moral behavior. One of these governs behavior having to do with reciprocity, and another regulates dominance hierarchies. Liberals and conservatives may be distinguished by a difference in the degree to which these modules drive moral evaluations. These theories may both sound far-fetched, but I think that they are moving in the right direction. It's highly plausible to suppose that liberals and conservatives embrace different grounding norms. Otherwise, debates between these two sides would be much easier to resolve, and the differences would diminish as the facts came in. For example, we might expect liberals and conservatives to converge on views about taxation once they came to agree on economic models. I doubt such convergence would occur. Conservatives value self-reliance, so they oppose using taxes to support a welfare state even if that is an economically sound policy, and liberals value equality over equity, so they tend to favor policies that involve redistribution of resources. Thus, the debate about tax policy won't go away.

If this is correct, insidious implications seem to follow. Debates between liberals and conservatives are really spurious. The same policy can be right on liberal values, but not right on conservative values. But "right" and "not right" are not incompatible, because the evaluative terms have different content in different contexts. Moreover, there is no transcendental position from which one can decide which value system is better. The value systems are simply different. To assess one system as better than the other is to make a value judgment, and that judgment must be made relative to a value system. The liberal will say that conservatism is worse, but this is just to assert liberal values. An intellectually honest liberal would have to admit that there is no position from which conservatism is objectively worse. A liberal who has come to this conclusion should find this unsettling. We strongly identify with our political views. To discover that our views are not objectively better than the views of those who oppose us is very humbling. It takes the steam out of our convictions.

This becomes even more unsettling when we consider the fact that our political values may be products of our upbringing. Liberals and conservatives tend to think members of the opposing political orientation must be evil or stupid. One's political opponents are either victims of bad reasoning, or they simply don't care enough to support the policies that good reasoning would entail. This attitude toward political opponents is arrogant and confused. It may turn out that both sides are reasoning perfectly, but starting with different first principles. More importantly, those first principles are not themselves the products of reasoning, at least many cases. The fact that some people are liberal and some are conservative is probably best explained by *biographical* facts. Liberals and conservatives are exposed to different influences. They grow up in different families and communities. They have different role models and peer groups. They experience different life events. These factors tend to shape political ideologies. Suppose you had grown up under different conditions. Your political convictions might have been entirely different. That's the kind of thought that should make it hard to sleep at night. Why should we get so worked up about political debates if our values are merely an outcome of upbringing?

Strictly speaking, these implications cannot be used as an argument against relativism. You cannot refute a descriptive theory by showing that it has unpleasant consequences. The truth is sometimes horrible. But the relativist should certainly be embarrassed by the unsavory implications. Relativism may be a pernicious thesis—a thesis that would undermine morality if people realized it was true. If relativism cannot be refuted, then at least, perhaps, it should be stamped out.

This, to me, is the most pressing challenge facing the relativist. The only thing worse than a false theory is a harmful one. Fortunately, I think that the relativist can say something in response. There are five points that I would like to make. First, there are some positive consequences of discovering that our values are not privileged. We may decide, for example, that we have been overly hasty in condemning people who do not share our values. In a word, relativism can promote tolerance. If our values are not privileged, then we should allow others to live in accordance with different values. When a secular community allows an Amish community to continue to live in traditional ways, the members of the secular community are showing tolerance. The Amish are showing tolerance for secularism by not imposing their values on others. This seems like a pretty good thing. That is a value judgment, of course. We value tolerance, so a theory that promotes tolerance is good.

I don't mean to imply that moral absolutists can't be tolerant. If there is a single true morality, there can still be doubt whether the values we currently have are correct, and that uncertainly opens up space for tolerance (Rachels, 1986:

ch. 2). But absolutism and relativism have a different relationship to tolerance. Absolutists tolerate other views because of epistemic uncertainly about which morality is right. Relativists are tolerant because they are certain that other views have equal claim to being right. Notice that, if an absolutist takes the uncertainty seriously, it could be motivationally withering. To be tolerant, the absolutist must think, "my morality may be mistaken." The relativist can be tolerant without losing moral certainty: "my views are right, and so are yours." Thus, ironically, relativist tolerance may be more compatible with strong moral conviction that absolutist tolerance. Moreover, when absolutists become certain of their views, intolerance often follows. Thus is it arguable that relativism offers a more satisfying form of tolerance, because it does not force a choice between debilitating self-doubt and arrogant self-assurance. Relativists can tolerate with certainty.

Admittedly, relativism does not entail tolerance. Relativism can even be used to defend intolerance. Suppose you have a sentiment of disapprobation toward tolerance. Then it's true on your value system that tolerance is wrong. Some relativists have tried to argue that relativists *shouldn't be* intolerant. David Wong (1984), for example, argues that we should not interfere with the actions of others unless we can justify that interference to them. Since multiple systems have equal claim to truth, for Wong, we cannot justify imposing our system on others. The problem with this argument is that Wong's non-interference principle is moral in character. Wong recognizes this, and he finds comfort in the fact that both Kantians and utilitarians would grant the non-interference principle. But, what Kantians and utilitarians would grant is irrelevant. The non-interference principle may be true on those moral systems, but its truth is relative. Suppose someone sincerely believes that we ought to interfere with those who do things we find repellent, even if we cannot justify our interference to them. If moral truth is determined by approbation and disapprobation, then the person who applauds interference is morally obligated to interfere.

Nevertheless, relativism does make intolerance difficult to sustain psychologically. People who applaud intervention usually do so because they think that their values are privileged. It's easy to be intolerant if you think you are in touch with a single true morality. If no such morality exists, you may find yourself becoming more open-minded about others' values. This is an empirical conjecture, of course, but I suspect it would be confirmed if tested. If I'm right, then relativism promotes tolerance, even if it doesn't entail tolerance. This can help counterbalance the worry that relativism has horrible implications.

Some people would question whether tolerance is really good. Let's consider a controversial example. In many parts of the world, women undergo one of several surgical procedures that opponents call female genital mutilation. I will use the neutral term "female circumcision." It is estimated that three million women are circumcised annually (UNICEF, 2005). The practice is performed in numerous countries by members of numerous religious and cultural groups. The surgical procedures involved vary considerably. In some cases, the exposed portion of the clitoris is removed; in others the entire clitoris and labia are removed. Some people would argue that we should not tolerate any of these procedures. I want to examine that claim.

There are some myths about female circumcision. One myth is that women who undergo the procedure lose all sexual response. This is false. Some versions of the procedure result in no reduction in sexual response, as measured by interest in sex, frequency of sex, frequency of initiation of sex, and frequency of orgasm (Okonofua et al., 2002). The authors of this study note that their findings undermine a standard argument used *in favor* of female circumcision: practitioners claim that the procedure reduces female interest in sex, and thereby increases the chances of premarital virginity, which they regard as desirable. The findings undercut that claim, but they also undercut the claim made by opponents—a claim frequently used against male circumcision—that the procedure diminishes sexual pleasure. That said, it's important to stress that there are versions of the procedure that impair sexual function. When the entire clitoris and labia are removed, sexual response may be seriously diminished. Some women also have their genitals surgically sealed, leaving only a small opening for urine and menstrual fluids. This procedure can cause significant pain, and it prevents women from having sexual intercourse, until the surgery is reversed (which usually happens at marriage). In all circumcision procedures there is also some risk of infection, and the more severe procedures can lead to reduced fertility rates (Almroth et al., 2005).

Another myth about female circumcision is that men impose the procedure on women, and that women are unwilling victims. In most cultures where female circumcision is performed, women evidently support and promote the practice. Women are often the ones who teach young girls about the importance of circumcision, and they are sometimes involved in performing the surgery. The reasons for circumcision are varied. They often involve reducing women's sexual behavior, but circumcised genitals are considered more attractive, constraints are considered good (as they are in many Western cultures), and undergoing the procedure is regarded as an important right of passage that confers membership within the community. It is possible that women pass on these values to their daughters under the influence of (or threat from) men who dominate them. My point is that this is an assumption that needs to be examined and may vary from culture to culture, and case to case.

Many Western liberals think that female circumcision is categorically wrong, and there have been worldwide campaigns to eliminate the practice. This may be entirely justified, but metaethical relativism invites us to examine such cases more closely. Perhaps the campaign to eliminate female circumcision is an imposition of Western values onto other cultures (Tamir, 1996; Shweder, 2000). Many members of the other cultures in question view these efforts as a threat to their autonomy. If Western liberal values are not privileged, then the campaign against female circumcision may be based on a mistake (the false belief that the practice is objectively wrong). In cultures where the "victims" of circumcision are willing, and where they see the goods as outweighing the harms, we may have to accept that our values simply don't apply. The story changes dramatically in cases where the "victims" are unwilling, or see the procedure as undesirable. In those cultures, the people in power are imposing values on women who do not share those values, and intervention may be appropriate (see, e.g., Nussbaum, 1999: ch. 4).

Vaginal circumcision is a very tough case. I do not want to suggest that we should abandon campaigns to illegalize it. Some forms of the procedure are truly horrifying. Perhaps our moral values demand of us that we intervene. What I want to suggest is that relativism should lead us to proceed with caution. We shouldn't deceive ourselves into thinking that we are helping female victims get what they really want. We should be open to the possibility that efforts to intervene may be based on such false premises. If we engage in this difficult exercise of open-mindedness, we may come to reevaluate intervention in some cases. After all, we are tolerant of other cultural practices that cause harm for the sake of cultural ideals of beauty. Scarification, lip plates, and neck extension come to mind. We also tolerate extreme diets and undernourishment of women in Western cultures. Perhaps a careful examination of vaginal circumcision, informed by an understanding of relativism, will lead us to tolerate genital surgery to the same degree that we tolerate lip plates.

I raise the issue of tolerance to show that relativism has a silver lining, even if cases like female circumcision tarnish that lining a bit. Tolerance is often very hard, but a strong commitment to relativism makes it easier. And relativism does not require that we tolerate everything. In cases where harms are brought against unwilling victims, we can protest. We can reason as follows: since there is not a single true morality, I will refrain from imposing my morality on others, because it has no claim over them; and likewise, I would hope that they don't impose their morality on people who do not share it; but if the victims of their actions do not share their morality, then my initial reason for not intervening doesn't apply. The factors that make it problematic to impose our values on those who do not embrace those values do not apply in the case of unwilling victims. Unwilling victims of practices that we condemn also condemn those practices. When we intervene in such cases, we are imposing our values on the perpetrators of the harms, but we are not imposing anything on the victims. A committed relativist can choose to assist people with similar values. The issue of female circumcision may ultimately rest on the question of whether the women who undergo the procedure are really willing. Of course, critics may contend that women are brainwashed into finding the practice acceptable. But this objection is hard to defend. In this context, the term "brainwashing" is simply a pejorative for enculturation. As far as I know, most women who have come to accept circumcision have not undergone any unusually coercive methods of indoctrination. They acquire their values the same way that we do.

If so, then the practice might be tolerated in those cases. Relativism promotes tolerance in cases where the "victims" are truly willing. This kind of tolerance, which relativism promotes, is a good thing by our own standards.

I want to turn to a second observation in response to the argument that relativism is pernicious. Earlier I said that relativism undermines convictions. On closer examination, I think this implication is doubly exaggerated. Critics of relativism overestimate how bad it is to lose convictions, and they overestimate the extent to which convictions must be abandoned if relativism is true. The case of female circumcision illustrates the first point. A person who becomes convinced that relativism is true may decide that her opposition to female circumcision is based on an untenable form of moral absolutism. If she loses her conviction that female circumcision is categorically wrong, that may not be a terrible consequence.

The second point can be illustrated with an analogy. Suppose that someone is a taste absolutist. She believes that chocolate is objectively, universally, and absolutely wonderful. Now imagine that her belief is corrected. She comes to recognize that taste is relative to the taster, and that, for some people, chocolate is dreadful. Trivially, this person will certainly lose her conviction that chocolate is absolutely wonderful, but she needn't give up the conviction that chocolate is wonderful *to her*. Likewise, if we discover that our moral values do not apply in other cultures, we can continue to be pleased that they apply to us. We may falsely believe that cannibalism is absolutely wrong, but we do not believe that cannibalism is wrong *because* it is absolutely wrong. It is wrong to us because we regard it as cruel, disgusting, and degrading to human life. All those things remain true, even if others do not regard cannibalism this way.

The point is that we embrace our values because they are our values. We value the things that we value. This tautology is the key to conviction. The fact that others do not value what we value is entirely moot unless our valuing something depends on the assumption that the value is universal. I think that is implausible. The critic who assumes that values must be universal to be worth having simply begs the question against relativism. Matters of taste are a glaring counterexample. Psychologically, valuing does not require universalizing. It is not obvious that moral valuing should depend on absolutist assumptions.

In the opening of this subsection, I said that relativism has two pernicious implications: it undermines convictions, and it renders debates spurious. I have just addressed the first concern. The second concern can be addressed by building on some resources from chapter 3. There, I gave some explanations for why people might engage in debates even if relativism is true. At the time, I was ostensibly interested in explaining why moral debates exist, not in showing that they make any sense. The worry about spuriousness is a worry about whether moral debates are justified. If relativism is true, aren't fundamental debates fundamentally confused? Aren't moral disputants just talking past one another? I think not. As expressivists have often pointed out, moral debates are often like practical debates (Stevenson, 1937; Blackburn, 1998). When practical interests clash, there is a genuine disagreement, because moral rules dictate action. As noted in chapter 3, people often have a vested interest in bringing others around to their moral views. If you really want to live in a society in which drugs are legal and I don't then there is a difference between us that we both have an interest in resolving (also recall the missionaries in Peru). When we have such debates we are disagreeing about what to do. Relativists can also mitigate concerns about spuriousness by providing a theory of how moral persuasion actually takes place. People with different value systems often have overlapping values. So when we debate with people who have different moralities, we can find a moral common ground. In debates with others, we can try to use shared values to get others to revise those values that we do not share. Thus, moral debates are not confused banter; disputants are not just talking past each other or quibbling about how to use moral words. Rather, they are trying to alter each other's practical behavior by identifying shared ends. On this picture, it would be misleading to say moral debates are completely spurious. This is my third point in defense against the objection from insidiousness.

My fourth point pertains to the claim that relativism puts all political values on equal footing. That may not be true. Relativism is incompatible with any political ideology that depends on the claim that there is one true morality. Not all ideologies require that. As a starting place, consider a political outlook that says: let everybody do what they want provided it does not infringe on those who want something else. The infringement clause is subordinate to the liberty clause; preventing infringement is a way to allow people to do what they want. Allowing people to do what they want is a way of converting relativism about values into a political outlook.

If one compares political conservatism with political liberalism, liberalism may come out ahead. Liberals, like conservatives, take certain values to be fundamental, self-evident, and inalienable. That may be problematic. But liberals also tend to promote tolerance to a greater degree than conservatives. They come closer to the political view that incorporates relativism. The relativist view says that we should protect privacy, free expression, and diversity—values that are more central to liberal thinking than to conservative thinking. Relativism may also be compatible with libertarian thinking, with isolationism, and with other political perspectives. My point is not that any single political view can be derived from relativism. The point is that relativism is not politically neutral. Certain policies, forms of government, and ideologies can be easily reconciled with the hypothesis that there is no absolute morality. Others are harder to reconcile with that hypothesis. Those who try to impose their values under the assumption that those values have exclusive claim to truth are making a mistake. Once we accept that our values are parochial, we may continue to have incentives to impose our values on others, but those who make such an imposition in the name of absolute truth should feel compelled to amend their ways once they accept relativism.

Against all this, one might wonder what to say about people who impose their values on others *without* assuming that there is a single true morality. They just want their values to spread, and they don't care that other values have equal claim to truth. Relativism does not have the resources to convince such evaluative imperialists that they are making a mistake. I have said that relativism does not entail toleration; it only promotes it psychologically. But can the relativist say anything about why we should prefer the tolerant view over the intolerant one, when the intolerant view is not based on false illusions of universal truth?

I think the relativist can say this much. If you impose your values on others knowing that your values have no greater claim to truth, then you must have a moral value according to which such an imposition would be acceptable. You must believe, for example, that you have the right to impose your preferences on people who do not share those preferences. Admittedly, there are probably some people who have values like that, but, I gather, many of us do not. So the claim that relativism promotes toleration is restricted to those who already have a moral value that imposing preferences on others is bad if preferences have no claim to truth. This restriction weakens the move from relativism to toleration, but it does not undermine it. If the imposition of preferences is something that people widely regard as wrong, then the discovery that relativism is true can promote toleration widely. I suspect that liberals and conservatives typically agree that it's wrong to impose preferences on others, if those preferences have no privileged claim to truth, and thus relativism may have implications for selecting between liberal and conservative perspectives on certain matters of policy, e.g., issues pertaining to privacy.

I have been addressing the concern that moral relativism entails political indifference. Some political values are more defensible than others. The point about political values can be generalized. Some moralities are better than others. In presenting concerns about the implications of relativism, I said that there is no transcendental stance from which we can adjudicate between competing moral systems. I think this claim is partially true and partially false. I think there is no transcendental stance from which one can determine which of two moralities is *morally* better. But there may be a transcendental stance from which one can adjudicate on non-moral grounds. I will not spell out the suggestion here, because it will be addressed in chapter 8. If I am right, this is a fifth reason for thinking that the implications of relativism are not as dire as they may initially appear.

To conclude, I think relativism is a coherent doctrine that enjoys ample support from anthropology and may even leave marks in the syntax of moral terms. It is a doctrine that may lead us to reconsider some of our moral convictions, but it is not insidious. Relativists can continue to care about morality.

In making these arguments, I have had occasion to describe some of the different values that can be found in cultural groups around the world. In chapter 6, I will inquire into the origin of morals, tracing the sources of some of the cultural differences that I discussed here. This genealogical exploration will reinforce the case for moral diversity, because it will show some of the mechanisms that can lead moral systems to develop in different ways. But critics may think I am overstating diversity, and they may look to biology to find some moral universals. In chapter 7, I will raise some doubts about that project. The question of where morals come from is interesting in its own right. It is one instance of the nature–nurture debate. But it also relates to some of the themes that have come up in this chapter. My inquiries into the origins of morals will expose further threats to moral confidence. Should we continue to moralize if we discover that moral values are products of bygone historical events? In chapter 8, I will argue that such discoveries may be helpful in making moral progress.

6

The Genealogy of Morals

Where do moral values come from? This question is not asked often enough. Philosophers are generally more interested in normative questions, rather than descriptive questions. The question of where our values come from is deemed irrelevant. Those who inquire into the origins of morality are sometimes accused of committing a genetic fallacy. The origin of a belief or value has no bearing, it is said, on its truth. I think this assumption needs to be reconsidered. Normative theories are often designed to encompass present-day intuitions. If those intuitions have ignoble origins, then perhaps they should not guide normative projects. This is a central theme in Nietzsche's critique of morality. Nietzsche sought to destabilize our values by exposing their past. As a constructive sentimentalist, I think morality is created by us, and, as a relativist, I think different societies create different moralities under different historical conditions. In this chapter, I examine that process.

I have two goals. I want to show that the genealogical method can be used effectively to investigate the origin of values. Doing so helps confirm that some moral convictions are products of social history. Nietzsche's own historical analyses were speculative, inflammatory, and probably deeply mistaken. More plausible genealogies have been proposed by anthropologists and historians. I consider some examples. My second goal is to determine whether genealogy can be used to support skepticism about current moral values. Nietzsche certainly used genealogy in this way, but I think his skepticism is overstated. Nietzsche also advocated the view that we should replace historically derived values with values that are more natural. I assess this aspect of his program in chapter 7, when I consider evolutionary ethics.

6.1 NIETZSCHE ON GENEALOGY

In nineteenth-century Germany, history was all the rage, and it is no surprise that German philosophers began emphasizing historical themes in their work. Nietzsche's interest in historical theme appears throughout his work and culminates in *On the Genealogy of Morals* (1887). To understand morality, Nietzsche argues, we must look into the origin of moral values. The project was not unprecedented. Nietzsche was influenced by the work of his close friend Paul Rée, who had published a book on *The Origin of the Moral Sensations* (1877). Rée's ideas were a blend of British moral philosophy, especially Hobbes and Mill, and Darwinian evolution. Nietzsche refers to Rée as a British psychologist in the *Genealogy*, despite the fact that Rée was a Pomeranian Jew who had never lived in England. According to Rée, moral terms, such as "good" and "bad," began as labels for positive and negative outcomes. More specifically, the terms refer to what is good and bad for the survival of the species. Eventually, through association and habit, those terms come to refer to the actions that cause positive and negative outcomes, rather than the outcomes themselves. We begin to think of cruelty as bad, for example, rather than recognizing that it is really the effects of cruelty that counted as bad in the original sense of the term.

Nietzsche rejected Rée's account, and devised a just-so story of his own. Like Rée, Nietzsche begins with an analysis of what one might call "natural good" and "natural bad"—the kind of good and bad that would be favored by human nature, unadulterated by history and culture. Rée had been convinced that Darwinian principles favored behavior that benefits others. Forecasting modern evolutionary ethicists, he regarded egoistic interests as compatible with selfless concern for others. Nietzsche thought that Darwinian principles lead to a less sanguine picture of natural good and bad. It is equally in our nature to seek power and to dominate those who are weaker. Nietzsche believed that these natural goods were enshrined in the morality of ancient Rome. Some of the values that Rée emphasized, including self-sacrifice, were not natural at all, according to Nietzsche. They were, instead, results of a power struggle in the ancient world.

In Rome, Christians were oppressed. They lived in poverty, and they resented their Roman oppressors (Nietzsche uses the French word, *ressentiment*, which also conveys feelings of hatred). To cope with their predicament, Christians began to demonize the values of their oppressors. They condemned power and domination, as well as wealth, freedom, and health. They called these things evil. They also began to regard their own dejected state as good, and made a virtue of poverty, weakness, and sickness. These values—celebrated in the Sermon on the Mount—were revolutionary. They reversed the Roman ideals, transforming Roman good into evil, and Roman bad into good. Nietzsche called this a slave revolt in morality. When Christians came to power, their moral system took a long and enduring hold. Nietzsche thought the values of nineteenth-century Europe were vestiges of early Christian resentment. He imagined a new dawn in which free-spirited Europeans would reinstate values of the kind that were celebrated in Rome. In *Zarathustra*, Nietzsche constructs a utopian vision in which the weak "drop off" and the strong assert their will to power (Nietzsche, 1885: 30, 58).

Nietzsche's moral philosophy is unsettling. His invective against Christianity is overwrought, his apotheosis of "aristocratic" values is offensive, and his invocation of the "blond beast" portends the rise of National Socialism in

Germany. In actuality, Nietzsche despised the anti-Semites of his day, and he would have been repelled by the herd mentality of Hitler's executioners. Indeed, Nazi morality is amenable to a Nietzschean critique. The Nazis were driven by resentment of Europe after the treaty of Versailles, and their anti-Semitism was probably an outgrowth of conversion tactics used by the early Church. St Paul tried to attract pagan converts by ruling that Christians did not need to follow Jewish Law, and St John tried to demonize Jews by blaming them for the crucifixion. The shift from Jewish customs led to a demonization of unconverted Jews in the Christian world, and the smear campaign made them into scapegoats during times of adversity. The result was two millennia of crusades, inquisitions, and pogroms. Nietzsche would have condemned the Nazis for appropriating a form of bigotry that was really a vestige of a bygone power struggle and mistaking it for scientific truth. Unfortunately, the Nazis mistakenly revered Nietzsche (along with Plato) as an ideological father of their political movement. This sometimes distracts from the philosophically interesting features of Nietzsche's *Genealogy*.

The most important lessons from Nietzsche can be summarized as follows. First, the values that we currently cherish have a history. Second, that history may not be pretty. It may not reflect a rational progression toward ideas that are truer or more beneficial. Instead, this history of morals, like history in general, often involves power struggles and questionable psychological motives (greed, resentment, xenophobia—to name a few). Third, our blindness to this history gives us a false sense of security in our values. We take our moral outlook to be unimpeachable. Fourth, we can do better. We can change morality radically, and adopt a system of values that has advantages over the values we were enculturated to accept. Nietzsche is not a moral nihilist. He thinks we need a new morality—a new system of norms.

Nietzsche's optimism about moral progress is built on two presuppositions. The first is that, when we discover the historicity of our values, we will have reason and ability to reject them. Second, Nietzsche thinks we can replace historically constructed values with values that are, in some sense, natural. I will assess this idea in chapter 7.

I will argue that Nietzsche is right about the historicity of morals, but that both his pessimism about existing values and his optimism about future values are misplaced.

6.2 NIETZSCHE NATURALIZED

6.2.1 Nietzsche on Christianity

Nietzsche's account of the origin of Christian values is highly speculative and probably mistaken. For example, Christian asceticism, which is an expression of the view that poverty is a virtue, may have its roots in ancient philosophical traditions in Greece, such as Stoicism and Cynicism, as well as ancient religious movements. There were ascetic cults in ancient Egypt, and Gnosticism, which probably emerged shortly before the dawn of Christianity, was a highly influential movement that urged chastity and the renunciation of the body. Gnosticism is believed to have had its origins in Persia, and it is unlikely that its asceticism derived from Roman oppression (Meeks, 1993).

The Christian preoccupation with charity may have had its origins in Jewish law (see, for example, Deuteronomy 15:11). Jews may have emphasized charity as the result of oppression, but there is no reason to think resentment or the apotheosis of poverty was a contributing factor. Aside from a few isolated sects, ancient Jews were not ascetics, and charity is a very sensible strategy for coping with oppression. From a game-theoretic point of view, sharing resources among members of a closely knit group can strengthen the group as a whole. This is a simpler explanation than Nietzsche's proposal about resentment.

These considerations lead me to conclude that the early Christians were not led to their moral outlook through resentment. Their ideology was appropriated from previously existing views. Of course, Nietzsche was aware that charity and ascetic movements predated Christianity. He might nevertheless argue that resentment led the early Christians to appropriate these values, rather than others. The impoverished Christians may have identified with the ascetics and they may have seen the Jewish concern for the needy as a mark of distinction from their Roman oppressors. The difficulty with this hypothesis is that early Christians may not have been impoverished. Stark (1996) argues convincingly that the movement was driven largely by the middle class and even the affluent.

Stark (1996) observes that new religious movements tend to be spread by financially secure individuals who have become disenchanted with their prior faith. Records suggest that many of the early converts were financially secure, and some were even members of the senatorial class in Rome. They were not victims of poverty or oppression. In any case, poverty and resentment cannot explain how Christianity spread. Christianity grew at an enormous speed in its first three centuries, probably at a rate of 40 percent per decade. People had been oppressed throughout the Roman Empire, but no religion of the oppressed ever displaced the pagan faith of the state. Stark thinks that oppression had little to do with it. Several other factors seem more plausible. First, Stark (1996) notes that there were two major plagues in the first centuries of Christianity, which decimated a large percentage of the Roman population. This could have led to disenchantment with Roman religion. Christianity offered a source of comfort by emphasizing life in the sweet hereafter. Moreover, Christian practices of caring for the needy (inherited from Judaism) may have resulted in greater survival rates during outbreaks of disease. That could have increased the Christian population and won over new converts.

Another important factor, Stark argues, is that Christianity offered better prospects for women than paganism. Pagan women were often married off by the time they were twelve, and there was little to protect them against male philandering and divorce. Christian women married older, and neither divorce nor philandering was permitted. So women were more secure. In addition, Christianity prohibited abortion, which at the time was highly dangerous to women and often imposed by men, and it also prohibited infanticide, which was a common method of killing unwanted female babies in Rome. The result is that women would have been attracted to Christianity, and once converted they would be much more likely to keep female offspring. This is very significant because women play a disproportionate role in the spread of religion. If Christian women married pagan men, they may have succeeded in converting those men or in raising their children as Christians. Stark shows that women were allowed to play ecclesiastical roles in the early Church, and he speculates that this added a further attraction to women and a further means by which women could spread the faith.

If Stark's account is on the right track, then Christianity spread largely because it empowered disaffected middle-class women. It was not a case of impoverished oppressed people turning their weaknesses into virtues. Rather, it was a case of financially comfortable people adopting a system of values that allowed for greater power and liberty. Hardly a slave revolt in morality. Once Christianity became the State religion, prospects for women seem to have diminished within the Church. For example, women could no longer serve in important ecclesiastic roles. We can safely assume that this transition in power, from middle-class women to male domination, was not driven by the destitute. The men who took over were the middle-class husbands of the women who spread Christianity, and members of Rome's ruling elite.

Even if Nietzsche's genealogy of Christian values is mistaken, the basic tenets of his approach can be defended. Moral values have undoubtedly been influenced by historical factors, and those factors are not always rational or noble. We should regard every moral value as a cultural artifact with a history just waiting to be discovered. Rather than speculating about the history of morals, we can call on the resources of social science. Of special value is historical anthropology. Anthropologists often engage in something resembling Nietzschean genealogy, but they support their origin stories with data. I will illustrate with some case studies. But first I will make a few remarks about the mechanisms of cultural transmission.

Nietzsche placed emphasis on power struggles and psychological factors: revolution and resentment. Resentment is not a *general* principle of cultural transmission, and, as I have just suggested, it may not have been especially important in the Christian revolution in morality. The idea of a power struggle is more general. But power struggles do not shed light on why values are passed on from generation to generation. Also, some values emerge slowly over time. It would be useful to begin with a more general framework for thinking about the genealogy of morals, before focusing on factors that may have been operative in particular cases.

6.2.2 Cultural Transmission

I will adopt the view that cultural transmission is a function of fitness (for related ideas, see especially Boyd and Richerson, 1985; Sperber, 1996). We need to identify factors that make cultural products especially suitable for spreading and being passed on. I will focus on three factors. These are not necessarily the only factors contributing to cultural transmission, but they are probably among the most effective. The probability that an evaluative belief will be culturally transmitted increases when:

(i) It yields material benefit to its believers or to the members of a culture who are in a position to indoctrinate others;

(ii) it is situated in a narrative context that is easy to learn because, e.g., it integrates with existing beliefs about the nature of the world or captures the imagination; or

(iii) it has emotional appeal, due to the intrinsic content of the belief or accompanying practices, such as emotional conditioning or emotionally intense religious rituals.

I will refer to these as material, narrative, and affective factors respectively. Each increases fitness in a different way. Material factors are most closely related to the idea of fitness that is used in evolutionary biology. A cultural element that has material benefits can increase prospects for survival and procreation. A materially beneficial belief can lead to an increase in the population size of people who hold that belief. Technological and medical knowledge are obvious examples. Cultures pass on knowledge of how to farm and how to treat wounds. But values can also have material costs and benefits. Consider two cases outside the moral domain. The desire for gold has played an important role in the geographic expansion of European society; it motivated European colonization of the New World and expansion across the North American frontier. This was good for the colonizers and bad for the indigenous people who were killed or displaced. In sharp contrast, the desire for silk may have contributed to the fall of the Roman Empire. Rome racked up a huge trade deficit with China, which made it more difficult to finance military conquests.

By narrative factors, I mean to refer to the rich, cohesive, verbal contexts in which values are sometimes presented. Narratives can take many forms: they can be histories (as in the case of the Judeo-Christian Bible), scientific theories (as in the pseudoscientific justification of racism), moral tales, or myths. There are a number of reasons why narratives can facilitate value transmission. First, people are better at memorizing stories than random lists of sentences (e.g., Black and Bern, 1981). Second, narratives can contain surprising elements that capture attention and enhance memory. Boyer and Ramble (2001) found that subjects in France, Gabon, and Nepal were all better at recalling stories in which physical expectations are violated (e.g., a being who can walk through walls) than stories in which nothing supernatural happens. Boyer and Ramble conclude that transmission of religious beliefs is facilitated when those beliefs are presented in counter-intuitive stories. Moral values are often conveyed through myths with supernatural elements, and this probably increases the chances that the values will be shared with others. Third, myths and stories are captivating to children, which leads to deeper processing and higher probability of recall and repetition. Fourth, narratives may facilitate information integration. By situating a value in a complex story, it may become linked to a large set of beliefs, including religious systems, cosmologies, and scientific theories. If a value is linked to broader belief systems, then it may be difficult to give up. Belief revision is a holistic process. To abandon a value grounded in a belief system may require abandoning large parts of that system, which would be epistemologically prohibitive. Fifth, narratives may contribute to the internalization of values by providing a resource for identity construction. People tend to think of themselves in terms of cohesive storylines, which may include autobiographical information as well as information about the historical past. It may be easier to adopt a set of values as mine if, for example, they are presented as having been discovered or given to my people, in the distant past. In each of these ways, narratives increase the probability of retention over time.

Affective factors facilitate memory as well. Emotions increase attention, and attention increases memory (e.g., MacKay et al. 2004). Emotions can also function as rewards. Positive affect is awarding, and a cultural element that induces positive emotions is, therefore, transmittable. Even negative emotions can increase transmission. For example, if rule violations are punished, fear of punishment can increase rule conformity, and this effect can be spread across generations. Moral emotions, such as guilt, can achieve the same effect. Moral sentiments are powerful tools for cultural transmission, because they assign emotional sanctions to rule violations, no matter who violated the rule (self or other; stranger or kin). In a very clever empirical study, Nichols (2002) demonstrates that emotionally implemented norms have greater potential for social transmission. Nichols compiled a list of rules listed in Erasmus's (1530) highly influential etiquette manual, *On Good Manners for Boys*. He then asked one coder to indicate which of these rules involves a prohibition against something that would naturally induce disgust (e.g., norms involving bodily fluids). Another coder was asked to indicate which of Erasmus's rules are still operative today. These two measures turned out to be highly correlated. Norms regulating behaviors that cause disgust are especially likely to endure.

The factors that effect cultural transmission often work in concert. Myths and rituals can be exciting, and sharing beliefs can promote feelings of affiliation and solidarity. Solidarity can increase material benefits by increasing cooperation, and material benefits can increase positive affect. A single belief is often bolstered by multiple factors. Consider the Christian idea of Heaven. This belief fits into a coherent cosmology that makes sense of worldly suffering, and it carries an emotional reward through hope. As suggested above, the optimistic message may have been attractive during times of plague, and it may have made people more likely to offer assistance to those in need, rather than taking flight. This, in turn, may have increased survival prospects. So belief in Heaven may be narratively compelling, emotionally seductive, and materially beneficial.

I invoked the notion of fitness in listing factors that contribute to cultural transmission. "Fitness" is a Darwinian term (introduced by Erasmus Darwin, and made famous by Charles). It suggests an analogy between cultural transmission and natural selection. Some authors have tried to get a lot of mileage out of this analogy. They argue that cultural elements (beliefs, practices, institutions, artifacts, etc.) are transmitted in much the way that genes are transmitted. Dawkins (1976) introduced the term "meme" to refer to such elements. Like genes, memes arise through mutations in previously existing cultures, they are replicated, and their capacity to spread depends on their fitness. Nevertheless, I hesitate to call this an evolutionary model of belief transmission.

There are some important contrasts between genes and alleged memes (see Sperber, 2000; Boyd and Richerson, 2001). First, unlike biological evolution by natural selection, beliefs are not necessarily formed by anything like random mutation. They may be formed intentionally. Second, it's not clear that the notion of replication applies. Belief transmission is not a matter of perfect mechanical copying. Beliefs are often transmitted intentionally. Change in beliefs can be intentional and abrupt. So there is great room for discontinuity in the ebb and flow of ideas. Third, cultural transmission is often horizontal as well as vertical. Cultural elements can be spread to individuals in the same generation. Genetic transmission is characteristically vertical (viral transmission of genes is an exception). Fourth, there is no obvious equivalent to the distinction between genotype and phenotype in cultural transmission. In biological evolution, genes work in concert with the environment to create phenotypical traits. Culturally transmitted evaluative beliefs are not necessarily the mechanisms by which anything else is produced. They are not underlying causes of more superficial traits. Dennett (1995) suggests that *Romeo and Juliet* and *West Side Story* have different semantic phenotypes and the same underlying semantic genotype (or "memotype"), but the analogy is far from perfect. Shakespeare's play has been faithfully reproduced (through umpteen printings), and subsequent authors have had to interact with the text in order to mimic it. Thus, one might just as well say that the play is like a genotype and the plot is like a phenotype.

For these reasons, evolutionary analogies should not be taken too far. Talk of memes is not especially helpful. It is important, however, to notice loose parallels between biological evolution and cultural transmission. The spread of cultural entities depends, in some sense, on success. Cultural entities must be transferable and they are especially likely to spread if they are materially beneficial or psychologically seductive. Beliefs that are accessible, exciting, or profitable have an advantage over those that are arcane, dull, or destructive. Likewise for institutions and practices. We should acknowledge the role of fitness in cultural transmission, without pushing the analogy to genetic transmission much further. In discussing the fitness of evaluative attitudes, I do not want to take on the theoretical baggage of memetics. I mean only to say that we can make sense of why certain attitudes come about, why they stay, and why others tend to disappear.

Given this framework, we can now gain some perspective on Nietzsche's explanatory constructs. Resentment is an affective factor, and, as such, it may be conducive to cultural transmission. If Nietzsche was right that the early Christians resented the Romans, this would help to explain the spread of Christianity. I suspect that other emotions, as well as narrative and material factors, were more important (see below). Nietzsche also mentions power struggles. These are not mentioned on my list of factors, because they are mechanisms of change, rather than factors of transmission. That said, I do think Nietzsche is right to highlight a link between power and morality. Several reasons may be cited.

First of all, those with power are in an especially privileged position when it comes to cultural transmission. There is a widespread "prestige bias": we are more likely to imitate people who are powerful or successful. Powerful people are salient, and we imitate them as a cognitively inexpensive way to increase prospects for our own success (Henrich and Gil-White, 2001). Second, people with power have control over institutions used in cultural transmission. The powerful control religious institutions, for example, and these are the source of locally entrenched cosmologies. Third, there is a sense in which all culturally transmitted beliefs *constitute* a form of power. Cultural beliefs play a major role in structuring our societies and organizing our lives. This is a Nietzschean point, but it has been brought out most forcefully by Foucault, who equates knowledge with power (see especially, Foucault, 1977). I will not dwell on these themes, but they will be in the background. My approach to genealogy may differ from Nietzsche's in emphasis, but the parallels would not be difficult to extrapolate.

6.2.3 Why Do People Eat Each Other?

To illustrate the naturalized genealogical method, I will focus on two examples: cannibalism and marriage. The analyses that I review are controversial, but they help to establish a broad methodological point: the history of human values can be empirically investigated. Nietzsche can be naturalized.

Let's begin with attitudes toward cannibalism. Few practices fill us with as much horror. Cannibalism is not just wrong, in our eyes; it is monstrous.

But this attitude has not always been the norm. In chapter 5, I remarked that cannibalism may be the default human practice. Before the emergence of modern societies, which are organized into states, cannibalism may have been quite widespread. Cannibal practices have been recorded, up until quite recently, in pre-state societies all over the globe. In Africa, examples of societies thought to have practiced cannibalism include the Mangbetu, Abadja, and the Mayi-Mayi tribes of contemporary Congo. In North America examples include the Iroquois, Huron, Algonkian, Kwakiutl, and, perhaps, the Anasazi. Documented examples in South America include the Akamara, Guiaca, Tupinamba, Panoans, and Yanomamö. There have been tribes in Papua New Guinea known to practice cannibalism, including the Fore, Baroi, Bimin-Kuskusmin, and Doboduras. In Polynesia, the Fiji islanders are believed to have been cannibals. In New Zealand, the Maori are reputed to have a history of cannibalism. Peggy Reeves Sanday (1986) estimates that cannibalism is quite common. In a representative sample of over 100 well-studied societies, spanning a time range of almost 4,000 years, she found that 34 percent engaged in cannibal practices.

Some skeptics have argued that tales of cannibalism in foreign lands are just sailors' stories designed to dehumanize members of other cultures (Arens, 1979). While I agree that some tales of cannibalism must be regarded with suspicion, skepticism about cannibalism is more insulting to other cultures than its denial; the urge to deny the existence of cannibalism stems from our own hegemonic conviction that cannibalism is unthinkably horrible. The evidence that cannibalism has been widely practiced is extremely strong. There are convergent eye-witness accounts from multiple, credible sources, including testimony from practitioners (Harris, 1985). There is also physical evidence: including human blood traces found on temple floors, charred human bones in cooking pots, human bones found cut in the same way as animal bones that were used for food, and human tissue found in human excrement (DeGusta, 1999; Turner and Turner, 1999; Marlar et al., 2000; Walker 2001). A bit more controversially, there is evidence that people across the globe have a gene that evolved to protect us against health risks associated with eating members of our own species (Mead et al., 2003). With extensive evidence from testimony and corroborating physical evidence, skepticism about cannibalism seems unfounded. I think we must come to terms with the fact that cannibalism was widespread, and we must explain that astonishing fact.

Cannibalism is documented to have taken different forms. Some societies have practiced mortuary endocannibalism, or eating of dead kin. But many other societies have practiced warfare exocannibalism, in which members of other social groups are eaten after being killed in battle. Mortuary cannibalism may be relatively easy to explain. Consuming the body of an ancestor may be a way to cope with the trauma of loss. It is a way to extend the life of the dead symbolically and transfer their vital powers. Mortuary cannibalism is also a way of coping with the problem of dealing with dead bodies. It eliminates potentially hazardous waste. But what about warfare cannibalism?

Marvin Harris (1985: ch. 10) offers a compellingly simple explanation in terms of costs and benefits. Let's suppose that two neighboring tribes get into a violent conflict with a nearby tribe over resources. One tribe wins the battle. Several members of the other tribe are killed, and several others are captured. Consider the dead first. The victors could leave the dead behind, or they could eat them. The second option often makes sense. To leave the bodies behind is wasteful—it reaps no benefits. Human flesh is nutritious. If the victors had to travel a distance to the location of the battle, they could carve up the flesh of the victims for the return journey or they could have a restorative victory feast on the battlefield. Either option is better than simply leaving edible meat behind. Now what about the captives? Here there are three options. They could let the captives go, allowing them to seek revenge at a later date. The victors could also enslave their captives, but then they would have to feed them and prevent them from rebelling. The benefits of keeping slaves outweigh the costs only when slaves can be used to produce significant revenue through farming or other chores. If the victors do not have advanced agriculture, slavery is a bad idea. Finally, they can kill the captives. This is the best option for non-agrarian societies, and, once the captives have been killed, the victors are faced with the initial choice: consume the dead or leave them to rot. Consumption is, again, the sensible choice. Moreover, the victors can march the captives back to their village and avoid the labor of carrying their bodies. They can kill them in the village and share the meat with villagers who were unable to participate in the battle. This makes economic sense. It may also make strategic sense. If a group of people is known to be cannibals, neighboring groups may be more reluctant to engage them in warfare. This is especially true if the cannibal victims are sacrificed in a painful and ostentatious way. It is not unusual for cannibal societies to torture their victims and to establish elaborate rituals around the consumption of flesh.

Harris's account of why people engage in cannibalism makes key predictions. It predicts that societies will be likely to engage in cannibalism if they are sufficiently organized to engage in warfare, have independent motives for going to war, and have insufficient infrastructure to benefit from taking slaves. The chiefdoms stand a good chance of being cannibalistic, especially if there are resource limitations and competition. States, however, are unlikely to be cannibalistic. States usually have agriculture, so they can benefit from having slaves. More importantly, states are sufficiently well organized to have systems for collecting taxes or tribute over large geographical areas. Once a society arrives at this point of development, there is little incentive to wage war with neighboring peoples. Neighbors can be taxed in return for protection or other resources. As long as neighbors are too weak to wage war against the state, it is more cost-effective to tax them than to conquer and eat them. Taxpayers yield more benefit than cadavers. Of course, neighbors are unlikely to be compliant if they think there is a high risk that they will eventually be conquered and eaten. So Harris's account predicts that cannibalism will not only diminish with the emergence of the state; cannibalism will actually be condemned. Indeed, it will become taboo. Otherwise people might give into their temptation to eat their neighbors. Harris argues that the taboo against people eating is like the taboo against eating horsemeat. Historically, horses were more useful as tools of war, than as food. To eat a horse was to threaten national security. This might be forgotten in a fit of hunger, of course, so societies that relied on horses for warfare established taboos to discourage capricious consumption of horsemeat. Likewise, for advanced societies, people in neighboring villages are more useful as taxpayers than as meals. By making people-eating taboo, societies added an emotional sanction against those who might otherwise give in to their murderous culinary temptations.

The hypothesis that cannibalism disappears with the emergence of the state is well supported by the anthropological record (see Sanday, 1986). There is, however, one glaring counterexample: the Aztecs. The Aztecs (who called themselves Mexica or Tenochca) had a highly organized state with powerful political alliances, and a capacity to collect tribute and trade with neighbors. These are just the kind of features that should have diminished the probability of cannibalism. Yet the Aztecs had the most extensive cannibal practices on record. This flies in the face of Harris's hypothesis. To solve the puzzle, Harris calls on the work of Michael Harner (1977). Harner chalks Aztec cannibalism up to nutrition. Unlike many other organized states, the Aztecs did not have well-developed agriculture. They grew corn, beans, tomatoes, peppers, and other foods, but they did not have plows or beasts of burden. They may also have had limited access to foods with high amounts of protein and fat. They got protein from eating insects, reptiles, waterfowl, and spirulina, but they had no domesticated animals. The Aztecs also endured long periods of drought and famine. Under these conditions, tidbits of human flesh may have been a welcome dietary supplement. Animal flesh was certainly considered a valuable award to the Aztecs, and human flesh, procured fortuitously in battles with neighboring territories, would have been a shame to waste. Enslaving captives after battles didn't make economic sense, because, without high-yield farming techniques, the costs of keeping slaves outweighed the benefits. Harner does not suppose that the Aztecs consumed enough human flesh to make a major nutritional difference, but he does suppose that the Aztecs had little incentive to eliminate cannibalism.

Critics of Harner and Harris argue that the Aztec diet was sufficiently rich to make cannibalism superfluous (Ortiz de Montellano, 1978; Sahlins, 1978, Garn, 1979). They also note that the victims of Aztec sacrifice were eaten by nobles, successful warriors, and their families. There was no distribution of human flesh to the masses. Moreover, victims were eaten during harvesting times, when festivals were held and when there was enough food supply to support battles. Victims were not eaten during times of great scarcity. These objections, strictly speaking, do not undermine the nutrition hypothesis, because Harner and Harris do not claim that cannibalism was necessary. They simply claim that the benefits may have outweighed the costs. But critics can weigh in with a more serious complaint. If cannibalism were just a matter of getting meat, why would it be so ritualized? Why didn't the Aztecs simply hunt humans like game meat and consume flesh without ceremony?

One answer to this question can be reconstructed from Harris's materialist account. Perhaps elaborate sacrificial rituals were designed to terrify people who were not loyal to the Aztec empire. Harris predicts that empires will not engage in cannibalism because they can collect tribute from conquered people, but some people may resist conquest. If the Aztecs lacked the military resources to police neighboring territories, then they could have promoted loyalty by threat of brutal sacrifice. Ingham (1984) argues that this is a likely possibility because the Aztecs had no good means of transportation, other than walking. Sending warriors to the distant villages would have been much more costly than scaring their inhabitants into submission through spectacularly brutal rituals.

This political domination account is plausible, but incomplete. It implies that sacrifice was no more than a show of power. This explains the function of sacrifice, but not the psychology. There is no reason to think that the Aztecs who participated in ritual sacrifice construed their practices in such strategic terms. It is much more likely that sacrifice was assigned religious significance.

Aztec mythology is awash in blood (Sanday, 1986; Carrasco, 1999). One myth tells of a monster goddess named Tlaltecuhtli, who was ripped in half by two other gods, Quetzalcoatl and Tezcatlipoca. Half of her body became the heavens and half became the Earth. Tlaltecuhtli was thought to provide nourishment on Earth only if fed a steady diet of human hearts. Quetzalcoatl and Tezcatlipoca were said to be at constant war with each other, and their battles had led to the creation and destruction of four suns. Each sun corresponds to an era in time, and each ended in cataclysm. The Aztecs believed they were living in the age of the fifth sun, which would also end in disaster. The fifth age was created when a minor god threw himself into a fire and became a fifth sun, named Tonatiuh. At first, Tonatiuh could not move across the sky, but then many other gods immolated themselves, and that gave him the power to move. Each night, however, he would be destroyed, and then recreated in the morning. Tonatiuh's head appears in the center of the Aztec calendar stone, with a protruding tongue in the shape of a sacrificial obsidian knife. The Aztecs believed that people came to life in the fifth era when Quetzalcoatl spilled his blood on the bones of people who had lived in earlier eras. Another major figure in the Aztec pantheon was the war god, Huitzilopochtli, who was sometimes regarded as a manifestation of Tonatiuh. Huitzilopochtli was created when his mother Coatlicue was impregnated by a ball of feathers that fell from the sky. Coatlicue had 400 prior children who felt dishonored by their mother's miraculous pregnancy, and they set out to kill her. When they attacked, Huitzilopochtli burst from his mother's womb and destroyed them all.

These myths have a common theme. All involve gods destroying gods, and cycles of revenge. But, more importantly, Aztec mythology promoted a sense of extreme vulnerability: there is an ongoing battle of divine forces, which will ultimately destroy the world. The Aztecs evidently believed that sacrifices were necessary to ward off inevitable doom. Sahlins (1978) and Sanday (1986) argue that cannibalism must be understood as part of this elaborate narrative structure.

The nutritional and political analyses of cannibalism do nothing to illuminate its religious significance. The nutritional analysis is probably best regarded as an account of how sacrifice emerged in the first place, but not why it stuck around. The Aztecs began as a poor, nomadic tribe that engaged in military conflicts with other groups. Cannibalism may have begun in this pre-state stage for nutritional reasons. But Harris and Harner do not explain how it became ritualized. One possibility has to do with the psychology of warfare. Warfare is emotionally charged, and warriors must go through training and psychological conditioning. Heightened emotions, repeated activities, and life-and-death situations, are the wellspring of religious ritual (Burkert, 1983). After a military victory, nomadic ancestors of the Aztecs would have likely felt relief, joy, and gratitude. If captives were taken for consumption, they would likely be eaten in the context of a victory celebration, which is, in itself, a kind of ritual. Such a celebration would mark the group's success in having escaped destruction through military success. Aztec cosmology probably emerged under these conditions. Rituals associated with victory were probably given mythic significance.

Once myths and rituals are created, they can take on a life of their own. Ritually killing a war captive is an intense, emotionally charged experience. Rituals that have a high level of emotional or sensory intensity are likely to be remembered and repeated (Whitehouse, 2000; McCauley and Lawson, 2002). Over time, the pageantry of Aztec sacrifice increased. Priests, sometimes clad in human skins, would hold up the hearts of their victims and then roll their bodies down the steps of great pyramids. The myths surrounding sacrifice probably increased the probability of cultural transmission. Aztec religion fuelled great anxiety about the future—anxiety backed up by periodic droughts, hurricanes, and other natural disasters. Ritual cannibalism was said to forestall doom. This, together with the political benefits, helps to explain why the practice endured past the period in which it could have yielded a significant nutritional advantage.

The Aztec religion is, in some respects, the opposite of Christianity. The gods were often regarded as enemies, rather than friends, and pleasing the gods was a way to ward off disaster, not a way to enter paradise. In both religions, humans were thought to be beneficiaries of a divine sacrifice, but, for the Aztecs, that favor needed to be repaid with human sacrifice, and, for Christians, human sacrifice was prohibited. In other words, Aztec religion preaches a message of anxiety whereas Christianity often preaches a message of hope. Both hope and anxiety are effective tools for transmission.

In discussing the Aztecs, I have invoked the factors of cultural transmission that I outlined above. First, I invoked material factors. Aztec cannibalism probably emerged because it was nutritionally cost-effective. The Aztecs were warring nomads before they achieved statehood, and cannibalism may be the default practice for societies with that profile. Cannibalism remained in place after the transition to statehood because it conferred political benefits, and the Aztecs lacked the kind of agriculture that would have rendered it cost-effective to keep war prisoners as long-term slaves. But these material factors may not have been explicitly recognized by the Aztec people. The Aztecs probably didn't regard cannibalism as merely an efficient way to scare conquered villages into paying tribute. It's more likely that the Aztecs interpreted their ritual practice in its cosmological context, and these religious beliefs together with the intense emotions evoked by lavish cannibal rituals were probably the primary means by which the practice was passed on from generation to generation. Cannibalism was sustained by an anxiety-inducing set of religious beliefs and emotionally evocative rituals. This cocktail of material factors, religious beliefs, and emotion is a potent force in the formation, transmission, and maintenance of values.

6.2.4 Marriage and the Christian Church

The case of cannibalism illustrates the viability of an empirically grounded genealogical program. We can make informed speculations about the factors that have led to the emergence, success, and ultimate disappearance of specific moral values. I want to shift from cannibalism to kinship. Cannibalism is an alien moral value. We no longer find it permissible. Indeed, cannibalism has been so successfully suppressed that it rarely occurs, and thoughts about cannibalism do not play an active regulative role in our lives. Kinship is different. Our lives are structured around operative norms governing familiar relations. The genealogy of kinship can be used to shed light on values that are central to our everyday practices. To illustrate, I want to consider the genealogy of modern Western values pertaining to marriage. Westerners believe that marriage should be monogamous. Polygamy is not only illegal in the West; it is considered immoral. Westerners also oppose marriage between kin, even beyond the immediate family. Marriage to a first cousin is regarded with disgust. Westerners also believe that marriage should be consensual: it should be based on love rather than pre-arranged.

These values are not universal. Monogamy is much less common than polygamy, in fact, and its global spread has been fairly recent. In a representative sample of 186 culturally independent societies, Murdock (1981) found that only 27, under 15 percent, are monogamous. A handful of polyandrous societies can be found in cross-cultural surveys (a woman can have multiple husbands), but the vast majority are polygynous (a man can have multiple wives). The distribution of these kinship systems is not random. Polyandry has arisen in environments with very scarce resources, such as the arid, mountainous lands of

Tibet and Nepal. The people of Tibet and Nepal traditionally practiced fraternal polyandry: a woman would marry all the brothers in a family. This system has certain advantages (Goldstein, 1987). Suppose, as is the case, that women in Nepal have on average three male children. If three brothers marry one woman, and that woman has three male children, and those three males marry one woman who has three male children, then the population will remain constant. If instead, each male child married a different woman, then male population size would grow exponentially. Exponential growth is fine in territories where there is room to expand, but less viable in the Himalayas. If it's difficult to set up a new household elsewhere, families will be under pressure to divide their estate among all heirs. If each family in Nepal has a farm that is passed down to male heirs, and all male offspring marry the same woman, than the family farm will remain intact rather than being divided into smaller parts with each generation. Males will have a strong incentive to remain in one household, because they will benefit from a more substantial inheritance, giving them greater comfort, freedom, and status. In sum, in an inhospitable climate where farmable land is limited, polyandry can be highly adaptive.

In most settings, however, polygyny has been the dominant form of marriage. That is not to say that most people across the world have engaged in polygyny; only that polygyny has been permissible in most societies. The convergence of three factors may be especially important in explaining the prevalence of polygyny (Grossbard-Schechtman, 1984; see also White and Burton, 1988): First, in many societies, there are few wage opportunities for women; in such societies, women cannot compete in the open marketplace and they depend on male wage earners. Second, in many societies, women and their children can participate in profitable domestic labor, including farming; in such societies, there is an economic advantage to having several women in a house. Third, in many societies there is considerable social stratification, so some men are much wealthier than others; in such societies, multiple women could survive on the income of one wealthy man. In short, if women depend on men and are profitable to men, and some men can support several wives, then polygyny is especially likely. These three factors have been extremely common through world history, which may help explain why polygyny has been so widespread. Polygyny was the norm in the ancient world. In ancient Greek, Egyptian, and Jewish society, wealthy men could have multiple wives. Solomon reportedly had 700 women in his harem (1 Kings, 11:3). Today, polygyny is less common in the West, but it remains widespread in the Third World.

Cousin-marriage is also quite common in certain parts of the world, especially in the Middle East, South Asia, and Sub-Saharan Africa. Bittles (1990) estimates that 20 percent of the world population lives in societies that promote or allow cousin-marriage. Cousin-marriage was allowed in Athenian Greece, in late Roman society, and in Judea (Thompson, 1967; Treggiari 1993; Goody, 1983). In the Old Testament, for example, Jacob is married to his mother's brother's two daughters (Genesis 29:10–30). Cousin-marriage has certain advantages, the most obvious of which is that it allows extended families to consolidate wealth.

Another feature of marriage that varies cross-culturally is consent. For us, consensual marriage is a highly moralized ideal, but it is far from universal. In many societies, marriages are arranged. This was true in ancient Rome and ancient Israel, and it remains true in parts of India, Japan, China, and in many African societies. There are obvious reasons why families might want a hand in choosing who their offspring marry. Love is often blind, and young couples may be drawn together by factors other than long-term economic advantage. When families arrange a marriage, they can select partners that will secure beneficial alliances, and prevent downward mobility.

The most striking fact about this cross-cultural comparison is that modern Western attitudes toward marriage seem to have emerged from societies with very different values. There is little precedent for modern values in Rome and Judea. This suggests that modern values were not inherited from a previous tradition; rather, they were invented. But why? There are various possible explanations. Consider a theory of monogamy that was proposed by Richard Alexander (1987). He argues that polygamy was outlawed as a way to avoid in-group conflict. In polygynous societies, there is fierce competition for women, because, if one man has multiple wives and gender ratios are equal, then some men will be condemned to a life of bachelorhood. This can lead to violent conflict, and imposed monogamy diminishes male–male violence by giving men more equal opportunity on the marriage market. It should also be noted that monogamy reduces conflicts between co-wives, and conflicts between children over inheritance, because monogamous marriages yield fewer children than polygynous marriages. Monogamy diminishes violence. Sanderson (2001) has surveyed evidence consistent with Alexander's hypothesis. He notes that monogamous societies are larger, wealthier, and more internally peaceful, suggesting that monogamy laws may have permitted societies to flourish and grow. Only 10 percent of pre-state societies have imposed monogamy versus 46 percent of large states.

Alexander's theory of monogamy is intuitively plausible, and it may help to explain why monogamy has become so widespread, but it is not the only available explanation. It is important to bear in mind that different explanations may be operative in different cases, and it is important to consider each case individually before settling on a theory of how a social institution emerged in any particular culture. Jack Goody (1983) advances a provocative hypothesis about how monogamy got off the ground in the West. Pre-Christian European peoples usually tolerated polygyny, or equivalently, they allowed men to have concubines whose offspring could inherit wealth. The Romans were officially monogamous, but they allowed a man to have a concubine if his wife was infertile. The Romans also allowed couples to divorce and remarry, which amounts to "serial polygamy," because people could have multiple spouses over the lifespan. Remarriage was even required during some periods in late Roman history. The monogamous system minimized conflicts over inheritance, because it kept family sizes down and eliminated competition between co-wives. But toleration for divorce and remarriage meant that a man who had no heirs with his first wife could leave her and try to have children with another. Things changed, Goody argues, with the rise of Christianity. Polygyny and consanguinity (marriage to close relatives) were banned by the Church in the fourth century, after Constantine's conversion. Arranged marriages were discouraged by the Church, and bans were introduced on marriage among clergy, divorce, and widow-inheritance (wherein widows would marry close relatives of their deceased husbands). The Church also condemned recreational sex and adoption. It took some time for many of these rules to take hold as the influence of the Church expanded through Europe, but they ultimately led to a significant transformation in attitudes toward marriage. On the face of it the new rules do not have much in common, but closer examination reveals a startling fact. All of them work to reduce family size and increase heirlessness, and heirlessness, Goody argued, was profitable for the Church.

In a polygynous marriage, there are multiple wives, and thus more offspring who can inherit wealth. The prohibition of polygyny led to a great decrease in the number of heirs. The ban on adoption made it impossible to compensate for that decrease. Prohibitions against consanguinity, including cousin-marriage, decreased easy access to spouses and prevented families from consolidating wealth. Familial wealth consolidation was further limited by the ban on arranged marriage. Strategic kinship ties were broken, and individuals were forced to find their own partners. The ban on divorce prevented couples from re-marrying and having more offspring (serial polygamy), and restrictions on widow marriage had a similar effect. The ban on recreational sex meant there were fewer accidental pregnancies, and hence fewer offspring. The net result was that many families ended up with no heirs. With high rates of mortality and no treatments for infertility, monogamous couples could easily end up heirless. Goody estimates that heirlessness may have been as high as 20 percent during some periods. When a family had no heirs, the estate was inherited by the Church. Because clergy could not marry, property going to the Church had no way of being filtered back out to the non-clerical population. It's not clear from Goody's analysis whether all of this was a strategy devised by Church leaders or a coincidence, but it is clear that the Church benefited enormously from increased heirlessness. With these policies in place, the Church became one of the largest landowners in Europe. Starting with no property, the early Church eventually came to possess some 25 percent of all Gaul.

Goody's hypothesis is controversial (see, e.g., Verdon, 1988), but it isn't crazy. It shows how attitudes toward marriage might have emerged. Like Harris and Harner on cannibalism, Goody emphasizes material factors. Strict rules on who could get married led to direct benefits. But there is a difference. In the case of cannibalism, benefits were accrued by the cannibals. In the case of marriage laws, benefits were accrued by the Church, on Goody's hypothesis, not necessarily by the individuals who were married. This is a historically stable scenario, however, because the Church is a primary purveyor of values. Values that benefit the Church are likely to be spread and sustained, because the Church plays a central role in moral education. But Goody's hypothesis faces a challenging question. Why would people have bought into the Church's marriage reforms if those reforms effectively reduced their capacity to accumulate wealth? The answer may involve the means of transmission. Christian attitudes toward kinship were spread through interpretations of biblical texts. Jesus' teaching and the story of the Fall put the values into a narrative context, and the rhetoric of sin and impurity helped to make illicit unions emotionally repellent.

The general shift in attitudes toward sexuality was heavily influenced by St Augustine and St Paul. After a debauched youth, Augustine came to believe that sex should be used only for procreation. He based this on ancient Greek philosophical traditions that tie moral goodness to natural functions. Sex has the function of procreation, so misuses of sex are unnatural. If something is unnatural, it is wrong. St Paul taught that all sex was sinful, because devotion should be reserved for God. Monogamy was the best thing next to celibacy, because it reduced sex to a minimum. By tying sex to sin, Augustine and Paul gave marriage restrictions a foundation in theology and natural law. By labeling certain sexual acts as unnatural, Church leaders may have been able to tap into parishioners' biological dispositions to disgust. Disgust obeys a logic of contamination. If sex is construed as dirty, then sex with multiple partners can be seen as a way to spread impurity. By cultivating squeamish attitudes toward sexuality, Church leaders could have more easily transmitted norms against polygamy, divorce, and remarriage.

Disgust may also have been exploited in advancing prohibitions against consanguineous marriages. People are often repelled by the idea of incest, and, therefore, any union that is labeled as incestuous may be regarded as repellent. Cousin-marriage was commonplace in the ancient world, but the medieval Church banned cousin-marriage up to the seventh degree. To this day, people enculturated in the West are uncomfortable with cousin-marriage, and the dominant reaction seems to be disgust.

More positive emotions may have factored into the transmission of consensual marriage. Early Church leaders encouraged people to make marriage decisions on the basis of love. This gave people greater autonomy and a very significant emotional payoff. The idea of consensual marriage resonates with the individualistic ideals that emerged in the course of Western history. The Church traditionally construes individuals as free, and Christian eschatology is based on the idea that one could gain access to heaven by making the right choices in life. Arranged marriage is ideologically difficult to fit into that picture.

In sum, the early Church may have implemented its revolutionary changes in kinship customs by embedding them in a compelling belief system with strong emotional content. These suggestions are sketchy and highly speculative. An adequate genealogical analysis would systematically examine the rhetoric used to disseminate marriage laws in the early centuries of the Church. But the main point should be clear. Radical changes in attitudes toward marriage may have been transmitted through a combination of material, narrative, and affective factors. Preachers and parishioners were probably oblivious to the economic impact of revised marriage laws, but emotional and philosophical attitudes can be traced by examining historical documents. Naturalized genealogists can use such records (just as naturalized epistemologists use psychological research) as empirical data in developing theories of how each of our moral values emerged.

6.3 GENEALOGY AS CRITIQUE

These case studies in the history of morals are instructive. They show that moral values can be viewed historically. For every moral value that we possess, there is a story to tell about how we came to possess it. In chapter 7, I will explore the possibility that these stories sometimes have a biological dimension. The examples discussed in this chapter owe more to cultural development. In some cases, new moral values emerge quickly, and in others transformation is slower. As Nietzsche suggested, the rise of Christianity may have been rapid enough to call a revolution. The disappearance of cannibalism may have been comparatively slow in some societies. If Harris is right, cannibalism tended to disappear as chiefdoms shifted over to sophisticated forms of agriculture and evolved into states. In these cases, human sacrifice and cannibal practices may have gradually been replaced by animal sacrifices, and, ultimately, symbolic "sacrifices," including everything from the burning of effigies and totems to the Christian Eucharist. Aztec cannibalism ended quickly because the Spanish conquistadors decimated the Aztec Empire in a single generation. This power shift, and subsequent efforts by missionaries, promoted relatively rapid change in Mesoamerica, but indigenous societies often managed to retain vestiges of their traditional ways as they converted to the belief systems of their conquerors.

Such historical dynamics are certainly interesting in their own right. They teach us something about why we believe what we do, and why others have different beliefs. But one can justifiably wonder whether they have any philosophical ramifications. What do they prove about the status of morality? Nietzsche believed that genealogical analysis could be used to criticize morals. By exposing the history of Christian values, in particular, he sought to erode their credibility. In this section, I want to ask whether such skeptical conclusions are warranted.

Let's begin by considering a strong version of the claim that historicity undermines morality. By "historicity," I mean to refer to values that emerged as a consequence of historical events, rather than through a process of, say, direct moral intuition, revelation, or rational deduction of normative principles. With respect to such values, one might be tempted to endorse the following genealogical principle:

> (G1) If a belief in a moral value emerged as a consequence of historical events, then the moral value is false.

For the purposes of this discussion, I will be thinking of moral values as evaluative propositions, of the form "ϕ-ing is morally bad" or "ϕ-ing is morally good." Thus, (G1) says that beliefs about what's good and bad can be discredited simply in virtue of the fact that they arose through historical, rather than, say, rational processes. I doubt that Nietzsche or anyone else would defend anything like this. (G1) commits a straightforward genetic fallacy: it is a mistake to treat a defect in how a proposition came to be believed as direct evidence against that proposition. Suppose I win the lottery by selecting numbers that correspond to the birthdays of my friends and family. This method of guessing has no bearing on the mechanisms that determine the winning numbers (e.g., a contraption that randomly spits out numbered spheres). But my guess is nevertheless accurate.

Here one might be tempted to argue that there is an important disanalogy between the lottery case and the case of morals. In the lottery case, there is a mind-independent mechanism by which numbers are selected. The mechanism does not depend on how we form beliefs about which numbers will win. But in the case of morals, I have argued that truth depends on us. The truth of a moral value is linked, in that sense, to the method of belief fixation. The gap between fact and belief is very narrow in the moral domain. This distinguishes the moral case from the lottery case, but it does not make (G1) defensible. If truth depends on us, then historical facts about how we came to take a moral value as true also establish that the value is true. Genealogical analyses could only undermine the truth of a moral value if they revealed that we don't really believe what we profess to believe. If Nietzsche had established that Christians don't really believe that charity is good, he would have been able to refute that moral value within Christian culture. This was not his intention. The genealogical method tends to take moral beliefs as a fixed point, and then explain their origins.

We need a weaker principle. Perhaps we should abandon the focus on truth, and switch to something more epistemological in character:

> (G2) If a belief in a moral value emerged as a consequence of historical events, then that belief is unwarranted.

This is an improvement. It seems to avoid the genetic fallacy. The way a belief is obtained can bear on whether a belief is justified. For example, medieval doctors believed that many plants had healing powers, and they often assumed that a plant was especially able to heal the body part that it most resembled. A gourd, for example, might be used to treat a swollen limb. That belief is unwarranted because it's based on a false premise. But suppose that a particular kind of gourd, by chance, can reduce swelling to some degree, and suppose that, over time, that gourd continues to be used medicinally, while others are not, in virtue of its past success. The belief that the gourd can heal came about in a bad way, but it stuck around for good reason, and is now endorsed with warrant. This kind of example shows that a belief might be initially unwarranted because of how it came about, but warranted later on, because of, for example, its success in guiding behavior. Ignoble origins are, to that extent, compatible with warrant.

(G2) faces another objection as well. I have argued that moral concepts refer to response-dependent properties. It follows that moral judgments (at least those that express grounding norms) are self-justifying. If I make a judgment that something is wrong, and that judgment is made under epistemic conditions in which I have accurately accessed my long-term memory and discovered a sentiment of disapprobation toward that thing, then my belief is warranted because WRONG refers to that toward which I have such a sentiment. If this account is right, it applies even if my response-dispositions are set up as a consequence of historical events. Warrant is cheap if constructive sentimentalism is true.

In response, one might concede that moral judgments are always warranted when made under good epistemic conditions, while insisting that they should be abandoned. When warrant is cheap, warrant may be insufficient to support conviction. By analogy, suppose you like a particular genre of music simply in virtue of having listened to it during formative years of your youth. Now, it's trivially warranted for you to say that this music is likeable to you. The fact that it brings you pleasure makes it the case that it's likeable, even if that pleasure is the result of a contingent biographical fact that has nothing to do with the intrinsic qualities of the music. You might decide that your preference should be abandoned, because it is the product of inculcation, and you might take steps to alter your musical taste. Applied to the moral domain, this suggests the following principle:

> (G3) If a belief in a moral value emerged as a consequence of historical events, then that belief *should be abandoned.*

(G3) is weaker than the preceding principles, because it does not make claims about truth or warrant. But it is no more defensible. Historicity can motivate us to revise values, but it need not. Returning to the music example, the fact that our preferences are influenced by prior exposure is not sufficient grounds for revision. The very fact that you like certain music now, no matter what the cause, is, all other things being equal, a perfectly good reason to listen to it. The aesthetic analogue of (G3) implies that every acquired taste should be abandoned. Imagine if someone told you that you should stop eating chocolate simply because your preference for chocolate is a contingent consequence of your biography. That's an odd policy in the aesthetic domain and equally odd, one might think, in the domain of moral values.

One might try to defend (G3) by arguing that morality differs from music in crucial respects. For one thing, we do not recognize that our moral values are historical. Discovering their origins reveals that we have been mistaken about them. Even if this is true, I don't see why it matters. Suppose I believe that I like jazz because it has certain intrinsic qualities, but, in reality, I like jazz because I listened to it during formative years of my life. If I discover that my preference results from this biographical fact, it does not seem to follow that I have a reason to give up my taste for jazz. For that to follow, there would need to be a further premise according to which love of jazz was worthwhile only if had a purely objective basis. This premise is hard to support. It is also hard to support in the moral case. A value may be worth retaining because it is entrenched and difficult to change, because it is useful, or simply because I value it.

It's tempting to try to salvage (G3) by drawing a distinction between two kinds of origins. Some values come about through events that are innocuous, and others come about through events that we find contemptible in hindsight. For example, some values may be driven by unseemly motives such as greed or resentment, and some might be imposed on us by others who have more power. Nietzsche wanted to undermine Christian values by proving that they were reactionary. If we can show that a value is not only historical, but that its origins are ignoble, then perhaps that is a reason for dropping the value. Thus:

(G4) If a belief in a moral value emerged as a consequence of ignoble historical events, then that belief should be abandoned.

This is beginning to sound more Nietzschean, but it is not very satisfying. "Ignoble" is an evaluative term. Nietzsche sometimes said that there is an objective moral standpoint from which we can evaluate the history of Christian morals—the natural standpoint of those free spirits who openly embrace the will to power. This is an aspect of Nietzsche's program that we would do well to drop. In the next chapter, I will raise doubts about a transcendental natural stance. If the word "ignoble" cannot be applied objectively, then it too may be a product of history. If historicity is a ground for skepticism, then we should be skeptical of attempts to undermine moral values by saying that they have morally dubious histories. By introducing a moral term (G4) might be self-defeating.

One might try to save (G4) by arguing that it can be used to diagnose the hypocrisy of moralizers. Perhaps Nietzsche wants Christians to realize that their values derive from factors that are despicable by their own standards. If a moral system arose in a way that the system itself demands that we condemn, then the system may undermine its own foundations. Perhaps. But the apologist for the moral system in question could simply reply that the road to heaven is paved with bad intentions. The ends justify the means. (G4) is just another instance of the genetic fallacy.

At this point, a faithful Nietzschean may make a very different move. When Nietzsche talks about the ignoble origins of Christianity, he is not merely making a point about the past. He thinks that the questionable motives that led to the Christian revolution in ethics also sustain Christian values in the present. Contemporary defenders of those values are driven by resentment. If that is right, then contemporary moralizers can be labeled hypocrites, and, by their own standards, hypocrisy is a bad thing. On this interpretation, skepticism does not rest on historicity as such. Rather genealogical analysis is designed to reveal something about the psychological foundations of contemporary morals (cf. Gemes, 2006). We should give up Christian values because they are sustained by emotions that we consider a bad basis for values. It is okay to like chocolate because it is pleasurable, but bad to like it because you resent chocolate-haters. This is an evaluative judgment of course, but it is a judgment that the person who presently likes chocolate would be willing to make. If you can convince the chocolate lover that chocolate loving is reactionary, that might prompt efforts to overcome the love of chocolate. Here, I think, we come closest to the strategy underlying Nietzsche's genealogical program. For him, diachronic methods are a tool for doing synchronic psychology. Genealogy is a ladder to be kicked away.

I think this approach to genealogy is too limited. For one thing, I doubt very much that Christians are (or were) motivated by *ressentiment*. We do not need fancy psychodynamic machinery to explain why people have the values that they do. Cultural conditioning is enough. Emotions play a role in this, but their contribution may be much simpler than it is on Nietzsche's model. We learn moral values through emotional training, and the values that are most easily spread are the ones that are most amendable to such techniques. I argued above that Christian norms against polygyny were easy to transmit, in part, because it is easy to promote disgust when it comes to bodily interactions. The idea of plural sexual contact can make one feel a bit queasy if one frames it in terms of impurity, contamination, and violations against nature. If the history of polygyny reveals anything about contemporary psychology, it shows that some people find polygyny disgusting. Accusing people of basing their moral values on disgust is very different from accusing people of basing their moral values on resentment. The former accusation wouldn't necessarily lead people to change their morals. A dedicated monogamist might even retort that polygyny is wrong precisely because it's disgusting. Putting this differently, Nietzsche assumes that we will experience cognitive dissonance when we discover the emotions that undergird our moral values; but I see no reason to think that will be the case.

Thus, genealogy will not always reveal hidden psychological motives that would embarrass those who moralize. But genealogy can embarrass moralizers in another way. If you told opponents of polygyny that their preference for monogamy came about through a real-estate grab by the early Church, that might give them pause. This revelation is not a sufficient reason for dropping the move against polygyny—perhaps there are good reasons to favor monogamy—but it does motivate a reassessment. Some moral values spread because they benefit those who hold them. Others spread because they benefit a powerful institution that has a privileged role in influencing local morality. When we discover that one of our values falls into the second category, rather than the first, we have reason to ask whether the value is worth maintaining. This suggests the following principle:

> (G5) If a belief in a moral value emerged as a consequence of ignoble historical events, then we should *consider* abandoning that belief.

In talking of cases where the history is ignoble, I am imagining cases where the dissemination of a value did not hinge on any obvious benefit (moral or otherwise) to the moralizer. In these cases, we can justifiably ask whether the value is doing anything beneficial for us in the present. A negative answer to this is not a sufficient reason for dropping the value. Moral values can be maintained even if they do not have any payoffs. Some moral values may even be costly for some people. But in cases where no benefits are discovered, reassessment becomes appropriate. In some cases we may discover that a value is doing more harm than good, and, in these cases, moral change becomes desirable.

(G5) depicts genealogy as a critical tool, though perhaps a blunter tool than Nietzsche's hammer. Values are not necessarily vitiated by their historicity, but historical analyses give us a tool for assessing whether our values serve functions that we still care about. In discussing (G2), I said that warrant comes cheap for moral values, because they refer to response-dependent properties. There I was talking about evidential warrant: factors that support the truth of a belief. I believe that ϕ-ing is bad in virtue of having a sentiment of disapprobation toward ϕ-ing; such sentiments are truth-makers for moral claims, so the very fact that I believe that ϕ-ing is bad supports the conclusion that ϕ-ing is bad in my value system. But warrant can also be instrumental (Sinnott-Armstrong, 1996). I may find a value that I have to be useful in some way. It may serve a function that I care about. I have argued that moral values often emerge because of some role that they played in the past. That role may matter to me, or it may not. Genealogical analysis provides a tool for seeing what function values have played, and that can be helpful in determining whether our moral values are helping or hindering us in pursuit of our non-moral ends.

Let's consider some examples. I suggested that the cannibalism taboo arose because we developed ways to use our neighbors as taxpayers rather than food. We should probably keep this taboo in place. To allow cannibalism, even in cases where people die of natural causes, might lead to a slippery slope. The rule would be easy to exploit, the potential for corruption would be great, and the payoff would be negligible. Moreover, our opposition to cannibalism has become constitutive of our identity as "civilized." It is the result of our attaining that status. To lift the taboo would potentially alter identity in a way that would have unforeseen negative consequences. Since the cannibalism taboo does not cause serious harm or otherwise conflict with values that we cherish, there is little reason to abandon it. In any case, the historical reasons underlying that taboo remain in place today. We are still better off taxing our neighbors than eating them.

Contrast this with monogamy. Suppose our transition from polygyny really was a conspiracy of the early Church. Should we stop valuing monogamy? That's a difficult question. We know that giving up monogamy would have costs. Our social systems and institutions have been structured around monogamy, and systems that are not monogamous often have features that we disvalue on other grounds. Polygamous societies are usually polygynous, and polygyny hinges on a double-standard that discriminates against women. Furthermore, monogamy is fulfilling to those who value it (compare: jazz is enjoyable to those who like it). Perhaps that is the result of social conditioning, but so too is taste in music, fashion preferences, affection for sports, the languages we speak, and much else. If we were conditioned to appreciate monogamy for dubitable reasons, it does not *follow* that monogamy is a bad institution. If we cannot find anything horribly wrong with monogamy, and we happen to value it, we might as well continue valuing it. On the other hand, we might not want to require monogamy by law, because some people may have the desire and ability to live in non-exploitative polygamous relationships. It is generally assumed in our culture that polygamy is categorically wrong. Indeed, some people argue against gay marriage on the grounds that allowing homosexual unions would initiate a slippery slope and lead to the legalization of polygamy. It's not obvious to me that either of these marriage types should be prohibited. The fact that monogamy and prohibitions on gay marriage are both products of history is not a sufficient reason to give up either for those who still value them, but, if these marriage norms no longer serve any function that we care about, then we should not impose them on others. For an interesting genealogy of attitudes toward gay marriage, see Boswell (1994).

The conclusion is even more obvious if we turn to cousin-marriage. To many of us, cousin-marriage sounds repellant. We think it is morally wrong and, in some sense, unnatural. But now we discover that cousin-marriage is common, and our own disdain for it is an artifact of history. That fact leads us to reassess our moral condemnation of cousin-marriage. In the centuries since it was banned, *post hoc* arguments have emerged for thinking cousin-marriage is wrong. We are taught that children of cousins are likely to have birth defects. This belief turns out to be false (Bennett et al., 2002). It is an urban legend marshaled in favor of a moral agenda. And, in any case, risk of birth defects does not make it morally wrong to marry someone. Therefore, there is no strong reason to maintain norms against cousin-marriage. We may also decide that there are good reasons to favor cousin-marriage. Perhaps cousins are more likely to share things in common and to forge stable relationships. If so, we should be receptive to a value change.

Let's conclude with a more controversial example: abortion. I noted above that abortion was condemned by the early Christian Church. This position may have been inherited from Judaism. Ancient Jews had two good reasons to oppose abortion: abortion was very risky to women in ancient times, and prohibiting abortion increased fertility, which is a virtue for a small religious community in constant risk of extinction. The Church later relaxed its anti-abortion stance. Augustine reverted to the Aristotelian view that the undeveloped fetus could not support a soul. Abortion was considered wrong only after quickening, the time when the mother feels the first movement in her womb. Augustine's position on abortion became Church Canon Law, reversing the earlier view that all abortion is wrong. One possible reason for the change is that, by the fifth century, the Church had a stake in reducing the number of heirs born to any family. This remained the official position of the Church for centuries. In 1588, Pope Sixtus V banned abortion briefly but Pope Gregory XIV repealed the ban three years later. The anti-abortion stance regained some popularity in the seventeenth century, but it was not until the nineteenth century, however, that the official doctrine of the Church turned against abortion. In 1869, Pope Pius IX added a ban on abortion to Church Canon Law, and that has been the official position of the Roman Catholic Church ever since. There is scant biblical support for this position, so cynics cite ulterior motives. One conjecture, entertained by abortion rights activists, is that the Church banned abortion to increase the size of the French army. The population in France was dwindling, and Emperor Napoleon III wanted to increase birth rates in his Catholic nation. Napoleon III publicly recognized the infallibility of the Pope in the same year as the abortion ban. Another conspiratorial hypothesis is that the Church began to oppose abortion again in order to keep women in their traditional roles. The ban coincided with the rise of the women's suffrage movement. Critics of women's suffrage often argued that women were ill-equipped to vote because the demands of motherhood kept them away from work and school, and promoted dangerous tendencies toward pacifism. The Vatican banned abortion in the same year that England gave women the right to vote in local elections—a right that was unprecedented in Western Europe.

I will not try to assess these historical analyses here. I am skeptical about the claim that the anti-abortion stance was simply a ploy against women's suffrage; Italy didn't give women the right to vote until 1925. I am also skeptical about the claim that abortion was banned to augment the French army; Pope Pius IX might not have regarded that end as advantageous to Rome and, in any case, it's incredibly presumptuous to assume that he would have changed Canon Law under political pressure. Moreover, the idea that life begins at conception had been popular for 200 years.

Rather than answering the thorny question about why the Church banned abortion, I want to consider a hypothetical question. Imagine a person, call her Smith, who opposes abortion because it is the doctrine of the Church. Now imagine that Smith comes to believe that the abortion ban was actually introduced as a deliberate tool in a campaign against women's suffrage. On learning this, would Smith instantly change her mind about abortion? Probably not. Values are difficult to change. But Smith *should* reassess her position. If Smith believed that abortion was wrong *because* it was a violation of an authoritative interpretation of holy texts, and now the authority of that interpretation is cast into doubt by the discovery of ulterior motives, then Smith's reason for opposing abortion has been discredited. She will have to rely on other reasons or treat opposition to abortion as a foundational grounding norm.

Genealogy is a powerful critical tool, because it forces us to see held convictions in a new light. We tend to think fairly superficially about our moral values. We take our values to be obvious or received truths. We regard immoral behavior as unnatural. When we adopt a historical stance we alter our epistemic stance toward values. In ordinary discourse, we either take moral values as foundational, hence immune to interrogation, or as justified by appeal to values that are foundational. When we offer justifications they are typically circular, thin, or formulaic. Any trained philosopher could devise credible arguments for either side of a moral debate. Perhaps one side always has the better argument in the end, but it is incredibly unlikely that every moralizer is in possession of knockdown arguments for each of her moral convictions.

When we view morals historically, we put aside questions of justification and engage in a form of auto-anthropology. We do not ask, "Why should I believe P?", but rather, "Why do I believe P?" Nietzsche's heretical suggestion is that the latter descriptive question can have some bearing on the apparently normative question. If the moral convictions tend to rest on foundational intuitions or half-baked justifications then asking the question "Why should I believe P" is an invitation to self-deception. We tend to fall back on pat answers. The question "Why do I believe P" can expose those cases where we have come to a moral conviction in the absence of decent reasons. I submit that this is the *usual* condition. In many cases, our cherished moral values emerged under conditions that no longer apply. Genealogy can be used to critically reassess these values. In some cases, however, moral values will withstand genealogical critique. Some of our values have managed to be passed on to us because they are helpful or successful. This is a possibility that Nietzsche does not fully appreciate. His pessimism is overblown. But Nietzsche is right to think that some of our moral values have questionable histories. Some get passed on, not because they work, but because they serve those who are in a position to disseminate values. When we encounter cases like this, we face a challenging choice. We can retain the value in question or we can try to overcome it. Overcoming values is not trivial task, as we will see in chapter 8.

In this chapter, I had two goals. I wanted to illustrate the genealogical method. If moral values are sentimentally constructed and culturally relative, then there must be an explanation of how we came to have each of our values. Genealogy is a method of uncovering such explanations. My second goal was to assess the implications of genealogy. Nietzsche thinks that genealogy can be used to promote skepticism about cherished moral values. I argued that he is overly pessimistic, but I agree that genealogy helps us determine when a value is especially suitable for reassessment. I said very little here about how that reassessment is supposed to take place. From what vantage point can we decide whether a value is worth keeping? Nietzsche can be read as supposing that there is a transcendental position from which we can assess morality and choose new values. He implies that we can base morality on human nature. Herein lies Nietzsche's optimism. In chapter 7, I will raise serious doubts about this, and, in chapter 8, I will defend an alternative approach. The interim moral is that genealogy is an under-utilized tool for moral critique. Nietzsche's pessimism about current morality and his optimism about natural morality are both exaggerated, but he is certainly right to think that historical analyses can be valuable in moral revision.

7

The Limits of Evolutionary Ethics

7.1 EVOLVED NORMS

7.1.1 Nietzsche's Myth

Nietzsche's ethical theory has two components: one negative, the other positive. The negative component is his genealogical program. Its primary function is critical and destructive. Nietzsche wanted to undermine deeply held values by exposing their sordid history and base underlying motives. The positive component is captured in Nietzsche's (1885) myth of the *Übermensch*—a being who is capable of living in a world beyond the good and evil dichotomy of contemporary morality. The *Übermensch* is a free spirit who affirms life and embraces values that are, in some sense, more natural than those of modern men.

The theme of natural values appears in *On the Genealogy of Morals*. There, Nietzsche says that our current values are reactive, or reactionary. They are fueled by resentment of Roman oppressors. Roman values, however, are active. They are not defined in opposition to anything else. Nietzsche also uses the rhetoric of natural values in *The Antichrist*, where he suggests that the ancient Israelites had values that were more natural than the Christians, and hence better:

Originally, and above all in the time of the monarchy, Israel maintained the right attitude of things, which is to say, the natural attitude. Its Yahweh was an expression of its consciousness of power, its joy in itself, its hopes for itself. . . . But . . . the conception of him was changed—the conception of him was denaturalized. . . . Morality is no longer a reflection of the conditions which make for the sound life and development of the people; it is no longer the primary life-instinct; instead it has become abstract and in opposition to life. (Nietzsche, 1888: 25)

Thus, early Israeli values, like Roman values, can be regarded as precursors to the values that the *Übermensch* will re-instill. Nietzsche's considered view is that Israeli and Roman values are not a perfect manifestations of human nature, but only an approximation. In *The Will to Power*, he writes,

[T]here has never yet been a natural humanity. The scholasticism of un- and *anti*-natural values is the rule, is the beginning; man reaches nature only after a long struggle—he never "returns". . . More natural is our first society, that of the rich, the leisure class: they hunt each other, love between the sexes is a kind of sport in which marriage furnishes an obstacle and a provocation; they amuse themselves and live for pleasure; they esteem physical advantages above all, are curious and bold.   (Nietzsche, 1883–8: 120)

Moral progress will come, on this reading of Nietzsche, when we shed our reactive values, and return to more ancient forms of flourishing. Nietzsche implies that we can even outdo the Romans, and develop a system of values that is even more natural, and ahistorical. To move beyond good and evil, we can take inspiration from the past, but doing so is not so much a form of nostalgia, but a strategy for stepping outside of time. The ancients were not better because they preceded the Christians; they were better because their values were more expressive of our fundamental constitution as human beings.

This idea, that some values are historically constructed and others are more natural, is very seductive. It is embodied in the Romantic ideal of the noble savage, and it is also central to Hume's distinction between natural and artificial virtues. Unlike Nietzsche, Hume did not want to reject the artificial ones, but he did think that natural virtues are privileged; he thought that artificial virtues must be grounded in natural virtues to have any authority. The theme of natural values is also popular in recent moral philosophy. Today's philosophers do not invoke Nietzsche's myth of the *Übermensch*, but some are attracted to the idea that we have a suite of norms that come to us naturally. In particular, it is supposed that some norms are products of natural selection; these norms were forged in our ancestral past, and they continue to play a role in guiding our moral behavior. Defenders of evolutionary ethics rarely contrast these biologically based norms with other norms that are not biologically based, but they might as well. All of the cultural variations that I have been discussing in the last two chapters, all of the historical contingencies may just be a dispensable overlay concealing a set of values that lie outside of the history. These natural values belong to a different timescale, and it is tempting to think they are privileged. Unlike historically constructed values, naturally evolved values are selected for, they are universal, and they may be immutable. Perhaps relativism and historicism can be escaped. Perhaps we can simply shed the values that I have been discussing in the last two chapters and restrict ourselves to the values that are woven into our nature as human beings. This would be a significant departure from the constructive sentimentalism that I have been favoring. There is room for an evolutionary sentimentalism, but what should we make of such a view? Is it possible that our moral sentiments are naturally directed toward some things and not others, and that this natural fact privileges those values over those that emerge through cultural processes?

In this chapter, I will raise some doubts about that suggestion. I will concede that we are biologically prone to have certain kinds of values, but I will deny that there is an innate morality (for more discussion, see Prinz, 2007; forthcoming *b*). Our biological predispositions have no authority over values that have a cultural origin, and they can be embellished and overturned under the influence of culture. Moreover, I will argue that our biological predispositions do not qualify as *moral* rules without cultural elaboration. Morality is artificial all the way down. Taken literally, "evolutionary ethics" is a myth. It is Romanticism reborn as crass scientism, no more plausible than Nietzsche's *Übermensch* and perhaps no less insidious. Before getting to that critique, let's see what evolution has to offer.

7.1.2 Back-scratching

Contemporary discussions of evolutionary ethics customarily attempt to distinguish the theories that are currently in vogue from the theory advocated by Herbert Spencer in the nineteenth century. Spencer coined the phrase "survival of the fittest," and saw human social progress in evolutionary terms. Spencer (1857) believed that each of us has an innate right to seek happiness provided we do not trample on the will of others. Laws requiring us to help those who are less fortunate qualify as state-imposed violations of this basic principle. Spencer adamantly opposed laws that enforce charity, because he believed that such laws infringe the rights of the wealthy. He also believed that such laws promote laziness among people who are perfectly able to work, and they diminish the natural sympathies we would have for those genuinely in need. Spencer suggests that we should help those who are destitute due to circumstances beyond their control, but, in less guarded passages, he notes that herd animals benefit from the fact that the weak and sickly can be killed off by predators, allowing fitter animals to thrive.

Spencer's social Darwinism can be construed as a moral theory. Spencer thinks that we have a moral sense for discerning right and wrong, but the right and wrong that we perceive has its basis in fitness. Spencer presumes that all evil, whether natural or moral, involves an incongruity between an organism and its environment. Social ills arise because we evolved to cope with the barbarous and competitive conditions that predate civilization. Now we must evolve more civilized patterns of behavior, and we must let those who fail to adapt, drop off. It is wrong to interfere with the process of natural selection, because natural selection is intrinsically progressive. Evil naturally fades away.

Contemporary evolutionary ethicists repudiate Spencer. They do not think that Darwinian principles can be used to justify the idea that the strong should be allowed to thrive, leaving behind the weak. "Survival of the fittest" should not be used to dictate social policy. Spencer tried to turn natural selection into a moral law. Contemporary evolutionary ethicists typically regard natural selection as morally neutral. Instead of making normative claims, they investigate the moral psychology that selection has conferred. Evolution has engendered a moral capacity in us. That moral capacity is not based on the triumph of the strong over the weak. Rather, it is based on the desire to help those in need, even at our own expense. Evolution has made us altruistic (see Sober and Wilson, 1998).

On the face of it, this conclusion looks quite unlike the egoistic morality of Spencer. But the contrast should not be exaggerated. Spencer believed that, in adapting to social existence, we must evolve to care for those in need. Spencer's views on social policy were driven by his moralization of Darwinian principles, but his account of moral psychology anticipates contemporary trends. The main difference between Spencer and contemporary moralists is that he regarded altruism as an adaptation to civilization. Contemporary theorists discern more ancient origins.

Altruistic behavior is everywhere in nature. Male honeybees will eviscerate themselves by leaving their stingers in creatures that threaten the hive. Female octopuses don't eat while guarding their eggs, and by the time those eggs hatch, the mother is generally so weak that she dies or falls victim to predation. A squirrel will give an alarm call when a predator nears, rendering itself vulnerable to save others of its kind. These behaviors are initially puzzling from a Darwinian perspective. If behavior is driven by the genes, why would genes lead a creature to sacrifice itself for others? Such a creature would be less likely to live to reproductive age, and its noble genes would stand a diminished chance of replication. This puzzle of altruism has a simple solution (Hamilton, 1964). In each of the cases mentioned here, the altruistic creature is sacrificing itself for the safety of its close relatives. Genes that lead creatures to protect their kin are likely to survive, because kin share genes. If the genes of one honeybee cause it to sacrifice itself for a genetically similar honeybee, duplicates of those genes will survive in the other honeybee. If mother octopus dies for her progeny, her progeny will stand a better chance of reaching maturity and producing further copies of mother's genes. Likewise for the squirrels who help their brethren. It turns out that a squirrel is more likely to help another squirrel if the two are closely related (Sherman, 1977).

The same is probably true for us. We'd rather help kin than strangers. Hamilton argued that kin selection—aiding individuals who bear similar genes—lies at the heart of human altruism. This proposal may be right, but it is widely regarded as incomplete. The difficulty is that we do sometimes help strangers. That fact reintroduces the puzzle of altruism. Admittedly, kin selection might lead us to help strangers accidentally, e.g., if biologically based altruism uses dumb mechanisms that cannot distinguish kin from non-kin (Joyce, 2006: 21), but it's hard to believe that kindness to strangers is just a biological blunder. We are kind to non-kin even when we know that they are non-kin, and our kindness to non-kin is considerably greater than that observed in most species. Human kindness is sufficiently widespread that one might even think that it would be selected against. If you sacrifice yourself for someone who does not share your genes, you do nothing to increase the chances that your genes will survive. This raises a serious problem for the hypothesis that moral values have a biological basis. After all, moral values often compel us to help non-relatives. One wonders how such values ever emerged if they are so contrary to the interests of our genes.

Trivers (1971) devised an answer to this challenge. Instead of assuming that we have evolved self-sacrificing mechanisms for helping strangers, one can suppose that we have evolved mechanisms for helping strangers in reciprocal contexts. If we evolved to reciprocate, then helping a stranger is a good strategy for getting assistance from that individual on a future occasion. Trivers calls this reciprocal altruism. As long as we don't kill ourselves in the process, helping strangers can increase our own chances of survival in the long term if favors are reliably reciprocated. To get such behavior off the ground, we must develop both a tendency to help others and a tendency to reciprocate when we've been helped. We must also evolve a capacity to identify, avoid, and perhaps punish those who don't reciprocate. Scratching the back of someone who will not scratch yours is a losing strategy. A population of reciprocal altruists can be overtaken by an invading population of free riders.

Trivers makes the point using the tools of game theory. Consider a standard prisoner's dilemma game in which players can cooperate or defect. One such game involves back-scratching (figure 7.1). If you and I scratch each other's backs, we will both come out happy, but we will both have to work for our happiness. If I could get you to scratch my back without having to scratch yours in return, I would be even happier. Of course, the same is true for you. If neither of us scratches the other's back, we won't get any reward, but neither will we have to endure the cost of back-scratching. If you examine this arrangement of utilities, ranked numerically in figure 7.1, you will notice that refusing to scratch any backs is the dominant strategy. It comes out ahead of back-scratching no matter what the other player does. This all but guarantees that neither of us will scratch the other's back. Neither of us will help the other. Thus, the matrix cell in the lower right is the outcome if we make our decision in a purely rational way. This is an unfortunate outcome, because both of us would be better off if we were both to scratch each other's backs. The cell in the upper left is more desirable. The dilemma arises, because we know we are better off cooperating, but it is more rational to not cooperate, because cooperation is risky.

With this incentive structure, reciprocity could never get off the ground. No one would be trustworthy. But reciprocity is often beneficial. A world of

	Me	
	I scratch your back	I don't scratch your back
You scratch my back	2 for me; 2 for you	3 for me; 0 for you
You don't scratch my back	0 for me; 3 for you	1 for me; 1 for you

Figure 7.1. Expected utilities in a back-scratching version of the prisoner's dilemma

cooperators is better than a word of conspirers. This creates a problem. How do we attain cooperative interactions given the payoffs of defection? Trivers surmises that this problem was solved by the genes. We evolved cooperative instincts and intolerance toward cheaters. This effectively increases the payoff of cooperation (it feels good to scratch your back) and increases the cost of defection (it feels bad not to reciprocate). If we catch and punish defectors, the balance can be tipped even farther in the direction of cooperation. Since evolution selects for traits that are beneficial, it would have selected for traits that promote reciprocal altruism in this way.

This story about the evolution of altruism has been the major inspiration behind recent work on evolutionary ethics. It explains how we might have evolved to be caring, and also how we may have evolved to penalize those who do not care about others sufficiently. We evolved to be good and punish the bad. This story also fits in nicely with the emotionist framework that I have been defending. We certainly don't deliberate about the future of our genes when choosing to behave altruistically. The genetic advantage of decency is invisible to the decent. In fact, we would criticize a person who chose to treat others kindly only because she believed it would benefit her genes to do so. Altruistic tendencies are evidently implemented by simpler psychological mechanisms. We treat others well because it gives us pleasure to do so, and because we become distressed when we see someone in need. We feel guilty when we don't return favors and angry when our own good deeds go unreciprocated. We love cooperation and detest defection. Evolutionary ethicists believe that genes promote altruism by causing their bearers to have emotions that lead to altruistic behavior (Trivers, 1971; Frank, 1988). We do not do good deeds as the result of selfishly calculating the genetic payoffs; we do good deeds because we love the good. According to evolutionary ethicists, this is the essence of morality. The root cause is selfish, but the proximate psychological mechanisms are anything but.

7.1.3 Beyond Altruism

Evolutionary ethicists have focused on reciprocal altruism. They regard our evolved desire to incur personal costs in assisting others as the primary biological source of morality. This focus has limited discussion in two respects. First, reciprocity may be an umbrella term for several interestingly different kinds of behaviors. It is a good idea to consider these separately. Second, while reciprocity is an important aspect of moral behavior, it certainly doesn't exhaust the domain. There are other moral norms that may have a basis in biology. In this section I will present a range of normative domains that may be informed by natural selection. In the next section, I will begin to look at these more critically. The primary point here is that evolutionary ethicists should not restrict themselves to altruism when searching for the biological roots of morality.

Altruism can be defined as any act wherein an organism confers a benefit on another individual while incurring a cost. The concept of reciprocal altruism is based on the idea that such favors can be returned. On this model, altruistic acts are parts of social exchanges. One organism receives benefits at the cost of another, and then subsequently incurs costs while conferring benefits. This very abstract characterization explains why altruism may have evolved, but it obscures the fact that social exchanges are not restricted to a single behavioral capacity. At a minimum, altruism requires behaviors of conferring benefits and repaying those who have conferred benefits in the past. Evolutionists argue that altruism also requires a capacity to keep track of those who haven't repaid—a capacity to detect cheaters. In advanced creatures, there may also be more sophisticated ways of keeping tabs. When we are rewarded for costs that we incur, we expect the reward to be fair. The reward should be proportionate to the cost incurred and proportionate to the rewards that others receive for incurring similar costs.

We can see already that altruism involves a number of capacities: doing and returning favors, detecting cheaters, and assessing fairness. These capacities are themselves complex and varied. Fairness assessment involves keeping track of what benefits two individuals have received for the same costs. Brosnan and de Waal (2003) have argued that capuchin monkeys can do this. If a capuchin is offered a cucumber for performing a task, and then sees another capuchin receive a more desirable grape, for performing the same task, it will refuse to take the cucumber. Brosnan and de Waal interpret this as a protest against inequitable pay (though see below). In the context of reciprocal altruism, a sense of fairness could be used to determine whether each act of reciprocation is proportionate to the act being reciprocated.

Cheater-detection is an important and separate component of reciprocal altruism. If altruistic animals cannot detect cheaters, they can be overtaken by a population of free riders. Specially evolved capacities for cheater-detection have been observed in vampire bats (Wilkinson, 1984). Vampire bats live off of blood, and, after one bat finds a meal, it regurgitates blood to share with others. Bats detect cheaters by looking for conspecifics that have distended bellies but fail to regurgitate.

Fairness and cheater-detection are specialized capacities that support reciprocal altruism. Reciprocal altruism is constituted by the doing and returning of favors. This is not a single capacity. In introducing reciprocal altruism above, I casually mentioned two very different kinds of cases. On the one hand, there are norms that lead us to aid those in need. On the other hand, we have norms governing ventures in which there is an exchange of resources. Jim Moore (1984) refers to such behaviors as helping and sharing, respectively. Helping and sharing are similar at an abstract level, but they are behaviorally distinct. Crucially, sharing involves exchange of goods, and helping does not. Presumably, these distinct behaviors involve some distinct psychological mechanisms. For one thing, they may be promoted by different emotions. When we help someone in need, we are typically prompted by feelings of concern or empathetic distress. Sharing is more likely to be prompted by feelings of affiliation or trust. For another thing, helping and sharing subsume different ranges of behaviors. The class of sharing behaviors includes giving gifts, providing services, and trading. Evidence for the biological roots of these behaviors comes from field observations of chimpanzees. Chimp hunters share their food with the troop, groomers groom those who groom them, and male chimps trade food for sex (de Waal, 1997; Stanford et al., 1994). Helping behaviors are equally diverse. They include nurturing injured conspecifics, protecting against aggression, and assisting others in the pursuit of their goals. These too can be observed in chimps (de Waal, 1996). Such specific behaviors probably evolved separately, and we can find species that exhibit one kind of altruism, but not another. We should resist the temptation to treat reciprocal altruism as if it were implemented by a single behavior. Those interested in the evolution of morality should be sure to examine the full range of behaviors that involve conferring benefits on non-kin. Reciprocal altruism is an abstract principle that explains why self-sacrificing behaviors might have evolved, but, if one is interested in the origin of specific human norms, rather than the origin of morality in general, it's essential to distinguish the different forms that reciprocity might take.

In addition to the complex range of behaviors associated with reciprocal altruism, there are morally relevant behaviors that are difficult to analyze in terms of reciprocity. I will now consider two other domains wherein moral rules can be found. First, there are rules pertaining to social dominance hierarchies. Most human societies are stratified to one degree or another, and power is almost never equally shared. Violations of rank are often considered very serious. We have emotions that underwrite rank relations, such as deference, respect, and, perhaps, feelings of submission. Violations of rank are enforced by one of the cardinal moral emotions: contempt (Rozin et. al, 1999). We have contempt for those who disrespect authorities, those who vie for undeserved social station, and those who abuse power.

Rank norms almost certainly owe something to evolution. Dominance hierarchies are found in many species, including great apes. Gorilla societies are organized around a single silverback male who has a harem of multiple females and exclusive sexual access. In chimps, groups have multiple males and females, and the females, who come initially from other groups, mate with most of the males. But dominant males have greater access to females, and occasionally demand exclusive access for short periods. Females are dominated by males, and, among both males and females, there is a rank hierarchy. Among bonobos, the power structure is reversed with females dominating males (de Waal and Lanting, 1997). All apes establish and maintain their dominance hierarchies by brute force, though bonobos are comparatively docile.

Rank norms involve patterns of deference. Subordinates bow down, often literally, to dominant animals. High-ranking animals are granted various entitlements. But they do not necessarily take without giving. Rank can interact with reciprocity. High-ranking animals may reciprocate favors done by animals of lower rank and, in chimpanzees, higher-ranking animals actually share more than animals of lower rank. This may help sustain their authority. If everyone is indebted to the alpha male, insurrection is less likely.

Less attention has been paid to the evolution of rank than to the evolution of reciprocity, but it's easy to spin evolutionary stories about rank. When members of a social species pursue the things that they desire, conflicts arise. If these conflicts go unchecked, the species will destroy itself. A successful group needs mechanisms to prevent dog-eat-dog doom. Those mechanisms can take different forms. A species might evolve to be egalitarian. That would presumably be a fairly stable outcome, but it would require amazing restraint on desires. Another adaptation would be to show restraint when and only when one's efforts to fulfill desires were thwarted by a more powerful animal. If creatures evolved a capacity to relent when defeated, then some animals would dominate others. A dog-eat-dog world can avoid doom if weaker animals respect authority. Just as Hobbes argued that a sovereign can protect people from unending murder and chaos, deference to an alpha animal can prevent animal societies from destroying themselves.

Another place where morality seems to get a boost from the genes is the domain of sexual relations. Sex is highly moralized. Sex norms can be found across the globe and throughout the animal kingdom. I will focus on norms governing who can sleep with whom. There are also norms pertaining to when sex can take place, and what kinds of sexual acts are appropriate, but these have been less well investigated in an evolutionary context. Many species have preferred sexual positions, and many restrict sex to periods when females are in estrus, but we, like the bonobos, seem to be relatively free from such biologically imposed constraints. We are not free, however, from constraints on sexual partner selection. Two kinds of norms seem to be especially well entrenched. In many cases, we are not permitted to choose sexual partners who are already sexually involved with someone else, and, among uncommitted sexual partners, we are not permitted to have sex with close relatives. We have infidelity norms and incest norms.

Let's begin with infidelity. Nobody likes to be cheated on, but it rarely occurs to us that the preoccupation with sexual fidelity might be a biologically programmed response. Why would we have evolved to hate infidelity? One answer is captured in the word "cheating" itself. A cheater, recall, is someone who reaps benefits without paying the requisite costs. Evolutionary psychologists like to view sexual liaisons as a form of exchange, and they typically argue that men and women face distinct costs and benefits (e.g., Buss, 2000). Men, on this view, provide support and protection in exchange for exclusive sexual access. Women provide exclusive sexual access in exchange for support. (Evolutionary psychologists are willing to accept that biology is sometimes politically incorrect.) Sexual exclusivity is especially important to men. If a woman is sexually involved with someone other than her primary partner, her offspring may end up being genetically unrelated to her primary partner. If he invests in those offspring, he will have guaranteed the survival of the adulterer's genes at the expense of his own. This could lead to the proliferation of adulterers. That wouldn't be good news for men or women. Adulterers will, by their nature, be less likely to offer stable and protective long-term alliances. If all men were adulterers, women could not rely on them for support. That would decrease female survival rates, and bode badly for the species. Thus, evolution should select for males who guard against infidelity.

Infidelity norms are underwritten by romantic jealousy. When we suspect that our partners have been unfaithful, we become jealous. Evolutionary psychologists try to support their conjectures about the biological basis of infidelity norms by examining gender differences in jealousy. If men and women have different motives when it comes to sexual liaisons, their pattern of jealousy should differ. Women want support and men want exclusive sexual access. Buss et al. (1992) reason that men should be more bothered by sexual infidelity than by emotional infidelity. Men are biologically programmed to guard against investing in other people's genes. If a man's sexual partner has sex with others, he cannot be sure whether her offspring carry his genes. Women never need to worry about accidentally investing in someone else's genes. Any baby that a woman has will certainly be hers! But women do need to worry about losing the support of their male partners. Emotional infidelity poses a greater risk, in this respect, than sexual infidelity. As predicted, Buss et al. (1992) find that men and women do indeed respond differently to the question of which is worse, emotional or sexual infidelity. Men are much more likely than women to say that sexual infidelity is worse than emotional infidelity. This may contribute to an explanation of a widespread double standard. Male sexual infidelity is often tolerated more than female sexual infidelity, and vastly more societies are polygynous (over 80 percent) than polyandrous (fewer than 1 percent).

Biology probably also contributes to moral attitudes toward incest. Incest avoidance is very common among non-human animals, including most of our close relatives. Baboons banish young males from their troops, forcing them to breed elsewhere. A similar pattern is observed in gorillas, and young male chimpanzees leave their initial troops as well. Goodall (1986) reports that adolescent male chimpanzees sometimes make sexual advances toward their mothers, but mothers resist. The same is true among macaques. Mother–son incest is even rare among bonobos, who are famously hypersexual (de Waal and Lanting, 1997). Father–daughter incest is harder to track among apes, because fathers tend not to participate in childrearing and many apes are sexually promiscuous. Gibbon fathers are reported to mate with their daughters if other females are not available, but this is not the default option (Bagemihl, 1999). Among human beings, incest avoidance has become a full-blown taboo. In many cultures, incest is strictly forbidden.

Why would we have evolved to avoid incest? One possibility is that incest avoidance is a byproduct of infidelity avoidance. Parent–child incest is typically a form of infidelity. When a parent and child become romantically involved, the two individuals are cheating on the other parent. This would not explain prohibitions against brother–sister incest, however. A more common explanation involves the genetic risks of inbreeding. Evidence suggests that the offspring of two immediate family members are often less fit than the offspring of more distant relatives. Inbreeding allows recessive traits to emerge, and recessive traits tend to be more harmful than dominant traits. Dominant traits come under heavier selection pressure, because they are more likely to dictate phenotypic expression. When animals with the same recessive traits reproduce, it is often bad news for the offspring. Species that avoid inbreeding are also more likely to produce offspring with novel combinations of genes, and this genetic diversity can diminish chances of distinction and promote adaptation. If an environmental catastrophe threatens individuals with a particular genetic makeup, individuals with a different makeup may survive.

The existence of widespread incest avoidance raises a question of implementation. To avoid relatives, we need a way of knowing who our relatives are. For contemporary human beings, that is not difficult. We keep a close track of kinship relations, and we understand the concept of genetic relation. We can conceptually distinguish those who share our genes from those who don't. If incest avoidance is an evolved response, however, it needs to be implemented in a way that does not require knowledge of modern science. Westermarck (1891) proposed a simple mechanism. He speculated that avoidance might be triggered by childhood cohabitation: two people who grow up in the same household will lack sexual interest in each other. This proposal enjoys some support. One study found that non-relatives raised together on Israeli kibbutzim were significantly less likely to marry each other than to marry those from outside the community (Shepher, 1971). Similar effects were found in northern Taiwan, where there is a system of "minor marriages" (Wolf, 1970). Rather than arranging a marriage for their sons in adulthood (a "major marriage"), parents will sometimes adopt a daughter and raise her in the household with the intention of arranging a marriage between her and their son later in life. Minor marriages turn out to be less successful than major marriages; they are three times as likely to end in divorce (Wolf and Huang, 1980). Recently, the Westermarck hypothesis was put to a more direct test. Lieberman et al. (2003) asked college students what they thought of brother–sister marriage. Subjects who had lived with opposite-sex siblings were more opposed than those who had not, even if their same-sex siblings were adopted and not genetically related. The study found that men who had lived with sisters during their teenage years were especially likely to disapprove of brother–sister incest.

I think some of this evidence needs to be critically reassessed. Below, I will reconsider some of the claims that I have just been surveying, and I will argue that the biological contributions to morality have, on occasion, been misidentified or exaggerated. But even if the specific findings don't hold up to scrutiny, the basic message is hard to deny. Natural selection has probably furnished us with a variety of behavioral and affective dispositions that contribute to the emergence of moral values. I have discussed three broad domains: altruism (including helping and sharing), rank, and sex. These domains are examples of the three kinds of ethical systems identified in the anthropological work of Richard Shweder and his colleagues (Shweder et al., 1997). As we saw in chapter 2, Shweder finds that the moral rules found throughout the world tend to divide into three categories. Some rules involve the domain of autonomy. We prohibit crimes against individual persons. Violations of reciprocity generally fall into this category. Cheating is a harm against a person. The standard emotional response to free riders is anger. Violations of rank are what Shweder would call crimes against community. Social hierarchies are the basic organizing principles of communities, and breaking a hierarchical rule threatens that organization. The default emotional response to those who disrespect the social order is contempt. Those who disrespect the rules of a courtroom are held in contempt. Those who consider the prevailing authorities to be unworthy are said to have contempt for authority. Violations of sex norms are said to be unnatural acts. Shweder places these in his ethics of divinity, which, I suggested, might better be regarded as an ethics of the natural order. Incest is an "unnatural act," and is regarded with disgust. Infidelity can evoke disgust as well, through thoughts of contamination, but it is also a crime against the person whose trust is violated. So infidelity is a violation of both a nature norm and an autonomy norm.

This is not intended as an exhaustive list of norms that have some basis in the genes. There may be others. Indeed, there is a trivial sense in which every norm we have owes something to our biological makeup. The survey here highlights cases where the biological contribution to morality has been especially well investigated. Altruism, which has attracted the most attention, is not the only domain amenable to an evolutionary analysis. Evolutionary ethicists should diversify, and take comfort in knowing that each of the major classes of ethical rules on Shweder's model can boast some biological backing.

7.2 LIMITATIONS OF EVOLUTIONARY ETHICS

7.2.1 Does Natural Entail Good?

Let's assume that all the evolutionary conjectures in section 7.1 are correct. Rules pertaining to reciprocity, rank, and romance are products of natural selection. These are central domains of human morality. If they are evolved, then ethics is, in part, natural. Despite all the cultural variation canvassed in chapters 5 and 6, we can find a common core written by Darwinian design into our bioprograms.

Perhaps these aspects of our moral lives are privileged. Perhaps we can dispense with the cultural contaminants and base morality on natural norms. This might be a strategy for achieving objectivity. The anti-objectivist claims of chapter 4 may have been premature.

In order to make this stick, naturally derived norms would have to have some special kind of authority. They would have to be good in virtue of being natural. Is there any way to defend this moralization of nature? Evolutionary ethicists do not offer a uniform answer. They are divided over the status of natural norms. Some believe that the evolutionary origin of moral values can be used to support a skeptical conclusion (e.g., Ruse 1991; Joyce, 2001). Ruse (1991: 506) says that, "Morality is no more than a collective illusion fobbed off on us by our genes." Morality is an illusion, on this view, because we presume that our sense of moral obligation derives from a deeper source. We think we are under some kind of special obligation to help others, and we think that this obligation is independent of contingent facts about our own history as a species. Ruse speculates that this objectivist assumption is hard-wired; we are biologically compelled to believe that moral claims are objective and true. But this belief is an illusion. The fact that morality has a basis in human nature explains why we make moral judgments, and once we realize that such judgments are hard-wired, we need not worry about postulating moral facts.

In contrast to Ruse's skepticism, one might take evolved values very seriously. One might argue that any norm that is the result of evolution is both true, in some sense, and privileged over norms that are culturally constructed. This kind of thinking is evident in Spencer and Nietzsche, but it can also be given a more modern interpretation and defense. I suggested that both Spencer and Nietzsche have been accused of making a fairly flatfooted inference from natural to good. But there are ways to endow such an inference with a degree of plausibility. Let's suppose that some of our values are products of natural selection. Natural selection works on a principle of fitness. The innate traits that we have inherited were traits that proved successful for our ancestors. If a norm has come down through natural selection, then it has done so in virtue of conferring fitness. If evolved norms are fitness-enhancing, then perhaps this endows them with normative authority. We ought to do what's good for us. On this reading, evolutionary ethics makes moral obligation a special case of prudential obligation. Far from undermining morality, this gives morality indubitable validity. Prudence is the gold standard underlying the currency of moral convictions. Things are selected for their positive payoffs, and thus those things that we naturally regard as good really are good, in a prudential sense. I'm not sure if any one has actually defended this line, but it has some intuitive appeal.

Thus, an evolutionary approach can lead to either skepticism or realism, depending on how it's described. Realists and skeptics disagree about whether natural entails good, but they often seem to agree on a further question. They think that evolution-backed norms are privileged with respect to cultural norms.

Ruse thinks that they are privileged because they are fixed and inescapable (though see Joyce, 2001). Darwinian realists think that naturally evolved morals are privileged because they are products of fitness rather than fiat.

I think both of these views—Darwinian skepticism and Darwinian realism—are mistaken. Let's begin with skepticism. I think Ruse's version of this view suffers from two fatal flaws. First, Ruse is wrong to think that evolved moral beliefs are fixed. As I will show below, there is ample reason to believe that we can alter and even overturn evolved evaluative intuitions through the process of enculturation. If I am right, this undermines the skeptic's best reason for thinking that evolved norms are privileged. Second, I reject Ruse's argument for the conclusion that moral claims are false. On one reconstruction, the reasoning goes like this: evolution furnishes us with beliefs about what is good; once these beliefs are explained, there is no reason to postulate a class of moral truths underlying these beliefs; therefore, our moral beliefs do not refer to moral facts. I take issue with the second premise. In chapter 3, I argued that moral concepts represent response-dependent properties. The good is that which causes moral approbation. If evolution gives us moral beliefs, it thereby produces a class of moral facts.

It's interesting to compare Ruse's strategy to Nietzsche's genealogical strategy, which I endorsed in a qualified form in chapter 6. Like Nietzsche, Ruse is attempting to discredit morality by showing that moral values have a historical origin (not in the scale of human history, but in the scale of evolutionary history). In discussing Nietzsche, I said that historical analyses can help us assess whether norms are worth keeping, and the same principle applies here. If an evolved norm is no longer instrumentally justifiable, then we might consider giving it up. But that is not the way Ruse uses evolution to criticize morality. Ruse differs from Nietzsche in two key respects. First, he uses history (of our species) to argue that moral values are good for us, whereas Nietzsche uses history (of our culture) to argue that moral values are bad for us. Second, Ruse is trying to show that moral beliefs are false, whereas Nietzsche can be interpreted as a moral realist—moral rules are social constructions that are true in the way that social facts, such as economic facts, are true. I think Ruse is wrong on both counts. I already suggested that he is wrong to think that moral beliefs are false; moral truth is secured by the fact that moral concepts refer to response-dependent properties. The supposition that evolved moral values are good for us can also be challenged. Ironically, Ruse, a Darwinian skeptic, shares this supposition with Darwinian realists. So let's turn to that approach now.

According to Darwinian realism, our evolved moral beliefs are true and privileged over culturally based norms, because they emerged through natural selection, and natural selection is fitness-enhancing. I'm not sure if anyone has seriously defended this view. Richards (1986) argues for the related idea that evolved norms are morally authoritative because they lead us to care for members of our communities (see also Joyce, 2006, for a compelling critique of this and other attempts to defend the normative authority of evolved norms). What I have in mind here is more general than that. It's the idea that fitness is an intrinsic good, and any norms evolved through natural selection are, thereby, designed to increase the good. It is intuitively plausible that this very fact vindicates evolved norms. Despite its appeal, Darwinian realism collapses under scrutiny, and it's instructive to see why.

First, evolution does not optimize. It does not produce traits that are best, but only traits that are good enough. There are many systems of rules that could lead to reproductive success. The ones that we happen to have inherited through evolution are sufficiently efficacious for mating and raising offspring, but, if prudential merit is the gold standard, than we can certainly do better. There are non-natural rules that might increase our success. Consider rank. We may have evolved to vie for higher rank through aggressive confrontation with our superiors. We may also have evolved to respectfully accept our social station when stronger individuals get a bigger piece of the pie. It's not clear that either of these polar options is maximally fit. Perhaps we'd be better off eliminating rank, and dividing everything up equally regardless of physical merits. Darwinian realists may be right to say that natural entails good (in the sense of fitness), but that discovery actually undermines any privileged status that evolved norms might have, because natural does not entail best. Culturally devised values may be more beneficial.

Second, biological fitness is not always advantageous to us as individuals. Biological fitness is most fundamentally defined in terms of genetic fitness: that which allows genes to replicate. What's good for our genes is not necessarily good for us. Joyce (personal communication) gives the example of parricide: if you kill your parents in order to increase your chances for survival, you thereby increase the fitness of your parents' genes, but you certainly don't increase the fitness of your parents.

Third, even if evolved traits increased fitness in the past, they may not be advantageous now: what was fit for our ancestors is not necessarily fit for us. As skeptics have pointed out, evolution tends to provide norms that are quite parochial. If altruism is driven by reciprocity, then we are probably biologically inclined to assist only those who can reciprocate. We may have an evolved tendency to withhold aid from the feeble, the poor, or those in distant lands. This policy may have been advantageous in the evolutionary past, but societies have grown, and, to achieve social stability in large groups (or in a global network of groups), it may be vitally important to respect the interests of those who cannot reciprocate. A main incentive for joining a large social collective is that they will offer protection in times of adversity.

Fourth, Darwinian realism conflates two kinds of goods. It tries to reduce moral goodness to biological goodness, but, to do so is to change the topic. For even if moral goods are biologically good (i.e., fitness-enhancing), we can still wonder if they are morally valuable. The concept of biological goodness has a different sense and reference from moral goodness. That it has a different sense can be inferred from the fact that the standard concept of moral goodness has a motivational kick. To judge that something is morally good is to be motivated to do it. In contrast, we can judge that something would increase our reproductive success (not using birth control, for example) without being motivated to do it. The fact that these concepts refer differently can be inferred from the fact that our category of moral goods can be altered by culture. Perhaps our Pleistocene ancestors moralized only those things that were fitness-enhancing. We don't restrict morality in that way and, consequently, the evolutionary analysis of the origin of morals cannot offer an adequate analysis of what morality has come to include. In sum, even if natural entails good, it does not entail morally good.

The upshot of all this is that we can draw no inference from the existence of an evolved norm to either its falsity or its truth (compare Sober, 1994). Evolution confers no special status, positive or negative, on morality. Thus, the project of distinguishing natural norms from culturally shaped norms, which Nietzsche encourages, may not be worth the effort. In the next section, I will argue that such a distinction is even more vexed than I have already implied. I will argue that there is no use in distinguishing natural and cultural norms, because culture shapes all norms, even when they have a natural foundation. I will also argue that no evolved norms qualify as moral norms, so, strictly speaking, there is no such thing as an evolutionary ethics.

7.2.2 Do Primates Have a Moral Sense?

In section 7.1, I offered a list of evolved norms that contribute to morality. In this section, I want to examine the entries on that list more critically. I will not retract my claims about evolved norms, but I will recast them. I will argue that evolved norms do not constitute an innate morality. They are, instead, flexible constraints within which morality emerges. In this section I will focus on comparative research. I will argue that researchers have not established the existence of moral capacities in non-human primates. Failure to find such capacities weakens the case for an evolved moral sense.

Let's begin with reciprocal altruism, which is supposed to underwrite moral norms having to do with sharing and helping. The first thing to notice is that reciprocal altruism is actually rare in other animals (Pusey and Packer, 1997). It carries fairly demanding cognitive prerequisites, which may be difficult for most creatures to achieve (Stevens and Hauser, 2004). But there is certainly evidence for reciprocal altruism in non-human primates. Apes and monkeys reciprocate, help, and share. Primates have clearly evolved altruistic behavioral tendencies. But, as Sober and Wilson (1998) point out, we cannot infer altruistic motives from altruistic behavior. Apes could be driven by a moral desire to do good things, or they could be driven by less noble concerns. I think the latter possibility is more likely.

There are various interpretations of altruistic behavior that do not require postulation of altruistic motives. First, primates may do good things for each other out of a selfish desire to reap rewards. For example, there is little reason to think that apes are driven by altruistic motives when they exchange goods, because the donor receives a payoff in return (e.g., food for sex trading in bonobos). In this context, it's worth noting that psychopaths will engage in tit-for-tat reciprocation when playing prisoner's dilemma games (Widom, 1976). Psychopaths are probably not motivated by a concern for fairness; they simply recognize that doing a favor for someone else may lead to higher returns. Second, some cases of apparent altruism may occur under duress. According to one theory, apes' sharing is actually tolerated theft; apes may allow conspecifics to steal in order to avoid violent assaults (Blurton-Jones 1987). Third, some acts of apparent altruism may be a strategy to achieve popularity when surplus resources are available. Alpha males often distribute more food than other apes, and this helps them to be viewed favorably by members of the troop. When apes share, they are not necessarily incurring a serious personal loss. If apes were driven by altruistic concerns, we might expect them to be more self-sacrificing, and we might expect them to be more even-handed in their efforts to share. Even the most generous chimps donate to only about half of those who beg for food (de Waal, 1996). More strikingly, Silk at al. (2005) have shown that chimps do not reliably share under conditions where sharing has no cost. They created an apparatus in which a chimp could pull one rope to get a food reward or pull a different rope to get that same food reward and deliver food to another chimp. Chimps in the study showed no preference for the generous rope over the selfish rope, even though there was no difference in personal rewards, and despite the fact that all the chimps had lived together for fifteen years.

Non-human primates also show strangely selective patterns of helping. They assist those with whom they have formed strong attachments, but they occasionally show bizarre indifference to the suffering of conspecifics. De Waal (1996) recounts an anecdote in which an adult rhesus threatened to hit a screaming infant rhesus whose arm got caught in the spokes of a spinning wheel. Though anecdotal, such examples raise questions about whether non-human primates help each other out of deeply felt moral concern. Their tendency to confer benefits may be driven by motives that we would not find especially praiseworthy. To prove otherwise, it would be important to show that primates regularly help each other when there is little chance of reciprocation. This, as far as I know, has not been shown. In contrast, human beings frequently help others when there is no reciprocation. We send donation checks to distant charity organizations, protest injustices that do not affect us directly, and support intervention in far-away lands. Sometimes these acts are chalked up to "indirect reciprocity" (Alexander, 1987), with the thought that by helping distant others, we enhance our reputation, and attain benefits at home. Perhaps, but such behaviors certainly aren't *explicitly* motivated by the desire to look good (no one watches when you send Oxfam checks), and they are probably implemented by moral concern. The fact that we don't see this kind of behavior regularly in other primate species suggests that moral concern may be uniquely human, and if it's uniquely human, then we cannot use the comparative method to show that this trait is evolved, rather than culturally constructed.

Similar doubts can be raised about the primate sense of fairness. Recall Brosnan and de Waal's (2003) study in which a capuchin monkey refused a cucumber award after seeing another monkey receive a grape for the same work. Rather than interpreting this as a nascent sense of social inequity, one might surmise that monkeys simply pass up mediocre rewards when they see that better rewards may be available. This is a well-known effect in ethology. Tinklepaugh (1928) showed that monkeys turn down an otherwise desirable food reward (lettuce), when a more desirable reward has been observed (bananas). Wouldn't you pass up a cracker for a piece of chocolate cake? This more modest interpretation of the Brosnan and de Waal results is supported by the fact that capuchins pass up their cucumber reward in a control condition in which a grape is placed in an empty cage nearby, rather than being given to another monkey (Wynne, 2004).

Clearly caution must be exercised when interpreting animal behavior. There is a temptation to attribute human-like motives even in cases where other explanations are available. To take one more example, de Waal (2000) argues that apes who have been fighting try to make peace afterwards in order to repair a damaged relationship. In a reanalysis of the data, however, Silk (2002) argues that peacemaking is motivated by a desire to reap immediate rewards, rather than a desire to secure long-term relations. If Silk is right, apes are shortsighted and selfish, not deeply concerned with social harmony. Likewise, the motives underlying apparently moral acts may be entirely amoral. When apes do each other favors, they may simply be trying to gain allies, reap benefits, or avoid being attacked. They may even be blindly programmed. To make the case that non-human primates are psychologically altruistic, one would need to show that they have a desire to be helpful out of genuine concern for other animals, especially unrelated animals. But—and this is an important point—even if it could be established that apes have genuine altruism, that would fall short of showing that they have morality.

We often say that genuine altruism is a form of moral behavior. But the phrase "moral behavior" is ambiguous. It can mean either behavior that we find morally praiseworthy or behavior that is driven by moral evaluations. Suppose apes help each other out of genuine concern. This would show that apes do something morally praiseworthy, and, if we were interested in the origins of morally praiseworthy behavior in human beings, we might take such findings as evidence for the conclusion that such behaviors predate our species. This tells us something about the evolution of moral decency, but it tells us nothing, I submit, about the evolution of morality. Morality is a system of rules and values used to assess actions, agents, and attitudes. A creature could behave in noble ways without any capacity to judge that actions are good. If apes had morality, they would not only help each other out of concern, they would help each other because that's what they morally *ought* to do. These are different. To echo Kant, there is a difference between conforming to a moral rule and acting under a moral rule. Kant thinks that the latter involves recognition of a categorical imperative. As a sentimentalist, I reject this requirement, but I do think there are important psychological prerequisites on having ought-thoughts, or "oughtitudes." For an ape to think that he ought to share, he must have a moral sentiment toward sharing. That means he must feel guilty if he doesn't share. He must also feel angry at those who do not share with him. This kind of motivation differs from what evolutionary ethicists call altruistic motivation. Altruistic motivation involves concern, a sentiment that is underwritten by emotions like sympathy and attachment. These emotions are not necessary and sufficient for moral judgments. The evidence for altruistic motivation in non-human primates is still pretty weak, given all the alternative interpretations. The evidence for moral motivation, or oughtitudes, is even weaker.

Trivers (1971: 50) suggests that the evolved tendency to reciprocate is driven, in part, by an innate tendency to feel guilty when we defect (see also Frank, 1988). Against that theoretical background, it is tempting to interpret reciprocity in apes as evidence for the conclusion that apes feel guilt, and this, in turn, would support the contention that they can have oughtitudes. But, as we have seen, ape charity can easily be explained without appeal to guilt. Indeed, there is good reason to think that non-human primates *lack* oughtitudes; no studies have demonstrated simian analogues of guilt or its cousin shame. Coe and Rosenblum (1984) report that low-ranking male macaques will copulate with females while the alpha male is away, and then they will be unusually submissive when the alpha male returns. De Waal (1996: 110) invites readers to interpret this submissive behavior as a sign of guilt, but it may be better interpreted as fear of reprisal. If low-ranking macaques really felt that it was wrong to copulate with females, they probably wouldn't try at every opportunity. More generally, if non-human primates felt guilt and shame, we should expect them to exhibit helping and sharing behavior more consistently and evenhandedly. Apes and monkeys often show astonishing indifference to the well-being of their peers.

I suspect that non-human primates lack guilt and shame, and, therefore, they cannot have oughtitudes. In addition, they probably lack two other psychological traits that figure prominently in healthy human morality. First, apes probably lack meta-emotions. We do not only feel guilty about violating rules of conduct; we also feel guilty if we don't feel guilty. Parents subject their children to "guilt trips" and they tell naughty children, "You should be ashamed!" There is no solid evidence for first-order moral sentiments in apes, much less second-order sentiments. Second, apes probably lack robust third-party concerns. Human moralizers get angry at wrongdoers even if they are not affected by the transgression. We even have concerns for third parties who are outside of our communities.

Our performance on tasks that test for comprehension of the moral/conventional distinction suggest that we think moral rules hold in societies that have no contact with our own. Hitting innocent people would be wrong in an isolated village even if the villagers approved of it. Notice that such long-distance concerns defy the logic of reciprocal altruism. People in distant places are not in a position to reciprocate. This kind of concern for unrelated others is not observed in apes. One ape may intervene in a conflict between two others (de Waal, 2000), but, when this is done, the intervening ape usually has a stake in the conflict or an attachment to one of the conflicting parties.

In sum, there is little reason to believe that apes have anything like human moral attitudes. Morality may be a uniquely human capacity (compare de Waal, 1996; Hauser, 2001). If that is correct, there are two possibilities. The capacity to moralize could be an evolved adaptation that occurred after we split from the ancestor that we share with chimpanzees. Or alternatively, the capacity to moralize could be a byproduct of other capacities, which evolved for other purposes. I will briefly consider both of these options, and I will conclude that the latter is more plausible.

7.2.3 Is Morality Innate in Humans?

Is there any solid evidence for the claim that morality is innate in human beings? Surprisingly little work has been done on this question. In developmental psychology there is a massive effort to identify core knowledge in a number of domains, but comparatively little effort to determine whether there are core moral beliefs that might be innate. This oversight is likely to change. There is a growing interest in moral cognition, and some authors are beginning to argue explicitly for moral nativism. I will consider four arguments here (for more discussion, see Prinz, 2007; forthcoming *a–b*).

The first argument is based on a recent line of research examining pro-social behavior in infants. Warneken and Tomasello (2006) wanted to see whether eighteen-month-olds would spontaneously help adults in need. In their study, infants watched as an adult tried to do something unsuccessfully (e.g., reach for a fallen object, stack a pile of books, open a cabinet, and so on). In comparison to control conditions in which adults did not display trying behavior, infants were likely to help spontaneously. For example, infants retrieved a fallen object and handed it to the adult. Young chimps were also tested in the study, and they showed some degree of helpfulness in the reaching scenarios, but otherwise showed no significant tendency to help. The authors suggest that humans may have evolved stronger helping tendencies than chimps. The fact that these tendencies are evident at eighteen months might be taken as support for the claim that humans have an innate moral sense.

Warneken and Tomasello do not make the inference from innate helpfulness to innate morality, and they are right to resist that temptation. As I have already argued, being helpful is not evidence for either pro-social motivations (helping out of concern) or moral judgments (helping because morality requires it). There is no evidence that infant helpfulness is driven by noble intentions. For similar reasons, we should not jump to conclusions when we read studies showing that infants console adults who display distress. Infants catch distress from those around them, and consolation behaviors may be an automatic program for stress management. Even family pets console their grieving masters (Preston and de Waal, 2002; Zahn-Waxler et al., 1984). The helping behaviors observed by Warneken and Tomasello may not even be innate. By eighteen months, infants have probably had a fair amount of experience with adults making requests: "Can you give me the marker?", "Can you open the cabinet?", "Can you stack the books?" Games in the first year of life often seem to involve tasks of this kind. In addition, infants are good at discerning trying behavior, and eighteen-month-olds spontaneously imitate behaviors that adults have merely attempted unsuccessfully (Meltzoff, 1995). What looks like helping behavior may just be one special instance of infants' general tendency to imitate and complete unsuccessful actions. Rather than being part of an innate moral capacity, this tendency to imitate is probably a mechanism for social learning.

A second argument for moral nativism focuses on our capacity to detect cheaters. Recall that reciprocal altruism raises free rider problems. When you are kind to someone, there is always a risk that the recipient of your kindness will not reciprocate. Consequently, we have a serious stake in finding and punishing cheaters: those who reap benefits without paying the cost. We are not the only creatures who can detect cheaters. As noted earlier, much has been made about cheater-detection in vampire bats. Vampire bats live on blood, and they can starve to death after two days without feeding. To increase their odds, groups of bats living together engage in food-sharing: a bat that has been successful in finding a victim will regurgitate blood for other bats in its group to eat. Wilkinson (1990) observed that bats are more likely to feed bats that have been good reciprocators. They can spot greedy bats by looking for non-sharers whose bellies are distended from eating. There is no reason to infer from this example that innate cheater-detection mechanisms exist in human beings. After all, human cheaters cannot be identified by simple perceptual cues, like distended bellies. But it's natural to suppose that we have our own version of a cheater-detection mechanism. In principle, one could detect cheaters without making moral judgments (as presumably is the case in vampire bats), but human cheater-detection tends to be moralistic. When we catch a cheater, we appraise him as morally bad. Thus, evidence for an innate cheater-detection mechanism in humans might be taken as support for an innate moral sense.

A number of evolutionary psychologists—most famously Cosmides and Tooby (1992) and their colleagues—have argued for an innate cheater-detection mechanism by studying human reasoning. Humans are notoriously bad at reasoning about descriptive conditionals of the form: If a is B, then a is C. In contrast, we are very good at reasoning using conditionals that involve social exchanges of the form: If *a* has received benefit B, then *a* must have paid cost C. The contrast can be shown by considering conditionals that have the same surface grammar, but either a descriptive or a social exchange interpretation. Here is an example based on materials used by Stone et al. (2002). Suppose you read a study in the newspaper that says children who watch a lot of TV are also especially tidy. In particular, the headline says "If a child watches more than two hours of TV a day, it must be that her or his room is clean." You are trying to decide if this true. To find out, which of the following do you need to check: (a) kids who watch more that two hours; (b) kids who watch less than two hours; (c) kids who have dirty rooms; (d) kids who have clean rooms? With examples like this, most subjects pick (a) and very few pick other options. Significantly, subjects overlook (c). They don't realize that they need to consider kids who have dirty rooms. These are cases in which the consequent of the conditional is false. A descriptive conditional is false when and only when it has a true antecedent and a false consequent, so it's logically imperative to check both cases like (a), with true antecedents, and cases like (c), with false consequents, if you are charged with determining the truth of the conditional in question. The fact that subjects overlook the false antecedent cases shows that subjects are prone to making a logical error.

Now consider a different problem. You are a parent, and your children are not allowed to watch a lot of TV unless they clean their rooms. Your household rule says: "If a child watches more than two hours of TV a day, it must be that his room is clean." When asked whom to check when enforcing this rule, subjects pick both (a) and (c). Subjects immediately recognize that they must check the kids with dirty rooms to make sure that they haven't watched a lot of television. This is the correct answer, and we get it in the social exchange case, but not the descriptive case. When subjects are charged with catching rule violators ("cheaters"), they reason more successfully. Evolutional psychologists explain this result by saying that we have an evolved module dedicated to detecting cheaters (Cosmides, 1989; Gigerenzer and Hug, 1992).

I find this evolutionary explanation unconvincing. I cannot review the vast literature on this topic, but let me articulate a principled reason for skepticism. The basic problem with the experiments that evolutionary psychologists use to contrast social and descriptive conditionals is that the two tasks, though superficially similar, are actually entirely different. When asked to assess the descriptive conditional in the newspaper case, your task is to determine whether it is true. This is a confirmation problem. It is like trying to determine whether all ravens are black. To do that efficiently, it's a good idea to check the ravens that we encounter, but a total waste of time to check all things that aren't black. The logical fallacy of avoiding the (c)-cases above is actually a good inductive strategy. In contrast, when presented with the parenting case, we assume the conditional is true; it is a rule of the household, and rules are true even if they are not always followed. The task is not to confirm or disconfirm the conditional, but to find violators. A violator is, by definition, someone who hasn't done what's required. So we are immediately oriented to (c)-cases. The task demands draw our attention to people who haven't done what's required of them. This does not show an innate specialized capacity for detecting cheaters. It merely shows that we are good at reasoning about conditionals when the task demands make us sensitive to cases that confirm the antecedent (as in (a)) and to cases that deny the consequent (as in (c)). Social exchange conditionals have this feature, but descriptive conditionals do not.

The alternative explanation for the experimental results is quite simple: there is an intrinsic difference between the task of assessing descriptive conditionals, in which case we are looking for counterexamples, and the task of assessing social exchange conditions, in which case we assume the conditional is true and look for violators. On this alternative story, we do not need to postulate a domain-specific module for reasoning about cheaters, but rather domain-general reasoning systems that apply differently when we are performing confirmation tasks and norm-violation tasks. This alternative predicts that people will generally perform successfully on conditionals that they interpret as norms, even when those conditionals have nothing to do with cheating or morality. Consider prudential conditionals. Suppose we learn that extended exposure to television exposes viewers to dangerous levels of radiation unless they sit more than five feet away. This fact about health hazards can be expressed as a conditional rule: "If a person watches more than two hours of TV a day, it must be that she or he sits five feet away." This conditional is not a moral norm; it's a norm about safety. If our ability to reason about cheater-detection is based on a domain-general capacity to reason about all normative conditionals, we should find that people are adept at reasoning about prudential conditionals. That is just what studies have shown (Manktelow and Over, 1990). If you are asked to protect people from the hazards of radiation, you will immediately recognize that you should check anyone who is sitting too close to a TV to find out how long that person has been sitting there.

Of course, it *could be the case* that we have one innate module for reasoning about cheaters and another innate module for reasoning about prudential norms, and these modules *just happen to* endow us with equally good capacities for thinking about conditionals in each of these domains. This would be an extravagant interpretation of the data, but it's the interpretation that evolutionary psychologists prefer. To support the conjecture that there are two modules—one for prudence norms and the other for cheater-detection—Cosmides and Tooby have joined up with collaborators in neuroscience to establish that there is a dissociation between the ability to reason about cheaters and the ability to reason about prudential norms (Stone et al., 2002). They examined a patient with injuries in the ventromedial prefrontal cortex who has a seriously impaired capacity to reason about social exchange conditionals (such as the parental rule case), but intact capacity to reason about prudential conditionals (such as the health risk case). To prove that these are independent reasoning capacities, evolutionary psychologists would need to show a double dissociation: they would need to find patients who are bad at prudence and good at detecting cheaters. No such patient has been found, but Stone et al., argue that the ventromedial patients offer preliminary support for the domain specificity of cheater-detection because they establish one of the two dissociations that must ultimately be found if separate modules are at work. The problem is that patients with ventromedial injuries do not have a selective deficit in cheater-detection; they have many other problems. For example, they are impulsive, they have abnormal emotional responses, and they are bad at detecting social *faux pas*. Given their profound suite of deficits, we cannot infer that they have a deficit in a cheater-detection module. The patient in the Stone et al. study may have a general deficit in thinking about social situations, and consequently he may not appreciate what's involved in enforcing social rules. His emotional deficits may also make it difficult for him to assign emotional incentives to catching cheaters. Without a capacity to understand fully or care about the subtleties of the social domain, this patient may simply fail to comprehend the demands placed on him in the reasoning task. For all we know, he may even misconstrue social exchange conditionals as descriptive conditionals. Thus, the Stone et al. study does not prove that there are cognitive resources dedicated to cheater-detection. No such evidence has been found. Without good evidence, I think we should reject the hypothesis that there is an innate cheater-detection module.

The third argument for moral nativism is put forward by Sue Dwyer (1999). To argue for innateness, Dwyer borrows a strategy from linguistics (see also Rawls, 1971; Harman, 2000; Mikhail, 2000). Linguistic nativism is usually supported by arguments that appeal to the poverty of the stimulus. Linguists claim that children obey grammatical rules that they could not have learned through experience, because the primary linguistic data to which they are exposed (adult speech, and adult corrections of their speech) do not provide enough information to help the child select between myriad possible rules. By parity, Dwyer argues that children do not receive enough primary moral data to explain their understanding of the moral domain. In particular, she says that children do not receive enough input from adults to distinguish between moral and conventional rules. The moral/conventional distinction is present by the third year of life, and it isn't explicitly taught. Parents do not tell their children which rules are moral and which are merely conventional, and they punish children for both. Children are punished for hitting and biting *and* for violating rules of etiquette. Yet, somehow they recognize that moral rules are different. By early childhood, they treat moral rules as more serious and less dependent on authorities. Hitting and biting would be wrong no matter what anyone says, but putting your elbows on the table would be okay if given permission. Children all around the world draw this sort of contrast without being explicitly taught.

Dwyer's argument has considerable prima facie plausibility, but I don't think it holds up (see also Nichols, 2005). Even if parents do not explicitly teach children the difference between moral and conventional rules, there are striking implicit differences in how such rules are transmitted. Parents treat moral norm violations as more serious and they enforce them more harshly (Smetana, 1989; Grusec and Goodnow, 1994; Nucci and Weber, 1995). Moral rules are often punished using power assertion and empathy induction, while conventional rules are supported by reasoning and appeals to social standards and social order. Moral rule violations also tend to be more emotionally charged because they often involve a victim. If little Sally bites Billy, Billy will cry, and Billy's parents will become very upset. When children judge that moral rules are not dependent on authority, it may be because they have internalized these rules emotionally. When they imagine biting, they become upset because biting has led to intense negative emotions in the past. As a result, children say it wouldn't be okay to bite even if authorities said it was okay. In sum, children are exposed to sufficient corrective feedback to differentiate between moral and conventional rules.

Let me turn to a final argument for moral nativism, which has been pushed forward by Hauser et al. (forthcoming), echoing ideas in Harman (2000) and extending experimental work by Mikhail (2000; 2002). Using an Internet questionnaire, Hauser et al. collected thousands of subjects' moral intuitions about a variety of different trolley cases (recall chapter 1). In one scenario, subjects are asked whether it would be okay to push someone into the path of a trolley in order to save five people who are lying further down on the track. In another case, subjects are asked whether it would be okay to pull a lever that would cause a trolley to switch from its current track, where it would hit five people, to an alternate track, where it would hit only one. Hauser et al. found that 11 percent of subjects think the pushing case is morally permissible and 89 percent of subjects think the switching case is morally permissible. Subjects also had robust and largely consistent intuitions across a wide range of other cases. This is striking because subjects have never heard trolley cases before. If people give consistent answers to novel cases, that can be taken as evidence for innate rules.

This argument works on the same principle as Dwyer's. The authors identify a feature of moral judgment that is widespread, but not explicitly taught. But I don't think that is an adequate argument for innateness (see also Nichols, 2005). Everyone agrees that we are explicitly taught not to harm people. If a child bites, hits, or otherwise attacks someone, the punishments will be serious. We also learn helping norms. We are taught that it is good to assist people in need. Helping behavior may have some basis in biology, but biological helping instincts are probably directed toward kin and close affiliates. We are taught that it's good to help strangers (a point I will come back to below). These two norms—avoiding harm and helping—come into conflict in trolley cases. So the question is, how do we decide which norm to apply? Is this determined by innate principles?

In chapter 1, I argued that trolley intuitions are driven by emotions. We think it's bad to push someone into the tracks, because that's an intensely negative emotion elicitor, and we think it's okay to switch the track, because that action seems more benign. This analysis predicts that trolley intuitions will fluctuate with the salience of harm. That prediction seems to be borne out by other scenarios used in Hauser et al.'s study. In one scenario, subjects are asked to consider a case in which you can pull a switch that will cause a trolley to move onto a looping track where a heavy man is standing; the looping track connects back up with the main track where the trolley would kill five people, but the heavy man will stop the trolley in its tracks. In this scenario, 55 percent say it's permissible to switch the tracks. These intuitions lie in between the original pushing case and the switch case, because, while it is not a paradigmatic case of killing, the fact that the heavy man is used as a human barrier makes his death quite salient. In a fourth case, Hauser at al. presented the looping track scenario with a minor variation: the heavy man on the track is standing in front of a heavy object. Subjects are told that the heavy object will serve as the barrier, preventing the trolley from hitting five people, and the heavy man will be killed in the process. Now 72 percent of subjects think it's okay to pull the switch, because, I submit, attention is drawn away from the victim and onto the heavy object.

The salience story may not explain every intuition about trolley cases, but it certainly seems to explain the ones that Hauser et al. present, and it does so without supposing that we have innate rules. As long as we can explain why people are taught helping norms and harming norms, we can explain all the varied intuitions about how these norms interact in trolley cases. The variation in our intuitions does not reflect a precise set of innate rules—a grammar of morals—rather the variation reflects how easily learned sentiments can shift as a function of salience.

One final consideration should be brought to bear against all these nativist arguments. It is tempting to assume that we arrive at moral insights without much instruction. That would be a serious mistake. Caregivers spend an enormous amount of energy teaching children how to behave. Hoffman (2000: 141) calculates that, between the ages of two and ten, caregivers correct children's behavior every six to nine minutes! That amounts to fifty lessons in conduct every single day. If morality were innate, all this instruction should be unnecessary. Clearly nurture is making a contribution to morality.

In sum, I think there is little pressure to say that human beings have an innate moral sense. Some of the leading arguments for moral nativism strike me as implausible. Of course, this is not an exhaustive survey of such arguments, so I don't take the considerations presented here as decisive evidence against moral nativism. I think the best way to defeat nativism in this domain and others is to present an alternative account. I think morality is a byproduct of other capacities. If morality can be explained as a byproduct of other capacities, there is little pressure to say that it is innate. I will begin my case for the byproduct view by considering some of the non-moral cognitive capacities that may play an important role in the acquisition of morality.

7.3 A BIOCULTURAL APPROACH TO MORALITY

7.3.1 Morality as a Byproduct

There are many human capacities that are nearly universal but not innate. Examples include art, clothing, the use of fire, constructed shelters, mortuary practices, religion, marriage, and complex tools. All of these distinctively human inventions are presumed to result from cognitive capacities that evolved for other purposes. We don't have a clothing module; we just get cold and are clever enough to solve that problem by making things to cover our bodies. We don't have a religion module; we just have tendencies to attribute mentality to non-living things and a penchant for stories that violate expectations (Boyer and Ramble, 2001). My conjecture is that morality falls into this category. It is a byproduct of capacities that are not themselves evolved for the acquisition of moral rules.

A variety of non-moral capacities may be important for acquiring a moral sense. First and foremost, we need to have certain emotions: other-directed emotions such as anger, contempt, and disgust, as well as self-directed emotions such as shame and guilt, which, I argued earlier, may be related to embarrassment and sadness. Second, one needs the ability to formulate rules. During moral development, we must *transfer* the negative emotions that we are conditioned to experience when we misbehave *to* the misbehavior. In so doing, we generate a mental representation that disposes us to have negative feelings about a type of behavior regardless of who is performing it. This may be the basis of our capacity to have moral attitudes toward third parties, even when we are not directly involved. It would be interesting to explore whether rule formation of the kind required is a uniquely human ability. In addition, healthy moral development may require memory. We very often catch wrongdoers well after a transgression has taken place. Other animals may have to catch each other red-handed in order to recognize that they have done something undesirable, and that minimizes opportunities to shape behavior through punishment. More speculatively, morality may depend on the capacity to imitate. When children are punished, they not only feel badly about what they have done; they also acquire the disposition to punish others for performing the actions that got them into trouble.

A fifth capacity that contributes to human morality is "mind-reading": the ability to attribute mental states to others. This ability allows us to experience genuine empathy as opposed to vicarious distress—we experience another person's misery and recognize that our misery results from theirs. This promotes pro-social behavior and allows for the acquisition of norms pertaining to mental states: e.g., we can think it's bad to cause suffering. Mind-reading also allows us to acquire norms about norms: moral educators can recognize our emotions and urge us to feel sorry for our bad behavior. This form of training increases the probability that we will behave in accordance with norms. We behave in accordance with norms because we would feel guilty otherwise, and the disposition to feel guilty has considerable stability, because we would feel guilty if we didn't feel guilty. Norms about how to feel establish meta-emotions and meta-emotions are like an extra insurance plan against misbehavior.

Meta-emotions may not be essential to having a moral sense—people with autism moralize despite an impairment in mind-reading—but they may play a fundamental role in the emergence of morality through cultural evolution. Using game-theoretic models, Henrich and Boyd (2001) have argued that widespread cooperative behavior would not be sustained and transmitted over generations if it were not for punishment; a society of cooperators would be overtaken by defectors. The same point can be articulated in terms of moral norms; a society would not continue to conform to moral norms generation after generation if wrongdoers were not punished (Sripada and Stich, 2006). If community members didn't punish wrongdoers, wrongdoers would not alter their behavior and regard wrongdoing as wrong. Here, the notion of punishment should be defined as any action that imposes a cost on those who violate a norm. Punishment can be physical, but it can also include psychological tactics such as love withdrawal and empathy induction, which I discussed in chapter 1. All of these methods lead people to conform to moral rules. Boyd et al. (2003) argue that the need for punishment introduces a serious puzzle. It is costly to punish. People who punish have to exert energy and put themselves at risk. It is very tempting, therefore, to try to get away without punishing anyone, and hope that others do the dirty work (as when one parent lets another parent play bad cop). This creates a second-order free rider problem. First-order free riders try to get away with violating moral rules, while second-order free riders try to get away with not enforcing first-order rules. Successful free riders are always better off than those who pay their dues, so a situation that is tempting for free riders can escalate into a situation in which everyone is trying to get away with doing less. If there are some second-order free riders from the outset, they may eventually radically outnumber the second-order cooperators, i.e., those who punish violators of first-order norms. But, a reduction of second-order cooperators entails a proliferation of first-order free riders, because there aren't enough people to keep those first-order free riders in check. This is tantamount to moral collapse, because, in this situation, there aren't enough people around to transmit moral rules. Boyd et al. argue that this predicament can be prevented by punishing second-order free riders; this is called meta-punishment. If we punish people who neglect to punish misbehavior, then there will be an incentive to punish, and morality will be able to get off the ground.

I think meta-emotions have a central role to play in this story. I said that first-order norms are inculcated by emotionally conditioning people to act in certain ways. Well, how are punishment norms inculcated? One possibility is that they are inculcated as a special class of first-order norms: we condition people to engage in punishment behaviors. But it's important to bear in mind that punishment is being defined broadly here to cover techniques of emotion conditioning such as love withdrawal. If you want to train people to be good at withdrawing love, you *could* train them just to behave as if they were withdrawing love, *or* you could train them actually to withdraw love. In short, you could train people to be disappointed (or angry or disgusted, etc.) when other people misbehave. The latter strategy seems more direct, and hence more efficacious. If I am right, then the best way to implement meta-punishment is to show disappointment (or anger or disgust etc.) at those who do not react to misdeeds with these negative emotions. When we do that, we effectively condition people to feel badly about not feeling badly about bad behavior. Thus meta-emotion is a form of meta-punishment because it assigns an emotional cost to anyone who fails to have punitive emotions toward those who transgress. Meta-emotions also have the advantage of being easy to transmit. We often condition people to have meta-emotions explicitly by punishing those who have the wrong attitudes ("You should be ashamed of yourself!"), but this may not even be necessary. There is a general desire that people have to share attitudes with members of their social group. People who think differently are regarded as deviant and are less successful at forging social alliances. Thus, failure to have the same first-order emotions as others is construed as a defect, and that promotes negative emotions toward non-conformist first-order emotions. In other words, meta-emotions are both explicitly transmitted and implicitly transmitted through a generalized desire to fit in (Boyd et al. invoke a "conformity bias"). If this basic story is right, then meta-emotions may be a principal tool used to implement meta-punishment, and, as such, they may play an essential role in maintaining moral rules across generations. If a population lacked meta-emotions (e.g., individuals with autism), then, even if they could acquire moral norms, they might not be able to maintain and transmit these norms stably over time.

The upshot of all this is that human beings are equipped with a range of non-moral tools, such as emotions, memory, rule-formation, imitation, and mind-reading, that could collectively give rise to a moral capacity. When emotions are conditioned in the context of behavior, sentiments are formed and affect-backed rules result (compare Nichols, 2004*a*). The business about punishment and meta-punishment shows that these relatively simple resources are quite powerful. In principle, any form of behavior could be subjected to a form of emotional conditioning that would result in the formation of a moral rule (Sripada and Stich, 2006). On this picture, morality is not innate; it is a powerful byproduct of other innate capacities.

The story that I have been sketching says nothing about the content of moral rules. It is a story about how moralization emerges, not a story about what we moralize. The research that has been done under the rubric of "evolutionary ethics" differs in this respect. That research usually concerns the content of norms. Evolutionary ethicists emphasize helping, sharing, reciprocating, and other forms of behavior. I objected that these behaviors can occur in the absence of any moral sense, and, to qualify as moral, they need to be regarded as good and motivated by that regard. Sharing is moral only if we share *in order to do the right thing*. Since biological dispositions to share may not be implemented by moral attitudes, evolutionary ethics may fail in its effort to demonstrate that we have innate moral rules. Now, however, we are in a position to see what evolutionary ethicists can contribute to an account of the origins of moral cognition. Moral rules are not innate, but once we learn to take a moral stance, the behaviors emphasized by evolutionary ethicists are especially likely to be moralized. We share a non-moral tendency to share, to help, and to reciprocate with our primate cousins, and these tendencies become objects of moral praise in us. We *learn* to view these things as good. We can develop moral attitudes toward other behaviors, but the behaviors emphasized by evolutionary ethicists are typically central to human moral life.

This raises a question. If we are naturally prone to share, help, and reciprocate, why do we ever moralize these behaviors? If we are instinctively charitable, why do we ever bother moralizing charity? Moralization is a means of fostering behavior, and there is no need to foster what we would do naturally. The answer to this question may involve the growth of human societies (Boyd and Richerson, 1985). In non-human primates, sharing, helping, and reciprocating tend to be restricted to the members of small groups. One animal will confer benefits on another only if they are either relatives or allied members of a troop. Very small-scale human societies may not require moral rules, because members of those societies are close enough to be naturally inclined to treat each other well. As population size grows, however, we find ourselves in contact with people who are not close friends or family. In large societies, there are often group projects, such as collective building and farming, that depend on cooperation. Mechanisms must be put in place to make sure that no one slacks off. If helping behaviors evolved in contexts where cooperative relationships were dyadic, the evolved mechanisms may not be sufficiently powerful to ensure cooperation with groups of strangers. The factors that compel us to be nice to our neighbors (affection, iterated tit-for-tat exchanges, fear of getting caught, etc.) may not apply when we are dealing with more distant collaborators. Moralization may have emerged as a technique to ensure that people didn't slack off as societies grew. Expansion places pressure on cultures to devise ways of extending our natural niceness to strangers. Moralization offers a solution. This suggestion resembles Hume's (1739) suggestion that the concept of justice emerges with the need to extend natural sympathies to large societal groups.

7.3.2 Biocultural Norms

If I am right, then moral rules are not innate. Rather, they emerge through interactions between biology and culture. Biologically based behavioral dispositions get extended through enculturation, especially as social groups grow larger. Enculturation can re-shape those behavioral dispositions in various ways, and, in some cases, even override them. In chapters 5 and 6, we saw many examples of moral diversity across cultures. The framework introduced in this chapter can deepen our understanding of cultural diversity, by recognizing that some of our moral rules are informed by biological tendencies to behave in certain ways. Biologically based behaviors are not quite a constraint on the genealogy of moral rules, because culture can override them, but they are often a central ingredient. We can understand many human moral norms as culturally specific variations on the same biological themes.

In most cultures, kindness tends to be greatest for members of the in-group, which is just what biological predispositions would predict, but there is considerable variation in how in-groups are defined. In medieval Japan, there was a strict social hierarchy, and social status played a role in determining who should be kind to whom. Limitations on out-group kindness in Japan can be illustrated by a practice called *tsujigiri*, wherein a samurai would test out a new sword by slicing a random peasant in half (see Midgley (1981) for a philosophical discussion). Here, moral concern is vertically bounded: high-ranking groups show little regard for people of lower rank. Moral concern can also be horizontally bounded. In pre-colonial New Guinea, neighboring tribes were often in competition for resources, and violent conflicts were commonplace. Based on ethnographic records, Wrangham (2004) calculates that 20–38 percent of men in highland tribes died of homicide. In these cases, we don't find rich people killing poor people, but rather one tribe waging war on another. Rank is not a factor. Sometimes, violence occurs between villages of the same tribe. The Yanomami of the Amazon basin live in villages that engage in a never-ending cycle of tit-for-tat brutality. One village will raid a neighboring village, killing men, and raping women, and then the neighboring village will plot revenge (Chagnon, 1968). The Yanomami are interesting because they war against each other despite a shared culture. They define the in-group by locale. Other societies define the in-group by culture, despite massive geographical distribution. Christianity has traditionally worked on this principle; Christians work to help other Christians, even if they are on the other side of the world. Christians also try to help non-Christians, but the charity campaigns are often conjoined with missionary efforts, which increase the probability that aid will end up in the hands of fellow Christians. In this case, the in-group is not defined by village borders or class, but by shared faith, which makes it much more encompassing. Historically, when Christians have encountered groups that won't convert, the policy of charity is replaced by a somewhat less friendly stance, as in the Inquisition and the Crusades. In contemporary society, globalization, pluralism, and cosmopolitanism are leading to new conceptions of group membership. These conceptions are more inclusive than past conceptions, in theory, but they pose a serious threat to groups that do not want to identify with a global collective. In sum, when our biological tendency to be kind to members of an in-group is converted into a moral rule, it can take a wide variety of forms. The rule is applied in different ways as cultures define and renegotiate conditions on group membership.

Under certain conditions, the biological tendency to be kind to members of one's in-group can be eroded. According to Turnbull (1972), the Ik of Uganda became vicious when drought and forced relocation led them to the brink of starvation. The Ik engaged in constant deception, they pried food from the mouth of an ailing villager, and they laughed with delight when a child burnt herself in a fire. Turnbull claims that the Ik continued in their miserable ways even after their economic situation improved, as if they had been corrupted by extreme poverty. Turnbull's analysis is controversial (see Heine, 1985), but it wouldn't be surprising if cultural conditions could lead people to abandon natural tendencies to be kind to their friends and family. Destitution can make competitors out of would-be friends. Once such cruel indifference enters the fabric of a culture, it can be passed on (for more examples, see Edgerton, 1992).

Let's turn from kindness to fairness, where cultural variations are also easy to demonstrate. Henrich et al. (2001) discovered this when they asked members of different cultures to play an ultimatum game. Two players are required. Player 1 is given a lump sum of money (say $100) and told that she has to offer a portion of it to Player 2. If Player 2 accepts the offer, the money is distributed in accordance with the offer. But Player 1 is also warned that neither player will receive any money if Player 2 rejects the offer. The players do not know each other, and they are told that they will never play with each other again. It would be rational for Player 1 to make an offer of $0.01 and keep $99.99 for herself. After all, this would maximize payoffs, and Player 2 would be rationally forced to accept the inequitable offer because $0.01 is better than receiving nothing. In fact, however, players in the game usually offer much more—typically around 40 percent of the pot—and grossly inequitable offers are rejected. It seems that we would rather punish those who make unfair offers and receive nothing than receive an unfair offer. This is true cross-culturally, and it is true when the starting pot is considerably greater than $100. Still, Henrich et al. found considerable cross-cultural variation. On average, the Machiguenga of Peru make and accept offers of 26 percent of the pot rather than 40 percent. The reason may be economic. The Machiguenga have a slash-and-burn economy that does not require much cooperation outside the family, so they are not in the practice of cooperating with strangers. Norms that promote fairness have never been very important for them. Contrast this case with the Gnau and Au people of Papua

New Guinea. The average offers made by these people are close to the offers made by American subjects, but, unlike us, they often reject offers that are hyperfair (offers over 50 percent). The reason for this seems to be that they have a cultural practice of gift-giving, in which receiving a gift strongly requires reciprocation. A generous offer can be a burden, because it has to be reciprocated. The Gnau and Au seem to have moralized reciprocity so deeply that failure to reciprocate is considered a very grave offense.

Further evidence for cross-cultural differences in attitudes toward fairness can be found by presenting subjects with questions about resource allocation. There are a number of principles that can be used to determine how to distribute resources. One could give to the needy, to those who have done the most work, or to everyone equally. These strategies, dubbed need, equity, and equality, have been extensively investigated in cross-cultural studies (Smith and Bond, 1998). In one study, Berman et al. (1985) asked Indian and American subjects to decide whether a bonus should be given to an affluent worker who worked especially hard, or to a moderate worker who was financially needy, or whether the bonus should be divided equally between them. Half of the American subjects said that the bonus should be allocated on the basis of equity to the hard worker, and only 14 percent said the money should go to the needy worker. Indian respondents had the opposite response: half allocated the bonus to the needy and only 14 percent allocated on the basis of equity. This difference in values may be related to the fact that there is more poverty in India, and people there regard care for the needy as an important value. In another study, Leung and Bond (1984) found that Chinese subjects prefer equal divisions over equitable divisions when they are dividing goods among friends, and American subjects preferred equity over equality. One explanation for this effect is that Americans tend to have individualist values, which emphasize self-efficacy and achievement. People in China care about these things too, but they tend to have a collectivist orientation, which means that group harmony, especially among friends and family, can be more valuable than individual success.

So far, I have been focusing on cultural variations in kindness and fairness. These are two of the areas in which there is evidence for biologically prepared behavioral dispositions, and I have argued that cultures extend those dispositions in various ways. Culture can also affect the specific form that our behavior takes. Consider reciprocity. Among many non-human animals, reciprocation behavior is highly stereotyped. A vampire bat reciprocates by regurgitating blood. Chimps reciprocate by grooming, food-sharing, or forming alliances for aggression and defense. But what about us? There seems to be no fixed pattern. We can reciprocate in the way that chimps do, but also in many other ways. A genetic program for reciprocation would be woefully inadequate in our case. If the genes provided us with specific instructions about how to reciprocate, that would be far too rigid. And if the genes provided us with the generic command "reciprocate!", that would be too vague to translate into action. Rules of reciprocation are highly specific, but they are neither stereotyped nor fixed. What gifts require reciprocation? It would be bizarre to reimburse an institution for conferring an achievement award. Who must reciprocate? In the Far East, debts can be passed down from generation to generation. How much payback is enough? Do we return the same favor or do something entirely different? It might be distastefully unthoughtful to give the same birthday gifts that we received. The subtle and variable rules governing human reciprocation suggest that culture is making an essential contribution. In apes and bats, reciprocity can be identified with specific behavioral dispositions. In our own case, it must be much more plastic.

This suggests that the biological contribution to human reciprocity is not a command that we could ever carry out on its own. If we had nothing but biology to go on, the impulse to reciprocate might not be behaviorally specific enough to issue in action. We wouldn't know how to reciprocate. Instead, the biological contribution may be more like a scaffold upon which we build executable norms. For example, we might be born with an innate sense of gratitude when our desires have been fulfilled by others. An innate sense of gratitude would not issue directly into action. To show our gratitude, we would have to learn culturally specific ways of repaying our debts.

In sum, I propose that biologically based behaviors pertaining to kindness, fairness, and reciprocity are culturally malleable and insufficient to guide our behavior without cultural elaboration. I think culture makes two contributions to the biological inputs. First, it converts these behaviors into moral norms, by grounding them in moral emotions. Second, it takes the biologically based norms that have highly stereotyped, and limited, behavioral effects in our primate cousins and alters them into culturally specific instructions for what we should do to whom. It's this latter aspect of cultural elaboration that I'm emphasizing in this discussion of reciprocity norms.

Culture makes a parallel contribution to rank and sexuality. The first thing to notice about rank is that it is highly variable across cultures. Some cultures are highly stratified, and some are egalitarian. Egalitarian cultures are not devoid of social dominance hierarchies, but dominant individuals do not wield a disproportionate amount of power or possess more assets. In egalitarian societies, dominant individuals (almost always male) are the ones who gain respect through wisdom, skills, charisma, or generosity. These high-status individuals are known in anthropology as headmen. Headmen do what everyone else does; they just work harder and give more away. They are not in a position to rule by force. Their judgments about what the group should do are taken as recommendations, not authoritative commands. Marvin Harris (1989) describes the emergence of stratification as societies evolve from egalitarian bands to states. In some societies, individuals will try to outperform each other with feats of generosity. They will get close friends and family to gather together so they can put on lavish feasts for members of their villages. The one who puts on the most lavish feast becomes a big man. The big man is able to recruit more supporters and followers, and he can thereby maintain his status in the face of competition. In societies where there are abundant, non-perishable sources of food, the leader can create storehouses and redistribute food during times of scarcity. Such leaders achieve a new level of respect and authority. They become chiefs. Their role as providers is vital, and villagers reward them with tribute, special goods and services. Special rewards are given to those who offer the most loyal support. Chiefs no longer need to hunt or gather food. They accumulate wealth and pass it on to their offspring, who are said to have a divine right to carry on leadership when the chief has died. To increase their pot, chiefs organize armies, wage war against neighbors, and expand the society. Systems of tribute can be extended to neighboring villages, enforced by military control. As group size increases, labor diversifies, and those serving different roles accumulate different degrees of wealth. The state is born.

At each stage of this process, rank takes on new meaning. By the end, there can be multiple levels of dominance based, not on age or gender, but on accumulated resources, strategic alliances, and social roles. Such stratification is an outgrowth of a biological predisposition to have rank systems, but it is culturally transformed. Cultures also determine the means by which one can change in rank. It can be a matter of merit, or training, or marriage. In some societies, movement between social strata is virtually impossible. In India, changing castes was traditionally forbidden. Castes were said to be fixed at birth and associated with different levels in the cycle of reincarnation. To change caste would be a grotesque form of line-skipping in the ascent to nirvana. This cosmological justification may have a political history. Though controversial, it is widely believed that the Indian subcontinent was invaded by Europeans some time around 1500 BCE. The indigenous population was suppressed, and the caste we know as the untouchables was created. Now, more than two millennia later, genetic tests show that upper-caste Indians are genetically closer to Europeans than lower-caste Indians (Bamshad et al., 2001). This suggests centuries of very successful prohibitions against upward mobility.

The Indian caste system certainly isn't innate, but it may be reinforced by a natural toleration of dominance hierarchies. It is a biocultural institution, reinforced by emotions of obedience, deference, and superiority. The emotions pertaining to rank are probably universal, but their expressions can vary. Feelings of deference are widely marked by bowing, hat tipping, kneeling, or other forms of body-lowering, which may be culturally adapted symbolic outgrowths of the head-lowering gestures seen in animal deference studies.

Culture can play a role in determining the prevalence of emotions pertaining to dominance hierarchies. Egalitarian societies tend to suppress feelings of superiority. When studying the !Kung, Lee (1969) bought a large ox and offered it as a present. The recipients complained that the ox was too lean to fill their bellies. In reality, they dismissed the gift as valueless because they didn't want Lee to feel that he was superior (cited in Harris, 1989).

As with superiority, cultures also seem to vary in the extent to which they encourage feelings of obedience. Recall the Milgram (1974) experiments discussed in chapter 4. Subjects inflicted electric shocks when they were asked to do so by an authority figure. These results were uniform across different personality types, gender, and social groups. But they were not uniform cross-culturally. Whereas American subjects were fully obedient 65 percent of the time, German subjects were fully obedient 85 percent of the time (Mantell, 1971). This fits the cultural stereotype that Germans are prone to obey orders. A contrasting pattern was observed when a Milgram-style study was conducted in Australia: there, only 40 percent of the male subjects and 16 percent of the female subjects were fully obedient (Kilham and Mann, 1974). This tendency to disregard authorities may carry over from Australia's days as an uncharted frontier, far away from the arm of European law.

These examples testify to the plasticity of the human predisposition to form social ranks. There is little evidence that our genes tell us how to organize social groups. Rather, they furnish us with obedience, the capacity to compete, and status-related emotions, which make us susceptible to hierarchy formation. Cultural factors determine which traits warrant high rank and the degree of stratification. Rank norms emerge through biocultural interaction. These norms are often moralized. It is regarded as morally wrong to act inappropriately for your rank in society; for example, we think it is wrong for a teenager to talk disrespectfully to a teacher without warrant. In chapter 2, I noted that we hold those who violate rank in contempt, which is a blend of anger and disgust. These moral sentiments toward rank violations are widespread, but they probably aren't innate. The blend of anger and disgust that we use to enforce rank norms may be a byproduct of how we transmit such norms in human society. Within simian societies, rank is enforced by power assertion and favors. Ruling apes are stronger and more generous. Those who vie unsuccessfully for power feel deferential, and, perhaps, a sad sense of defeat (see Price et al., 1994 on the evolutionary origins of depression). Among humans, rank is not established merely by power; it is taught. We are told to respect authority. We are told that certain individuals (parents, leaders, elders, etc.) are *entitled* to their high social station. People who don't obey this rule are not just imprudent (as in the ape case); they are violating the rights of people in power. On this conceptualization, a rank violation is a crime against another person, and crimes against persons elicit anger. We also tend to conceptualize our dominance hierarchies as if they were part of the natural or supernatural order. Consider the divine rights of kings, or the Indian caste system, or the more general fact that people are *born* into social classes, or the fact that some forms of authority are correlated with biological facts (parenthood or age, for example). On this conceptualization, to violate rank is to transgress against nature or divinity. Unnatural acts elicit disgust. Thus, both anger and disgust are inevitable consequences of rank violations, because of the way that cultures conceptualize rank. Anger and disgust blend into contempt.

Apes have rank hierarchies without moralization, and, as far as we know, they do not experience contempt.

Let me turn, now, to sexual morality, beginning with infidelity. Primates differ in the degree to which relationships are regarded as exclusive. Gorillas have their harems, but chimps and bonobos are quite promiscuous. Dominant animals, like any desirable partners, often get first picks. Male macaques and baboons often fight violently for rights to sexual access, and liaisons with subordinates are severely punished. Of course, infidelity does occur. Monkeys will have secret trysts when they can, and even bird species known for their long-term monogamous relationships often sneak in some romance on the side. There is no evidence that non-human animals regard such behaviors as immoral, rather than merely risky. Non-human animals do not seem to exhibit third-party concerns when it comes to infidelity. In stark contrast, we condemn adulterers even when we are not directly affected by their acts. We don't always make adulterers wear scarlet letters around their necks, but we make them feel ashamed by publicly expressing the view that infidelity is terribly wrong. I think that moral attitude is a learned add-on to the sexual politics found in other primates. Apes and monkeys fight for sexual access, and sexual entitlement is governed by might rather than right. Humans have moved beyond this system. We create institutions, such as marriage, for restricting sexual access and these institutions are grounded in contracts, laws, and, above all, sentiments. We promote fidelity by moralizing it.

A nativist about infidelity norms might object to this analysis by arguing that we have an innate, domain-specific psychological mechanism for responding to infidelity: romantic jealousy. But the claim that jealousy is an innate emotion can be called into question. I think jealousy is actually an acquired blend of anger, fear, sadness, and disgust (Prinz, 2004). All of these emotions naturally arise in the context of infidelity. We are enraged when our trust is violated, frightened about facing competing suitors, saddened by the potential loss of a lover, and disgusted by the prospect that a lover has been contaminated. Thus, these emotions inevitably blend together when we have been romantically betrayed, and we use the term jealousy to label that blend. We do not need evolution to furnish us with an emotion that is dedicated for this function. Nor do we need to postulate innate gender differences to explain why women are more concerned about emotional infidelity than sexual infidelity. In most societies, woman still depend on men for material support. To lose a male partner is almost always a financial hardship for women. Notice, however, that this may not have been true in the Pleistocene. Perhaps there, as in some primate and human societies, children were raised by whole communities without any disproportionate contribution from the one male who happened to be progenitor. Some contemporary hunter-gatherer societies have such arrangements (Kelly, 1995). If early human societies were organized in this way, then the assumption that men are biologically programmed to worry about uncertain paternity and women are programmed to worry about keeping the bread-winner around is ludicrous. One can also take issue with the claim that women care more about emotional fidelity than sex (C. R. Harris, 2004). This experimental finding may merely show that women are discouraged from expressing interest in sex. That well-known fact may be a culturally driven product of male domination (see, e.g., Hrdy (1999) on the biological evidence for a strong female sex-drive). When women are given a cognitively demanding memory task just before being asked the question about infidelity, they respond more like men. The memory task prevents them from censoring their knee-jerk response, which is that sexual infidelity is worse than emotional infidelity (DeSteno et al., 2002). Moreover, responses to the infidelity question vary across cultures. In Holland, where there is greater sexual liberty and a high degree of employment for women, male and female answers look very similar (Buunk et al., 1996). They all say that emotional infidelity is worse than sexual infidelity. Perhaps the Dutch are concealing their real answers, or perhaps, for them, sex just isn't a very big deal. Either way, the pattern of results does not support the contention that we have an emotion especially evolved to enforce infidelity norms.

This is not to deny that we have an evolved tendency to punish infidelity. We probably do. My point is rather that moral rules against infidelity, and the emotions that ground them, reflect biocultural interaction. The most direct evidence for this comes from cultural variation in infidelity norms. In most cultures, infidelity is forbidden, but, in many, men are given more latitude. Evolutionary psychologists would have us believe that this double standard is a cultural capitulation to the innate desire that each man has to spread his seed. If infidelity in monkeys and birds is any indication, however, women are equally covetous of multiple partners. The double standard is better explained, therefore, by male dominance in political power. A pro-male bias in the courts is no more a product of evolution than a pro-white bias. Furthermore, there are societies in which women are allowed to have extramarital partners. For example Wood (1999) reports that, among the Gabra nomads of East Africa, married women are encouraged to have lovers. Ironically, the Gabra still have a double standard. Unmarried men are allowed to have sex, but when unmarried women have sex, they are banished. Marriage is the key to sexual liberation among the Gabra. This is the inverse of our infidelity norms.

Equally surprising variation can be found when it comes to incest. Taboos against incest vary dramatically. Among the Zaroastrians, sexual unions within the immediate family were reportedly regarded as morally preferable to exogamous unions (Slotkin, 1947). The Na of China have a system of open sexuality before marriage, and they don't keep track of paternity, so it is possible for a woman to end up in bed with her biological father (Hua, 2001). Thonga men in East Africa are said to have sex with their daughters before hunting lions (Junod, 1962). Among the Burundi, women sleep with their newly married sons as a treatment for impotence (Albert, 1963). Sexual relations between mothers and sons are also alleged to occur from time to time in modern Japan. According to reports, which may be greatly exaggerated, some mothers appease their son's sexual appetites so that they don't get distracted by dating girls their own age when they are studying for their all-important exams. In the 1980s concerns about mother–son incest reached a fevered pitch akin to concerns about father–daughter incest in Western nations (Allison, 2000).

Brother–sister incest is perhaps the most common form of culturally sanctioned sex between immediate family members. Among Incan, Hawaiian, and Egyptian royalty, it was often prescribed. Many of the Julio-Claudian emperors had incestuous relationships. Caligula had a sexual relationship with his sister, Agrippina, who married her uncle, Claudius, whose daughter married her son, Nero. In Ptolemaic Egypt, as many as 21 percent of the recorded marriages among Greek and Roman immigrants were between siblings. They may have been emulating the Ptolemaic rulers, eight of thirteen of whom married their sisters. It's also plausible that these Greek and Roman citizens were encouraged to have incestuous relationships in order to consolidate power. The Ptolemies ruled Egypt like an apartheid state, and imposed laws preventing Greeks and Romans from marrying native Egyptians; if an Egyptian took on a foreign name, it was a capital offense. Once forced to marry within their own national groups, Greeks and Romans, who lived scattered across large cities, were left with few potential marriage partners from whom to choose. By encouraging incest, leaders undercut any temptation that these immigrants might have had to marry into the indigenous population (Shaw, 1992).

Though unusual, these cases cast some doubt on Westermarck's hypothesis that a strong aversion to incest is triggered by being raised in the same household. That hypothesis is also challenged by the fact that, in some small-scale societies, villagers who are raised in close proximity end up marrying each other. The empirical evidence used to support the Westermarck hypothesis can also be challenged. First, there was the high failure rate among Taiwanese minor marriages, wherein girls are adopted into families at a young age and then raised to be the wives of male children in those families. The problem with this finding is that the failure rate may stem from factors that have nothing to do with incest avoidance. Minor marriages are arranged by poor families who cannot afford to pay a brideprice, and poverty may lead to marital instability; because no money is at stake, parents of children in minor marriages have less financial interest in seeing them succeed (Harris, 1989: 201); minor marriages are regarded as unusual and inferior to major marriages; and minor marriages allow the bride and groom to exercise less choice in picking a marriage partner. The second line of evidence for the Westermarck hypothesis was furnished by the low marriage rates among men and women who were raised together on Israeli kibbutzim. In response, Harris (1989) points out that the marriage rate between members of the same kibbutz is actually pretty high, when one includes couples who were not schooled in the same class. The fact that men and women in the same class did not marry can be explained by the fact that men married women who were three years younger than themselves on average. Moreover, we shouldn't be surprised if there were hardly any marriages between people raised together on a kibbutz, because young people typically leave home to serve in the military and attend universities, and they often don't go back; thus, people who are raised on kibbutzim have left by the time they begin looking for marriage partners. Finally, there was Lieberman et al.'s finding that negative attitudes toward sibling incest are higher for people raised with opposite sex siblings. Here there is a simple explanation. Prohibitions against sibling incest are inapplicable to people who don't have siblings. Those that do have siblings are more likely to be told about the prohibition (through explicit instruction or, more likely, expression of emotion when the topic comes up), and they are under more pressure to internalize it. Teenage males who are interested in sex are especially likely to come under social pressure to behave properly with their sisters; hence it is no surprise that they are especially squeamish about sibling incest.

The Westermarck hypothesis also fails to explain the scope of the incest taboo, which in most societies extends to kin who are not members of the household. In current Western society, people are repelled by cousin-marriage, even though cousins in the West are reared far apart. There are many societies that extend incest taboos to affinal family (related only by marriage). Up until recently, it was illegal in Korea to marry someone with the same last name. This indicates that incest taboos are not merely a codification of an innate disposition to revile those with whom we cohabitate during development. And, correlatively, culturally based incest taboos could not be devised merely to protect against inbreeding. Indeed, risks of inbreeding may be exaggerated. If a small group of people reproduce together over a very long period of time, they can weed out deleterious recessive genes. Small tribes of hunter-gatherers (not to mention purebred animals) are often very healthy despite a profound lack of genetic diversity.

I don't mean to infer from all this that there is no biological disposition to avoid incest in humans. There probably is. I'm just not convinced by the evidence for the Westermarck hypothesis. An alternative hypothesis is that when children reach sexual maturity, they develop a sexual interest in people outside the family. Such exogamous preferences would protect us against the potential risks, but they would also confer another benefit: if we were to stay in one group all our lives, and that group befell a terrible fate through disease, disaster, or predation, then the genes in the group would die out; if, however, offspring were to change groups, the family genes would be spread out geographically, and survival prospects would be increased. Whatever the evolutionary function of exogamy, it seems to be the pattern in our closest animal relatives. Chimpanzees leave natal communities before seeking sexual partners. In the case of common chimps, it's the females who leave, and in the case of bonobos, it's the males. In humans, there is no apparent asymmetry in sexual wanderlust. Both male and female humans may form a desire to leave home in search of mates around the onset of puberty. Or perhaps we have an innate switch that can be set differently in matrilocal and patrilocal societies.

Exogamous breeding preferences would explain incest avoidance. It's a typical feature of sexual preferences that you will be repelled by the idea of sex with people whom you do not overtly desire. Disinterest breeds disgust. If you are not attracted to someone sexually, the thought of sex with them is repellent, regardless of whether they are related or not. I think that the disgust response associated with incest avoidance is simply an instance of this more general tendency. If we are biologically programmed to be exogamous, then we won't be attracted to kin, and, if we are not attracted to kin, we will be disgusted by them. On this story, the disgust response has nothing special to do with incest. The innate machinery that's specific to incest is the bit we share with apes: an attraction to people outside the group. In one respect this proposal is quite similar to the Westermarck hypothesis: incest avoidance involves a lack of sexual interest in those with whom one has cohabitated. But there are some key differences. On the present proposal, the incest taboo is not a function of early childhood cohabitation, which is a central component for Westermarck, and it is not primarily manifested as a disgust response to siblings. Rather, incest avoidance is a consequence of exogamous desire. That desire manifests itself as an attraction to partners outside the group in which one grows up. Where Westermarck focused on cohabitation, the exogamy account is neutral about how groups get defined (e.g., the group can be the natal household or the whole village). It is possible that culture has a hand in determining the relevant group boundaries.

If this story is on the right track, then the biological incest-avoidance mechanism is not a moral norm—it is not equivalent to an incest taboo. It's one thing to avoid a behavior and quite another to condemn that behavior. With a natural tendency to avoid incest, moral rules seem to be unnecessary. We don't need moral rules against eating rotting meat or slicing off our genitals. It's not surprising, then, that only 44 percent of societies have explicit rules against sex with kin (Thornhill, 1991). But this raises a question. Why does incest avoidance ever get moralized? There may be multiple factors, but one likely possibility is that incest rules are culturally constructed to encourage the formation of strategic alliances with other families, and to restrict consolidation of wealth within any one family (Thornhill, 1991). If it's taboo to sleep with relatives, and sex is linked to marriage, then it will be difficult to keep wealth within a single family. Consistent with this economic analysis, Thornhill points out that societies with greater degrees of social stratification tend to have harsher penalties for incest. The ruling classes want to prevent commoners from consolidating wealth by imposing tough incest rules that apply to everyone except the members of the royal household. The ruling classes can make it even harder to consolidate wealth by defining a large class of relations as incestuous, including relations with cousins and affinal kin. Economic strategies may also underlie rules that are the inverse of the incest taboo: prohibitions against out-group marriage. In some groups, such as the Bedouins, individuals are expected to marry their first cousins. This is a good way to keep wealth within the group.

In sum, there is reason to believe that incest taboos have a biocultural origin. We have an innate tendency to avoid incest through exogamy, but this tendency guides behavior in culturally sensitive ways. First of all, exogamy requires leaving the group, but group boundaries in human beings are culturally defined. Second of all, it is possible that both men and women are disposed to be exogamous, but, in some cultures that disposition is expressed in only one sex. Third, and most importantly, biological incest avoidance is not a moral norm. It only gets moralized under certain cultural conditions, having to do with the consolidation of power and wealth. When avoidance becomes taboo, cultures often extend the definition of family to include individuals who are not subject to biological aversion.

The moralization of incest probably works by capitalizing on the human capacity for disgust. Disgust is the default negative emotion for things relating to the body. It evolved to protect us from contamination. Sex involves physical contact with another body and transfer of bodily fluids. All bodily fluids (except tears) can elicit core physical disgust. This is not a moral response, but a hygienic response, furnished by natural selection. When incest is moralized, hygienic disgust is recast as a moral emotion. Through moral education, we come to see cousin-marriage and other benign relationships as repellent. With moralization, incest also becomes shameful. Shame arises when we feel that we need to conceal our bodies, and a body that has been contaminated by unsanctioned sexual conduct is just the sort of thing that one might want to conceal.

In this discussion, I have been emphasizing the diversity of human morality, even in cases where our moral norms have some basis in biology. Along the way, I have tried to present evidence for two conclusions. First, the naturally evolved norms that I introduced in section 7.1 may not qualify as *moral* norms in their natural state. I think that moralization, including the emergence of Shweder's three kinds of ethical systems, is the result of cultural development. Second, naturally evolved norms can be embellished, expanded, and perhaps suppressed under cultural influence. Cultural influences are not limited to a fixed range of outcomes, but are open-ended.

This point about open-endedness deserves special emphasis. In this context, I want to defuse one possible objection. These days, everyone seems to be an interactionist. Moral nativists are often willing to admit that environment contributes to morality; they say that most of our psychological phenotypes are a blend of nature and nurture. Thus, it may appear that there is no difference between my view and the prevailing view among defenders of evolutionary ethics. But appearances deceive. I think evolutionary ethicists systematically underestimate the contributions of culture. This is certainly true of evolutionary psychologists. In claiming to be interactionists, they often give examples that suggest a very minimal role for the environment. For example, Cosmides and Tooby (1997) suggest that a good model of environmental influences can be found in the blue-headed wrasse. These fish travel in groups with one male and multiple females. If the male dies, the largest female changes into a male. That looks like an extraordinary case of environmentally driven alteration in phenotype. The environment causes a sex change! The problem is that this is really just a case of gender-bending genetic determinism. The wrasse's genes work like a switch. Depending on the environment, the switch toggles very predictably from male to female. The environment is not adding anything of substance. It is simply triggering an outcome that has been predetermined by the genes. The environmental influences that I am interested in are decidedly un-wrassey. Variations in morality are not restricted to a fixed set of pre-established settings on an internal switch. The environment has a much more substantive impact on us than it does on the blue-headed wrasse. The open-endedness of morality suggests that the cultures in which we live actually contribute to the content of our moral rules, rather than selecting from a set of rules that are pre-coded in the genes. Culture does not merely activate innate programs; it rewrites our moral software.

If I am right, then it is a gross exaggeration to say that moral rules are products of evolution. Evolved norms can be thought of as schematic guidelines, which get filled out through interaction with our cultural environments. We may have evolved to be kind to members of the in-group, but the identity of the in-group members needs to be worked out culturally. We may have evolved to respect authorities, but the degree of stratification and the criteria for status need to get worked out culturally. We may have evolved to avoid sex with kin, but the scope of the ban and the seriousness of violations need to be worked out culturally. Culture tells us how to apply our natural norms, and, in some cases (Zaroastrian incest? Ik reciprocity?), it even overrides them. One might put the point by saying that humans instinctively take their cues from culture. Culture also converts our biological norms into moral norms—norms that are grounded in sentiments and extended to third parties. Evolution is not the source of morality; it is at best a toehold by which we can make our moral ascent.

7.3.3 Conclusion: Against Nature

What if we could somehow shed all the influences of culture and return to our premoral values—the values we would have in our natural state? To do this, we would have to eliminate marriage and property, we would have to abandon concerns about global justice, and we would have to tolerate corporal punishment, and perhaps some opportunistic cannibalism and rape. We would still behave in some ways that might be described as respectable. Our natural values would lead us to groom each other if we had been groomed. We would respect authority. We would avoid having sex with our siblings. Our lives would probably be fairly predictable. Unlike the Nietzschean self-creating *Übermensch*—a fantasy concocted under the spell of Romanticism—we would probably be a lot like chimps.

Perhaps we could sustain this chimpish existence for a while. Perhaps early human populations were like this. But not for long. Our ancestors had dwellings, clothing, and tools. They engaged in battles with each other, organized hunting expeditions, and devised political organizations for their clans. Once these things are in place, natural values can no longer serve as straightforward guides to action. We need to decide what constitutes rank, what goods to give when we reciprocate, and what romantic bonds are off limits.

Are we worse off for this? Should we strive to return to the mythical savannah? The answer is obvious. For one thing, we cannot return to a pure state, uninformed by the knowledge and technologies we have accumulated over millennia of cultural evolution. For another, there is no way to justify the claim that our natural state is better simply in virtue of being more natural. Our natural state fosters the construction of social institutions and values. Our values are now, and will always be, products of both nature and nurture. Evolutionary ethics, that misnomer, provides a pinhole view on moral life. It is fascinating to expose the broad biological boundaries within which morality grows, but an investigation of those boundaries is grossly incomplete and utterly devoid of normative implications.

8

Moral Progress

8.1 IS PROGRESS POSSIBLE?

8.1.1 Two Kinds of Nihilism

Nietzsche is sometimes called a moral nihilist, and not without warrant. He wanted to undermine Christian morality, but he did not want to eliminate morality altogether. He wanted to replace existing values with better values. Nietzsche's formula for improvement was to identify values that are active rather than reactive, or natural rather than historically constructed. I raised some doubts about this project in chapter 7. I think all morality is constructed. This forecloses one avenue for moral progress. Indeed, it may make progress look downright impossible. If every moral system is a cultural construction, and none has greater claim to absolute truth, what grounds do we have for saying any one system is better than any other? I briefly raised this question in chapter 6. Here I will have a bit more to say.

To pose the challenge of progress more precisely, let us distinguish two kinds of moral nihilism. According to the first, all moral systems are empty: the claims they make are false. Error theories of morality are nihilistic in this sense, including the theories of Mackie or Ruse. Morality is an illusion. I have argued against error theories (chapter 3). I think that moral claims can be true. Moral concepts are indexicals that refer to response-dependent properties. The good is that which is an object of approbation in a moral observer, and the bad is an object of disapprobation. As long as we morally approve and disapprove, we secure the existence of moral facts. The problem is not that moral claims are false, but rather that too many moral claims are true.

There are probably thousands of moralities throughout the world, and an unbounded number of merely possible moralities. Each of these has a claim to truth. If moral claims are relativized to culturally inculcated systems of values in moral observers, then any claim about what morality demands can come out true. There is always a possible moral system where some action is permissible, no matter how heinous it might be relative to our own system. One culture's good can be another culture's evil. In actual fact, there is probably a lot of convergence across cultures, but, as we have seen, there is also a lot of moral diversity. The problem is that while we may have preferences for our own moral systems over the moral systems of others, there seems to be no sense in which our preferences are better than the preferences of others. The fact that they are *our* preferences does not make them better preferences, except to us.

This brings us to a second kind of nihilism. No moral system, it turns out, is better than any other moral system. Claims to moral truth are essentially parochial. My moral assertions are true, but no truer than their denial when uttered by a member of another community. If this is the case, then it is hard to see how one can ever talk about moral progress. As we move from slave states to slave-free states, as we struggle for gender equity, as we renounce torture and imperialism, are we not doing better than we did before? Our current values seem to be an improvement over the values of the past, and moral humility leads us to hope for continued improvement. If moral truth is shallow in the way that I have been describing, then moral change is not a move forward, but a lateral repositioning in a space of equally acceptable options. This is a nihilism of directionless abundance. Must we settle for that?

8.1.2 Beyond Good and Evil

I believe that moral progress is possible, but I don't think we can succeed in moving forward by stepping outside our current values and weighing alternatives. I don't think there is a transcendental stance from which we can assess competing moral theories. There is no view from nowhere. We must always assess progress from the inside. In this respect, morality is not different from science. In Otto Neurath's familiar trope popularized by Quine, theory revision is like rebuilding a raft while we are afloat at sea. We cannot simply abandon our current raft and start anew; we must replace the planks on the raft we already have. This is equally true in the evaluative domain. We cannot simply abandon our current values. The racist cannot imagine loving the members of the reviled race any more than we can imagine reveling in torture. We must retool our values from within.

Ordinarily, when we assess alternative values using the values that we already possess, the result is rejection. Alternative values are perceived as defective, corrupt, or otherwise worse than our own. In these cases, progress is possible only in an empty backward-looking sense. From the present, we always seem to have better values than we had in the past for the trivial reason that we embrace our present values and no longer embrace our past values. The interesting cases are the ones in which we consider the possibility that an alternative value is better than a value we currently possess. This kind of comparison is progressive, or forward-looking. We can see that the moral future might be better than the moral present. But how is this possible from the inside? Doesn't it require a transcendental stance?

To address this question, it will help to think about how moral debates are conducted *between* individuals. One standard technique is norm-pitting. If you think one ought to ϕ, and your interlocutor has an opposing value, you can try to bring her over to your side by looking for some other value in her repertoire that can be used to build a case in favor of ϕ-ing. In other words, we use one norm to veto another. We can do something like that in our own case. We can bring different norms together on the same issue, and give one norm precedence when two come into conflict. The key to moral change is to pit current values against each other. We often live quite complacently with inconsistencies in our values, but we are embarrassed when they are brought to our attention. When confronted with an inconsistency, we have an incentive to eliminate one of the conflicting values and find a replacement.

Norm-pitting presupposes that our norms are sometimes inconsistent. It requires that we can possess two norms that lead us in conflicting directions. There is good reason to think such conflicts are possible. Moral systems are not built or acquired in one sitting. They are cobbled together piecemeal over time. Different rules are devised to serve different purposes and to govern different aspects of our lives. There is a philosophical preoccupation with finding a single moral rule that dictates all of our judgments (see Williams (1985) for a critique). The rule of utility and the categorical imperative are examples. Even the command "Do as the virtuous person would do" is highly reductive. Such philosophical proposals are hopelessly flawed if we take them to describe how ordinary moral psychology works. The rules we follow are more concrete and varied: say "thank you"; don't spit in public; tip well; be kind to strangers; clean up after yourself; don't skip ahead in a line; apologize when you take out a bad mood on someone you love. We rarely step back and try to place these daily dicta under an overarching principle. When we search for principles, we sometimes find that many apply. These rules conform to the principle of humanity, to the rule of utility, and to the behavior of virtuous persons; yet they are products of none of these. Each norm has its own history, and, consequently, there is always a chance that two norms will clash.

Imagine someone who thinks it is okay not to help people who are dying of starvation in underdeveloped parts of the world. We can point out that this moral attitude is at odds with the injunction to be kind to strangers. On the face of it, the two attitudes are inconsistent. There are several ways of coping with the inconsistency. For example, one can revise one's view about the permissibility of ignoring world hunger. Alternatively, one can add a restrictive quantifier to the norm about strangers: be kind to strangers whom you happen to encounter. Notice that one probably wouldn't drop the rule about being kind to strangers entirely. That would be a more radical revision than the conflict requires. It might also violate other values that one has, including values about character traits: be nice, be caring, be charitable, be sympathetic, and so on. We can value traits as much as we can value actions.

This example illustrates a general point about moral values. We expect our moral systems to have some of the same theoretical virtues as our beliefs. Above all, they should be consistent. When revising, in the face of inconsistency, we usually prefer conservative revisions. Conservatism manifests itself in several ways. We aim for maximally consistent sets of norms, and we don't change more than we have to. Peripheral tweaking is better than radical overhaul. We also try to avoid changing values that may be bolstered by other related values—values that lie at the center of our evaluative webs (compare Quine and Ullian, 1978). We may also factor in the intensity with which we hold conflicting values. It is hard to drop a value about which we feel especially passionate.

We can already see the beginning of an answer to the problem of moral progress. The example under consideration illustrates a way in which one moral system can be better than another. One system may be more consistent. We prefer consistent systems to inconsistent systems. Showing that we are committed to inconsistent moral values, can spur revision. In weighing alternative moral systems from inside a system that we already possess, we also have a preference for those that are closer to the ones that we possess. Conservative revisions are more desirable.

Inconsistency is not the only thing that can motivate moral revision. There are a number of other standards by which one might assess one's moral values. Consider the following list.

Some rules are backed up by appeal to false factual knowledge. Opponents of women's suffrage claimed that women are too psychologically delicate for politics. This was probably a *post hoc* excuse for male dominance, but by resting the case against suffrage on a false factual claim, opponents opened up the door to moral revision through belief correction. (Ironically, when suffrage finally came, it did not come by convincing people to give up this factual premise. Rather, in many states, white male voters agreed to let women vote because they believed that US-born white women would use their votes to dilute the corrosive impact of immigrant and African American voters. The point here is that belief correction *could* have changed attitudes toward women's suffrage.)

Some rules are relatively easy to carry out. Others are demanding and difficult to impose on others. Moral revision may be possible when we discover that a current value is too demanding. Changing attitudes toward premarital sex may be a case of diminishing demands.

Some rules lead to greater social stability. We value freedom from anxiety, and we disvalue disruptive change. Rules that lead to the persecution of people within a society are the most likely to produce unrest.

Some rules increase our welfare; they protect us from pain and increase our pleasure. Prohibitions against harms are the most obvious examples.

Some rules increase our subjective sense of well-being; they help to provide us with lives that are fulfilling, above and beyond our basic creature comforts. For example, rules can be designed to promote education, provide a range of life choices, and support the development of personal relationships.

Some rules are more general than other rules. They deliver advice for a broad range of cases. The rule "Tip well" applies under very special conditions. Rather than treating it as a grounding norm, we might prefer the rule: "Show gratitude for services rendered." This rule can be used to derive more specific injunctions, including the tipping rule, when combined with knowledge of local customs.

Some rules are more universal than others. They would be regarded as sensible by a large number of people, rather than a few. This is an advantage, because moral rules are used to coordinate behavior within sizable populations.

Some rules are less vulnerable to genealogical critique. Rules about giving to the needy are still (*pace* Nietzsche) valuable even if they emerged under ignoble circumstances.

Some rules are more consistent with our premoral biological norms. They allow us to help and share, to install worthy authorities, and to protect our bodies against contamination. Such rules were the topic of chapter 7.

Each of these points can be treated as a standard of assessment. Each provides a sense in which one rule can be better than another. In that respect, they provide us with tools for measuring moral progress. Of two competing moral rules, the one that does better by these standards will be judged the better rule. This is an empirical claim. The list is subject to empirical alteration.

There are several things to notice. First, the standards can compete. For example, the most beneficial systems (those that increase welfare and well-being) are not necessarily the easiest to implement. That does not undermine the utility of these standards, because they do not *always* lead to inconsistent advice. Rules that are universally appealing are likely to promote stability, which is likely to promote well-being.

Second, all of these standards of assessment are themselves values. Consistency, coherence with facts, stability, ease of implementation, welfare, well-being, completeness, universality, genealogical impunity, and conformity to biological norms are all things about which we care. If we did not value these things, they would not be seen as advantages when weighing moral rules. Even our preference for consistency is a value judgment.

Third, the standards may vary across cultures. For example, there is some cultural variation in what promotes well-being. When compared to people in Eastern cultures, Westerners derive greater well-being from self-satisfaction, positive emotions, and personal enjoyment; Easterners care more about fulfilling obligations, working toward goals, and doing good things for others (Diener et al., 2003; see also Tiberius, 2003). There are even cultural differences in the degree to which people care about consistency. In the Far East, where dialectical reasoning is praised, consistency is considered less important (Nisbett, 2003).

Fourth, the standards under consideration are not moral standards. Consistency, stability, well-being, and even conformity to biological norms are things we value in an extramoral sense. When we deploy these standards in assessing moral systems we are stepping outside of morality. We are going beyond the categories of good and evil. A moral system that is farther along one of these dimensions is not more moral. Nor is it any truer. Recall that moral truth comes cheap. The dimensions I have been discussing are largely pragmatic, prudential, and hedonic. An ape or even a psychopath might care about many of these standards.

When Nietzsche said we should move beyond good and evil, he meant that we should return to the standards of assessment that preceded the Christian inversion of Roman values. This is not what I am recommending. But there is a grain of truth in Nietzsche's advice. When revising morality we should keep an eye on all the things we value. Just as we can pit moral norms against each other, we can pit extramoral norms against moral norms. Since we are forced to revise morality from the inside, we should avail ourselves of all resources. Everything we care about is potentially relevant in deciding how to improve our current system of morals.

Using extramoral criteria, it is easy to see that some moral values are suboptimal even from the point of view of those who endorse them. Consider the Tasmanians, one of many cultures where men have had extreme dominance over women (Edgerton, 1992). Tasmanian women were treated as male property and they had to procure the vast majority of food. Women were probably indoctrinated into accepting their lower status, but they certainly would have recognized that this system of values had negative consequences for their well-being. The system of exploitation also made the society vulnerable to devastating instability. When European settlers came, Tasmanian men traded many of their women for dogs. The result was a serious reduction in food supply, since women were the main providers, and a significant increase in violence, since men began to fight more in competition for the remaining women. The Tasmanian story is not unusual. Many societies (including our own) have some values that fuel violence, promote inequality, and deplete valuable resources (Diamond, 2004).

The Tasmanians were ultimately eradicated by European settlers, so they never had an opportunity to revise their values. But one can speculate that as things went from bad to worse, they might have inaugurated a program of moral reform. But notice that values in Tasmania had remained in place for many generations before the settlers arrived. The reason for this is not clear, but it may stem from the fact that men were largely comfortable in Tasmanian society, before they began to sell off the women. Since men had power and men were comfortable, there was little interest in reform. This is a sobering observation, because it suggests that reform will be difficult as long as the people in power are not suffering.

The question arises: can a person who is not suffering detect dysfunctional values and push for reform? Let's consider a test case. Suppose that Smith is a well-to-do, mid-nineteenth-century, white American who believes that it is permissible to have slaves. Smith thinks that people of African descent are inferior, and that slavery is a good way to expose them to Christian values, which will lead to their moral improvement and entitle them to a place in heaven. He also thinks slavery is perfectly fair. Like the ancients, he sees it as a kind of lottery.

If you are unlucky enough to be captured and enslaved, you just have to put up with it, unless of course you escape. Any one could be a slave. Slavery is also necessary, Smith might argue. There must be a division of labor in society, and, to guarantee economic progress, large numbers of people must work without pay.

On reflection, Smith might reconsider his attitudes toward slavery. He might discover that the presumed racial inferiority of Africans is based on bad science, and he'd have to recognize that Christian indoctrination of Africans is possible (for better or worse) without enslavement. Smith might also come to recognize that keeping slaves is inconsistent with other moral values that he practices in daily life. Smith is kind to strangers; he won't beat his dog; he pays his grocer; he rewards people for their merits; he cherishes freedom. It is at least questionable whether slavery can be morally reconciled with these other values. It is also questionable whether slavery is a stable arrangement. Slaves can revolt. It is possible to maintain slave economies for centuries, but other social arrangements may be more stable. In any case, slavery is difficult to maintain. It requires a forced imposition of values on people who are likely to resist very strongly. Slavery also reduces general welfare and well-being. It profoundly reduces the quality of life of the slaves, which conflicts with universality, and it may also reduce the quality of Smith's life, insofar as he is naturally sympathetic to the suffering and moved by the biological predisposition to help people in need.

Smith might also gain perspective by reflecting on the genealogy of the slave trade. Slavery in Europe can be traced back to ancient times when there were military conflicts with other nations, motivated by competition over resources or the desire for new territory. This was the case in Rome, and Roman slavery was not illegalized by the Church; it merely evolved, with economic changes and the waning of imperialism, into the system of indentured servitude and serfdom. Criminals were sometimes sold as slaves. In the Islamic world, slavery continued, and African slaves were taken as domestic workers, concubines, and miners. When the Portuguese came to Africa in search of gold, they adopted the practice of buying slaves in Africa to sell to the Muslims there, who controlled many of the trading ports. In the meantime, settlers in the New World had been enslaving conquered Native Americans to work on farms. The Native Americans proved to be bad slaves because they would often revolt or escape. Imported African slaves were easier to catch when they escaped, because they stood out and didn't know the land, and they were more immune to such deadly diseases as malaria. They also came with impressive skills from their homelands, which had comparatively advanced agriculture and crafts. As agriculture grew in southern states, South America, and the Caribbean islands, the demand for African slaves increased. These slaves initially worked alongside white tenant farmers and were treated similarly, but tenant farming decreased and treatment declined because slaves were cheaper. With the rise of cotton farming after the Revolution, the demand for slaves grew to a fevered pitch. Only a small percentage of southern whites had slaves, but some had such large plantations that black Africans outnumbered whites in many parts of the South. This was used to political advantage, because slaves were counted in the census rolls, giving southern states a large number of Electoral College votes, which increased the chances that US presidents would be friendly to slavery. This history shows that there was an evolution in slavery from the use of vanquished people to the intentional capture of human beings for use as property. This led to a degradation in status for slaves, and increased toleration for grotesque abuse. Slavery continued because it was big business: cotton constituted half the American export trade by the time of the Civil War. By 1808, slave-importing was banned, and the domestic slave trade turned to individuals who were American-born. Slavery had once been a consequence of military defeat, but now slaves were bred like cattle and forced to lead miserable lives of labor so that plantation owners could line their pockets. By the nineteenth century, standard arguments justifying slavery were inapplicable. Romans said slavery was a just system, because slaves were born with equal opportunity and were fairly defeated in battle; but in the Americas, slaves were bred, and they were born into a life of unimaginable oppression. Arguments for the economic necessity of slavery were also losing credibility: by the mid-nineteenth century, there were highly profitable non-slave economies throughout the world, and urban America had a sizable middle class.

Even after reflecting on these things, a nineteenth-century American like Smith probably wouldn't become an abolitionist overnight. He would be in the grip of the view that slavery was morally permissible, and few of the historical facts just outlined speak directly to the morality of slavery. But Smith would probably start to suspect that slavery is bad in an extramoral sense. This change in view would be a first step toward a new set of moral values about slavery—values that Smith would recognize as better. Once he started to form negative emotional attitudes toward slavery on extramoral grounds, he would be primed for moral reconditioning.

This fictional example of moral conversion may correspond to some actual cases. Before the nineteenth century, slavery was regarded by whites as a progressive institution that would allow societal expansion, accumulation of wealth, and a modern economic system based on global trade. In the nineteenth century, moral attitudes changed, and slavery began to look retrograde (Davis, 1984). It would be nice to think that this transition was driven, for some, by a recognition that slavery failed to meet some of the standards that I have been discussing, especially moral consistency. Evidence for the increased recognition of moral inconsistency can be found in the fact that the nineteenth century saw a dramatic rise in efforts to ground racism in science (Gould, 1981). In the American South, religious leaders preached that people of color were products of a separate creation (Fredrickson, 1971). This suggests that people implicitly recognized a tension between their attitudes toward slavery and their beliefs about human dignity. Nevertheless, it would be misleading to say that the opposition to slavery was driven by the kind of reflective process that I attributed to Smith.

In England, opposition to slavery coincided with the industrial revolution, and some scholars have argued that this economic transition sparked the emergence of an ideology that favored wage labor and the hegemony of the middle class (Davis, 1984). In the United States, slavery lagged on a long time. First came a ban on importing slaves, but this may have been motivated by avarice and fear (Bender, 2006). Virginia, the most populous and politically powerful state in the union, was yielding fewer and fewer crops, and Virginians had more to gain financially from selling slaves than from using slaves to farm. They knew they could drive up the value of slaves by illegalizing slave imports. In addition, there had been a massive slave revolt in Haiti (the Haitian revolution) at the turn of the nineteenth century, and leaders in Washington were afraid that slaves imported from that region would spread the word and incite insurrection in America; they banned importation soon after. It took almost fifty more years and a bloody civil war to achieve emancipation, and those who opposed slavery often had questionable reasons. In the South, some opposition to slavery was driven by a desire to increase employment for whites; slaves were seen as taking white jobs. The North had a complicated relationship to slavery, because New York financiers and the New England textile industry benefited from cotton production, but there was also an active abolitionist movement. Abolitionism, Davis (1984) points out, had two forms, secular and religious. The secular arguments focused on the inefficiency of slave labor as compared to wage labor, and the religious abolitionists argued that slavery required slave owners to sin by adopting god-like control over other human beings. It's not clear that either of these positions emerged out of the kind of assessment process that I have been describing. Slavery was clearly recognized to be at odds with some extramoral values, but they were not necessarily the values on my list. Rather, slavery was criticized for economic inefficiency and incompatibility with a Christian conception of human brotherhood. In sum, I don't present my account of how moral values might be changed as an accurate portrayal of how values actually have changed in the past. Rather, I offer the list of extramoral standards as a possible tool for change in the future.

The extramoral methods of assessment on my list could be used to shed light on contemporary controversies. Is it okay to kill and eat animals? Is pornography okay? Is it okay to retain one's entire post-tax income rather than giving large portions away to fight world hunger? Is it okay to have a career that doesn't save lives or reduce suffering? Is it okay to support corporations that promote globalization? Are bans of polygamy morally defensible? Many people would answer affirmatively to these questions. They are consistent with prevailing values. But perhaps our current values are not consistent. Or perhaps other pragmatic and prudential considerations would argue in favor of moral revision. I am not advancing a verdict on any of these issues. I am simply pointing out that moral claims can generally be assessed along the dimensions I have been considering.

The upshot is that there are ways in which we can compare moral claims. We cannot make moral progress by asserting that certain moral claims are *truer* than others; what's false here may be true elsewhere. Nor can we make progress by saying that certain moral values are *morally* better than other moral values; when we say that a moral value is morally good, we simply reveal that we have internalized that value, rather than values that have been internalized by others. Progress requires moving beyond our current moral commitments. To adopt new moral values, it is important to move beyond good and evil. "Moral progress" cannot be interpreted as a transition from one set of values to a morally better set of values. Every time our values change, we see our new values as morally better than our old, but this is an illusion: we no longer embrace the old values, so we see them as bad. To make progress that is not illusory, we seek moral values that are better in an extramoral sense.

8.2 MAKING PROGRESS

8.2.1 Coherent Evil

One worry immediately arises for the proposal that we can measure progress by appeal to extramoral standards. When faced with the discovery that your current values fail to satisfy some extramoral standard, there are usually multiple avenues of revision available. Each possible revision is an improvement, on the proposal that I am peddling, if it does better on one of these standards. For example, if you discover you have two conflicting values, it's an improvement to drop one of them, because that will increase consistency. The problem with this proposal is that this strategy allows for—even encourages—changes that might be pretheoretically regarded as regressive rather than progressive.

Let's consider an example. Most of us believe that all people deserve equal opportunity regardless of sex, but there is empirical evidence that, in spite of this moral conviction, there is rampant bias against women. In one study, Rudman and Kilianski (2000) demonstrated that people unconsciously harbor negative attitudes toward women in authority positions even if they are not aware of those attitudes explicitly; pictures of women in high-status jobs (e.g., doctor) prime negative words, and pictures of women in low-status jobs (e.g., waitress) prime positive words. In another study, Steinpreis et al. (1999) sent out identical job candidate CVs to psychology professors, but they put a male name on some of them and a female name on others; the professors were more than 50 percent more likely to judge that the male candidate was hirable. Suppose you discover that you value gender equality explicitly, but you harbor an implicit bias against women. These values conflict. Using the standard of consistency, you can improve your morality by dropping one of these two values. But which one? If you use extramoral principles, such as consistency, it seems there is no fixed answer to this question. You'd improve your morality equally by working to exorcise your gender bias *or* by abandoning your conviction that we should not discriminate against women. Intuitively, however, these two options are not equally good. One would be an improvement, and the other would be a step backwards.

I think this worry can be addressed by looking at the example more closely. I reject the contention that no extramoral considerations can help us decide between consistent chauvinism and consistent gender egalitarianism. Notice, first, that chauvinism may hinge on false assumptions about differences between the sexes, such as the assumption that women have less aptitude in certain cognitive domains than men. Chauvinism is also harder to universalize than egalitarianism, and it may lead to a decrease in well-being (certainly for women). Genealogical analyses can be used to criticize chauvinism as well. The world's societies differ in how they regard women. Women enjoy very high status and considerable power in some parts of the world, and very low status in others. Harris (1993) argues that the primary determinants of women's status are, genealogically speaking, economic. In societies where physical strength is the basis of material wealth (and hence power and respect), men come out ahead. Where that is not the case, women can gain a greater degree of equality. Consider an example. In West Africa, agriculture was traditionally based on the hand-held hoe, rather than the plow. In India, it was based on the plow. Plows, yokes, and the animals that pull them are very heavy and difficult to handle. In plow economies, men were naturally more capable of producing wealth, and they rose in power. In hoe economies, women can produce as much as men, and consequently, women tend to have more equality in West African societies than they do in India. The exception is Kerala society, in southern India, which has a warmer climate and is thus less dependent on the plow. Moist soil can be farmed without heavy gear, and southern India is dominated by small rice farms. In our contemporary society, we depend on neither hoe nor plow. These constraints on wealth are outmoded. Male chauvinism may be an outgrowth of the fact that the European economy was plow-based early in development. This resulted in men having more money, more control of commerce, more literacy, and more political power. Attitudes of male superiority are based on factors that are no longer relevant. Egalitarianism makes more sense in our economy than male chauvinism.

But this story raises another objection. The last few remarks imply that gross gender inequities were appropriate when we had a plow economy. That is an embarrassing and perhaps offensive suggestion. It also threatens to undermine my claim that we have made moral progress. Chauvinism was appropriate when economic conditions were different, and it is inappropriate now. So, I am forced to say that the move toward greater liberation for women has not been a move forward; it has just been a lateral transition from one good moral system to another equally good moral system.

This objection presupposes that there is nothing else wrong with moral systems that tolerate gender inequities. In many such systems women are denied liberties that have nothing to do with their capacity to farm, and everything to do with men using economic power to secure greater control. The fact that women get lower yield in the fields when plowing does not mean that women should be treated as male property. In such societies where that happens, female well-being is diminished and norms of respect are applied inconsistently. So gender inequity can still be condemned on extramoral grounds. That said, we must distinguish gender inequity from division of labor. Extramoral standards give us tools to criticize societies that discriminate, but they may not have the power to criticize societies in which men and women play different roles. A society that did not oppress women, but simply assigned different economic roles on the basis of gender would not necessarily be worse, in any extramoral sense, than a society that made the same economic options available to men and women. A hunter-gatherer society, where men hunt and women gather, is not necessarily worse than a postindustrial society where most jobs are available to both men and women. I don't think this is a counterintuitive result. It's not obvious that the transition from hunter-gatherer lifestyles to postindustrial lifestyles was a moral improvement. Moral systems are tools for social coordination and, as such, they should be tailored to the varying material conditions of culture.

Still, one might object, I have said nothing to guarantee that an utterly abhorrent system of values couldn't be better, on the standards I have been considering, than a system of values that is humane. There is, after all, room for coherent evil. Those who pursue genocide often construct elaborate moral systems that are more consistent than the liberal moralities they replace (compare Nazi morality to the morality of the Weimar Republic). In response, we need only remind ourselves that coherence isn't everything. A coherent moral system may be better in that respect than a collection of inconsistent values. But it may be far worse in other respects. The assessment standards are not limited to logical constraints. These alone could not distinguish benevolence from brutality. We assess moral progress by appeal to welfare, well-being, universality, and social stability. Genocide is hard to reconcile with these goals. I grant that a wicked society might not be concerned with any of these extramoral values, but we are certainly concerned about these things, and, therefore, we would not regard the adoption of a genocidal value system to be progressive, even if it scored high on the standard of consistency.

We can assess moral systems by asking how well they are suited to providing lives that we would find desirable. Of course, people may vary in what they find desirable, and, hence, in what they regard as moral progress. If I value interpersonal relationships and you value wisdom, then our conceptions of well-being come apart. A moral system better suited to proliferating wisdom at the price of community will strike you as an advance, but it will appear otherwise to me. If standards of progress are evaluative, progress is itself relative. That's fine. The relativist does not need to show that there are absolute standards of progress. The initial challenge was to explain how progress is possible *at all.*

Divergent assessments of progress are commonplace. What the liberal extols as moral maturation, the conservative might regard as moral decay. Some of these debates about progress are intractable. But they are not all intractable. When the liberal and conservative assess progress, they may find common ground in some of the standards I have been discussing. Have our values become more consistent? Has social cohesion been increased? Are we thriving? These are just the sorts of considerations that liberals and conservatives regularly bring to bear when they are having debates about public policy. Relative to a shared set of extramoral values, there may be a fact of the matter about which political outlook promotes the better moral system.

8.2.2 Pitfalls En Route to Progress

There are a number of pitfalls en route to progress. We sometimes think we are making progress when the reverse is true. When embarking on moral reform, it is crucial that we keep that in mind. I will mention four pitfalls here, though there are surely others.

I alluded to the one pitfall earlier, when I referred to a backward-looking sense of progress. From within any moral system, other systems appear immoral. If we look at the values held by our cultural forbearers, they seem defective. In some cases, that impression may be justified, but it is unreliable. The past looks morally defective when viewed through the moral lens of the present. This gives rise to illusions of progress. One example is illustrated in Foucault's (1977) discussion of the penal system. He argues that the transition from public executions to incarceration was not a moral advance motivated by concern for prisoners, but rather a new form of control, driven by a reconceptualization of criminals as abnormal or deviant. Because of the ideological shift that occurred with the rise of the human sciences, we now see past methods of punishment as deeply immoral, while failing to appreciate the oppressive character of contemporary methods. That illusion of progress is hard to escape. Most of us think that we now are in touch with the moral truth. We think those in the past were backward, and we say that those who long for the past are reactionary. This conceit would be defensible if moral progress were an inevitable consequence of history. It is not.

A second pitfall arises when we let ends justify means. It is likely that some of Pol Pot's loyalists were victims of a hideous error when they murdered a large percentage of the Cambodian population. They believed that they could increase harmony and well-being by forcibly creating an agrarian communist state. Killing thousands of "intellectuals" (often just people who wore glasses or spoke two languages) seemed a necessary cost. That cost might have been avoided if the members of the Khmer Rouge had not made a gross miscalculation. In devising their utopian vision, they assumed that people would find life more fulfilling in post-revolutionary Cambodia. They assumed that people would be happy to lead bucolic agrarian lives. But the error in this assumption was instantly manifest. Thousands of people had to be forced to work on farms, and those who resisted were killed. Had Pol Pot's campaign succeeded in creating a communist utopia in Cambodia, would it have been a case of moral progress? Perhaps. Killing all your opponents is a bloody shortcut to social stability. But the mass executions of the Khmer Rouge probably qualified as evil by the standards of those who carried them out. If we apply the standards that I have been discussing to means as well as ends, we can see that brutality in the service of good is a kind of moral inconsistency. By the same token, we can look back with hindsight on the various acts of genocide against the indigenous populations of the Americas and Australasia and ask whether our comfortable lives now justify what European colonizers did in the past. There is a collective sense of guilt associated with these old atrocities, and, while we may feel that we've made great progress in terms of well-being and stability, we are deeply bothered, I hope, by the moral hypocrisy of our achievement.

The third pitfall is that we may become corrupt. To see how easily this can happen, consider a classic study in social psychology (Haney et al., 1973). In 1971, Philip Zimbardo and his collaborators paid a small group of college students to participate in a role-playing "prison" experiment at Stanford, in which some would play guards and others would play prisoners. After six days, the planned two-week experiment had to be stopped because the students acting as guards had become seriously abusive. They humiliated prisoners, stripped them, had them simulate sex acts, deprived them of food, put them in solitary confinement, and made them urinate and defecate in buckets. Those very students would have condemned abusive behavior before the experiment, but the situation led them unwittingly to abandon their values. Eerily similar abuses occurred in the Abu Ghraib military prison in Iraq. This is a sober reminder of the fact that moral corrosion is often easier than moral improvement. Progress requires vigilance.

The final pitfall is that we are always in danger of viewing morality as immutable. When we regard moral rules as objective and unassailable, we forget that moral progress is possible. One prophylactic strategy is to view morality instrumentally. It is a way a securing other goals, such as social cohesion, welfare, and well-being. It is difficult to view morality instrumentally, because our sentiments present our basic moral values to us as if they were intrinsically good. If we remember that morality is a tool and not a window into absolute truth, we can be open to the possibility of moral growth. We would be wise to recalibrate our sentiments regularly with extramoral standards.

Assessing progress is hard. I may even have fallen prey to these pitfalls myself in this chapter. With talk of slavery, women's rights, and colonialism, I have given the impression that the morality in the present is an improvement over the morality of the past. I've implied that we have moved unequivocally forward, and I have not emphasized ways in which we can do better. This is troubling because it implies a deep vulnerability to self-deception about progress. When we reason about whether things have improved and whether further improvement is possible, we are subject to the confirmation bias: a tendency to cherry-pick evidence that will support our current convictions.

Against this very serious concern, I can only urge hard labor. We must constantly remind ourselves that our values are not reflections of an absolute truth which, like items in a science text book, have been uncovered through careful investigation over time. Morals are inculcated, and often shaped, as Nietzsche would say, by power struggles and happenstance. Reminding ourselves of this deep contingency of morality is just a first step. We must also subject our values, including those we treasure, to rigorous reconsideration in light of extramoral concerns. For example, we should examine our attitudes toward democracy, capitalism, free speech, punishment, marriage, and infanticide. Conservatives and liberals should both explore the possibility that their values are the result of inculcation, and those who criticize the values of others should examine their own complicity in contributing to the world's woes. I won't embark on this exercise of self-examination here. There is a long line of radical reformers who have tried to shake people from complacency and instigate moral revolutions. Some of these reformers (Marx and Nietzsche, for example) have met with mixed success, but others had considerable impact on the conscience of people living in the Western world (leaders of the civil rights movement and the women's movement come to mind). Relativists who believe in progress must be open to the possibility that current values can be improved.

8.2.3 Progress and Normative Ethics

In earlier chapters, I expressed doubts about prevailing normative ethical theories, including theories advanced by Kant, Mill, and Aristotle. Ironically, all three have resurfaced in my standards of assessment for morality. I said that we want our moral rules to be as universal as possible; this is a central tenet of Kant's program. I also said that we prefer rules that increase welfare; this echoes the Millian concern with utility. I also invoked the broader construct of well-being; this is a modern word for Aristotle's notion of *eudaimonia*, which lies at the center of his conception of a virtuous life. The invocation of these ideas may cast doubt on my earlier remarks about Kant, Mill, and Aristotle. The theories that I was very quick to dismiss are now being used to decide which moral rules are best. Up until now, the protagonists of this story have been Hume and Nietzsche. It would be embarrassing to discover that Kant, Mill, and Aristotle are really running the show. Let me explain why this isn't the case.

First, it is important to see that Hume and Nietzsche are doing something very different from Kant, Mill, and Aristotle. Hume is providing an account of what it is to value something morally, and Nietzsche is offering an account of where our current values come from. Both projects are descriptive. Hume's is psychological, and Nietzsche's is a blend of psychology and history. Kant, Mill, and Aristotle are offering normative theories: theories of what we should value. In this sense, their contributions are compatible with Humean moral psychology and Nietzschean genealogy. Hume says that to value something morally is to have a sentiment of approbation toward it. Nietzsche tells us how our current sentiments came to be. Kant, Mill, and Aristotle are telling us what we should value instead. They may have believed that we already do value duty, utility, and *eudaimonia*, but it is debatable whether they need to make such descriptive claims. Indeed, such descriptive claims are not incompatible with the descriptive claims made by Nietzsche and Hume.

It is also important to see that the standards of assessment that I have been discussing are different from the standards urged by Kant, Mill, and Aristotle, even if there is some resemblance. I speculated that many moralizers have a preference for rules that are more universal. This does not entail Kant's claim that morality should be based on principles of practical rationality and that universalization provides the crucial test for moral permissibility. My suggestion that people want rules that increase welfare falls short of Mill's maxim that utility is the final arbiter of the good. And unlike Aristotle's *eudaimonia*, my appeal to well-being has no essential link to the notion of virtue. I also remarked that conceptions of well-being may vary; they are not dictated by human nature. My standards of assessment are, at best, pale shadows of these elaborate normative theories, or perhaps they are the seeds that give normative theories their intuitive appeal.

In addition, my invocations of universality, welfare, and well-being are not intended as categorical norms. I have not provided an argument for the claim that these are absolute standards that anyone must accept. I am first and foremost making a descriptive claim, subject to empirical test, that these are standards by which we would judge one set of values to be better than another. In so doing, I am demonstrating that moral progress is intelligible within a relativist framework. Were I to make any normative claim about these standards—were I to recommend them—it would be an expression of the fact that I accept these standards, and of the hope that you accept them too. Unlike classic normative theories, I think the normative claims must always be made from within a value system. We cannot find a transcendental litmus test for morality.

Another difference between the account of moral progress that I am advancing and prevailing theories in normative ethics is that I think the standards by which moral progress is judged are not themselves moral standards. It is important for progress that we can step outside morality. Otherwise, our current values would always dictate our moral preferences, and progress would be impossible.

Therefore when I say, for example, that we prefer moral theories that lead to greater well-being, I am not making a moral claim. Well-being is neither necessary nor sufficient for moral goodness. Someone who does something that results in great happiness has not necessarily done a morally good thing, and someone can do the morally good thing (i.e., do something that we regard with moral approbation) even though it does not bring about happiness. Likewise for the "goods" put forward in classical normative theories. I am claiming that these are extramoral goods. They reside outside of morality, though they can be used to improve morality.

In addition, I would reject the claim that any of the goods put forward by classical normative theories is foundational. None is the source from which all other goods flow. More generally, I don't think any of the standards of assessment that I have been discussing is more fundamental than the others. Nor do I think that these standards of assessment are more fundamental than the moral rules that they assess. Moral rules are not derived from these standards. It assessing moral theories, as in doing science, we must be holistic. We must keep all of our values in view, we must know where they stand in relation to our web of moral convictions, and we must bear in mind the extramoral principles that matter to us as well. Some moral principles are more basic than others, insofar as some are general principles and others are applications. But, when it comes to the revision of the general principles (our grounding norms), all of our convictions, moral and non-moral, are potentially relevant. And, just as extramoral principles might be used to revise morality, moral principles might weigh in as we revise our extramoral values.

This holism goes hand in hand with pluralism. All too often moral philosophers seek to reduce morality to a single principle. Doing that would be a breathtaking achievement. The great normative theories are stunningly elegant and ambitious. Indeed, they are ambitious to a fault. Human morality is multifaceted. We have a range of different rules that cannot be unified under any single principle. Most philosophers focus on rules having to do with harms, justice, or rights. These are all different constructs, and they are only a fraction of the moral pie. They all belong to the ethics of autonomy, in Shweder et al.'s (1997) phrase, leaving out the domains of community and divinity/nature. Shweder believes that autonomy norms have taken on special prominence in Western individualist cultures. Collectivist cultures, such as those in the Far East, may place comparatively more emphasis on community norms, including those that have to do with rank. Non-secular societies emphasize community too, and also place emphasis on rules pertaining to religious and sexual purity. Rules pertaining to rank and sex are less salient to us, but they certainly exist. They cannot be captured under the rubric of autonomy without considerable contrivance. Some philosophers would have us believe that rules of rank and sex are not bona fide moral rules because they cannot be justified by appeal to prohibitions against harm or other principles of autonomy. But this attitude is a form of moral myopia, brought on by Western individualism and socialization in professional philosophy. Moral domains outside autonomy have fallen off the cultural radar even though they exercise considerable influence on our daily lives. We live in a world of class, authority, and norms of respect. We form our most intimate relationships on the basis of kinship rules and norms of sexual propriety. The morality of daily life may have more to do with these things than with harms, rights, and justice. We need moral theories to be more inclusive. Philosophers end up being overly parochial by ignoring moral values that they consider too parochial.

The pluralism that I have been describing is a pluralism of moral domains. Within those domains, there is also likely to be a pluralism of rules. For example, we have multiple sexual mores (incest, bestiality, necrophilia, public masturbation, etc.) that cannot be reduced to one overarching taboo. Each rule has its own biocultural history. Broad principles are likely to be an outgrowth of specific rules, rather than the converse. In addition to a plurality of moral domains and moral rules, I have advocated a plurality of standards of assessments for morality. There is no single litmus test for moral progress. We can find pale shadows of Kant, Mill, and Aristotle in the litany of standards by which progress is assessed, but we cannot find any way to tie these shadows together. The imperialistic ambition of these authors has no place in the present account of moral progress.

In sum, classic normative ethical theories are not vindicated by anything I've said, nor are they refuted. These theories stand as worthy recommendations for action. Perhaps a steady commitment to moral progress will ultimately lead us to adopt some components of the classic theories. Adoption of Kantian, Millian, or Aristotelian ethics might count as moral progress by the standards I have enumerated. Perhaps moral values will evolve to incorporate lessons from these approaches. But I doubt that any culture will ever succeed in inculcating pure Kantian, Millian, or Aristotelian values. Human life is too varied, and morality is too complex, to be guided by such streamlined ethics.

8.2.4 Should We Forgo Morality?

In the scheme I have been discussing, there are two levels of evaluation. At one level, we have moral values. These are defined by moral sentiments and the constituent moral emotions. At another level, we have extramoral values. I haven't said much about how these are implemented, but it is easy enough to imagine a collection of goals, desires, preferences, and theoretical decision procedures that weigh certain features above others. I have been suggesting that extramoral values can play a key role guiding moral change. And this raises an important question: Why bother with morality at all? Can't we get by with our extramoral values? Isn't the moral layer unnecessary?

On one reading, Nietzsche can be interpreted as recommending that we abandon morality, and replace it with something else. I tend to read him as suggesting that we replace one morality with a superior morality, but both interpretations find textual support. More surprisingly, one can read Kant, Mill, and Aristotle as recommending a flight from morality. If the meaning of "morality" is captured by our everyday use of moralizing terms such as "good" and "evil" or "right" and "wrong," then the classic normative ethicists are recommending an alternative. I have argued that ordinary moral vocabulary is linked essentially to the sentiments. Moral terms of praise and blame express emotional dispositions. Traditional normative ethicists tend to be skeptical about approbation and disapprobation. They think sentiments are bad guides to conduct. Instead, we should act in accordance with duty, utility maximization, or virtue. All of these things are very hard to do, and the demands they place on us are often counterintuitive. The fact that there can be a clash between ordinary moral intuitions and the demands of normative ethics is an indication that normative ethics is in the business of usurping morality. If that is the case, then leading figures in the history of normative ethics align with Nietzsche. They are radical revisionists.

I doubt we could simply abandon morality if we tried. Moral sentiments may be inevitable products of human psychology, and moral rules are deeply entrenched. But suppose we could somehow eliminate them. Should we? I don't think so. Moral sentiments serve a number of important functions.

For one thing, moral sentiments play a key role in *motivation*. When we judge that something is good, we are motivated to act because we are disposed to feel certain motivating emotions. Of special import are the punitive emotions. The threat of guilt and shame help us resist temptations. Anger, contempt, and disgust help regulate the behavior of others. Without morality, rules of conduct might become dispassionate, and dispassionate rules are easy to ignore. Consider the rule against jaywalking. We all know that this rule exists and it comes to mind every time we walk against the light, but, for many of us, it has no motivational impact. Rules that are not sentimentally grounded are not especially effective in guiding conduct.

Second, the *transmission* of rules is greatly facilitated by moral sentiments. We can get our children to conform to operative norms by conditioning their emotions. Rules based on anything other than sentiments are harder to pass on. Emotions command attention and facilitate memory. They serve as punishments and rewards. If we simply gave our children books of rules, I suspect that they would have a hard time learning what morality requires of them, and an even harder time learning to conform.

A third closely related point is that moral sentiments can be used to *internalize* rules. By training our sentiments, conduct that would not otherwise appeal to us begins to seem natural and automatic. Morality becomes a central part of our self-conceptions. We identify with moral rules, and we like to affiliate with people whose values are similar to our own. Dispassionate beliefs tend not to be internalized in this way. We can lose beliefs without losing our sense of self.

Fourth, moral sentiments allow us to *extend* morality. Through sentimental education, the welfare of other people becomes a matter of personal concern. The idea of moral extension relates to Hume's conception of artificial virtues (Hume, 1739: III.ii). According to Hume, we are naturally disposed to be benevolent, but our natural benevolence is constrained by self-love, and reserved for those who are close to us, similar to us, or who have qualities that we happen to value. We are not naturally benevolent to strangers and, thus, have no natural bias against stealing their property when it suits us. On reflection, however, this would be a bad idea. If we did not respect the property rights of others, they wouldn't respect ours. Thus, we would ultimately lose out in a society that tolerated theft. We benefit from rules protecting property ownership (what Hume call's "justice") along with other rules, such as promise-keeping, that are unnatural. Self-love drives us to create such artificial rules. We cultivate moral sentiments toward justice, because we know that it is in our interest to do so. Hume does not fully explain how these sentiments are cultivated in the first place, but he suggests that parents can teach children to love justice, to condemn promise-breakers, and so on. Had Hume been more cynical, he might have realized that some artificial virtues do not originate in the recognition that certain unnatural rules are beneficial. Some may emerge, as Nietzsche suggested, through power struggles and historical happenstance. But the core idea in Hume's account of artificial virtues seems right. Many of our rules involve the application of sentiments to things that would not naturally elicit approbation or disapprobation. Sentiments are valuable because they can be extended to new cases.

For these reasons, I think it would be disastrous to abandon the moral sentiments that constitute morality. If we could replace our passionate rules with cool principles, there would be hideous consequences. Suppose we could take pills that eliminate anger, contempt, disgust, guilt, and shame. We might initially be relieved to be rid of these unpleasant emotions. But, in so doing, we would lose our motivation to avoid antisocial behavior, we would undermine our capacity to transmit rules easily, we would eliminate our self-conceptions as moral agents, and we would risk becoming indifferent to the needs of distant others. Moral sentiments are like a vaccine that protects us from virulent psychopathy.

It is time to take stock. I have been defending constructivist sentimentalism, which is a form of sensibility theory according to which moral facts are products of our moral rules, moral rules are constituted by sentiments, and sentiments are established through biocultural interactions. Because morality is a construction, it is possible for us to take the reins. We can exert some control in determining the course of moral change. Once we recognize that morality exists to serve our wants and needs, we can try to adjust current morals so that they serve us better. We cannot do this from a transcendental position. We have to use our current values to guide us. But moral values cannot be used to guide moral change, because moral values are self-affirming; we always think our current convictions are noble. To make moral progress, we need to consult our extramoral values. Extramoral values cannot illuminate the path to a single true morality, but they can help us see how our current values fail to achieve ends that matter to us greatly. It might be tempting to dispense with morality and let extramoral values guide behavior without recruiting moral sentiments. That would be a grave mistake. Sentiments are better suited for the regulation of behavior than any dispassionate alternative. They are the safeguard against vicious indifference.

References

Adams, R. M. (1976). Motive Utilitarianism. *Journal of Philosophy*, 73: 467–81.

Albert, E. M. (1963). Women of Burundi: A Study of Social Values. In D. Paulme (ed.), *Women of Tropical Africa*, pp. 179–216. London: Routledge & Kegan Paul.

Alexander, R. D. (1987). *The Biology of Moral Systems*. Hawthorn, NY: Aldine De Gruyter.

Allison, A. (2000). *Permitted and Prohibited Desires: Mothers, Comics and Censorship in Japan*. Berkeley, CA: University of California Press.

Almroth, L., Elmusharaf, S., El Hadi, N., Obeid, A., El Sheikh, M. A., Elfadil, S. M., and Bergström, S. (2005). Primary Infertility after Genital Mutilation in Girlhood in Sudan: A Case-Control Study. *The Lancet*, 366: 385–91.

American Psychiatric Association. (1994). *Diagnostic and Statistical Manual of Mental Disorders* (4th edn.). Washington, DC: American Psychiatric Association.

Annas, J. (2003). Virtue Ethics and Social Psychology. *A Priori*, 2: 20–59.

Anscombe, G. E. M. (1957). *Intention*. Oxford : Blackwell.

Arens, W. F. (1979). *The Man-Eating Myth: Anthropology and Anthropophagy*. New York, NY: Oxford University Press.

Aristotle, (350 BCE/1988). *The Nicomachean Ethics*, trans. D. Ross, ed. J. L. Ackrill and J. O. Urmson, Oxford: Oxford University Press.

Arnold, M. B. (1960). *Emotion and Personality*. New York, NY: Columbia University Press.

Arsenio, W. F., and Lover, A. (1995). Children's Conceptions of Sociomoral Affect: Happy Victimizers, Mixed Emotions and Other Expectancies. In M. Killen and D. Hart (eds.) *Morality in Everyday Life: Developmental Perspectives*, pp. 87–128. Cambridge: Cambridge University Press.

Audi, R. (2004). *The Good in the Right: A Theory of Intuition and Intrinsic Value*. Princeton, NJ: Princeton University Press.

Ayer, A. J. (1952). *Language, Truth, and Logic*. New York, NY: Dover

Bagemihl. B. (1999). *Biological Exuberance: Animal Homosexuality and Natural Diversity*. New York, NY: St. Martin's Press.

Baier, K. (1967). Fact, Value, and Norm in Stevenson's Ethics. *Noûs*, 1: 139–60.

Baille, J. (2000). *Hume on Morality*. London: Routledge.

Bamshad, M., Kivisild, T., Watkins, W. S., Dixon, M. E., Ricker, C. E., Rao, B. B., Naidu, M. J., Prasad, R. B. V., Reddy, G. P., Rasanayagam, A., Papiha, S. S., Villems, R., Redd, A. J., Hammer, M. F., Nguyen, S. V., Carroll, M. L., Batzer, M. A., and Jorde, L. B. (2001). Genetic Evidence on the Origins of Indian Caste Populations. *Genome Research*, 11: 994–1004.

Barrett, K. C., Zahn-Waxler, C., and Cole, P. M. (1993). Avoiders Versus Amenders: Implication for the Investigation of Guilt and Shame During Toddlerhood? *Cognition and Emotion*, 7: 481–505.

Baumeister, R. F., Stillwell, A. M., and Heatherton, T. F. (1994). Guilt: An Interpersonal Approach. *Psychological Bulletin*, 115: 243–67.

Bender, T. (2006). *A Nation among Nations: America's Place in World History*. New York, NY: Hill and Wang.

Bennett, R. L., Motulsky, A. G., Bittles, A., Hudgins, L., Uhrich, S., Doyle, D. L., Silvey, K., Scott, C. R., Cheng, E., Mcgillivray, B., Steiner, R. D., and Olsen, D. (2002). Genetic Counseling and Screening of Consanguineous Couples and their Offspring: Recommendations of the National Society of Genetic Counselors. *Journal of Genetic Counseling*, 11: 97–119.

Ben-Ze'ev, A. (2000). *The Subtlety of Emotions*. Cambridge, MA: MIT Press.

Berman, J. J., Murphy-Berman, V. A., and Singh, P. (1985). Cross-Cultural Similarities and Differences in Perceptions of Fairness. *Journal of Cross-Cultural Psychology*, 16: 55–67.

Berthoz, S., Armony, J. L., Blair, R. J. R., and Dolan, R. J. (2002). An fMRI Study of Intentional and Unintentional (Embarrassing) Violations of Social Norms. *Brain*, 125: 1696–1708.

Bittles, A. H. (1990). Consanguineous Marriage: Current Global Incidence and Its Relevance to Demographic Research. Research Report No. 90–186, Population Studies Center, University of Michigan.

Black. J. B., and Bern, H. (1981). Causal Inference and Memory for Events in Narratives. *Journal of Verbal Learning and Verbal Behavior*, 20: 267–75.

Blackburn, S. (1980). Opinions and Chances. In D. H. Mellor (ed.), *Prospects for Pragmatism*, pp. 175–96. Cambridge: Cambridge University Press.

——(1984). *Spreading the Word: Groundings in the Philosophy of Language*. Oxford: Oxford University Press.

——(1985). Errors and the Phenomenology of Value. In T. Honderich (ed.), *Morality and Objectivity*. London: Routledge & Kegan Paul.

——(1988). Attitudes and Contents. *Ethics*, 98: 501–17.

——(1998). *Ruling Passions*. Oxford: Oxford University Press.

Blair, R. J. R. (1995). A Cognitive Developmental Approach to Morality: Investigating the Psychopath. *Cognition*, 57: 1–29.

——(1997). Moral Reasoning and the Child with Psychopathic Tendencies. *Personality and Individual Differences*, 26: 731–9.

Blair, R. J. R., Colledge, E., Murray, L., and Mitchell, D. G. (2001). A Selective Impairment in the Processing of Sad and Fearful Expressions in Children With Psychopathic Tendencies. *Journal of Abnormal Child Psychology*, 29: 491–8.

Blair, R. J. R., Jones, L., Clark, F., and Smith, M. (1997). The Psychopathic Individual: A Lack of Responsiveness to Distress Cues? *Psychophysiology*, 34: 192–8.

Blass, T. (2004). *The Man Who Shocked the World: The Life and Legacy of Stanley Milgram*. New York, NY: Basic Books.

Blurton-Jones, N. G. (1987). Tolerated Theft: Suggestions About the Ecology and Evolution of Sharing, Hoarding, and Scrounging. *Social Science Information*, 26: 31–54.

Boswell, J. (1980). *Christianity, Social Tolerance and Homosexuality*. Chicago, IL: University of Chicago Press.

Boswell, J. (1994). *Same-Sex Unions in Pre-Modern Europe*. New York, NY: Villard Press.

Boyd, R. N. (1988). How to be a Moral Realist. In G. Sayre-Mccord (ed.), *Essays on Moral Realism*. Ithaca, NY: Cornell University Press.

Boyd, R., and Richerson, P. J. (1985). *Culture and the Evolutionary Process*. Chicago, IL: University of Chicago Press.

—————— (2001). Memes: Universal Acid or a Better Mouse Trap. In R. Aunger (ed.), *Darwinizing Culture: The Status of Memetics as a Science* (pp. 143–62). Oxford: Oxford University Press.

Boyd, R., Gintis, H., Bowles, S., and Richerson, P. J. (2003). The Evolution of Altruistic Punishment. *Proceedings of the National Academy of Sciences*, 100: 3531–5.

Boyer, P., and Ramble, C. (2001). Cognitive Templates for Religious Concepts: Cross-Cultural Evidence for Recall of Counter-Intuitive Representations *Cognitive Science*, 25: 535–64.

Brandt, R. B. (1954). The Definition of an 'Ideal Observer' in Ethics. *Philosophy and Phenomenological Research*, 15: 407–13.

—— (1967). Ethical Relativism. In P. Edwards (ed.). *Encyclopedia of Philosophy*, vol. 3, pp. 75–8. New York, NY: Macmillan.

Brink, D. (1989). *Moral Realism and the Foundations of Ethics*. Cambridge: Cambridge University Press.

Brogaard, B. (forthcoming). Moral Contextualism and Moral Relativism. *The Philosophical Quarterly*.

Brosnan, S. F., and De Waal, F. B. M. (2003). Monkeys Reject Unequal Pay. *Nature*, 425: 297–9.

Burkert, W. (1983). *Homo Necans: the Anthropology of Ancient Greek Sacrificial Ritual and Myth*, trans. P. Bing. Berkeley, CA: University of California Press.

Buss, A. H. (1989). Personality as Traits. *American Psychologist*, 44: 1378–88.

Buss, D. M. (2000). *The Dangerous Passion: Why Jealousy Is as Necessary as Love and Sex*. New York, NY: Simon & Schuster.

Buss, D. M., Larsen, R. J., Westen, D., and Semmelroth, J. (1992). Sex Differences in Jealousy: Evolution, Physiology, and Psychology. *Psychological Science*, 3: 251–5.

Buunk, B. P., Angleitner, A., Oubaid, V., and Buss, D. M. (1996). Sex Differences in Jealousy in Evolutionary and Cultural Perspective: Tests From the Netherlands, Germany, and the United States. *Psychological Science*, 7: 359–63.

Cappelen, H., and Lepore, E. (2005). *Insensitive Semantics*. Oxford: Blackwell.

Carlsmith, J. M., and Gross, A. E. (1969). Some Effects of Guilt on Compliance. *Journal of Personality and Social Psychology*, 11: 232–9.

Carlsmith, J. M., Darley, J. M., and Robinson, P. H. (2002). Why Do We Punish? Deterrence and Just Deserts as Motives for Punishment. *Journal of Personality and Social Psychology*, 83: 284–99.

Carrasco, D. (1999) *City of Sacrifice: The Aztec Empire and the Role of Violence in Civilization*. Boston, MA: Beacon Press.

Caughlin, J. P, Huston, T. L., and Houts, R. M. (2000). How Does Personality Matter in Marriage? Anxiety, Interpersonal Negativity and Marital Satisfaction. *Journal of Personality and Social Psychology*, 78: 326–36.

Chagnon, N. A. (1968). *Yanomamö: The Fierce People*. New York, NY: Holt, Rinehart and Winston.

Cleckley, H. M. (1941). *The Mask of Sanity: An Attempt to Reinterpret the So-Called Psychopathic Personality*. St Louis, MO: The C. V. Mosby Company.

Coale, A. J., and Banister, J. (1994). Five Decades of Missing Females in China. *Demography*, 31: 459–79.

Coe, C. L., and Rosenblum, L. A. (1984). Male Dominance in the Bonnet Macaque: A Malleable Relationship. In P. Barchas and S. P. Mendoza (eds.), *Social Cohesion: Essays toward a Sociophysiological Perspective*, pp. 31–64. Westport, CT: Greenwood Press.

Cohen, A. B., and Rozin, P. (2001). Religion and the Morality of Mentality. *Journal of Personality and Social Psychology*, 81: 697–710.

Cohen, D., and Nisbett, R. E. (1994). Self-Protection and the Culture of Honor: Explaining Southern Violence. *Personality and Social Psychology Bulletin*, 20/5: 551–67.

Colby, A., Kohlberg, L., Gibbs, J., and Lieberman, M. (1983). A Longitudinal Study of Moral Judgment. *Monographs of the Society for Research in Child Development*, 48, nos. 1–2.

Cooper, D. (1978). Moral Relativism. *Midwest Studies in Philosophy*, 3: 97–108.

Cosmides, L. (1989). The Logic of Social Exchange: Has Natural Selection Shaped How Humans Reason? Studies with the Wason Selection Task. *Cognition*, 31: 187–276.

Cosmides, L., and Tooby, J. (1992). Cognitive Adaptations for Social Exchange. In J. H. Barkow, L. Cosmides, and J. Tooby (eds.), *the Adapted Mind: Evolutionary Psychology and the Generation of Culture*, pp. 163–228. New York, NY: Oxford University Press.

Cosmides, L., and Tooby, J. (1997). *Evolutionary Psychology Primer*. Http://www.psych.ucsb.edu/research/cep/primer.html

Costa, P., and Mccrae, R. (1992). *Revised NEO Personality Inventory (NEO-PI-R) and NEO Five Factor Inventory (NEO-FFI): Professional Manual*. Odessa, FL: Psychological Assessment Resources.

Crimmins, M. (1989). Having Ideas and Having the Concept. *Mind and Language*, 4: 280–94.

D'Arms, J., and Jacobson, D. (2000). Sentiment and Value. *Ethics*, 110: 722–48.

———— (2006). Sensibility Theory and Projectivism. In D. Copp (ed.), *the Oxford Handbook of Ethical Theory*, pp. 186–218. New York: Oxford University Press.

Damasio, A. R. (1994). *Descartes' Error: Emotion, Reason, and the Human Brain*. New York, NY: Gossett/Putnam.

Damasio, A. R., and Van Hoesen, G. W. (1983). Emotional Disturbances Associated With Focal Lesions of the Limbic Frontal Lobe. In K. M. Heilman and P. Satz (eds.), *Neuropsychology of Human Emotion*. New York, NY: Guilford Press.

Darby, B. W., and Jeffers, D. (1988). The Effects of Defendant and Juror Attractiveness on Simulated Courtroom Trial Decisions. *Social Behavior and Personality*, 16: 39–50.

Darley, J. M., and Batson, C. D. (1973). From Jerusalem to Jericho: A Study of Situational and Dispositional Variables in Helping Behavior. *Journal of Personality and Social Psychology*, 27: 100–8.

Darwall, S. (1998). Empathy, Sympathy, Care. *Philosophical Studies*, 89: 261–82.

Darwall, S., Gibbard, A., and Railton, P. (1992). Toward Fin De Siècle Ethics: Some Trends, *Philosophical Review*, 101: 115–89.

Davidson, D. (1974). On the Very Idea of a Conceptual Scheme. *Proceedings and Addresses of the American Philosophical Association*, 47: 5–20.

—— (1975). Thought and Talk. In S. Guttenplan (ed.), *Mind and Language*, pp. 7–24. Oxford: Oxford University Press.

Davidson, R. J., and Irwin, W. (1999). The Functional Neuroanatomy of Emotion and Affective Style. *Trends in Cognitive Sciences*, 3: 11–21.

Davies, J. G. V., and Maliphant, R. (1971). Autonomic Responses of Male Adolescents Exhibiting Refractory Behavior in School. *Journal of Child Psychology and Psychiatry*, 12: 115–27.

Davis, D. B. (1984). Slavery and Human Progress. New York, NY: Oxford University Press.

Davis, D. L., and Whitten, R. G. (1987). The Cross-Cultural Study of Human Sexuality. *Annual Review of Anthropology*, 16: 69–98.

Dawkins, R. (1976). *The Selfish Gene*. Oxford: Oxford University Press.

De Gelder, B., Vroomen, J., Pourtois, G., and Weiskrantz, L. (1999). Non-Conscious Recognition of Affect in the Absence of Striate Cortex. *Neuroreport*, 10: 3759–63.

De Waal, F. B. M. (1996). *Good Natured: The Origins of Right and Wrong in Humans and Other Animals*. Cambridge, MA: Harvard University Press.

—— (2000). Primates: A Natural Heritage of Conflict Resolution. *Science*, 289: 586–90.

—— (1997). The Chimpanzee's Service Economy: Food for Grooming. *Evolution and Human Behavior*, 18: 375–86.

De Waal, F. B. M., and Lanting, F. (1997) *Bonobo: The Forgotten Ape*. Berkeley, CA: University of California Press.

DeGusta, D. (1999). Fijian Cannibalism: Osteological Evidence from Navatu. *American Journal of Physical Anthropology*, 110: 215–41.

Dennett, D. C. (1991). Lovely and Suspect Qualities. In Enrique Villanueva (ed.), *Consciousness*, pp. 37–43. Atascadero, CA: Ridgeview.

—— (1995). *Darwin's Dangerous Idea*. New York, NY: Simon and Schuster.

DeSteno, D. A., Bartlett, M. Y., Salovey, P., and Braverman, J. (2002). Sex Differences in Jealousy: Evolutionary Mechanism or Artifact of Measurement? *Journal of Personality and Social Psychology*, 83, 1103–16.

Diamond, J. (2004). *Collapse: How Societies Choose to Fail or Succeed*. New York, NY: Viking Press.

Diener, E., and Oishi, S. (2003). Are Scandinavians Happier Than Asians? Issues in Comparing Nations on Subjective Well-Being. In F. Columbus (ed.), *Politics and Economics of Asia*, vol. 15, pp. 187–219. Hauppauge, NY: Nova Science Publishers.

Diener, E., Oishi, S., and Lucas, R. E. (2003). Personality, Culture, and Subjective Well-Being: Emotional and Cognitive Evaluations of Life. *Annual Review of Psychology*, 54: 403–25.

Diener, E., Scollon, C. N., and Lucas, R. E. (2004). The Evolving Concept of Subjective Well-Being: The Multifaceted Nature of Happiness. In P. T. Costa and I. C. Siegler (eds.), *Advances in Cell Aging and Gerontology*, vol. 15, pp. 187–220. Amsterdam: Elsevier.

Dion, K., Berscheid, E., and Walster, E. (1972). What Is Beautiful Is Good. *Journal of Personality and Social Psychology*, 24: 285–90.

Doris, J. M. (1998). Persons, Situations and Virtue Ethics. *Noûs*, 32: 504–30.

—— (2002). *Lack of Character*. Cambridge: Cambridge University Press.

Downing, F. G. (1972). Ways of Deriving "Ought" From "Is". *The Philosophical Quarterly*, 22: 234–47.

Dreier, J. (1990). Internalism and Speaker Relativism. *Ethics*, 101: 6–26.

—— (2006). Was Moore A Moorean? In T. Horgan and M. Timmons (eds.), *The Legacy of G. E. Moore: 100 Years of Metaethics*. Oxford: Oxford University Press.

Dretske, F. I. (1988). *Explaining Behavior: Reasons in a World of Causes*. Cambridge, MA: MIT Press.

Dwyer, S. J (1999). Moral Competence. In K. Murasugi and R. Stainton (eds.), *Philosophy and Linguistics*, pp. 169–90. Boulder, CO: Westview Press.

Edgerton, R. B. (1971). *The Individual in Cultural Adaptation: A Study of Four East African Peoples*. Berkeley, CA: University of California Press.

—— (1992). *Sick Societies: Challenging the Myth of Primitive Harmony*. New York, NY: The Free Press.

Ehrlich, P. R. (2000). *Human Natures: Genes, Cultures, and the Human Prospect*. Washington D.C.: Island Press.

Eisenberg, N. (2000). Emotion, Regulation, and Moral Development. *Annual Review of Psychology*, 51: 665–97.

Ekman, P. (1972). Universals and Cultural Differences in Facial Expressions of Emotion. In J. Cole (ed.), *Nebraska Symposium on Motivation 1971*, pp. 207–83. Lincoln, NE: University of Nebraska Press.

Ekman, P., and Friesen, W. V. (1986). A New Pan Cultural Facial Expression of Emotion. *Motivation and Emotion*, 10: 159–68.

Erasmus, D. (1530/1985). *On Good Manners for Boys*. In B. Mcgregor (trans.) and J. Sowlands (ed.), *Collected Works of Erasmus*, vol. 25. Toronto: University of Toronto Press.

Ehrlich, P. R. (2000). *Human Natures: Genes, Cultures, and the Human Prospect*. Washington D.C.: Island Press.

Fehr, E., and Gächter, S. (2002). Altruistic Punishment in Humans. *Nature*, 415: 137–40.

Firth, R. (1952). Ethical Absolutism and the Ideal Observer. *Philosophy and Phenomenological Research*, 12: 317–45.

Flanagan, O. (1991). *Varieties of Moral Personality: Ethics and Psychological Realism*. Cambridge, MA: Harvard University Press.

Fodor, J. A. (1975). *The Language of Thought*. New York, NY: Cromwell.

—— (1990). *A Theory of Content*. Cambridge, MA: MIT Press.

Fogas, J. P., and Bower, G. H. (1987). Mood Effects on Personal Perception Judgments. *Journal of Personality and Social Psychology*, 51: 53–60.

Foot, P. (1972). Morality as a System of Hypothetical Imperatives. *Philosophical Review*, 81: 305–16.

Forsyth, D. R. (1980). A Taxonomy of Ethical Ideologies. *Journal of Personality and Social Psychology*, 39: 175–84.

Foucault, M. (1977). *Discipline and Punish: The Birth of the Prison*, trans. A. M. Sheridan-Smith. New York, NY: Vintage.

Fowles, D. C., (1980). The Three Arousal Model: Implications of Gray's Two-Factor Learning Theory for Heart Rate, Electrodermal Activity, and Psychopathy. *Psychophysiology*, 17: 87–104.

Frank, R. H. (1988). *Passion within Reason: The Strategic Role of the Emotions*. New York, NY: Norton.

Fredrickson, G. M. (1971). *The Black Image in the White Mind*. New York, NY: Harper & Row.

Freeman, M. M. R. (1971). A Social and Ecologic Analysis of Systematic Female Infanticide among the Netsilik Eskimo. *American Anthropologist*, 73: 1011–18.

Frei, T. (2005). *Implications of the Categoricity of the Hypothetical Imperative*. Doctoral Thesis, Department of Philosophy, University of North Carolina, Chapel Hill.

Garn, S. M. (1979). The Noneconomic Nature of Eating People. *American Anthropologist*, 81: 903.

Geach, P. T. (1965). Assertion. *Philosophical Review*, 74: 449–65.

Gemes, K. (2006). We Remain of Necessity Strangers to Ourselves: The Key Message of Nietzsche's *Genealogy*. In C. Acampora (ed.), *Nietzsche's On the Genealogy of Morals: Critical Essays*. New York, NY: Rowman & Littlefield.

Gewirth, A. (1994). Is Cultural Pluralism Relevant to Moral Knowledge? *Social Philosophy & Policy*, 11: 22–43.

Gibbard, A. (1990). *Wise Choices, Apt Feelings*. Cambridge, MA: Harvard University Press.

—— (2003). *Thinking How to Live*. Cambridge, MA: Harvard University Press.

Gigerenzer, G., and Hug, K. (1992). Domain-Specific Reasoning: Social Contracts, Cheating, and Perspective Change. *Cognition*, 43: 127–71.

Goldman, A. I., and Sripada, C. S. (2005). Simulationist Models of Face-Based Emotion Recognition, *Cognition*, 94: 193–213.

Goldstein, M. H. (1987). When Brothers Share A Wife. *Natural History*, 96: 39–49.

Goodall, J. (1986). *The Chimpanzees of Gombe: Patterns of Behavior*. Cambridge, MA: Harvard University Press.

Goody, J. (1983). *The Development of the Family and Marriage in Europe*. Cambridge: Cambridge University Press.

Gould, S. J. (1981). *The Mismeasure of Man*. New York, NY: Norton.

Gray, J. A. (1987). *The Psychology of Fear and Stress*. Cambridge: Cambridge University Press.

Gray, N. S., Macculloch, M. J., Smith, J., Morris, M., and Snowden, R. J. (2003). Forensic Psychology: Violence Viewed By Psychopathic Murderers. *Nature*, 423: 497–8.

Greene, J. D., and Haidt, J. (2002). How (and Where) Does Moral Judgment Work? *Trends in Cognitive Sciences*, 6: 517–523.

Greene, J. D., Lindsell, D., Clarke, A. C., Nystrom, L. E., and Cohen, J. D. (forthcoming). What Pushes Your Moral Buttons? Modular Myopia and the Trolley Problem.

Greene, J. D., Sommerville, R. B., Nystrom, L. E., Darley, J. M., and Cohen, J. D. (2001). An fMRI Investigation of Emotional Engagement in Moral Judgment. *Science*, 293: 2105–8.

Greenspan, P. (2000). Emotional Strategies and Rationality. *Ethics*, 110: 469–87.

Grossbard-Shechtman, A. (1984). A Theory of Allocation of Time in Markets for Labour and Marriage. *The Economic Journal*, 94: 863–82.

Grusec, J. E., and Goodnow, J. J. (1994). Impact of Parental Discipline Methods on the Child's Internalization of Values: A Reconceptualization of Current Points of View. *Developmental Psychology*, 30: 4–19.

Haidt, J. (2001). The Emotional Dog and Its Rational Tail: A Social Intuitionist Approach to Moral Judgment. *Psychological Review*, 108: 814–34.

—— (2003). Elevation and the Positive Psychology of Morality. In C. L. Keyes and J. Haidt (eds.), *Flourishing: Positive Psychology and the Life Well-Lived*, pp. 275–89. Washington, DC: American Psychological Association.

Haidt, J., and Joseph, C. (2004). Intuitive Ethics: How Innately Prepared Intuitions Generate Culturally Variable Virtues. *Daedalus*, 133: 55–66.

Hamilton W. D. (1964). The Evolution of Social Behavior. *Journal of Theoretical Biology*, 7: 1–52.

Haney, C., Banks, C., and Zimbardo, P. (1973). Interpersonal Dynamics in A Simulated Prison. *International Journal of Criminology & Penology*, 1: 69–97.

Hardin, C. L. (1991). *The Hare Psychopathy Checklist—Revised.* Toronto: Multi-Health Systems.

—— (1993a). *Color for Philosophers: Unweaving the Rainbow.* Indianapolis, in: Hackett Publishing Company.

—— (1993b). *Without Conscience: The Disturbing World of the Psychopaths among Us.* New York, NY: Pocket Books.

—— (1998). Psychopathy, Affect and Behavior. In D. J. Cooke, R. D. Hare, and A. E. Forth (eds.), *Psychopathy: Theory, Research, and Implications for Society*, pp. 105–37. Dordrecht: Kluwer.

Harman, G. (1975). Moral Relativism Defended. *Philosophical Review*, 84: 3–22.

—— (1977). *The Nature of Morality.* Oxford: Oxford University Press.

—— (1999). Moral Philosophy Meets Social Psychology: Virtue Ethics and the Fundamental Attribution Error. *Proceedings of the Aristotelian Society*, 99: 315–31.

—— (2000) Moral Philosophy and Linguistics. In G. Harman, *Explaining Value*, pp. 217–25. Oxford: Oxford University Press.

—— (2001). Virtue Ethics without Character Traits. In A. Byrne, R. Stalnaker, and R. Wedgewood (eds.), *Fact and Value: Essays on Ethics and Metaphysics for Judith Jarvis Thomson*, pp. 117–27. Cambridge, MA: MIT Press.

Harner, M. (1977). The Ecological Basis for Aztec Sacrifice. *American Ethnologist*, 4: 117–35.

Harris, C. R. (2004). The Evolution of Jealousy. *American Scientist*, 92: 62–71.

Harris, M. (1985). *Good to Eat: Riddles of Food and Culture.* New York, NY: Simon and Schuster.

—— (1989). *Our Kind.* New York, NY: Harper Collins.

—— (1993). The Evolution of Human Gender Hierarchies: A Trial Formulation. In B. D. Miller (ed.), *Sex and Gender Hierarchies*, pp. 57–79. Cambridge: Cambridge University Press.

Harris, M. B., Benson, S. M., and Hall, C. (1975). The Effects of Confession on Altruism. *Journal of Social Psychology*, 96: 187–92.

Hauser, M. D. (2001). *Wild Minds: What Animals Really Think.* New York, NY: Henry Holt.

Hauser, M. D., Young, L., and Cushman, F. (forthcoming). Reviving Rawls' Linguistic Analogy: Operative Principles and the Causal Structure of Moral Actions. In W. Sinnott-Armstrong (ed.), *Moral Psychology, Vol. 2: The Cognitive Science of Morality.* Cambridge, MA: MIT Press.

Heekeren, H. R., Wartenburger, I., Schmidt, H., Schwintowski, H. P., and Villringer, A. (2003). An fMRI Study of Simple Ethical Decision-Making. *Neuroreport*, 14: 1215–19.

Heine, B. (1985). The Mountain People: Some Notes on the Ik of North-Eastern Uganda. *Africa*, 55: 3–16.

Henrich, J., and Boyd, R. (2001). Why People Punish Defectors: Weak Conformist Transmission Can Stabilize Costly Enforcement of Norms in Cooperative Dilemmas. *Journal of Theoretical Biology*, 208: 79–89.

Henrich, J., and Gil-White, F. (2001). The Evolution of Prestige: Freely Conferred Status as a Mechanism for Enhancing the Benefits of Cultural Transmission. *Evolution and Human Behavior*, 22: 1–32.

Henrich, J., Boyd, R., Bowles, S., Camerer, C., Gintis, H., Mcelreath, R., and Fehe, E. (2001). In Search of Homo Economicus: Experiments in 15 Small-Scale Societies. *American Economic Review*, 91: 73–9.

Herdt, G. (1987). *The Sambia: Ritual and Gender in New Guinea*. New York, NY: Holt, Rinehart, and Winston.

Hill, T. (1973). The Hypothetical Imperative. *The Philosophical Review*, 82: 429–50.

Hoffman M. L. (1983). Affective and Cognitive Processes in Moral Internalization. In E. T. Higgins, D. N. Ruble, and W. W. Hartup (eds.), *Social Cognition and Social Development: A Sociocultural Perspective*, pp. 236–74. Cambridge: Cambridge University Press.

—— (1998). Varieties of Empathy-Based Guilt. In J. Bybee (ed.), *Guilt and Children*, pp. 91–112. New York, NY: Academic Press.

—— (2000). *Empathy and Moral Development: Implications for Caring and Justice*. Cambridge: Cambridge University Press.

Horgan, T., and Timmons, M. (1990–1). New Wave Moral Realism Meets Moral Twin Earth. *Journal of Philosophical Research*, 16: 447–65.

House, T. H., and Milligan, W. L. (1976). Autonomic Responses to Modeled Distress in Prison Psychopaths. *Journal of Personality and Social Psychology*, 34: 556–60.

Hrdy, S. (1999). *Mother Nature: A History of Mothers, Infants, and Natural Selection*. New York, NY: Pantheon Books.

Hua, C. (2001). *A Society without Fathers or Husbands: The Na of China*, trans. A. Hustvedt. New York, NY: Zone Books.

Hume, D. (1739/1978). *A Treatise of Human Nature*, ed. P. H. Nidditch. Oxford: Oxford University Press.

—— (1751/1998). *An Enquiry Concerning the Principles of Morals*, ed. T. L. Beauchamp. Oxford: Oxford University Press.

—— (1757/1993). On the Standard of Taste. In *Selected Essays*, ed. S. Copley and A. Edgar, pp. 133–54. Oxford: Oxford University Press.

Hupka, R. B. (1981). Cultural Determinants of Jealousy. *Alternative Lifestyles*, 4: 310–56.

—— (1991). The Motive for the Arousal of Romantic Jealousy: Its Cultural Origin. In P. Salovey (ed.), *the Psychology of Jealousy and Envy*, pp. 252–70. New York, NY: Guilford Press.

Hutcheson, F. (1738/1994). *An Inquiry into the Original of Our Ideas of Beauty and Virtue*. In *Philosophical Writings*, ed. R. S. Downie. London: J. M. Dent.

Ingham, J. M. (1984). Human Sacrifice at Tenochtitlan. *Comparative Studies in Society and History*, 3: 379–400.

Isen, A. M., and Levin, P. F. (1972). The Effect of Feeling Good on Helping: Cookies and Kindness. *Journal of Personality and Social Psychology*, 21: 384–8.

Jaffee, S., and Hyde, J. S. (2000). Gender Differences in Moral Orientation: A Meta-Analysis. *Psychological Bulletin*, 126: 703–26.

James, W. (1884). What is an Emotion? *Mind*, 9: 188–205.

Jang, K. L., Livesley, W. J., and Vernon, P. A. (1996). Heritability of the Big Five Dimensions and their Facets: A Twin Study. *Journal of Personality*, 64: 575–91.

Johnston, M. (1989). Dispositional Theories of Value. *Proceedings of the Aristotelian Society Supplementary Volume*, 63: 139–74.

Joyce, R. (2001). *The Myth of Morality*. Cambridge: Cambridge University Press.

—— (2006). *The Evolution of Morality*. Cambridge, MA: MIT Press.

Junod, H. A. (1962). *The Life of a South African Tribe*, vol. II: *Mental Life*. New York, NY: University Books.

Kagan, S. (1989). *The Limits of Morality*. Oxford: Oxford University Press.

Kamtekar, R. (2004). Situationism and Virtue Ethics on the Content of Our Character. *Ethics*, 114, 458–91.

Kant, I. (1785/1998). *Groundwork of the Metaphysic of Morals*, ed. Mary J. Gregor. Cambridge: Cambridge University Press.

Kaplan, D. (1989). Demonstratives: An Essay on the Semantics, Logic, Metaphysics, and Epistemology of Demonstratives and Other Indexicals. In J. Almog, J. Perry, and H. Wettstein (eds.), *Themes from Kaplan*, pp. 481–563. Oxford: Oxford University Press.

Kawabata, H., and Zeki, S. (2004). Neural Correlates of Beauty. *Neurophysiology*, 91: 1699–1705.

Kelly, D., Stich, S., Haley, K., Eng, S., and Fessler, D. (2007). Harm, Affect and the Moral/Conventional Distinction. *Mind & Language*, 22: 117–31.

Kelly, R. C. (1977). *Etoro Social Structure: A Study in Structural Contradiction*. Ann Arbor, MI: University of Michigan Press.

Kelly, R. L. (1995). *The Foraging Spectrum: Diversity in Hunter-Gatherer Lifeways*. Washington D.C.: Smithsonian Books.

Kilham, W., and Mann, L. (1974). Level of Destructive Obedience as A Junction of Transmitter and Executant Roles in the Milgram Obedience Paradigm. *Journal of Personality and Social Psychology*, 29: 696–702.

Kluegel, J. R., and Smith, E. R. (1986). *Beliefs about Inequality: Americans' Views of What Is and What Ought to Be*. New York: Aldine De Gruyter.

Knobe, J. (2003). Intentional Action in Folk Psychology: An Experimental Investigation. *Philosophical Psychology*, 16: 309–24.

Kochanska, G., Casey, R. J., and Fukumoto, A. (1995). Toddlers' Sensitivity to Standard Violations. *Child Development*, 66: 643–56.

Kochanska, G., Gross, J. N., Lin, M., and Nichols, K. E. (2002). Guilt in Young Children: Development, Determinants, and Relations With A Broader System of Standards. *Child Development*, 73: 461–82.

Kohlberg, L. (1984). *The Psychology of Moral Development: Moral Stages and the Life Cycle*. San Francisco, CA: Harper & Row.

Kölbel, M. (2003). Faultless Disagreement. *Proceedings of the Aristotelian Society*, 104: 53–73.

Kompa, N. (2002). The Context Sensitivity of Knowledge Ascriptions, *Grazer Philosophische Studien*, 64: 79–96.

Korsgaard, C. M. (1996). *The Sources of Normativity*. Cambridge: Cambridge University Press.

Kripke, S. (1980). *Naming and Necessity*. Cambridge, MA: Harvard University Press.

Krueger, R. F., Caspi, A., and Moffitt, T. E. (2000). Epidemiological Personology: The Unifying Role of Personality in Population-Based Research on Problem Behaviors. *Journal of Personality*, 68: 967–98.

Kuper, A. (2002). Incest, Cousin Marriage, and the Origin of the Human Sciences in Nineteenth-Century England. *Past and Present*, 174: 158–83.

Kupperman, J. (2001). The Indispensability of Character. *Philosophy*, 76: 239–50.

Lakoff, G. (2002). *Moral Politics: How Liberals and Conservatives Think*, 2nd edn. Chicago, IL: University of Chicago Press.

Lange, C. G. (1885/1922). *Om Sindsbevaegelser: Et Psyko-Fysiologisk Studie*. Kjbenhavn: Jacob Lunds. Reprinted in I. A. Haupt (trans.), *the Emotions*. Baltimore, MD: Williams and Wilkins Company.

Lasersohn, P. (2005). Context Dependence, Disagreement, and Predicates of Personal Taste. *Linguistics and Philosophy*, 28: 643–86.

Lazarus, R. S. (1991). *Emotion and Adaptation*. New York, NY: Oxford University Press.

Ledoux J. E. (1996). *The Emotional Brain*. New York, NY: Simon and Schuster.

Lee, R. B (1969). Eating Christmas in the Kalahari. *Natural History*, 78: 14, 16, 18, 21–2,60–3.

Leiter, B. (2001). Objectivity, Morality, and Adjudication. In B. Leiter (ed.), *Objectivity in Law and Morals*. Cambridge: Cambridge University Press.

Lepore, E., and Cappelen, H. (forthcoming). The Myth of Unarticulated Constituents. In M. O'Rourke and C. Washington (eds.), *Essays in Honor of John Perry*. Cambridge, MA: MIT Press.

Lerner, J., Goldberg, J., and Tetlock, P. E. (1998). Sober Second Thought: The Effects of Accountability, Anger, and Authoritarianism on Attributions of Responsibility. *Personality and Social Psychology Bulletin*, 24: 563–74.

Leung, K., and Bond, M. H. (1984). The Impact of Cultural Collectivism on Reward Allocation. *Journal of Personality and Social Psychology*, 47: 793–804.

Leupp, G. P. (1995). *Male Colors: The Construction of Homosexuality in Tokugawa Japan*. Berkeley, CA: University of California Press.

Levenson, R. W., Ekman, P., and Friesen, W. V. (1990). Voluntary Facial Action Generates Emotion-Specific Autonomic Nervous System Activity. *Psychophysiology*, 27: 363–84.

Lewis, M. (1998). Emotional Competence and Development. In D. Pushkar, W. M. Bukowski, A. E. Schwartzman, D. M. Stack, and D. R. White (eds.), *Improving Competence across the Lifespan*, pp. 27–36. New York, NY: Plenum.

Lewis, D. (1989). Dispositional Theories of Value. *Proceedings of the Aristotelian Society Supplementary Volume*, 63: 113–37.

Lieberman, D., Tooby, J., and Cosmides, L. (2003). Does Morality Have A Biological Basis? An Empirical Test of the Factors Governing Moral Sentiments Regarding Incest. *Proceedings of the Royal Society, London B*, 270: 819–26.

Locke, J. (1690/1979). *An Essay Concerning Human Understanding*, ed. P. H. Nidditch. Oxford: Oxford University Press.

Lynam, D. R., Caspi, A., Moffitt, T. E., Raine, A., Loeber, R., and Stouthamer-Loeber, M. (2005). Adolescent Psychopathy and the Big Five: Results from Two Samples. *Journal of Abnormal Child Psychology*, 33: 431–43.

Lyons, D. (1976). Ethical Relativism and the Problem of Incoherence. *Ethics*, 86: 107–21.

McCauley, R., and Lawson, E. T. (2002). *Bringing Ritual to Mind: Psychological Foundations of Cultural Forms*. Cambridge, MA: Cambridge University Press.

McCullough, M., Kilpatrick, S., Emmons, R., and Larson, D. (2001) Is Gratitude a Moral Affect? *Psychological Bulletin*, 127: 249–66.

McDougall, W. (1908). *An Introduction to Social Psychology*. London: Methuen & Co.

McDowell, J. (1985). Values and Secondary Qualities. In T. Honderich (ed.), *Morality and Objectivity*. London: Routledge & Kegan Paul.

—— (1987). Projection and Truth in Ethics, Lindsay Lecture, University of Kansas. Reprinted in S. Darwall, A. Gibbard, and P. Railton (eds.), *Moral Discourse and Practice: Some Philosophical Approaches*, pp. 215–27. New York: Oxford University Press.

MacFarlane, J. (2005). The Assessment Sensitivity of Knowledge Attributions. *Oxford Studies in Epistemology*, 1: 197–233.

Mackay, D. G., Shafto, M., Taylor, J. K., Marian, D. E., Abrams, L., and Dyer, J. R. (2004). Relations between Emotion, Memory, and Attention: Evidence from Taboo Stroop, Lexical Decision, and Immediate Memory Tasks. *Memory & Cognition*, 32: 474–88.

Mackie, J. L. (1977). *Ethics: Inventing Right and Wrong*. London: Penguin.

McMillen, D. L., and Austin, J. B. (1971). Effect of Positive Feedback on Compliance Following Transgression. *Psychonomic Science*, 24: 59–61.

McNaughton, D. (1988). *Moral Vision: An Introduction to Ethics*. Oxford: Blackwell.

Malle, B. F., and Bennett, R. E. (2002). People's Praise and Blame for Intentions and Actions: Implications of the Folk Concept of Intentionality. *Technical Reports of the Institute of Cognitive and Decision Sciences*, no. 02–2, Eugene, or.

Manktelow, K., and Over, D. (1990). Deontic Thought and the Selection Task. In K. J. Gilhooly, M. T. G. Keane, R. H. Logie, and G. Erdos (eds.), *Lines of Thinking*, pp. 153–64. London: Wiley.

Mantell, D. M. (1971). The Potential for Violence in Germany. *Journal of Social Issues*, 27: 101–12.

Marglin, F. A. (1985). *Wives of the God-King: Rituals of Devadasi of Puri*. Delhi: Oxford University Press.

Marlar, R. A., Leonard, B. L., Billman, B. R., Lambert, P. M., and Marlar, J. E. (2000). Biochemical Evidence of Cannibalism at a Prehistoric Puebloan Site in Southwestern Colorado. *Nature*, 407: 74–8.

Mayor, M. (1974). Fears and Fantasies of the Anti-Suffragists. *Connecticut Review*, 7: 64–74.

Mead, S., Stumpf, M. P. H., Whitfield, J., Beck, J. A., Poulter, M., Campbell, T., Uphill, J. B., Goldstein, D., Alpers, M., Fisher, E. M. C., and Collinge, J. (2003). Balancing Selection at the Prion Protein Gene Consistent With Prehistoric Kurulike Epidemics. *Science*, 300: 640–3.

Mealey, L. (1995). The Sociobiology of Sociopathy: An Integrated Evolutionary Model. *Behavioral and Brain Sciences*, 18: 523–99.

Meeks, W. A. (1993). *The Origins of Christian Morality: The First Two Centuries*. New Haven, CT: Yale University.

Mele, A. R. (1996). Internalist Moral Cognitivism and Listlessness. *Ethics*, 106: 727–53.

Meltzoff, A. (1995). Understanding the Intentions of Others: Reenactment of Intended Acts By 18-Month-Old Children. *Developmental Psychology*, 31: 838–50.

Merritt, M. (2000). Virtue Ethics and Situationist Personality Psychology. *Ethical Theory and Moral Practice*, 3: 365–83.

Midgley, M. (1981). On Trying out One's New Sword on a Chance Wayfarer. In M. Midgley, *Heart and Mind*. London: Methuen & Co.

Mikhail, J. (2000). Rawls' Linguistic Analogy: A Study of the "Generative Grammar" Model of Moral Theory Described By John Rawls in "A Theory of Just Ice". Doctoral Dissertation, Department of Philosophy, Cornell University.

—— (2002). Aspects of the Theory of Moral Cognition: Investigating Intuitive Knowledge of the Prohibition of Intentional Battery and the Principle of Double Effect. Georgetown University Law Center Public Law & Legal Theory Working Paper No. 762385.

Milgram, S. (1974). *Obedience to Authority*. New York, NY: Harper & Row.

Miller, R. S. (1996). *Embarrassment: Poise and Peril in Everyday Life*. New York, NY: Guilford Press.

Millgram, E. (1999). Moral Values and Secondary Qualities. *American Philosophical Quarterly*, 36: 253–5.

Millikan, R. (1984). *Language, Thought, and Other Biological Categories*. Cambridge, MA: MIT Press.

Mischel, W. (1968). *Personality and Assessment*. New York, NY: John J. Wiley and Sons.

Mitchell, P. G., Tetlock, P. E., Newman, D., and Lerner, J. (2003). Experiments behind the Veil: A Hypothetical Societies Approach to the Study of Social Justice. *Political Psychology*, 24: 519–47.

Moll, J., De Oliveira-Souza, R., Bramati, I., and Grafman, J. (2002). Functional Networks in Emotional Moral and Nonmoral Social Judgments. *Neuroimage*, 16: 696–703.

Moll, J., De Oliveira-Souza, R., and Eslinger, P. J. (2003). Morals and the Human Brain: A Working Model. *Neuroreport*, 14: 299–305.

Moody-Adams, M. (1997). *Fieldwork in Familiar Places: Morality, Culture and Philosophy*. Cambridge, MA: Harvard University Press.

Moore, G. E. (1903). *Principia Ethica*. Cambridge: Cambridge University Press.

Moore, J. (1984). The Evolution of Reciprocal Sharing. *Ethology and Sociobiology*, 5: 5–14.

Morris, J. S., Öhman, A., and Dolan, R. J. (1999). A Subcortical Pathway to the Right Amygdala Mediating "Unseen" Fear. *Proceedings of National Academy of Science*, 96: 1680–5.

Moscovitch, M. (1995). Confabulation. In Schacter, D. (ed.), *Memory Distortion*, pp. 226–54. Cambridge, MA: Harvard University Press.

Murdock, G. P. (1981) *Atlas of World Cultures*. Pittsburgh, PA: University of Pittsburgh Press.

Murphy, S., Haidt, J., and Björklund, F. (2000). Moral Dumbfounding: When Intuition Finds No Reason. Unpublished Manuscript, Department of Philosophy, University of Virginia.

Nagel, T. (1986). *The View from Nowhere.* Oxford: Oxford University Press.

Neuberg, S. L., Cialdini, R. B., Brown, S. L., Luce, C., Sagarin, B. J., and Lewis, B. P. (1997). Does Empathy Lead to Anything More Than Superficial Helping? Comment on Batson et al. (1997). *Journal of Personality and Social Psychology*, 73: 510–16.

Nichols, S. (2002). On the Genealogy of Norms: A Case for the Role of Emotion in Cultural Evolution. *Philosophy of Science*, 69: 234–55.

—— (2004a). *Sentimental Rules: On the Natural Foundations of Moral Judgment.* New York, NY: Oxford University Press.

—— (2004b). After Objectivity: an Empirical Study of Moral Judgment. *Philosophical Psychology*, 17: 5–28.

—— (2005). Innateness and Moral Psychology. In P. Carruthers, S. Laurence, and S. Stich (Eds.), *The Innate Mind: Structure and Content.* New York, NY: Oxford University Press.

Nietzsche, F. W. (1883–8/1968). *The Will to Power*, trans. W. Kauffman. New York, NY: Vintage.

—— (1885/1966). *Thus Spoke Zarathustra: A Book for None and All*, trans. W. Kauffman. New York, NY: Viking Penguin.

—— (1887/1967). *On the Genealogy of Morals*, trans. W. Kauffman. New York, NY: Random House.

—— (1888/1920). *The Antichrist*, trans. H. L. Mencken. New York, NY: Knopf.

Nisbett, R. E. (2003). *The Geography of Thought: How Asians and Westerners Think Differently and Why.* New York, NY: Free Press.

Nisbett, R. E., and Cohen, D. (1996). *Culture of Honor: The Psychology of Violence in the South.* Boulder, CO: Westview Press.

Nisbett, R. E., and Wilson, T. (1977). Telling More Than We Can Know: Verbal Reports on Mental Processes. *Psychological Review*, 84: 231–59.

Nucci, L. P. (2001). *Education in the Moral Domain.* Cambridge: Cambridge University Press.

Nucci, L. P., and Weber, E. (1995). Social Interactions in the Home and the Development of Young Children's Conceptions of the Personal. *Child Development*, 66: 1438–52.

Nunner-Winkler, G., and Sodian, B. (1988). Children's Understanding of Moral Emotions. *Child Development*, 59: 1323–38.

Nussbaum, M. C. (1999). *Sex and Social Justice.* Oxford: Oxford University Press.

—— (2001). *Upheavals of Thought: The Intelligence of the Emotions.* Cambridge: Cambridge University Press.

Oberg, K. (1934). Crime and Punishment in Tlingit Society. *American Anthropologist*, 36: 145–56.

Okonofua, F. E., Larsen, U., Oronsaye, F., Snow, R. C., and Slanger, T. E. (2002). The Association between Female Genital Cutting and Correlates of Sexual and Gynaecological Morbidity in Edo State, Nigeria. *British Journal of Obstetrics and Gynaecology*, 109: 1089–96.

Ones, D. S., Viswesvaran, C., and Schmidt, F. L. (1993). Comprehensive Meta-Analysis of Integrity Test Validities: Findings and Implications for Personnel Selection and Theories of Job Performance. *Journal of Applied Psychology*, 78: 679–703.

Ortiz De Montellano, B. R. (1978). Aztec Cannibalism: An Ecological Necessity? *Science*, 200: 611–17.

Panksepp, J. (1995). The Emotional Sources of "Chills" Induced by Music. *Music Perception*, 13: 171–207.

Patrick, C. J., Bradley, M. M., and Lang, P. J. (1993). Emotion in the Criminal Psychopath: Startle Reflex Modulation. *Journal of Abnormal Psychology*, 102: 82–92.

Paunonen, S. V., and Jackson, D. N. (2000). What Is Beyond the Big Five? Plenty! *Journal of Personality*, 68: 821–35.

Phan, K. L., Wager, T. D., Taylor, S. F., and Liberzon, I. (2002). Functional Neuroanatomy of Emotion: A Meta-Analysis of Emotion Activation Studies in PET and fMRI. *Neuroimage*, 16: 331–48.

Pitcher, G. (1965). Emotion. *Mind*, 74: 324–46.

Platner, S. B. and Ashby, T. (1929). *A Topographical Dictionary of Ancient Rome*. Oxford: Oxford University Press.

Preston, S. D., and De Waal, F. B. M. (2002). Empathy: Its Ultimate and Proximate Bases. *Behavioral and Brain Sciences*, 25: 1–19.

Price, J., Sloman, L., Gardner, R., Gilbert, P., and Rohde, P. (1994). The Social Competition Hypothesis of Depression. *British Journal of Psychiatry*, 164: 309–15.

Prinz, J. J. (2000). The Duality of Content. *Philosophical Studies*, 100: 1–34.

—— (2002). *Furnishing the Mind: Concepts and their Perceptual Basis*. Cambridge, MA: MIT Press.

—— (2004). *Gut Reactions: A Perceptual Theory of Emotion*. New York, NY: Oxford University Press.

—— (2007). Is Morality Innate? In W. Sinnott-Armstrong (Ed.), *Moral Psychology, Vol. 1: The Evolution of Morality*. Cambridge, MA: MIT Press.

—— (forthcoming *a*) Resisting the Linguistic Analogy. In W. Sinnott-Armstrong (ed.), *Moral Psychology, Vol. 2: The Cognitive Science of Morality*. Cambridge, MA: MIT Press.

—— (forthcoming *b*). Against Moral Nativism. In M. Bishop and D. Murphy (eds.), *Stich and his Critics*. Oxford: Blackwell.

Provine, R. R. (2000). *Laughter: A Scientific Investigation*. New York, NY: Penguin.

Pusey, A. E., and Packer, C. (1997). The Ecology of Relationships. In J. R. Krebs and N. B. Davies (eds.), *Behavioural Ecology: An Evolutionary Approach*, pp. 254–83. Oxford: Blackwell.

Putnam, H. (1975). The Meaning of "Meaning." in K. Gunderson (ed.), *Language, Mind, and Knowledge*, pp. 131–93. Minneapolis, MN: University of Minnesota Press.

—— (1980). *Reason, Truth and History*. Cambridge, MA: Cambridge University Press.

Quine, W. V. O. (1953). Two Dogmas of Empiricism. In *From a Logical Point of View*, pp. 20–46. Cambridge, MA: Harvard University Press.

—— (1969). Natural Kinds. In *Ontological Relativity and Other Essays*, pp. 114–38. New York, NY: Columbia University Press.

Quine, W. V. O., and Ullian, J. S. (1978). *The Web of Belief*, 2nd edn. New York, NY: Random House.

Rachels, J. (1986). *The Elements of Moral Philosophy*. Philadelphia, PA: Temple University Press.

Rawls, J. (1971). *A Theory of Justice*. Cambridge, MA: Harvard University Press.

Rée, P. (1877/2003). Origin of the Moral Sentiments. In *Basic Writings*, trans. R. Small. Champaign, IL: University of Illinois Press.

Richard, M. (2004). Contextualism and Relativism. *Philosophical Studies*, 119: 215–42.

Richards, R. (1986). A Defense of Evolutionary Ethics. *Biology and Philosophy*, 1: 265–93.

Rizzolatti, G., and Craighero, L. (2004). The Mirror-Neuron System. *Annual Review of Neuroscience*, 27: 169–92.

Roberts, B. W., and Delvecchio, W. F. (2000). The Rank-Order Consistency of Personality from Childhood to Old Age: A Quantitative Review of Longitudinal Studies. *Psychological Bulletin*, 126: 3–25.

Ross, L., and Nisbett, R. E. (1991). *The Person and the Situation: Perspectives of Social Psychology*. New York, NY: McGraw-Hill.

Ross, W. D. (1930). *The Right and the Good*. Oxford: Oxford University Press.

Rozin, P., Haidt, J., and Mccauley, C. (1993). Disgust. In M. Lewis and J. Haviland (eds.), *Handbook of Emotions*, pp. 575–94. New York, NY: Guilford Press.

Rozin, P., Lowery, L., Imada, S., and Haidt, J. (1999). The CAD Triad Hypothesis: A Mapping between Three Moral Emotions (Contempt, Anger, Disgust) and Three Moral Codes (Community, Autonomy, Divinity). *Journal of Personality and Social Psychology*, 76: 574–86.

Rozin, P., Millman, L., and Nemeroff, C. (1986). Operation of the Laws of Sympathetic Magic in Disgust and Other Domains. *Journal of Personality and Social Psychology*, 50: 703–12.

Rozin, P., and Singh, L. (1999). The Moralization of Cigarette Smoking in the United. States. *Journal of Consumer Psychology*, 8: 339–42.

Rudman, L. A., and Kilianski, S. E (2000). Implicit and Explicit Attitudes toward Female Authority. *Personality and Social Psychology Bulletin*, 26: 1315–28.

Ruse, M. (1991). The Significance of Evolution. In P. Singer (ed.), *A Companion to Ethics*, pp. 500–10. Oxford: Blackwell.

Sahlins M. (1978). Culture as Protein and Profit. *The New York Review of Books*, 25: 45–53.

Sanday, P. R. (1986). *Divine Hunger: Cannibalism as a Cultural System*. Cambridge: Cambridge University Press.

Sanderson, S. K. (2001). Explaining Monogamy and Polygamy in Human Societies: Comment on Kanazawa and Still. *Social Forces*, 80: 329–35.

Sanfey, A. G., Rilling, J. A., Aronson, J. K., Nystrom, L., and Cohen, J. D. (2003). The Neural Basis of Economic Decision Making in the Ultimatum Game, *Science*, 300: 1755–7.

Sayre-McCord, G. (1994). On Why Hume's "General Point of View" Isn't Ideal—and Shouldn't Be. *Social Philosophy & Policy*, 11: 202–28.

Schalling, D., and Rosen, A. S. (1968). Porteus Maze Differences between Psychopathic and Non-Psychopathic Criminals. *British Journal of Social and Clinical Psychology*, 7: 224–8.

Scherer, K. R. (1993). Studying the Emotion Antecedent Appraisal Process: An Expert System Approach. *Cognition and Emotion*, 7: 325–55.

Schnall, S., Haidt, J., and Clore, G. L. (2005). Disgust as Embodied Moral Judgment. Unpublished Manuscript, Department of Psychology, University of Virginia.

Schneebaum, T. (1969). *Keep the River on Your Right*. New York, NY: Grove Press.

Searle, J. R. (1964). How to Derive "Ought" From "Is". *Philosophical Review*, 73: 43–58.

Shaw, B. (1992). Explaining Incest: Brother–Sister Marriage in Graeco-Roman Egypt. *Man*, 27: 267–99.

Shepher, J. (1971). Mate-Selection among Second-Generation Kibbutz Adolescents and Adults: Incest-Avoidance and Negative Imprinting. *Archives of Sexual Behavior*, 1: 293–307.

Sherman P. (1977). Nepotism and the Evolution of Alarm Calls. *Science*, 197: 1246–53.

Shin, L. M., Dougherty, D., Macklin, M. L., Orr, S. P., Pitman, R. K., and Rauch, S. L. (2000). Activation of Anterior Paralimbic Structures during Guilt-Related Script-Driven Imagery. *Biological Psychiatry*, 48: 43–50.

Shweder, R. A. (2000). What about "Female Genital Mutilation"? And Why Culture Matters in the First Place. *Daedalus*, 129: 209–32.

Shweder, R. A., Much, N. C., Mahapatra, M., and Park, L. (1997). The "Big Three" of Morality (Autonomy, Community, Divinity), and the "Big Three" Explanations of Suffering. In P. Rozin and A. Brandt (eds.), *Morality and Health*. New York, NY: Routledge.

Silk, J. B. (2002). The Form and Function of Reconciliation in Primates. *Annual Review of Anthropology*, 31: 21–44.

Silk, J. B., Brosnan, S. F., Vonk, J., Henrich, J., Povinelli, D. J., Richardson, A. F., Lambeth, S. P., Mascaro, J., and Schapiro, S. J. (2005). Chimpanzees are Indifferent to the Welfare of Other Group Members. *Nature*, 435: 1357–9.

Singer, T., Seymour, B., O'Doherty, J., Kaube, H., Dolan, R. J., and Frith, C. D. (2004). Empathy for Pain Involves the Affective but not Sensory Components of Pain. *Science*, 303: 1157–62.

Singer, T., Seymour, B., O'Doherty, J., Sephan, K. E., Dolan, R. J., and Frith, C. (2006). Empathic Neural Responses are Modulated by the Perceived Fairness of Others. *Nature*, 439: 466–9.

Sinnott-Armstrong, W. (1996). Moral Skepticism and Justification. In W Sinnott-Armstrong and M. Timmons (eds.), *Moral Knowledge? New Readings in Moral Epistemology*. New York, NY: Oxford University Press.

Slotkin, J. S. (1947). On a Possible Lack of Incest Regulations in Old Iran. *American Anthropologist*, 49: 612–17.

Smetana, J. G. (1981). Preschool Children's Conceptions of Moral and Social Rules. *Child Development*, 52; 1333–6.

—— (1989). Toddlers' Social Interactions in the Context of Moral and Conventional Transgressions in the Home. *Developmental Psychology*, 25: 499–508.

Smetana, J. and Braeges, J. (1990). The Development of Toddlers' Moral and Conventional Judgments. *Merrill-Palmer Quarterly*, 36: 329–46.

Smith, A. (1759/2000). *The Theory of Moral Sentiments*. Amherst, NY: Prometheus Books.

Smith, M. (1994). *The Moral Problem*. Oxford: Blackwell.

Smith, P. B., and Bond, M. H. (1998). *Social Psychology across Cultures*. New York, NY: Allyn & Bacon.

Snarey, J. R. (1985). Cross-Cultural Universality of Social-Moral Development: A Critical Review of Kohlbergian Research. *Psychological Bulletin*, 97: 202–32.

Sober, E. (1994). Prospects for an Evolutionary Ethics. In *From A Biological Point of View*, pp. 93–113. Cambridge: Cambridge University Press.

Sober, E., and Wilson, D. S. (1998). *Unto Others: The Evolution and Psychology of Unselfish Behavior*. Cambridge, MA: Harvard University Press.

Solomon, R. C. (1976). *The Passions.* New York, NY: Doubleday.

Solomon, R. L. (1980). The Opponent-Process Theory of Acquired Motivation: The Costs of Pleasure and the Benefits of Pain. *American Psychologist,* 35: 691–712.

Spencer, H. (1857). Progress: Its Law and Causes. *The Westminster Review,* 67: 445–7: 451: 454–6: 464–5.

Sperber, D. (1996). *Explaining Culture: A Naturalistic Approach.* Oxford: Blackwell.

——(2000). An Objection to the Memetic Approach to Culture. In R. Aunger (Ed.), *Darwinizing Culture: The Status of Memetics as A Science,* pp. 163–73. Oxford: Oxford University Press.

Spinoza, B. (1677/1994). *Ethics.* In E. Curley (trans. and ed.), *A Spinoza Reader.* Princeton, NJ: Princeton University Press.

Sreenivasan, G. (2002). Errors about Errors: Virtue Theory and Trait Attribution. *Mind,* 111: 47–68.

Sripada, C. and Stich, S. (2006). A Framework for the Psychology of Norms. In P. Carruthers, S. Laurence and S. Stich (eds.), *The Innate Mind: Culture and Cognition,* pp. 280–301. New York: Oxford University Press.

Stanford, C. B., Wallis, J., Matama, H., and Goodall, J. (1994). Patterns of Predation by Chimpanzees on Red Colobus Monkeys in Gombe National Park, 1982–1991. *American Journal of Physical Anthropology,* 94: 213–28.

Stark, R. (1996). *The Rise of Christianity: A Sociologist Reconsiders History.* Princeton, NJ: Princeton University Press.

Steinpreis, R. E., Anders, K. A., and Ritzke, D. (1999). The Impact of Gender on the Review of the Curricula Vitae of Job Applicants and Tenure Candidates: A National Empirical Study. *Sex Roles: A Journal of Research,* 41: 509–28.

Sterelny, K. (1990). *The Representational Theory of Mind.* Oxford: Blackwell.

Stevens, D., Charman, T., and Blair, R. J. R. (2001). Recognition of Emotion in Facial Expressions and Vocal Tones in Children with Psychopathic Tendencies. *Journal of Genetic Psychology,* 162: 201–11.

Stevens, J. R., and Hauser, M. D. (2004). Why Be Nice? Psychological Constraints on the Evolution of Cooperation. *Trends in Cognitive Sciences,* 8: 60–5.

Stevenson, C. L. (1937). The Emotive Meaning of Ethical Terms. *Mind,* 46: 14–31.

Stone, V., Cosmides, L., Tooby, J., Kroll, N., and Knight, R. (2002). Selective Impairment of Reasoning about Social Exchange in a Patient with Bilateral Limbic System Damage. *Proceedings of the National Academy of Sciences,* 99: 11531–6.

Strack, F., Martin, L. L., and Stepper, S. (1988). Inhibiting and Facilitating Conditions of Facial Expressions: A Nonobtrusive Test of the Facial Feedback Hypothesis. *Journal of Personality and Social Psychology,* 54: 768–77.

Sturgeon, N. L. (1985). Moral Explanations. In D. Copp and D. Zimmerman (eds.), *Morality Reason and Truth,* pp. 49–78. Totowa, NJ: Rowan and Allanheld.

Svallfors, S. (1997). Worlds of Welfare and Attitudes to Redistribution: A Comparison of Eight Western Nations. *European Sociological Review,* 13: 283–304.

Tamir, Y. (1996). Hands off Clitoridectomy: What Our Revulsion Reveals about Ourselves. *Boston Review,* 21. http://bostonreview.net/BR21.3/Tamir.html

Thomas, K. (1983). *Man and the Natural World: A History of the Modern Sensibility.* New York: Pantheon.

Thompson, W. E. (1967). The Marriage of First Cousins in Athenian Society. *Phoenix*, 21: 273–82.

Thomson, J. J. (1976). Killing, Letting Die, and the Trolley Problem. *The Monist*, 59: 204–17.

—— (1997). The Right and the Good. *Journal of Philosophy*, 94: 273–98.

of:Thornhill, N. W. (1991). An Evolutionary Analysis of Rules Regulating Human Inbreeding and Marriage. *Behavioral and Brain Sciences*, 14: 247–93.

Tiberius, V. (2003). Cultural Differences and Philosophical Accounts of Well-Being. *Journal of Happiness Studies*, 5: 293–314.

Tinklepaugh, O. L. (1928). An Experimental Study of Representative Factors in Monkeys. *Journal of Comparative Psychology*, 8: 197–236.

Treggiari, S. (1993). *Roman Marriage*. Oxford: Oxford University Press.

Trivers, R. L. (1971). The Evolution of Reciprocal Altruism. *Quarterly Review of Biology*, 46: 35–57.

Turiel, E. (1983). *The Development of Social Knowledge: Morality and Convention*. Cambridge: Cambridge University Press.

Turnbull, C. (1972). *The Mountain People*. New York, NY: Simon and Schuster.

Turner II, C. G., and Turner, J. A. (1999). *Man Corn: Cannibalism and Violence in the Prehistoric American Southwest*. Salt Lake City, UT: University of Utah Press.

Tylor, E. B. (1871). *Primitive Culture*. New York, NY: Gordon Press.

UNICEF (2005). *Female Genital Mutilation/Cutting: A Statistical Exploration*. New York, NY: The United Nations Children's Fund.

Valdesolo, P., and DeSteno, D. (2006). Manipulations of Emotional Context Shape Moral Judgment. *Psychological Science*, 17: 476–7.

Vartanian, O., and Goel, V. (2004). Neuroanatomical Correlates of Aesthetic Preference for Paintings. *Neuroreport*, 15: 893–7.

Verdon, M. (1988). Virgins and Widows: European Kinship and Early Christianity. *Man*, 23: 488–505.

Vranas, P. (2005). The Indeterminacy Paradox: Character Evaluations and Human Psychology. *Noûs*, 39: 1–42.

Wagner, H. L. (2000). The Accessibility of the Term "Contempt" and the Meaning of the Unilateral Lip Curl. *Cognition & Emotion*, 14: 689–710.

Walker, P. L. (2001). A Bioarchaeological Perspective on the History of Violence. *Annual Review of Anthropology*, 30: 573–96.

Warneken, F., and Tomasello, M. (2006). Altruistic Helping in Human Infants and Young Chimpanzees. *Science*, 311: 1301–3.

Westermarck, E. (1891). *The History of Human Marriage*. London: Macmillan.

—— (1900). Remarks on the Predicates of Moral Judgment. *Mind*, 9: 184–204.

—— (1906). *The Origin and Development of the Moral Ideas*. London: Macmillan.

Wheatley, T., and Haidt, J. (2005). Hypnotically Induced Disgust Makes Moral Judgments More Severe. *Psychological Science*, 16: 780–4.

White, D. R., and Burton, M. L. (1988). Causes of Polygyny: Ecology, Economy, Kinship, and Warfare. *American Anthropologist*, 90: 871–87.

Whitehouse, H. (2000). *Arguments and Icons: Divergent Modes of Religiosity*. Oxford: Oxford University Press.

Widom, C. S. (1976). Interpersonal Conflict and Cooperation in Psychopaths. *Journal of Abnormal Psychology*, 85: 330–4.

Wiedemann, T. (1992). *Emperors & Gladiators*. London: Routledge.

Wiggins, D. (1987). A Sensible Subjectivism. In *Needs, Values, Truth: Essays in the Philosophy of Value*, pp. 185–214. Oxford: Blackwell.

Wilkinson, G. S. (1984). Reciprocal Food Sharing in Vampire Bats. *Nature*, 308: 181–4.

Williams, B. (1985). *Ethics and the Limits of Philosophy*. Cambridge, MA: Harvard University Press.

Witter, R. A., Stock, W. A., Okum, M. A., and Harding, M. J. (1985). Religion and Subjective Well-Being in Adulthood: A Quantitative Synthesis. *Review of Religious Research*, 36: 332–42.

Wolf, A. P. (1970). Childhood Association and Sexual Attraction: A Further Test of the Westermarck Hypothesis. *American Anthropologist*, 72: 503–15.

Wolf, A. P., and Huang, C. S. (1980). *Marriage and Adoption in China, 1845–1945*. Stanford, CA: Stanford University Press.

Woloch, N. (2000). *Women and the American Experience: A Concise History*, 2nd edn. New York, NY: McGraw Hill.

Wong, D. B. (1984). *Moral Relativity*. Berkeley CA: University of California Press.

Wood, J. C. (1999). *When Men Are Women: Manhood among Gabra Nomads of East Africa*. Madison, WI: University of Wisconsin Press.

Wrangham, R. (2004). Killer Species. *Daedalus*, 133: 25–35.

Wright, C. (1992) *Truth and Objectivity*. Oxford: Blackwell.

Wyatt-Brown, B. (1982). *Southern Honor: Ethics and Behavior in the Old South*. New York, NY: Oxford University Press.

Wynne, C. D. L. (2004). Fair Refusal by Capuchin Monkeys. *Nature*, 428: 140.

Zahn-Waxler, C., and Robinson, J. (1995). Empathy and Guilt: Early Origins of Feelings of Responsibility. In J. P. Tangney and K. W. Fischer (eds.), *Self-Conscious Emotions*, pp. 143–73. New York, NY: Guilford.

Zahn-Waxler, C., Hollenbeck, B., and Radke-Yarrow, M. (1984). The Origins of Empathy and Altruism. In M. W. Fox and L. D. Mickley (eds.), *Advances in Animal Welfare Science*, pp. 21–39. Washington D.C.: Humane Society of the United States.

Zajonc, R. B. (1984). On the Primacy of Affect. *American Psychologist*, 39: 117–23.

Zhong, C. B., and Liljenquist, K. (2006). Washing Away Your Sins: Threatened Morality and Physical Cleansing. *Science*, 313: 1451–2.

Index